A CONCISE DICTIONARY OF THE PERSIAN LANGUAGE

A CONCISE DICTIONARY OF THE PERSIAN LANGUAGE

PERSIAN – ENGLISH

E.H. PALMER

MANOHAR

2021

First published 1876
Reprinted 2021

ISBN 978-93-90729-70-8

Published by
Ajay Kumar Jain *for*
Manohar Publishers & Distributors
4753/23 Ansari Road, Daryaganj
New Delhi 110 002

Printed at
Replika Press Pvt. Ltd.

A CONCISE DICTIONARY OF THE PERSIAN LANGUAGE.

BY

E. H. PALMER, M.A.,

OF THE MIDDLE TEMPLE, BARRISTER-AT-LAW,
LORD ALMONER'S READER AND PROFESSOR OF ARABIC,
AND FELLOW OF ST JOHN'S COLLEGE IN THE UNIVERSITY OF CAMBRIDGE

THIRD EDITION.

LONDON
KEGAN PAUL, TRENCH, TRÜBNER & CO., LTD.
PATERNOSTER HOUSE, CHARING CROSS ROAD.
1891.

PREFACE.

THIS Dictionary is chiefly intended for the use of travellers and others in Persia, and will be found to contain all the words in use in colloquial Persian. With a view to making it available for beginners in the language, and especially for Candidates for the Indian Civil Service, all the words in the Gulistán and most of those occurring in other prescribed text-books have also been included. The principal works of which I have made use in the compilation are Johnson's Persian Dictionary, Nicolas' Dialogues Persans-Français, and the small Persian-French Vocabulary of Bergè.

E. H. PALMER.

ST JOHN'S COLLEGE, CAMBRIDGE.
June 30, 1876.

PRONUNCIATION.

The vowels are to be pronounced as in Italian, except ا *á*, which is sounded broad as in the word *awe.*

ح *Ḥá*, a strong pectoral aspirate.

خ *Khá*, a guttural, something like the Scotch *ch* in *loch.*

ژ *Zhé*, like the French *j* in *jour.*

ط *Ṭá*, a hard palatal *t.*

ع *'ain*, is a guttural vowel.

غ *Ghain*, is a guttural sound something between *gh* and *r.*

ق *Ḳáf*, like *ck* in *stuck* pronounced very gutturally.

گ *Gáf*, like the English *g*, but always hard before all vowels, as گی *gí*, *ghee* not *jee.* The Persians frequently pronounce it with a slight *y* sound, like the Cockney mode of pronouncing the *g* in *garden*, "*gyarden.*" When it occurs between two vowels it is often sounded like *y*, as اگر, pronounced *éyer.*

ه *Há*, at the end of words is frequently silent. Otherwise it is sounded like the English *h* in *hat*

ذ ز ض ظ, although differing widely in Arabic are all pronounced in Persian like the English *z* in *zone.*

Similarly ث س ص are all pronounced *s.*

The other consonants are pronounced as in English.

The capital letters before each word refer to the language to which it belongs, A. Arabic, P. Persian, H. Hindustani, G. Greek, T. Turkish.

A CONCISE DICTIONARY.

PERSIAN AND ENGLISH.

ا *alif.* The first letter of the Arabic and Persian Alphabet.

A. ا *a.* Oh! also a particle of interrogation.

آ *á.* Come thou.

P. آب *áb.* Water, moisture, humour, splendour, elegance, grace. The lustre of precious stones, polished steel, &c.

A. اب *ab.* A father, pl. آباء *ábá.*

A. اباً عن جد *aban 'an jadd.* From father to son, from generation to generation.

A. اباء *ibá.* Denial ابا كردن از *ibá kerdan az,* to refuse to....

A. اباحت *ibáhat.* Publishing, divulging a secret; permitting, giving liberty.

P. آباد *ábád.* A city; populous, cultivated.

P. آبادان *ábádán.* Flourishing, populous, cultivated, inhabited.

A. اباق *ibák.* Running away (as a slave), absconding, withdrawing.

P. آبان *'Abán.* The 10th day of the Persian month, and also the 8th month of the Persian year.

A. ابانت *ibánat.* Publishing, disclosing, declaring.

A. آبا و اجداد *ábá wa ajdád.* Ancestors.

A. اباهر *abáhir.* The feathers and quills of a bird, pl. of ابهر *abhar.*

A. آبائی *ábáí.* Ancestral, paternal.

A. ابت *abt.* Being warm, sultry; swelled with drinking.

P. آبتابه *ábtába.* An ewer, water-pot.

A. ابتار *ibtár.* Docking the tail, curtailing.

A. ابتدا *ibtidá.* Beginning commencement.

A. ابتداع *ibtidá'*. Invention, innovation.

A. ابتذال *ibtizál*. Carelessness, vileness, meanness.

A. ابتر *abtar*. Docked, ruined, confused; mutilated.

A. ابتسام *ibtisám*. A smile, smiling.

A. ابتلاء *ibtilá*. Temptation, trial.

A. ابتلاع *ibtilá'*. Devouring, swallowing.

A. ابتناء *ibtiná*. Building, constructing.

A. ابتهاج *ibtiháj*. Gladness, alacrity, cheerfulness.

A. ابتياع *ibtiyá'*. Buying.

A. ابتهال *ibtihál*. Supplication.

A. ابجد *abjad*. The Arabic alphabet arranged in numerical order.

A. ابحر *abhur*. Seas. pl. of بحر *bahr*.

P. A. اب حيات *ábi haiyát*. The water of immortality, nectar.

A. ابخر *abkhur*. Vapours, perfumes.

A. ابخل *abkhal*. More or most avaricious.

P. ابخورد *ábkh'urd*. Livelihood.

P. ابخوره *ábkh'ura*. A cup for drinking water.

P. ابخوری *ábkh'urí*. Halter, a watering place.

A. ابد *abad*. An age; eternity without end.

A. ابداء *ibdá*. Beginning, creating.

P. ابدار *ábdár*. Succulent, juicy, lustrous. A servant who attends to the provisions on a journey.

A. ابداع *ibdá'*. Producing something new, inventing; also halting, limping (as cattle from fatigue).

A. ابدال *abdál*. Mysterious beings who preside over the spheres. Hermits, saints, pious men.

A. ابدال *ibdál*. Change, exchange.

P. ابدان *ábdán*. A vessel for holding water.

P. ابدست *ábdast*. Ablution before prayer.

A. ابدی *abadí*. Eternal, without end.

P. ابدیده *áb-dída*. Tears, tearful.

P. ابر *abr*. A cloud.

A. ابر *abr*. A puncture; sting of a scorpion.

A. ابراء *ibrá*. Setting free, acquitting.

A. ابراح *ibráh*. Self-complacency, pride; honouring, surprising.

A. ابرار *ibrár*. Justification, acquittal.

A. ابرار *abrár*. Just, pious men. Pl. of بر *barr*.

A. ابراز *ibráz*. Manifestation, publication, divulging.

A. ابراص *ibráṣ*. Afflicting with leprosy.

A. ابرام *ibrám*. Importunity.

P. ابراه *ábráh*. A conduit, canal, watercourse.

A. ابراهيم *Ibráhím*. Abraham, also called خليل الله *Khalílu 'lláh*, the friend of God.

A. ابرج *abraj*. Having fine eyes.

A. ابرج *abruj*. Signs of the Zodiac.

A. ابرش *abrash*. A dapple-grey or piebald horse.

A. ابرص *abraṣ*. Leprous; a species of lizard.

A. ابرق *abrak*. Talc, piebald; name of a bird

A. ابرقوه *abar kúh*. A town in the Persian Irak, commonly supposed to be the ancient *Persepolis*. It is also called P. ابركوه *abar-koh*.

P. ابرنجين *abranjín*. A bracelet.

P. ابرو *abrú*. The eyebrow.

P. ابرو *ábrú*. Honour, renown, reputation, glory.

P. ابره *abra*. The outer side of a garment.

P. ابری *abrí*. Cloudy.

P. ابريشم *abrísham*
P. ابريشم *ábríshami* } Silk.

A. ابريق *ibrík*. An ewer.

P. ابزر *'Abzar*. A mountain near *Hamádán* in Persia, about 150 leagues west-ward of *Isfahán*.

P. اب زر *áb i zar*. White wine.

P. ابزن *áb-zan*. A medicated bath.

P. ابسال *ábsál*. A vineyard, a garden.

P. ابست *ábist*. Pregnant; a fœtus, a new-born child.

P. ابستن *ábistan*. To conceive, to be pregnant; *adjective* pregnant.

P. ابسته *ábista*. Pregnant, having conceived.

P. ابشار *ábshár*. A waterfall, cascade, cataract.

P. ابشار *ibshár*. Rejoicing at, or announcing, good news.

P. ابشخور *ábish-kh'ur*. A cistern, a reservoir of water; fortune, destiny.

P. ابشم *ábsham*. A silk-worm cocoon.

A. ابط *ibt*. The armpit.

A. ابطاء *ibṭá*. Delay, protracting.

A. ابطال *ibṭál*. Abolition, rendering void or useless.

A. ابعاد *ib'ád*. Removing to a distance.

A. ابعد *ab'ad*. Very distant.

A. ابق ábiḳ. Absconding (a slave).

A. ابقاء ibḳá. Establishment, perpetuating.

P. آبکار áb-kár. A wine-merchant or distiller.

P. آبکاری áb-kárí. A distillery; a duty levied on distilleries.

P. آبکش áb-kesh. Water-carrier.

P. آبگینه ábgína. A mirror, a decanter.

A. ابل ibl. The camel.

A. ابلاء ablá. Fatigued, emaciated (camel).

A. ابلاء iblá. Trial, proof.

A. ابلاغ iblagh. Conveying, delivering.

A. ابلق ablaḳ. Piebald, black and white.

A. ابله ablah. A fool, blockhead.

P. آبله ábila. A blister, pimple; the small pox. آبله کوبیدن ábila kobídan, to vaccinate.

A. P. ابلهی ablahí. Silliness, folly.

A. ابلیس Iblís. The devil.

A. ابن ibn. A son.

A. ابناء abná. Sons.

A. ابن السبیل ibn us sabíl. Son of the road (a traveller).

A. آبنوس ábnús. Ebony.

A. ابو abu. Father; (in composition) endowed with.

A. ابوان abawáni. Both parents. ابواه abawáhu, both his parents.

A. ابواب abwáb. Doors; chapters; (pl. of باب bab).

P. آب و دانه áb u dána. Livelihood.

P. A. آب و هوا áb u hawá. Climate.

A. ابو بکر Abu Bekr. The father-in-law, and first successor of Moḥammed.

A. ابهام ibham. The thumb.

P. آبی ábí. Watery, moist.

A. ابیات abyát. Verses, distichs, pl. of بیت bait.

A. ابیض abyaẓ. White.

T. اتابك Atábek. A preceptor; the dynasty of the Turkoman Kings of Shíráz.

T. اتالیق Atálíḳ. Guardian, tutor.

A. اتباع atbá'. Followers, clients; اتباع سفارت atbá' i safárat, attachés to the legation.

A. اتّحاد ittiḥád. Union, concord.

A. اتّخاذ ittikháẓ. Seizing, adopting.

A. اتّحاف ittiḥáf. Making a present of.

P. آتش átish. Fire; آتش زدن átish zadan, to set fire to; آتش کردن átish kerdan, to make a fire; آتش روشن کردن átish raushan kerdan, to light a fire.

P. آتشی *átishí.* Fiery, hot.

P. آتشک *átishak.* The venereal disease.

A. اتصاف *ittiṣáf.* Description, qualification; being endowed with anything.

A. اتصال *ittiṣál.* Contiguity, conjunction.

A. اتفاق *ittifák.* Union, agreement, chance, accident; باتفاق *ba ittifák,* with the consent of, together with.

A. اتفاقاً *ittifákan.* Accidentally, by chance.

A. اتفاقی *ittifákí.* Casual, fortuitous, accidental.

A. اتقاء *ittiká.* Dreading, shunning.

A. اتقیاء *atkiyá.* Pious men.

A. اتکاء *ittiká.* Reliance.

A. اتکال *ittikál.* Faith, confidence.

A. اتلاف *itláf.* Waste, loss.

A. اتم *atamm.* Very perfect.

A. اتمام *itmám.* Completion, end.

A. اتون *atún.* An oven, furnace.

A. اتهام *ithám.* Suspicion, false accusation.

A. اثاث البیت *aśáś ul bait.* Household furniture.

A. اثار *aśár.* Signs, marks, traces.

A. اثارت *iśárat.* Handing down by tradition.

A. اثام *áśám.* Sins.

A. اثبات *iśbát.* Confirmation, proof.

A. اثر *aśar.* Impression, mark.

A. اثقال *aśkál.* Burdens, loads.

A. اثم *iśm.* Sin.

A. اثمار *aśmár.* Fruits.

A. اثناء *aśná.* Middle, midst.

A. اثنان *iśnáni.* Two.

A. اجابت *ijábat.* Answering, consenting; اجابت کردن, to respond.

A. اجاره *ijárah.* Price, hire, rent, profit; a farm.

A. P. اجاره دار *ijárah-dár.* A farmer.

A. اجازت *ijázat.* Leave, permission.

A. اجبار *ijbár.* Force, constraint.

A. اجتباء *ijtibá.* Choice, selection.

A. اجتناء *ijtiná.* Gathering.

A. اجتناب *ijtináb.* Shunning, abandoning.

A. اجتهاد *ijtihád.* Care, diligence, effort.

A. اجحاف *ijḥáf.* Annoyance, molestation.

A. اجداد *ajdád.* Ancestors.

A. اجر *ajr.* A reward; hire.

A. اجراء *ijrá.* Giving effect or currency to anything; to put in force, execute.

A. اجرام *ajrám.* Bodies.

A. P. اجرای کار *ijrá e kár.* Executing a business.

A. اجرت *ujrat.* Reward, wages.

A. اجزاء *ajzá.* Parts, portions (pl. of جزء *juz'*).

A. اجسام *ajsám.* Solid bodies.

A. اجفان *ajfán.* Eyelids.

A. اجل *ajal.* An appointed time, the hour of death, doom.

A. آجل *ájil.* Procrastinating; of, or belonging to, a future state.

A. اجلّ *ajall.* More or most glorious.

A. اجلاف *ajláf.* Pl. of جلف *jilf*, tyrants, ignoble.

A. اجلال *ijlál.* Magnificence.

A. اجماع *ijmá'.* Congregation, collection.

A. اجمال *ijmál.* Abridgement, abbreviation.

A. اجمالاً *ijmálan.* Briefly.

A. اجمعين *ajma'ín.* All, the whole, universal.

A. اجناس *ajnás.* Kinds, sorts, species; goods, things.

A. اجنبى *ajnabí.* Foreign.

A. اجنحه *ajnihah.* Wings, fins.

A. اجوبه *ajwiba.* Answers, replies (pl. of جواب *jawáb*).

A. اجوف *ajwaf.* Concave, hollow.

A. اجير *ajír.* A mercenary, hired-labourer.

A. آچار *áchár.* Pickles, preserves.

A. آحاد *áhád.* Units (pl. of احد (*ahad*).

A. احاديث *ahádís.* The traditional sayings of Mohammed; reports.

A. احاطه *iháta.* Surrounding, comprehending; a fence.

A. احباب *ahbáb.* Friends, relations, &c.

A. احتباس *ihtibás.* Restraining, arresting; self-restraint.

A. احتذار *ihtizár.* Being cautious of.

A. احتراز *ihtiráz.* Avoiding, shunning.

A. احتراس *ihtirás.* Guarding, watching.

A. احتراق *ihtirák.* Conflagration.

A. احترام *ihtiram.* Veneration, respect.

A. احتساب *ihtisáb.* Esteeming, reckoning.

A. احتشام *ihtishám.* Pomp, splendour, retinue; shame, bashfulness.

A. احتمال *ihtimál.* Endurance, probability.

A. احتياج *ihtiyáj.* Want, indigenee, necessity.

A. احد *ahad.* One, an unit.

A. احتياط *ihtiyát.* Care, circumspection.

A. احداث *ihdás.* Invention.

A. احدب *ahdab.* Humpbacked.

A. احديت *ahadíyat.* Unity, singularity.

A. احذار *ihzár.* Care, caution.

A. احراق *iḥráḳ*. Burning, setting on fire.

A. احرام *iḥrám*. Putting on a pilgrim's habit; making unlawful.

A. احزان *iḥzán*. Grieving.

A. احسان *iḥsán*. Kindness, favour, beneficence.

A. احسانمند *iḥsánmand*. Grateful.

A. احسن *aḥsan*. More or most beautiful.

A. احسنت *aḥsanta*. Well done! bravo! (2nd per. sing. masc. of the Arabic verb حسن).

A. احصان *iḥṣán*. Continence.

A. احضار *iḥẓár*. Producing, presenting; summoning.

A. احقر *aḥḳar*. Most mean or contemptible.

A. احکام *aḥkám*. Orders, commands.

A. احمال *aḥmál*. Burdens, loads.

A. احمد *aḥmad*. More or most laudable.

A. احمر *aḥmar*. Red.

A. احمق *aḥmaḳ*. Stupid.

A. احمقی *aḥmaḳí*. Stupidity.

A. احوال *aḥwál*. Conditions, circumstances. احوال شما چه طور است *aḥwál i shumá chi ṭúr ast*. How are you?

A. احول *aḥwál*. Squinting.

A. احیا *iḥyá*. Reviving, animating.

A. احیاناً *aḥyánan*. Sometimes.

P. اخ *akh*. Bravo!

A. اخ *akh*. A brother

A. اخبار *akhbár*. News.

A. اخت *ukht*. A sister.

A. اختتام *ikhtitám*. End, conclusion.

P. اختر *akhtar*. A star, constellation.

A. اختراع *ikhtirá'*. Invention, artifice.

A. اختراق *ikhtiráḳ*. Tearing, rending.

A. اختصار *ikhtiṣár*. Contraction, abridgment.

A. اختصاص *ikhtiṣáṣ*. Peculiarity, speciality.

A. اختفاء *ikhtifá*. Concealment.

A. اختلاط *ikhtiláṭ*. Intercourse, association, confusion.

A. اختلاف *ikhtiláf*. Difference, contradiction.

A. اختلال *ikhtilál*. Trouble, revolution.

P. آختن *ákhtan*. To draw (a sword); to hang.

P. آخته *ákhta*. Drawn; trained; a gelding.

A. اختیار *ikhtiyár*. Choice, option.

A. اخذ *akhẓ*. Seizing, taking.

A. آخر *ákhar*. The end, last, final; at last.

A. آخر *ákhir*. Another, second, latter.

A. اخراج *ikhráj*. Expulsion, drawing forth.

A. اخراجات *ikhráját*. Tribute, revenue, expenses.

A. اخر الامر *ákhar ul amr.* At length, finally.

A. اخرت *ákhirat.* The future state.

A. P. اخر بین *ákhar-bín.* Provident, prudent.

A. اخرس *akhras.* Dumb.

P. اخشیجان *akhshíján.* The four elements.

A. اخص *akhaṣṣ.* More or most special.

A. اخضر *akhẓar.* Green.

A. اخفا *ikhfá.* Concealment.

P. اخگر *akhgar.* Embers.

A. اخلاص *ikhláṣ.* Candour, sincerity.

A. P. اخلاصمند *ikhláṣmand.* Sincere.

A. اخلاط *akhláṭ.* Humours.

A. اخلاق *akhláḳ.* Peoples, nature, ethics, morals.

A. اخوان *ikhwán.* Brothers.

A. اخوت *ukhúwat.* Brotherhood.

P. اخور *ákh'ur.* A stable, filth.

P. اخون *ákhún* } A tutor.
P. اخوند *ákh'und* }

A. اخوی *akhawí.* Brotherly; my brother.

A. اخیار *akhyár.* Excellent men.

اخیر *akhír.* Last, posterior.

P. ادا *adá.* Pronunciation, voice. خوش ادا *kh'ush-adá,* melodious.

A. ادا *adá.* Payment, performance.

A. اداب *ádáb.* Etiquette.

A. ادارہ *idára.* Administration.

A. ادات *adát.* An instrument.

A. ادام *adáma.* May he perpetuate. ادام الله ایامه *adáma 'lláhu aiyámahu,* may God prolong his days.

A. ادامت *idámat.* Perpetuating.

A. ادب *adab.* Politeness, etiquette, polite literature.

A. ادبار *idbár.* Calamity, adversity, defeat.

A. ادخال *idkhál.* Introducing, inserting.

A. ادرار *idrár.* Salary, pension.

A. ادراک *idrák.* Perception.

A. ادریس *Idrís.* Enoch.

A. ادعا *iddiʻá.* Pretending to, arrogating.

A. ادق *adaḳḳ.* More or most subtile.

A. ادم *ádam.* ادمخور *ádam khur,* cannibal.

A. ادهم *adham.* A dark-coloured (horse).

A. ادمی *ádmí.* Human, a man. ادمی بچه *admí-bacha,* child of man. ادمی زاده *admí-záda,* human.

A. ادميت ádamíyet. Humanity.

A. ادنى adna. Mean, low; base, least.

A. ادوات adawát. Instruments.

A. ادويه adwiyah. Medicines, drugs.

A. ادهان adhán. Oils, unguents.

A. اديان adyán. Religions. Pl. of دين dín.

A. اديب adíb. A tutor; polite.

A. اديم adím. Morocco leather. اديم السماء adím us samá, the expanse of heaven.

P. ادينه ádína. Friday.

A. اذان ażan. The call to prayers.

A. اذى ażá. Vexation, trouble.

A. اذر 'Azar. Fire, the fire-demon; name of the father of Abraham.

A. اذعان iż'án. Obedience.

A. اذل ażall. More or most base.

A. اذن iżn. Permission.

A. اذن użn. An ear.

A. اذيت ażíyet. Distress, injury.

P. ار ár. Bring thou.

P. ار ar. If; for اگر.

P. ارا árá. (In composition), ornamenting.

P. ارابه arába. A cart, carriage.

A. اراجيف arájíf. Rumours, false reports.

A. ارادت irádat. Inclination.

P. اراستگى árástagí. Decoration, order.

P. اراستن árástan. To adorn, to put in order.

P. اراسته árásta. Adorned, arrayed.

A. اراضى arází. Lands.

P. ارام árám. Repose.

P. ارامگاه árám-gáh. Resting-place.

P. ارامش árámish. Ease, tranquillity.

A. ارامل arámil. Widows (pl. of ارمل armal), poor persons.

P. ارامیدن árámidan. To rest, to repose; to appease.

P. ارای árái. Adorn thou.

P. ارائیدن áráídan. To ornament.

P. ارایش áráyish. Ornament.

A. ارباب arbab. Possessors, masters, lords.

A. ارتباط irtibát. Connexion, friendship.

A. ارتحال irtiḥál. Starting on a journey; decease.

A. ارتداد *irtidád.* Apostasy; refusing.

A. ارتشاء *irtishá.* Bribery.

A. ارتفاع *irtifá'.* Elevation, altitude.

A. ارتقاء *irtiḳá.* Ascending, promotion.

A. ارتکاب *irtikáb.* Perpetration; commission (of sins).

A. ارتیاح *irtiyáḥ.* Contentment, gaiety.

A. ارث *irṡ.* Inheritance.

P. اردشاهی *ardasháhi.* Artichoke.

P. ارج *arj.* Price, value.

P. ارجمند *arjmand.* Excellent, noble, precious.

A. ارحم *arham.* More or most merciful.

A. ارخی *arkhá.* More or most flabby, flaccid.

P. آرد *árd.* Meal, flour.

P. اردی بهشت *urdí-bihisht.* The second Persian month (April).

A. ارذل *arzal.* Mean, vile.

P. اردشیر بابکان *Ardashir Bábakán.* Name of the 1st King of the Sassanian dynasty, a contemporary of Commodus.

P. ارز *arz.* Price, value.

A. ارزاق *arzáḳ.* Provisions.

P. ارزان *arzán.* Cheap.

P. ارزانی *arzání.* Cheapness.

ارزانی داشتن *arzání dáshten.* To confer, grant.

P. ارزش *arzish.* Valuation.

P. ارزن *arzan.* Millet.

P. آرزو *árzú.* Desire, wish.

P. آرزومند *árzúmand.* Desirous, fond, eager.

P. ارزیدن *arzídan.* To be worth.

P. ارزین *arzín.* Tin.

P. ارژنگ *arzhang.* The portfolio of the Persian painter and heresiarch Manes.

P. ارژنگی *arzhangí.* *Adjective* from the above.

A. ارسال *irsál.* Remittance, despatch.

A. ارسطو *Arisṭú.* Aristotle.

P. T. ارسلان *arslán.* A lion.

A. ارشاد *irshád.* Direction, command.

A. ارض *arz.* The earth, land.

A. ارضه *araẓah.* The white ant, weevil.

A. ارضی *arzí.* Terrestrial, earthly.

P. ارغوان *arghawán.* Purple.

A. ارقام *arḳám.* Writings.

A. ارکان *arkán.* Pillars.

A. ارکان دولت *arkán i daulat.* Ministers of state.

A. ارم *Iram.* A fabulous earthly Paradise, said to have been constructed in Arabia Felix by Sheddád ibn 'Ad.

P. آرم *āram.* That I may bring.

P. ارمان *armán.* Desire, remorse.

P. ارمغان *armaghán.* A present, offering.

P. A. ارمن *arman.* Armenia.

P. ارمیدن *aramídan.* To rest, repose.

A. ارنب *arneb.* A hare.

P. ارنج *aranj.* The elbow.

P. ارنده *áranda.* One who brings, a carrier.

P. ارنه *ar-na.* If not; otherwise.

A. ارواح *arwáḥ.* Spirits, souls.

P. اره *arrah.* A saw.

P. اری *áre.* Yes, so. *árí,* thou mayest bring.

A. ارياح *aryáḥ.* Winds.

P. اريز *aríz.* Frost, hoar-frost.

A. اريكه *aríkah.* A throne.

P. از *áz.* Desire, avidity.

P. از *az.* From, of, by, for, &c.

P. ازاد *ázád* / P. ازاده *ázáda* — Free, liberated. ازادماهی *ázád-máhi,* a carp (fish).

P. ازادی *ázádí.* Freedom, liberty.

P. ازار *ázár.* Trouble; injury; sickness. In comp. tormenting. مردم ازار *mardum-azár,* tormenting mankind.

A. ازار *izár.* Trowsers, drawers.

A. P. ازاربند *izár-band.* The string of the drawers.

P. ازاردن *ázárdan.* To trouble; to hurt; to molest.

P. ازاری *ázárí.* A sick person.

A. ازالت *izálat.* Removing, causing to cease.

P. از پای *az pái.* Down.

P. از پای پست *az pái past.* Decayed, undermined.

P. از بر *az bar.* By heart, by rote.

P. از بس *az bas.* Much, many. از بسکه *az baski.* Inasmuch as.

P. ازدن *ázadan.* To prick with a needle, to sew.

A. ازدواج *izdiwáj.* Marriage.

P. اژدها *azhdahá.* A dragon.

A. ازدحام *izdiḥám.* A crowd, throng.

A. ازدياد *izdiyád.* Augmentation, increase.

P. ازردگی *ázardagí.* Uneasiness, displeasure.

P. ازردن *ázardan.* To injure; to displease.

P. ازرده *ázarda.* Afflicted; displeased.

A. ازرق *azraḳ.* Blue, cerulean. *azraḳ-pairáhan,* wearing a blue vest.

P. ازرم *ázarm.* Modesty, justice. ازرم جو tolerant.

P. ازرو *az rú.* On the ground, or score.

A. ازكيا *azkiyá.* Ingenuous, virtuous people.

P. ازكل *azkal.* a medlar.

A. ازل *azal.* Eternity without beginning.

A. ازلی *azalí.* Existing from all eternity.

P. ازما *ázmá.* Try thou; (in composition) examining.

A. ازمان *azmán.* Times.

P. ازمایش *ázmáyish.* Experience, trial.

P. ازمند *ázmand.* Greedy.

A. ازمنه *azminah.* Times, ages.

P. ازمودن *ázmúdan.* To try, prove, experience.

P. ازو *azú* } Of, from, or
P. ازوی *azvai* } than him.

A. ازواج *azwáj.* Pairs, spouses.

A. ازهار *az-hár.* Flowers.

P. ازین *azín.* From this.

P. ازین پیش *azín pesh.* Before this.

P. ازینجا *azínjá.* Hence, inasmuch.

A. اس *ás.* The myrtle.

P. اسا *ásá.* Like, resembling (in composition).

A. اسابیع *asábí'.* Weeks.

A. اساتیر *asátír.* Weights of 6½ drams.

A. P. اساتین *asátín.* Pillars.

A. اساس *asás.* Foundations.

A. اسافل *asáfil.* Inferiors.

A. اسالیب *asalíb.* Modes, methods, pl. of اسلوب *uslúb.*

A. اسامی *asámí.* Names; pl. of اسما *asmá.*

P. اسان *ásán.* Easy.

P. اسانی *ásání.* Facility, ease.

P. اسایش *ásáyish.* Rest, repose.

P. اسائیدن *ásá'ídan.* To rest.

P. اسپ *asp.* A horse. یک راس اسپ *yek rás asp,* one horse.

A. اسباب *asbáb.* Causes; baggage.

A. اسبق *asbak.* Previous, surpassing.

P. استاد *ustád.* A teacher, professor.

P. استادن *istádan.* To stand.

A. استاذ *ustáz.* A teacher.

P. استان *ástán.* Threshold.

A. استبرا *istibrá.* Cleansing.

A. استتار *istitár.* Concealing, covering.

A. استثنا *istisná.* Exception.

A. استحسان *istihsán.* Approving; considering as a favour.

A. استحقاق *istihkák.* Meriting; demanding one's rights.

A. استحکام *istihkám.* Firmness.

A. استخراج *istikhráj.* Extracting, deducing.

A. استخوان *ustukhwán.* A bone; kernel; a skeleton.

A. استدامت *istidámat.* Permanency.

A. استدعا *istid'á.* Supplication.

A. استدلال *istidlál.* Demonstration, proof.

P. استر *ástar.* The lining of a garment.

P. استر *astar.* A mule.

A. استراحت *istiráḥat.* Tranquillity.

A. استرخاص *istirkháṣ.* Leaving, asking leave.

A. استرداد *istirdád.* Repelling, restitution.

P. استردن *usturdan.* To shave.

A. استرضاء *istirẓa.* Acquiescence.

P. استره *ustura.* A razor.

A. استسقاء *istisḳá'.* The dropsy.

A. استشام *istishám.* Smelling.

A. استصواب *istiṣwáb.* Approbation.

A. استطاعت *istiṭá'at.* Obedience, power.

A. استظهار *istiẓhár.* Demanding aid or support.

A. استعاره *isti'árah.* Borrowing; a metaphor.

A. استعجاب *isti'jáb.* Astonishment.

A. استعانت *isti'ánat.* Asking aid.

A. استعجال *isti'jál.* Hastening, accelerating.

A. استعداد *isti'dád.* Skill, ability.

A. استعفاء *isti'fá'.* Asking forgiveness; resignation (of an office, &c.).

A. استعمال *isti'mál.* Practice, usage. استعمال كردن *isti'mál kerdan.* To use.

A. استغاثه *istighásah.* Seeking redress.

A. استغراب *istighráb.* Amazement.

A. استغراق *istighráḳ.* Immersion, overwhelming.

A. استغفار *istighfár.* Asking forgiveness.

A. استغفرالله *astaghfiru 'llah.* I ask pardon of God.

A. استغناء *istighná'.* Independence.

A. استفاده *istifádah.* Profit, result.

A. استفاضه *istifáẓah.* Superabundance.

A. استفسار *istifsár.* Inquiry.

A. استفتاء *istiftá'.* Demanding a legal decision.

A. استفتاح *istiftáḥ.* Opening, conquering.

A. استفهام *istifhám.* Interrogation.

A. استقامت *istiḳámat.* Rectitude, perseverance.

A. استقبال *istiḳbál.* The future; going out to meet a visitor.

A. استقرار *istiḳrár.* Confirmation, establishment.

A. استقراض *istiḳráẓ.* Borrowing.

A. استقصاء *istiḳsá'.* Curiosity.

A. استقلال *istiḳlál.* Irresponsible authority, despotism.

RUS. استكان *istakán.* Glass.

A. استكبار *istikbár.* Pride.

A. استلام *istilám.* Prostration, kissing the hand.

A. استكراه *istikráh.* Abhorrence, aversion.

A. استماع *istimá'*. Listening.

A. استكشاف *istiksháf*. Discovery, exploration.

A. استمالت *istimálat*. Consolation, comforting.

A. استمداد *istimdád*. Asking for aid.

A. استمرار *istimrár*. Continuance.

A. استمراری *istimrárí*. Perpetual.

A. استمزاج *istimzáj*. Asking after one's health.

A. استنباط *istimbát*. Drawing a conclusion, extracting.

A. استواء *istiwá'*. Equal, parallel.

P. استوار *ustuwár*. Strong, firm, brave.

P. استواری *ustuwárí*. Strength, firmness.

A. استهزاء *istihzá'*. Derision.

A. استیفاء *istífá'*. Performance of a promise.

A. استیلاء *istílá'*. Dominion, domination.

P. استین *ástín*. A sleeve.

A. استئناس *isti'nás*. Familiarity.

A. اسد *asad*. A lion; the sign Leo.

A. اسرار *asrár*. Secrets. *israr*. Acting secretly.

A. اسراف *isráf*. Prodigality.

A. اسرافیل *isráfíl*. The angel of death.

A. اسرع *asra'*. Swifter or swiftest, sooner.

G. اسطبل *istabl*. A stable.

G. اسطرلاب *usturláb*. An astrolabe.

A. اسعار *as'ár*. Prices.

A. اسعد *as'ad*. Happiest, auspicious.

G. اسفاناج *isfánáj*. Spinage.

A. اسفل *asfal*. Inferior, lowest.

A. اسقاط *iskát*. Causing to fall, abortion.

A. اسقام *askám*. Infirmities.

A. اسکندر *Iskandar*. Alexander.

A. اسکندریه *Iskanderíyeh*. Alexandria (in Egypt).

A. اسلاف *asláf*. Ancestors.

A. اسلام *islám*. Islam. The Mohammedan religion. Islamism.

T. اسلامبول *Islámbúl*. Constantinople; for استنبول *Istámbúl*.

A. اسلحه *aslihah*. Weapons, arms.

A. اسلم *aslam*. Safer, safest.

P. A. اسلم شقوق *aslam i shukúk*. The best course to pursue.

A. اسلوب *uslúb*. Manner, mode. pl. اسالیب *asálíb*.

A. اسم *ism*. A name, a noun.

A. اسماء *asmá'*. Names.

P. اسمان *ásmán*. The sky, heaven.

P. اسمانی *ásmání*. Heavenly. azure, cerulean.

A. اسمر *asmar*. Brown.

A. اسناد *asnád*. Documents. *isnád*. Attributing to.

A. اسنان *asnán.* Teeth; the points of spears. pl. of سن *sinn.*

A. اسوار *aswár.* Horsemen.

A. اسود *aswad.* Black, blacker.

P. اسودن *ásúdan.* To repose.

P. اسوده *ásúda.* Tranquil.

A. اسهال *ishál.* Diarrhœa, purging.

A. اسهل *ashal.* More or most easy.

P. اسپا *ásyá.* A mill. اسپای گردان *ásyá i gardán.* The revolving millstone.

P. اسپا باد *ásyá-bád.* A windmill.

P. اسپا بان *ásyá-bán.* Miller.

P. اسپا سنك *ásyá-sang.* A millstone.

P. اسپانه *ásyána.* A whetstone.

P. اسيب *ásíb.* Damage; detriment.

A. اسير *asír.* A captive.

A. اسيرى *asírí.* Captivity.

P. اش *ásh.* Potage, gruel.

A. اشارة *ishárah.* A sign, a hint.

A. اشاعت *ishá'at.* Diffusion, publication.

P. اشاميدن *áshámídan.* To drink.

A. اشباه *ashbáh.* Resemblances.

P. اشپز *ásh-paz.* Cook.

A. اشتباه *ishtibáh.* Doubt, ambiguity.

A. اشتداد *ishtidád.* Violence.

P. اشتر *ushtur.* A camel.

A. اشترا *ishtirá'.* Buying, purchase.

A. اشتراك *ishtirák.* Partnership.

A. اشتعال *ishti'ál.* Flaming, conflagration.

A. اشتغال *ishtighál.* Occupation, distraction.

A. اشتقاق *ishtiḳáḳ.* Derivation.

A. اشتمال *ishtimál.* Containing, comprising.

A. اشتهاء *ishtihá'.* Appetite.

A. اشتهار *ishtihár.* Publication, an advertisement.

P. اشتى *áshtí.* Peace, reconciliation.

A. اشتياق *ishtiyáḳ.* Longing, desire.

A. اشخاص *ashkhás.* Persons.

A. اشد *ashadd.* More or most vehement.

A. اشر *asharr.* Worse, worst.

A. اشراف *ashráf.* Nobles.

A. اشراق *ishráḳ.* Splendour; the rising of the sun.

P. اشردن *áshurdan.* To bruise, pound.

A. اشرف *ashraf.* Illustrious.

P. اشرفی ashrafí. A gold coin worth about 12s.

A. اشعار ash'ár. Poetry, verses. ish'ár. To inform.

A. اشعه ashi''ah. Rays.

A. اشغال ashghál. Affairs, occupations.

A. اشفاق ishfák. Compassion.

P. اشفتن áshuftan. To be uneasy, to disturb, infatuate.

P. اشفتگی áshuftagi. Perturbation.

P. اشفته áshufta. Enamoured; distracted.

P. A. اشفته حال áshufta ḥál. Distracted in condition.

P. اشفته کار áshufta kár. An intricate business.

P. اشفته موی áshuftá múy. Dishevelled hair.

P. اشقالنگ ishkálang. The leg, shank.

A. اشقیاء ashkiya. Wretched. pl. of شقی shakíy.

P. اشک ashk. A tear.

P. اشکار áshkár. Evident.

P. اشکارا áshkárá. Openly, publicly.

P. اشکبار ashk-bár. Shedding tears.

A. اشکال ashkál. Forms, figures.

A. اشکال ishkál. Perplexity, doubts. اشکال داشتن ishkál dáshtan. To be difficult (a question).

P. اشنا áshná. A friend.

P. اشوب áshúb. Confusion, tumult, from اشوفتن, see اشفتن (in comp.) confusing.

P. اشوردن áshurdan. To mix; to ferment.

A. اشهاد ash-hád. Witnesses.

A. اشهب ash-hab. Dun-coloured.

A. اشهر ash-har. More or most celebrated. ash-hur. Months.

A. اشیاء ashyá'. Things.

P. اشیان áshyán } A nest.
P. اشیانه áshyána }

A. اصابع aṣábi' } Fingers.
اصابیع aṣábí' }

A. اصح aṣaḥḥ. More or most true.

A. اصحاب aṣ-ḥáb. Companions. اصحاب کهف aṣ-ḥáb i kahf. The seven sleepers (of Ephesus).

A. اصدار iṣdár. Issuing; publishing.

A. اصداف aṣdáf. Shells.

A. اصرار iṣrár. Perseverance, obstinacy.

A. اصراف iṣráf. Expending.

A. اصطبل iṣṭabl. A stable.

A. اصطفاء iṣṭifá'. Selecting.

P. اصطخر Iṣtakhar. Persepolis.

A. اصطلاح iṣṭiláḥ. Idiom, technical term.

A. اصغاء iṣghá'. Listening to.

A. اصغر *asghar.* Smaller or smallest.

A. آصف *'Aṣuf.* Asof, name of King Solomon's vizier.

A. اصفار *aṣfár.* Ciphers.

A. اصفر *aṣfar.* Yellow, pale.

P. اصفهان *Iṣfahán.* The ancient capital of Persia.

A. اصفیاء *aṣfiyá.* Pure, holy (men). (pl. of صفی *ṣafiy*).

A. اصل *aṣl.* Root, origin.

A. اصلاً *aṣlan.* Not at all, never.

A. اصلاح *iṣláḥ.* Correction.

A. اصلح *aṣlaḥ.* Better, best; most advisable.

A. اصلی *aṣlí.* Radical, principal.

A. اصم *aṣamm.* Deaf; (in arithmetic) surds.

A. اصناف *aṣnáf.* Kinds; guilds, corporations.

A. اصوات *aṣwát.* Sounds, voices. (sing. of صوت *ṣaut.*)

A. اصول *uṣúl.* Roots; causes; elements. (pl. of اصل *aṣl.*)

A. اصیل *aṣíl.* Well-born, thorough-bred.

A. اضاعت *iżá'at.* Ruining, losing, squandering.

A. اضافت *iżáfat.* Adding, joining; construction of one noun with another. The relation of the genitive case expressed by *kesrah.*

A. اضافه *iżáfa.* Addition, augmentation.

A. اضداد *ażdád.* Opposites; contrary, opponent.

A. اضطراب *iżṭiráb.* Anxiety, agitation, trouble.

A. اضطرار *iżṭirár.* Misery, distress.

A. اضعف *aż'af.* More or most weak.

A. اضلاع *ażlá'.* Sides, ribs, districts.

A. اضلال *iżlál.* Seduction, leading astray.

A. اضواء *ażwá.* Lights.

A. اطاعت *iṭá'at.* Obedience, loyalty.

A. اطالت *iṭálat.* Extension.

A. اطباء *aṭibbá.* Physicians.

A. اطراف *aṭráf.* Sides, quarters, environs.

A. اطعمه *aṭ'ima.* Viands, victuals. (pl. of طعام *ṭa'ám.*)

A. اطفاء *iṭfá.* Extinction.

A. اطفال *aṭfál.* Infants.

A. اطلاع *iṭṭilá'.* Notice, information.

A. P. اطلاع کردن *iṭṭilá' kerdan.* To inform.

A. P. اطلاع داشتن *iṭṭilá' dáshtan.* To be informed.

A. اطلاق *iṭláḳ.* Setting at liberty; evacuation.

A. اطلس *aṭlas.* Satin.

A. اطناب *iṭnáb.* Prolixity, amplifying a discourse.

A. اطماع *iṭmá'.* Incitement.

A. اطمئنان *iṭmi'nán.* Tranquillity.

A. اطوار *aṭwar.* Modes, fashions.

A. اظہار *iẓhár.* Discovering, revealing.

A. اظہر *aẓhar.* More or most evident.

A. اعاجم *a'ájim.* Barbarians. (pl. of اعجم *a'jam.*)

A. اعاجیب *a'ájíb.* Prodigies. (pl. of اعجوبہ *u'júbah.*)

A. اعادة *i'ádat.* Returning, repetition.

A. اعانت *i'ánat.* Assistance, help.

A. اعتاق *i'ták.* Setting at liberty, giving leave.

A. اعتبار *i'tibár.* Esteem; credit.

A. اعتدال *i'tidál.* Moderation.

A. اعتذار *i'tiẕár.* Apologizing, excuse.

A. اعتراض *i'tiráẓ.* Opposition, objection.

A. اعتراف *i'tiráf.* Confession.

A. اعتزال *i'tizál.* Abdication, secession.

A. اعتصام *i'tiṣám.* Preserving one's self from sin; laying firm hold of (a rope, &c.).

A. اعتضاد *i'tiẓád.* Supporting.

A. اعتقاد *i'tiḳád.* Faith, confidence, belief.

A. اعتکاف *i'tikáf.* Restraining one's passion; constant devotions.

A. اعتلاء *i'tilá.* Height, exaltation.

A. اعتماد *i'timád.* Confidence, trust.

A. اعجاز *i'jáz.* A miracle; rendering (another) powerless.

A. اعجوبہ *u'júbah.* A prodigy.

A. اعداء *a'dá.* Enemies.

A. اعداد *a'dád.* Numbers.

A. اعدل *a'dal.* More or most just.

A. اعدی *a'dá.* More or most hostile.

A. اعذاب *i'ẕáb.* Tormenting.

A. اعراب *a'ráb.* The wandering Arabs.

A. اعرابی *a'rábí.* An Arab.

A. اعراض *i'ráẓ.* Dislike, avoiding.

A. اعراف *i'ráf.* Purgatory, the bridge between Heaven and Hell.

A. اعزاز *i'záz.* Respecting, honouring.

A. اعضاء *a'ẓá.* Members, limbs.

A. اعطاء *i'ṭá.* Bestowing.

A. اعطاف *a'ṭáf.* Bounties, favours.

A. اعظم *a'ẓam.* Superior, supreme.

A. اعلام *a'lám.* Flags, ensigns.

A. اعلام *i'lám* }
A. اعلان *i'lán* } Publication.

A. اعلی *a'lá.* Higher, loftier, loftiest.

A. اعمال *a'mál.* Works, actions. (pl. of عمل *'amal.*)

A. اعم *a'amm.* More common or general.

A. اعوان *a'wán.* Assistants. (pl. of عون *'aun.*)

A. اعيان *a'yán*. Nobles. (pl. of عين *'ain.*)

P. آغا *ághá*. Chief, master; eunuch.

P. آغاريدن *ághárídan*. To moisten, wet, macerate.

P. آغاز *ágház*. A beginning, commencement.

P. آغازيدن *ágházídan*. To begin, commence.

P. آغاليدن *ághálídan*. To excite; to satiate.

A. اغانى *aghání*. (pl. of اغنية) songs.

A. اغتشاش *ightishásh*. Rebellion, riot.

A. اغذيه *aghziyeh*. Aliments.

P. آغشتن *ághashtan*. To moisten; to pollute.

A. اغلب *aghlab*. Prevalent; mostly.

A. اغماض *ighmáz*. Connivance.

P. آغندن *ághandan*. To fill, to stuff.

A. اغنيا *agniyá*. Rich men. (pl. of غنى *ghaníy*).

A. اغوا *ighwá*. Evil suggestion, seducing.

P. آغوش *ághúsh*. The bosom; an emhrace.

A. اغيار *aghyár*. Strangers; others; rivals. (pl. of غير *ghair.*)

A. اف *uff*. Fie! for shame!

A. آفات *áfát*. Misfortunes, calamities.

A. افاده *ifáda*. Benefit.

A. افاضل *afazil*. Learned; virtuous. (pl. of افضل *afzal.*)

A. آفاق *áfák*. Horizons; tracts; quarters of the heavens, the world, &c. (pl. of افق *ufk.*)

A. افاقت *ifákat*. Convalescence, recovery.

A. افانين *afánín*. Paths, ways. (pl. of افنان *afnán*, which is itself a plural of فن *fann.*)

A. آفت *áfat*. Misfortune, calamity.

P. آفتاب *áftáb*. The sun.

P. آفتاب پرست *áftáb-parast*. A sun-worshipper.

P. آفتاب گردان *áftáb-gardán*. The sun-flower (tourne-sol).

طلوع آفتاب *tulú' i áftáb*. Sunrise.

غروب آفتاب *ghurúb i áftáb*. Sunset.

P. آفتابگير *áftáb-gír*. A parasol, umbrella.

P. آفتابه *áftába*. An ewer.

P. افتان *uftán*. Falling, stumbling. افتان خيزان *uftán khízán*. Limping.

A. افتتاح *iftitáh*. Opening; commencement.

P. افتادگى *uftádagí*. Humility.

P. افتادن *uftádan.* To fall, to happen.

A. افتخار *iftikhár.* Glorying, boasting.

A. افتراء *iftirá.* Calumny, falsehood.

A. افتراق *iftirák.* Separation.

A. افتقار *iftikár.* Poverty; needing.

A. افخم *afkham.* More or most grand.

P. افراختن *afrákhtan.* To elevate, to exalt. .

A. افراد *afrád.* Individuals. (pl. of فرد *fard.*)

P. افراز *afráz.* Exalting.

P. افراشتن *afráshtan.* To exalt, to extol.

A. افراط *ifrát.* Excess.

P. افروختن *afrúkhtan.* To illuminate; to inflame.

P. افروز *afrúz.* (In composition) illuminating.

P. افریدگار *'Afrídgár.* The Creator, God.

P. افریدگان *áfrídagán.* Creatures, created beings.

P. افریدن *áfrídan.* To create.

P. افرین *áfrín.* Praising, creating. افرین کردن *áfrín kerdan.* To applaud.

P. افریننده *áfrínanda.* Creator.

P. افرینش *áfrínish.* The creation.

P. افزا *afzá.* Increasing, multiplying.

P. افزائیدن *afzáídan.* To multiply, add, increase.

P. افزایش *afzáyish.* Increase, abundance.

P. افزودن *afzúdan.* To increase.

P. افزون *afzún.* Increasing.

P. افزونی *afzúní.* Increase, abundance; spare, surplus.

A. افساد *ifsád.* Spoiling.

P. افسار *afsár.* A bridle, halter, headstall.

P. افساریدن *afsárídan.* To speak obscenely.

P. افسانه *afsána.* A fable, romance.

P. افسردن *afsurdan.* To congeal; to wither.

P. افسر *afsar.* A crown.

افسر سر *afsar i sar.* The crown of the head.

P. افسرده *afsurda.* Withered, congealed.

P. افسوس *afsos.* Sorrow, alas! افسوس خوردن *afsos khwurdan.* To regret.

P. افسون *afsún.* Incantation, sorcery.

A. افشاء *ifshá.* Publication, divulging.

P. افشاردن *afshárdan.* To squeeze, to press.

P. افشان *afshán.* Scattering, diffusing.

P. افشاندن *afshándan.* To diffuse, disperse, scatter.

P. افشردن *afshardan.* To filter, to squeeze.

A. افصح *afṣaḥ.* More, or most, eloquent.

A. افضال *afẓál.* Virtues. (pl. of فضل *faẓl.*)

A. افضل *afẓal* } More
A. P. افضلتر *afẓal-tar* } excellent, or accomplished.

A. افطار *ifṭár.* Breaking a fast.

A. افعال *af'ál.* Actions. (pl. of فعل *fi'l.*)

A. افعی *af'á.* A snake.

P. افغان *Afghán.* Lamentation; an Afghan.

A. افق *ufḳ.* The horizon.

P. افکن *afgan.* Overthrowing, casting away.

P. افکندن *afgandan.* To throw, to throw down.

A. افلاح *ifláḥ.* Prosperity.

A. افلاس *iflás.* Poverty, bankruptcy.

A. افلاطون *Aflaṭún.* Plato.

A. افلاك *aflák.* The heavens. (pl. of فلك *falak.*)

A. افلج *aflaj.* Palsied.

A. افواج *afwáj.* Troops, armies. (pl. of فوج *fauj.*)

A. افواه *afwáḥ.* Mouths. (pl. of فم *famm* or فوه.)

A. افیون *ifyún.* Opium.

P. آقا *áḳá.* Master, sir! lord.

P. آقابانو *aḳábánú.* Muslin.

A. اقارب *aḳárib.* Relations, kinsmen. (pl. of قریب *ḳaríb.*)

A. اقاصی *aḳáṣí.* The extremes; remotest parts. (pl. of اقصی *aḳṣá.*)

A. اقالیم *aḳálím.* Climates, countries, zones.

A. اقامت *iḳámat.* Abode, dwelling; establishment.

A. اقبال *iḳbál.* Prosperity, felicity; approaching. دام اقباله *dáma iḳbáluhu.* May his prosperity be lasting.

A. P. اقبالمند *iḳbálmand.* Prosperous, lucky.

A. اقتباس *iḳtibás.* Quoting (especially from the Ḳorán.)

A. اقتدا *iḳtidá.* Following, imitating.

A. اقتدار *iḳtidár.* Power, authority. ذو الاقتدار *ẕu'l iḳtidár.* Powerful (prince).

A. اقتران *iḳtirán.* Coniunction; company.

A. اقتسام *iḳtisám.* Partitioning, division.

A. اقتصار *iḳtiṣár.* Abbreviation, abridgment.

A. اقتضا *iḳtiẓá.* Exigency, demand.

A. اقداح *aḳdáḥ.* Cups, bowls.

A. اقدام *aḳdám.* Paces, steps.

A. اقدام *iḳdám.* Presenting; pushing forward.

A. اقدس *aḳdas.* More or most pure or holy.

A. اقدم *aḳdam.* Prior, former.

A. اقرار *iḳrár.* Confession, agreement. اقرار نامه *iḳrár náma.* A bond.

A. اقران *aḳrán.* Equals, peers.

A. اقرب *aḳrab.* Nearer, nearest.

A. اقرباء *aḳribá.* Kindred, relation. (pl. of قریب *ḳaríb.*)

A. اقسام *aḳsám.* Sorts, kinds; oaths.

A. اقصی *aḳsá.* More or most extreme.

A. اقطار *aḳṭár.* Tracts, districts.

A. اقل *aḳall.* Few, least.

اقل قلیل *aḳall i ḳalíl.* At least.

A. اقلید *iḳlíd.* Key.

A. اقلیم *iḳlím.* A clime, country.

A. اکابر *akábir.* Great people.

A. اکارم *akárim.* Nobles, grandees.

P. آگاه *ágáh.* Vigilant; informed, aware.

P. آگاهی *agáhí.* Knowledge; vigilance.

A. اکبر *akbar.* Greater, greatest.

A. اکتساب *iktisáb.* Acquisition, gain.

A. اکتفاء *iktifá.* Sufficiency, enough.

A. اکتناه *iktináh.* Scrutinizing.

A. اکثر *akṡar.* More, many.

P. اگر *agar.* If.

A. اکرام *ikrám.* Honouring.

A. اکراه *ikráh.* Abhorrence, disgust.

P. اگرچه *agarchi.* Although.

A. اکرم *akram.* More or most noble or generous.

A. اکسیر *iksír.* An elixir; the philosopher's stone.

A. اکل *akl.* Eating.

A. اکمال *ikmál.* Perfecting.

A. اکلیل *iklíl.* A crown, garland.

A. اکمل *akmal.* More or most perfect.

A. اکناف *aknáf.* Environs; sides.

P. آگندن *ágandan.* To fill, stuff, cram.

P. آگنده پر *aganda par.* Stuffed with feathers.

P. اکنون *aknún.* Now, at present.

A. اکید *akyad.* More or most decided or urgent.

P. آگین *ágín.* Full (in composition).

A. آل *ál.* Family, race.

A. الا *illa.* But, unless, except.

P. الا تا *ala tá.* Beware! that...

A. آلات *álát.* Tools, instruments.

A. آلام *álám.* Pains, griefs.

A. الآن *al-án.* Now, the present moment.

A. الله *Alláh.* God.

P. آلايش *áláyish.* Pollution, corruption.

A. البته *albatta.* Certainly.

A. آلت *álat.* A tool, instrument.

A. التجاء *iltijá.* Taking refuge.

A. التزام *iltizám.* Expediency; necessity.

A. التفات *iltifát.* Attention, kindness, condescension.

A. التماس *iltimás.* Petition, request.

A. P. التمغا *at-tamghá.* Royal insignia.

A. التيام *iltiyám.* Healing; reconciliation.

A. الحاح *ilḥáḥ.* Solicitation, importunity.

A. الحاصل *al-ḥásil.* Upon the whole, to sum up.

A. الحاق *ilḥáḳ.* Annexation.

A. الحمد لله *al-ḥamdu lilláh.* Praise be to God!

الحال *al ḥál.* Now, at present.

A. الحان *alḥán.* Modulated notes. خوش الحان *kh'ush alḥán.* Melodious.

A. الزام *ilzám.* Conviction, proof.

P. الش *alush.* The remains of a repast.

A. الطاف *altáf.* Favours, benefits. (pl. of لطف *lutf.*)

A. الغرض *al-gharẓ.* Upon the whole; in short.

A. الغياث *al-ghiyás.* Clamour for justice.

A. الفت *ulfat.* Affection, familiarity.

P. الفختن *alfakhtan.* To acquire.

A. القاب *alḳáb.* Title, appellation. (pl. of لقب *laḳab.*)

A. القصه *al-ḳiṣṣah.* In short.

A. الم *alam.* Grief, anguish, pain.

A. الماس *almás.* A diamond.

P. النگ *alang* or } Intrenchment.
P. آلنگ *álang* }

A. الوان *alwán.* Colours; varieties. (pl. of لون *laun.*)

P. آلو بالو *álú bálú.* Sour cherry.

P. آلو بخار *álú-bukhár.* A sort of plum.

P. آلوچه *álúcheh.* A plum.

P. آلودن *álúdan.* To stain, to pollute.

A. الوداع *al-widá'.* Farewell, adieu!

P. آلودگی *álúdagí.* Pollution.

P. الوش *alúsh.* The remains of a repast.

P. الوند *Alwend.* Name of a high mountain in Hamadán.

A. الوف *ulúf.* Thousands.

A. الويه *alwiyeh.* (Pl. of لواء *liwá*) Standards, banners.

A. الوهيت *ulúhíyet.* Deity, Godhead.

A. الهام *ilhám.* Inspiration.

A. اللهم *Allahumma!* Oh God!

A. الهی *Iláhí*. Divine, O! God.

A. الی *ilá*. To.

A. الیم *alím*. Painful, grieving.

A. ام *umm*. A mother.

A. اما *ammá*. But, however, nevertheless.

P. اماج *ámáj*. A butt or mark.

A. اماجد *amájid*. Great nobles. (pl. of امجد *amjad*.)

P. اماده *ámáda*. Ready.

P. امادگی *ámádagí*. Readiness.

P. امادن *ámádan*. To prepare, make ready.

A. امارت *imárat*. A government; dominion. *amárat*. A sign-post.

P. اماس *ámas*. A swelling.

P. اماسیدن *ámásídan*. To swell.

A. اماکن *amákin*. Places, habitations. (pl. of مکان *makán*.)

A. امال *ámál*. Hopes, desires.

A. امام *Imám*. A leader, chief; priest.

A. امامت *imámat*. The office of Imam.

A. امام جمعه *Imám i Jum'ah*. Imam, who recites the prayer for the sovereign on Fridays in the mosque.

A. امان *amán*. Security, safety; quarter.

A. P. امامزاده *Imámzáda*. Son of an Imam. Mausoleum, where a descendant of the Prophet is buried.

A. امانت *imánat*. Deposit, trust, safety.

A. امانی *amání*. Protection.

A. امت *ummat*. A sect; religion.

A. امتثال *imtisál*. Conformity, obedience.

A. امتحان *imtihán*. Trial, examination.

A. امتداد *imtidád*. Prolongation.

A. امتزاج *imtizáj*. Union, conjunction.

A. امتلاء *imtilá*. Repletion.

A. امتناع *imtiná'*. Restraint, prohibition.

A. امتنان *imtinán*. Obligation, favour.

A. امتیاز *imtiyáz*. Distinction.

A. امثال *amsál*. Proverbs; resemblances. (pl. of مثل *masal*.)

A. امجد *amjad*. More or most laudable.

P. امد *ámad*. Income; arrival; he came.

A. امداد *imdád*. Aid, help.

P. امدن *ámadan*. To come, arrive.

P. امدنی *ámadaní*. Import; income; revenue.

P. آمد و شد *ámad u shud.* Access, coming and going.

A. امر *amr.* A thing; a command. امر و نهی *amr u nahy.* Command and prohibition

A. امرا *umará.* Nobles, grandees. (pl. of امیر *amír.*)

A. امراض *amráẓ.* Diseases, maladies.

A. امرد *amrad.* A beardless youth.

P. آمرزش *ámurzish.* Forgiveness, remission.

P. آمرزگار *ámurzgár.* Forgiver.

A. P. آمرزیدن *ámurzídan.* To forgive.

A. امساك *imsák.* Parsimony, grasping.

P. امروز *imrúz.* To-day.

T. امزك *amzek.* End of a pipe or tube; a spout.

P. امسال *imsál.* This year.

P. امشب *imshab.* To-night.

A. امضاء *imẓá.* Signature; causing to pass, transmitting.

A. P. امضاء داشتن *imzá dáshtan.* To sign.

A. امعان *im'án.* Reflecting, speculating. امعان نظر *im'án i naẓar.* Mature consideration.

A. امکان *imkán.* Possibility; hypothetical existence (opposed to واجب q. v.).

A. امکنه *amkinah.* Places, mansions.

A. امل *amal.* Hope, desire.

A. املاء *imlá.* Orthography; filling up.

A. املاك *amlák.* Goods, possessions.

A. املاك *imlák.* Property, possession.

A. امم *umam.* People; seeds.

A. امن *amn.* Tranquillity, safety.

A. اموال *amwál.* Wealth. (pl. of مال *mál.*)

A. امواج *amwáj.* Waves. (pl. of موج *mauj.*)

P. آموختن *ámúkhtan.* To teach, read, learn.

P. آمودن *ámúdan.* To fill; prepare.

A. امور *umúr.* Things, affairs.

P. آموزش *ámúzish.* Learning, teaching.

P. آموزگار *amúzgár.* A teacher; student.

A. امهال *imhál.* Delay; respiting.

A. امی *ummí.* Illiterate (an epithet of Mohammed, who appealed to the Ḳorán as a miracle in support of his prophetic assumptions, he not being able to read or write).

P. آمیختن *ámíkhtan.* To mix, compound.

P. امید *ummeid.* Hope, desire.

P. امدوار *ummeid-wár*. Hoping; a candidate.

A. امیر *amír*. A nobleman, prince. امیرزاده *amírzáda*. A prince, a young noble.

P. آمیز *ámíz*. Mixing, mixed.

P. آمیزش *ámízish*. Mixture, mixing.

A. امین *amín*. Safe; faithful; superintendent.

P. آن *án*. That.

A. اناء *iná*. A vessel.

A. انابت *inábat*. Repentance, penitence.

P. انار *anár*. A pomegranate; fireworks.

A. انارت *inárat*. Brilliancy.

A. انام *anám*. Mankind.

P. آنان *ánán*. Those.

A. انانیت *ananíyet*. Egoism.

A. انبار *ambár*. A heap, granary.

P. انبار *imbár*. This time.

P. انبارش *ambárish*. Stuffing, quilting.

P. انباز *ambáz*. Partner, associate.

P. انبازی *ambází*. Partnership.

P. انباشتن *ambáshtan*. To fill; to sprinkle.

P. انباغ *ambágh*. A concubine, extra wife.

P. انبان *ambán*. Soft leather.

A. انبساط *imbisáṭ*. Mirth, joy.

P. انبر or انبور *ambúr*. Pincers, forceps.

P. انبوه *ambúh*. Multitude, a crowd.

P. انبه *amba*. A mango.

A. انبیاء *ambiyá*. Prophets. (pl. of نبی *nabíy*.)

A. انبیق *ambíḳ*. An alembic; a still.

A. انتباه *intibáh*. Vigilance.

A. انتخاب *intikháb*. Selection.

A. انتزاع *intizá'*. Tearing up or out.

A. انتساب *intisáb*. Connexion, relation.

A. انتشار *intishár*. Dispersion.

A. انتظار *intiẓár*. Expectation, waiting.

A. انتظام *intiẓám*. Order, arrangement.

A. انتفاع *intifá'*. Utility, advantage.

A. انتقال *intiḳál*. Emigration; dying.

A. انتقام *intiḳám*. Revenge, vengeance.

A. انتہا *intihá*. The end, extremity.

P. آنجا *ánjá*. There, that place.

P. انجام *anjám*. The end, conclusion, result.

A. انجاح *injáḥ*. Success; giving success (God).

P. انجمن *anjuman*. Company, banquet, society.

P. آنچنان *ánchunán*. Such as that, in such a way.

P. آنچه *unchí*. Whatever.

P. انجیر *anjír*. A fig.

A. انجیل *Injíl*. The gospel.

A. انحاء *anhá*. Ways, kinds.

A. انحراف *inhiráf*. Change, deviation; declension (in astronomy). انحراف مزاج *inhiráf i mizáj*. Indisposition.

P. انداختن *andákhtan*. To cast, throw, shoot. بگردن انداختن *bagardan andákhtan*. To cast headlong.

P. انداز *andáz*. Quantity; throwing.

P. اندازه *andáza*. Estimation, reach.

P. اندام *andám*. The body.

P. اندر *andar*. In, into, within.

P. اندرز *andaraz*. Precept, admonition; will, testament.

P. اندرون *andarún*. Within, inside.

P. اندك *andak*. Little, few.

A. اندلوس *Andalús*. Spain.

P. اندوختن *andúkhtan*. To collect, gain.

P. اندودن *andúdan*. To incrustate; to plaster; to anoint.

P. اندوه *andúh*. Grief, sorrow.

P. اندوه‌گین *andúhgín*. Sorrowful, sad.

P. اندیش *andísh*. Considering, reflecting.

P. اندیشناك *andíshanák*. Thoughtful.

P. اندیشه *andísha*. Consideration.

P. اندیشیدن *andíshídan*. To consider, think.

A. انزال *inzál*. Seminal effusion.

A. انزواء *inziwá*. A solitary life.

A. انس *Ins*. Mankind; انس و جان *ins wa jánn*. Men and devils.

A. انس *uns*. Familiarity, sociality.

A. انسان *insán*. Man, mankind.

A. انسانیت *insáníyet*. Human nature; humanity; politeness.

A. انساب *ansáb*. Genealogies (pl. of نسب).

A. انسب *ansab*. More fitting.

A. انشاء *inshá'*. Elegance of style, composition; producing.

A. انشاء الله *inshá 'alláh*, (properly ان شاء الله). If it please God.

A. انصار *ansár*. Assistants, auxiliaries.

A. انصاف *insáf*. Equity, justice.

A. انصرام *insirám*. Being cut off, or finished.

A. انضباط *inzibát*. Maintaining, order.

A. انضمام *inzimám*. Adjoining. بانضمام *ba-inzimám*. Conjointly.

A. انعام *in'ám*. A present, favour.

A. انعام *an'ám*. Cattle.

A. انفاذ *infáz*. Transmitting; issuing an order; causing to penetrate. سیاحه، اشیا در جوف این مراسله انفاذ داشت *siyáha i ashyá dar jauf i ín muráselah infáz dásht*. He has enclosed a list of articles in this letter.

A. انفاس *anfás*. Breathings, sighs; spirits, persons.

A. انفاق *infák*. Expenditure.

P. انفختن *anfakhtan*. To acquire, to gain.

A. انفراق *infirák*. Being separated.

A. انفصال *infiṣál*. Separation, cutting off; settlement, decision.

A. انفعال *infi'ál*. Modesty, shame.

A. انقضاء *inkizá*. Expiration, conclusion.

A. انفيه *unfíyeh*. Snuff.

A. P. انفيه دان *unfíyah-dán*. A snuff-box.

A. انقراض *inkiráz*. Extinction of a family or dynasty.

A. انقلاب *inkiláb*. Revolution, change, alteration.

P. انقوزه *ankúza*. Assafœtida.

A. انقياد *inkiyád*. Obedience, submission.

A. انكار *inkár*. Denial, disavowal.

P. انكاشتن *angáshtan*. To think.

P. انكاريدن *angárídan*. To compute.

P. انكبين *angabín*. Honey.

P. انكختن *angikhtan*. To excite, rouse; to create.

P. انكژ *anguzh*. An instrument for driving an elephant.

A. انكر *ankar*. More or most odious.

A. انكسار *inkisár*. Humility.

A. انكشاف *inkisháf*. Detection, revelation.

A. P. انكشت *angisht*. Charcoal.

P. انكشت *angusht*. A finger.

P. انكشتانه *angushtána*. A thimble.

P. انكليز or انكليس *Ingilís* or *Ingilíz*. English.

P. انكشتري *angushtarí*. A ring.

P. انكور *angúr*. A grape.

P. انكوزه *anguza*. Assafœtida.

P. انكه *ángah*. Then, at that time.

P. انكيختن *angíkhtan*. To excite; to draw (a sword).

A. انوار *anwár*. Lights, splendours.

A. انواع *anwá'*. Sorts, kinds, varieties.

A. انوري *Anwarí*. Name of a celebrated Persian poet, died 586 A.H. = 1190 A.D.

P. انها *ánhá*. They, those.

A. انهزام *inhizám*. Defeat, rout.

A. انيس *anís*. A companion, friend.

A. انيقه *aníka*. A letter.

P. او *ú*. He, she, it.

P. اوارجه *awárja*. A journal, register, diary.

P. اواره *áwára*. Wandering; distressed.

P. اوارگی ávaragí. A state of wandering.

P. اواز awáz. A noise, sound, voice.

P. اوازه áwáza. Report, fame.

P. اوازیدن awázídan. To call out.

P. A. اوامر awámir. Orders, commands (pl. of امر amr).

A. اوان áwán. Times (pl. of ان).

A. اوایل awá-il. Beginnings.

A. اوباش aubásh. Blackguards, rabble.

P. اوباشتن aubáshtan. To fill, to devour.

A. اوج auj. The top, summit, altitude, zenith; the ascendant of a planet.

A. اوجب aujab. More incumbent.

A. اوداء awiddá. Lovers, friends.

A. اوراد aurád. Portions of the Korān recited at different hours (pl. of ورد wird).

A. اوراق auráḳ. Leaves.

P. اورد áward. Battle, conflict.

T. اوردك urdak. Duck.

P. اوردن áwardan. To bring; to relate; to adduce.

T. اوردو urdú. Camp; the Hindustáni language.

P. اورنك aurang. A throne, a crown; glory.

T. اورمك urmek. Silk-stuff.

A. اوزار auzár. The sails of a vessel; tools; weapons.

A. اوزان auzán. Weights, measures. (pl. of وزن wezn.)

P. اوستاد ustád. A teacher.

A. اوسط ausaṭ. The middle, medium.

A. اوصاف ausáf. Qualities; epithets; praises.

A. اوقات auḳát. Times, seasons, hours. (pl. of وقت waḳt.)

T. اوقيه úkíyah. An ounce.

A. اول awwal. First, beginning; principle.

P. اولاغ ulágh. A donkey.

A. اولى aulá. Better, best.

A. اولى awwalí. First.

A. اولى الالباب uli-l elbáb (obl. of اولو الالباب). Possessed of hearts or intellects.

A. اولاد aulád. Children, descendants.

A. اولياء aulíyá. Friends (of God), saints.

A. اولياء الدولة auliyá ed daulat. Ministers of state.

A. اولين awwalín. First, prior.

P. اوند áwand. Furniture; a vessel of any kind.

P. اويختن áwíkhtan. To suspend.

P. اويز áwíz. Suspending.

P. اويزش áwízish. Suspension; war, engagement.

P. آویزه *áwíza.* Pendulous; an ear-ring.

A. اه *áh.* Alas! a sigh.

A. اهالی *aháli.* Inhabitants; possessors.

A. اهانت *ihánat.* Abasing, scorn.

A. اهتمام *ihtimám.* Care, attention, diligence.

P. اهختن *áhikhtan.* To intend, design; to unsheath.

P. اهستگی *áhistagí.* Slowness.

P. اهسته *áhista.* Softly, slowly, step by step.

P. اهك *áhak.* Lime, plaster.

A. اهل *ahl.* Skilful; worthy people; spouse. اهل عشایر *ahl i 'asháïr.* Nomade tribe.

A. اهلاً وسهلاً *ahlan wa sahlan.* Welcome.

A. اهل بیت *ahl i beit.* Family.

A. اهلاك *ihlák.* Destruction.

A. اهلیت *ahlíyet.* Capability, skill, experience.

A. اهلیه *ahlíyeh.* A wife.

A. اهم *ahamm.* Very important.

A. اهمال *ihmál.* Neglect, delay, respite.

P. اهن *áhan.* Iron.

P. اهنربا *áhan-rubá.* A loadstone, magnet.

P. اهنك *áhang.* Intention; melody.

P. اهنگر *áhangar.* Blacksmith.

P. اهنکش *áhan-kesh.* A magnet, a loadstone.

P. اهنی *áhaní.* / P. اهنین *áhanín.* Made of iron. اهنین چنگال *áhanin-changál.* Iron-clawed.

P. اهو *áhú.* A deer; a defect.

P. اهو بره *áhú-bara.* A fawn.

A. اهویه *ahwiyeh.* Airs, atmosphere.

P. اهیختن *áhíkhtan.* To unsheath.

P. اهیز *áhíz.* Modestly, slowly; softly!

P. ای *ai.* The interjection, O! Oh!

A. ایا *ayá.* O! ho! holla!

P. ایا *áyá.* An interrogative particle.

A. ایات *áyát.* Signs, miracles; verses of the Korán.

A. ایادی *ayádí.* Hands; favours, benefits.

A. ایالت *iyálat.* Government.

T. ایاز *Aiyáz.* Name of a favourite of Sultán Mahmúd.

A. ایام *aiyám.* Days, times, seasons. (pl. of یوم *yaum.*).

A. ایت *áyat.* A mark; a verse of the Korán.

A. ایتام *aitám* (pl. of یتیم *yetím*). Orphans.

A. ايثار *ísár.* Bestowing, diffusing.

A. ايتلاف *ítiláf.* Amity, friendship.

A. ايجاب *íjáb.* Acquiescence.

A. ايجاد *íjád.* Invention.

A. ايجاز *íjáz.* Abbreviation.

A. ايذا *ízá.* Harming, injury; pain, distress.

A. ايراد *írád.* Bringing, adducing; objection, protest.

P. ايران *'Irán.* Persia.

P. ايرانى *'Irání.* Persian.

P. ايزد *'Izad.* God.

P. ايزدى *'Izadí.* Divine.

P. ايستادن *ístádan.* To stand.

P. ايشان *íshán.* They.

T. ايشك اقاسى *íshak-áḳásí.* Master of the ceremonies. ايشك اقاسى باشى *íshak-áḳási-báshí.* Grand master of the ceremonies.

A. ايضا *aiẓan.* Ditto, the same, also.

T. ايل *íl.* (pl. ايلات *ílát.*) A tribe (especially nomade).

T. ايلچى *elchí.* An ambassador.

T. ايلغار *elghár.* An expedition.

A. ايماء *ímá.* Allusion, signal.

A. ايمان *ímán.* Faith, religion, belief.

A. ايمان *aimán.* Oaths.

P. ايماندار *ímán-dár.* Faithful, honest.

LAT. T. ايمپراطور *ímperáṭúr.* Emperor.

A. ايمن *aiman.* Safe, secure.

A. ائمه *a-imma.* Imams.

A. اين *ain.* Where.

P. اين *ín.* This.

P. اينان *ínán.* These.

P. اينجا *ínjá.* Here, this place.

P. اينده *áyenda.* Coming, future; a comer.

P. اينك *ínak.* Behold!

P. ايوان *aiwán.* A palace.

A. ايهام *íhám.* Insinuation.

P. ائين *á-ín.* Regulation, customs.

P. ائينه *á-ina.* A mirror, a looking-glass.

P. ائينه دار *á-ina-dár.* A mirror-holder (a court-officer).

ب

ب *Bá.* B. The second letter of the Arabic and Persian Alphabet.

P. به ب *ba.* } With, in, to,
A. ب *bi.* } by, &c.

P. با *bá.* With, possessed of.

P. با انكه *bá-ánki.* Notwithstanding.

A. باب *báb.* A gate, a door; chapter of a book; affair, matter.

P. بابا *bábá.* Father.

A. بابت *bábat.* On account of.

P. بابر *bábar.* The autumn; the name of the second Mogul Emperor of Hindustan.

A. بابل *Bábel.* Babylon.

P. بابونه *bábúneh.* Camomile.

P. بابونهٔ شیرازی *bábúneh i Shírází.* Camomilla officinalis.

A. بابی *bábí.* A member of the Bábi sect

P. باج *báj.* Tribute, customs, duty, tax.

P. باجدار *báj-dár.* A tax-gatherer.

P. باجگذار *báj-guzár.* Tributary, taxed.

P. باجی *bájí.* Sister! miss; e.g. باجی خبردار *Bájí khabardár,* Look out, miss! to a married woman you say نه بیحش *nana-be-bakhsh,* pardon, ma'am!

P. A. با خبر *ba-khabr.* Intelligent.

P. باختر *Bákhtar.* The East or West; Bactria.

P. باختن *bákhtan.* To play; to lose at play.

P. باخته *bákhta.* Plaster; incrustation; played.

P. باد *bád.* The wind, air, breath; let it be so, so be it.

P. بادام *bádám.* An almond.

P. بادامی *bádámí.* Buff-coloured; oval.

P. بادبان *bád-bán.* The sail of a vessel.

P. بادپا *bád-pá.* Swift as the wind (a horse).

P. بادرنگ *bád-rang.* A cucumber.

P. بادصبا *bád i ṣebá.* The zephyr.

P. بادگرد *bád-gird.* A whirlwind.

P. بادکش *bád-kesh.* A fan.

P. A. باد مخالف *bád i mukhálif.* A contrary wind.

P. بادنجان *bádinján.* The egg-plant.

P. باد نما *bád-numá.* A weather-cock.

P. باده *báda.* Wine.

P. بادی *bádí.* Windy, flatulent.

A. بادی *bádí.* Foreign cause; author.

A. بادیه *bádiya.* A desert.

P. بار *bár.* A burden; pregnancy; fruit; once; admittance; great.

P. باران *bárán* Rain.

P. بارانی *báráni.* A riding-coat, cloak.

P. بار بار *bár bár.* Again and again, several times.

P. بار بردار *bár burdár.* A bearer of burdens; pregnant (female).

P. بار خدای *bár Khudáy.* The great God.

P. بار دار *bár dár.* Fruitful.

P. بار دیگر *bár i-díyar.* Another time.

P. بارش *bárish.* Rain.

P. A. بار عام *bár i'ám.* Public audience.

A. بارقه *bárika.* Flashing, glittering.

A. بارك الله *bárak alláh.* May God bless.

P. بار گاه *bárgáh.* A king's court.

P. بار کش *bár kesh.* A porter.

P. بارو *bárú.* Embrasure (in a tower or city wall).

P. باروت *bárút.* Gunpowder.

P. باروت خانه *bárút-khána.* Powder magazine.

P. بار ور *bár-war.* Producing fruit.

P. باره *bára.* Subject, behalf; battlements. در بارهٔ من *dar bára e man.* With regard to me.

P. بارها *bárhá.* Often.

P. باری *bárí.* One time, once.

P. باری چند *bárí chand.* Several times.

A. باریٔ *Bári.* The Creator.

P. بار یاب *bár-yáb.* Admittance (at court).

A. باریٔ تعالی *Bári ta'ála.* The Most High Creator.

P. باریدن *báridan.* To rain.

P. باریك *bárík.* Thin, fine.

P. باریك بینی *bárík-bíní.* Quickness of apprehension.

P. باریکی *báríkí.* Subtilty; fineness.

P. باز *báz.* A hawk; again; open; (in comp.) a player.

P. بازار *bázár.* A market.

P. بازاری *bázárí.* Belonging to a market.

P. باز امدن *báz ámadan.* To come back.

P. باز اوردن *báz áwardan.* To bring back.

P. باز پس *báz-pas.* Retrospection.

P. باز خواست *báz-kh'ást.* Investigation; retrospection.

P. باز خریدن *báz-kharídan.* To buy back, redeem.

P. باز دادن *baz dádan.* To give back.

P. باز داشتن *báz dáshtan.* To hold back, restrain.

P. بازرگر *bázargar.* A merchant.

P. باز کردن *báz kerdan.* To open; to undo.

P. باز کشیدن *báz keshídan.* To draw back.

P. باز زدن *báz zadan.* To strike again; to keep back.

P. باز گردیدن *báz gardídan.* To turn back.

P. باز گردانیدن *báz gardánídan.* To bring or turn back.

P. بازرگانی *bázargání.* Trade.

P. باز گشت *bázgasht.* Return.

P. باز گشتن *báz gashtan.* To return.

P. باز گفتن *báz guftan.* To reply.

P. باز ماندن *báz mándan.* To lag behind.

P. بازنده *bázanda.* A player.

P. بازو *bázú.* The arm, wing.

P. بازو بند *bázú-band.* An ornament for the arm.

P. بازی *bází.* Play, sport.

بازی در اورد از برای من *bází dar áward az baráyi man.* He has played me a trick.

P. باز یافتن *báz yáftan.* To resume.

P. بازیافت *bázyáft.* A receipt.

P. بازیچه *bázíchi.* Sport, a game.

P. بازیدن *bázídan.* To play.

P. بازیگر *bazígar.* A juggler.

A. بأس *bá's.* Might, prowess.

A. باسق *básiḳ.* Tall (a palm-tree).

A. باش *básh.* Stay, let it be.

A. باسط *básiṭ.* Spacious, plain.

P. باشد *báshad.* Let it be so.

P. باشنده *báshanda.* An inhabitant.

P. باشه *básha.* A sparrow-hawk.

P. باشیدن *báshídan.* To be; to stand, stay, dwell.

A. باصره *básira.* The sight, vision.

A. باطل *bátil.* False, absurd.

A. باطن *báṭin.* Inward part; hidden, concealed.

A. باطنی *bátíni.* Internal.

A. باعث *bá'iṡ.* Cause, motive, occasion, subject.

P. باغ *bágh.* A garden.

P. باغبان *bághbán.* A gardener.

P. باغچه *bághcha.* A little garden.

P. باغستان *bághistán.* Garden-ground, vineyard.

A. باغی *bághi.* A rebel, a sinner.

P. بافتن *báftan.* To weave; to plait; to twist.

P. بافته *báfta.* Woven; twisted; a kind of cloth.

P. بافنده *bafenda.* A weaver; a twister.

A. باقلا *báḳilá.* Bean.

A. باقی *báḳí.* Remainder, balance; durable.

P. باك *bák.* Fear.

P. باکه *bá ki.* With whom?

A. باکره *bákira.* A virgin.

A. باکی *bákí.* Weeping.

P. بال *bál.* An arm, wing.

A. بال *bál.* Spirit, mind.

سرور البال *surúr el bál.* Joyous.

P. بالا *bálá.* Above, summit.

P. بالا پوش *bálá-posh.* A coverlet, a quilt.

P. بالا خانه *bálá-kháná.* An upper chamber, balcony.

P بالا گرفتن *bálá-giriftan.* To get the upper hand.

P. بالای *bálá-í.* Above, up.

A. بالله *billáh.* By God.

A. بالجمله *bi'l-jumla.* In short, to sum up.

P. بالش *bálish.* A cushion, pillow.

A. بالضرورة *biẓ.ẓurúrat.* Necessarily.

A. بالفعل *bi'l-fi'l.* Actually; at the present.

A. بالغ *báligh.* Mature; arrived; adult.

A. بالکل *bil-kull.* Wholly, all.

P. بالکانه *bálkána.* A lattice-window.

P. بالدگی *bálidagí.* Growth; pride.

P. بالدن *bálídan.* To grow up.

P. بالین *bálín.* A pillow, cushion.

P. بالین تربت *bálín i turbat.* Head of a tomb.

T. بالیوز *bályúz.* A consul.

P. بام *bám.* The terrace, roof of a house; the morning.

P. بامداد *bámdád.* The morning, dawn.

P. بامدادان *bámdádán.* The next morning.

P. با مزه *bá-maza.* Sweet, savoury.

P. بام گاه *bám-gáh.* The morning.

A. بان *bán.* A kind of tamarisk tree (the myrolaban).

P. بانك *báng.* A noise, sound.

HINDUST. بانات *bánát.* Woollen cloth.

P. بانو *bánú.* Princess, lady.

P. با نوا *bá-navá.* Rich, fortunate.

A. بانی *báni.* Builder, maker.

P. A. باوجود *ba-wajúd.* Notwithstanding.

P. باور *báwar.* Faith, belief, credit.

P. باورچه *báwarche.* A cook.

P. باوصف *bá-wasf.* Notwithstanding.

P. باوی *bá-vai.* With him.

P. باه *báh.* Virility, sperm.

A. باهر *báhir.* Manifest, clear, open.

P. باهم *báham.* Together.

P. باهم دیگر *báham dígar.* Together, with each other.

P. باهم امدن *báham ámadan.* To get in a passion.

P. باید *báyad.* Necessary; it behoves.

P. بایست *báyist.* Fit, incumbent.

P. بایستن *báyistan.* To be necessary.

P. بایزید *Báyezíd.* A proper name.

A. بائع *bá'i.* A seller.

P. ببر *babar.* A lion.

P. بت *but.* An idol, image.

P. بت پرست *but-parast.* Idolator.

P. بت *bat.* A score or mark.

P. بتاشه *batásha.* A sweetmeat.

P. بت تراش *but tarásh.* A statuary.

P. بتر *bat-tar.* Worse. (for بدتر).

P. بت کده *but-kedah.* } An
P. بت خانه *but-khána.* } idol-temple, pagoda.

P. بثره *basra.* A pimple.

P. بجا *ba já.* In place; proper, fit, right.

P. بجا اوردن *bajá áwardan.* To perform.

P. بجان *baján.* Heartily.

P. بجان امدن *baján ámadan.* To be wearied out, disgusted.

P. بجان رنجیدن *baján ranjídan.* To cut to the heart, vex.

P. بجای *ba jái.* Instead of.

H. بجره *bajara.* A barge.

P. بجز *bajuz.* Except; besides.

P. بچگان *bachagán.* Children.

A. بجد *bajidd.* Diligently, eagerly.

A. بجنس *bajins.* In the same kind. بجنسه *bijinsihi.* The thing itself.

P. بچه *bacha.* The young of any animal; an infant.

P. بچه *bachi.* Why? wherefore?

A. بحار *biḥár.* Seas.

A. P. بحال *bahál.* Proper state or condition.

A. بحث *baḥs.* Argument, controversy.

A. P. بحدی *baḥaddí.* In that degree, to such an extent.

A. بحر *bahr.* The sea. بحر قلزم *Baḥr i Kulzum.* Red Sea. بحر محیط *Baḥr i Muḥíṭ.* Ocean. بحر یونان *Baḥr i Yúnán.* Ægean Sea. بحر خزر *Baḥr i Khazr.* Caspian Sea. بحر سفید *Baḥr i Sufeid.* Mediterranean.

A. بحران *buḥrán.* The crisis of a disease.

A. بحری *baḥrí.* Marine, maritime.

A. P. بحسب *ba ḥasb.* In conformity with.

A. P. بحضور *baḥuzúr.* In presence of.

A. P. بحکم *baḥukm.* In accordance with, by force of.

P. بحل کردن *biḥil kerdan.* To absolve, forgive.

A. بحور *buḥúr.* Seas.

A. بخار *bukhár.* Vapour, steam.

P. بخت *bakht.* Fortune, prosperity.

P. بخت بر گشته *bakht-bar-gashta.* Unfortunate.

P. بختمندی *bakhtmandí.* Good fortune.

P. بختاور *bakhtáwar.* Happy, rich.

P. بختی *bukhtí.* The two-humped Bactrian camel.

P. بختیار *bakht-yár.* Fortunate, rich.

P. بخدا *ba Khudá.* By God, to God.

P. بخرد *ba khird.* Intelligent, sagacious.

P. بخردی *ba khirdí.* Wisdom, sagacity.

P. بخش *bakhsh.* Part, share.

P. بخشایش *bakhsháyish.* Forgiveness, compassion.

P. بخشایشگر *bakhsháyishgar.* Merciful.

P. بخشاینده *bakhsháyenda.* Bountiful.

P. بخشبندر *bakhsh-bandar.* A royal custom-house.

P. بخشش *bakhshish.* A present, gift.

P. بخشندگی *bakshandagí.* Munificence.

P. بخشنده *bakhshanda.* A giver, bestower.

P. بخشودن *bakhshúdan.* To have pity on.

P. بخشی *bakhshí.* Paymaster.

P. بخشیدن *bakhshídan.* To give, bestow; to pardon.

A. بخل *bukhl.* Parsimony, avarice.

P. بخله *bukhla.* A bean.

P. بخور *bakhúr.* Perfume, odour.

A. بخیل *bakhíl.* Avaricious; miser.

A. بخیلی *bakhílí.* Parsimony, stinginess.

P. بخیه *bakhya.* Strong quilting.

P. بد *bad.* Bad, wicked.

A. بدء *bad'a.* Beginning.

P. بد اختر *bad-akhtar.* Ill-starred.

P. بدخشان *Badakhshán.* A country of Central Asia celebrated for rubies.

A. بداهت *badáhat.* An impromptu.

P. بدان *badán.* Know thou (imp. of دانستن); with that.

P. بد اندیش *bad-andesh.* Malicious.

P. بدایت *badáyat.* Commencement.

A. بدایع *badá'i'.* New, strange, rare things.

P. بدبخت *bad-bakht.* Unlucky.

P. بدتر *bad-tar.* Worse.

P. بد خوی *bad-khúy.* Ill-tempered.

A. بدر *badr.* The full moon.

P. بدر *badar.* Out of doors.

P. بدر امدن *badar ámadan.* To come out.

P. بدر رفتن *badar raftan.* To go out.

P. بدر رو *badar-rav.* A drain, a sewer.

P. بدرستی *ba-durustí.* Indeed, truly, certainly.

P. بدرقه *badraka.* A guard, escort.

P. بدر کردن *badar kerdan.* To eject.

P. بدرود *bidrúd.* (See پدرود) farewell.

A. بدره *badra.* A bag of money.

P. بد روزگار *bad-rozgar.* Unfortunate; wicked.

P. بد زندگانی *bad-zindagáni.* Bad living.

P. بدستور *ba-dastúr.* According to rule, as formerly.

P. بدست اوردن *badast áwardan.* To gain possession of.

P. بد سگال *bad-sigál.* Malevolent, malignant.

A. بدعت *bid'at.* Oppression, violence; heresy.

P. A. بد عهد *bad-a'hd.* A traitor, faithless.

P. بد فرجام *bad-farjám.* Unsuccessful; of evil tendency.

P. بد کیش *bad-kísh.* Irreligious.

P. بد کار *bad-kár.* Ill-doing; adulterous.

P. بدکاری *bad-karí.* Evil; adultery.

A. بدل *badal.* A substitute, change.

P. بدگو *badgú.* Evil speaker.

P. بد گوهر *bad-gauhar.* } Of bad quality.
P. بد گهر *bad-guhar.*

A. بدلا *badlá.* Substitute; succedaneum.

P. بد مست *bad-mast.* Refractory; intoxicated.

P. بد مهر *bad-mihr.* Unkind, unfriendly.

A. بدن *badan.* The body.

P. بد نام *bad-nám.* Infamous.

P. بد نما *bad-numá.* Bad-looking.

P. بد نهاد *bad-nihád.* Ill-disposed, perfidious.

P. بدو *badú.* To him.

A. بدون *bidún.* Without, besides.

P. بده *ba-deh.* Give thou.

P. بدی *badí.* Wickedness, malignity.

A. بدیع *badí'.* Wonderful, rare, strange.

P. بدین *badín.* For به این *ba-ín,* in this.

A. بدیهت *badíhat.* An impromptu.

A. بدیهی *badíhí.* An axiom, extempore.

A. بذر *bażr.* Seed.

A. بذل *bażl.* Munificence.

A. بذله *bazla.* A jest, pleasantry.

A. P. بذله گو *bazla-gú.* A wit.

P. بر *bar.* Above, on, upon; the bosom; fruit.

A. بر *barr.* Dry land; a desert.

P. برابر *barábar.* Equal, alike; level, up to; opposite.

A. برات *barát.* An assignment, commission. برات بر شاخ اهو *barát bar shákh i áhú.* Vain promises ("a draft on Aldgate pump").

P. برادر *birádar.* A brother.

P. برادر خواندگی *birádar khwándagí.* Professions of brotherly love.

P. برادر رضاعی *birádar-rizá'í.* Foster-brother.

P. برادری *birádarí.* Brotherhood.

A. براده *buráda.* Filings, sawdust.

A. برار *bar ár.* Peace, concord.

A. براز *baráz.* An extensive open plain.

A. براز *biráz.* Fighting; human ordure.

A. براعت *bará'at.* Excellence, preeminence.

A. براق *barrák.* Brilliant, flashing.

A. براق *burák.* The celebrated animal on which Mohammed is said to have ascended to heaven on the night of the معراج *mi'ráj.*

P. بر امد *bar ámad.* Appearance, coming out; impeachment.

P. برامدن *bar ámadan.* To

come up, emerge; cope with; succeed.

P. برامدگی bár-amadgí. Pre-eminence.

P. برآمیختن bar ámíkhtan. To mix up.

P. بر ان bar án. On that.

P. بر ان شدن bar án shudan. To agree to...

P. برانام bar án am. I obey.

P. بران burrán. Cutting, sharp.

P. برانیدن buránídan. To put to flight.

P. براورد bar-áward. An estimate. براورد کردن bar-áward kerdan. To make a valuation.

P. بر اوردن bar áwardan. To raise, to perform; to heave (a sigh).

P. بر اویختن bar áwíkhtan. To suspend.

A. براهمة baráhima. Brahmins.

A. براهین baráhín. Proofs, arguments.

P. برای baráyi. For, on account of.

P. برای چه biráyi chi. Why? for what?

A. برایا baráyá. Peoples, creatures.

P. بر پا bar pá. Fixed, established.

P. بر باد bar bád. Ruined, destroyed.

P. بر بر bar bar. Upon the breast, above.

P. بر بست bar bast. According to rule.

P. بر بستن bar bastan. To pack up.

A. بربط barbaṭ. A harp or lute.

A. بربط سرای barbaṭ saráy. A harper.

P. بر تافتن bar táftan. To twist, to turn.

P. برت barat. On thee.

P. برتر bartar. Higher.

P. A. بر تقدیر bar taḳdír. On supposition.

P. برتله bartula. A gift, present.

A. برج burj. A tower; a sign of the zodiac.

P. برجا bar já. In place, properly placed; prostrate.

P. برجستن bar jastan. To leap, to bound.

P. بر جستگی bar jastagí. Springing upon; an eruption.

P. بر جسته bar jasta. Befitting, proper.

A. برجیس Birjis. The planet Jupiter.

P. بر چیدن bar chídan. To pluck; gather up; to remove.

A. برح barḥ. Affliction, distress.

P. A. برحق bar ḥaḳḳ. In truth.

P. برخ barkh. Somewhat, a little.

P. بر خاست bar khást. Adjournment; dismissal from office; rise.

P. بر خاستن *bar khástan.* To rise, arise.

P. برخفچه *barkhafch.* The nightmare.

P. A. برخلاف *barkhiláf.* Contrary, opposite.

P. برخواندن *bar khwándan.* To recite, repeat.

P. برخوردار *barkhwurdár.* Happy, enjoying the fruits of life (a child).

P. بر خوردن *bar khwurdan.* To enjoy, to meet.

P. برخی *barkhí.* Somewhat, a little.

P. بر خیز *bar khíz.* Get up! (imp. of برخاستن).

A. برد *bard.* Cold, frigid.

P. بردار *burdár.* A carrier, a bearer.

P. بردار *bardár.* Suspended, hanged.

P. بردار کشیدن *bar dár keshídan.* To hang.

P. بر داشتن *bardáshtan.* To elevate; to carry off.

P. بردبار *burd-bár.* Forbearing; patient.

P. بر دریدن *bar darídan.* To rip up.

P. بردن *burdan.* To carry; to win at play.

P. برده *barda.* A prisoner of war.

P. برده *burda.* Borne, carried.

P. بر رفتن *bar raftan.* To climb; to proceed; to surpass.

P. برز *barz.* Seed.

P. برز *burz.* A trowel; a mace.

P. برزغه *barazgha.* A saddle-cloth.

P. برز گر *barz-gar.* An agricultural labourer.

P. برزن *barzan.* A street, lane.

P. برس *bars.* A halter.

HIND. برسات *barsát.* The periodical rains.

P. برسام *bar-sám.* The pleurisy.

P. بر سر *bar sar.* On or at the head, end, &c.

P. برشتن *burushtan.* To fry, to broil.

P. بر شدن *bar shudan.* To mount, to rise.

P. برشك *barshak.* A wine- or oil-press.

HIND. برشکال *barshakál.* The periodical rains.

P. برشکستن *bar-shikastan* (pronounced ورشکستن). To become bankrupt, to fail.

A. برص *baraṣ.* The leprosy.

P. A. بر طرف *bar ṭaraf.* Dismissed.

P. A. بر عکس *bar 'aks.* Inversely.

P. برف *barf.* Snow. برف باریدن *barf báridan.* To snow.

P. برف اب *barf-áb.* Iced water.

P. بر فروختن *bar farúkhtan.* To light up, kindle.

P. برفزودن *bar fuzúdan.* To increase.

P. بر فشاندن *bar fishándan.* To squeeze up; to snap (the fingers).

A. برق *bark̤.* Lightning.

P. A. بر قرار *bar k̤arár.* Established, firm.

A. برقع *burk̤a'.* A veil.

A. P. برقنداز *bark̤-andáz.* A matchlock man.

P. برگ *barg.* A leaf.

A. برکات *barakát.* Blessings.

A. برکه *birkeh.* A pool.

A. برکت *barakat.* Prosperity, blessing.

P. بر گردیدن *bar gardídan.* To be inverted. To depart. To turn away from.

P. برگ ریزی *barg rízí.* The fall of the leaf; autumn.

P. بر گزیدن *bar guzídan.* To choose, to select.

P. بر گرفتن *bar giriftan.* To take up; remove; to attain.

P. بر گزیده *bar guzída.* Chosen, selected.

P. بر گستوان *bar gustuwán.* Horse-armour.

P. بر گسلانیدن *bar guslánídan.* To snatch, wrench off.

P. بر گسلیدن *bar guslídan.* To snap off.

P. بر کشادن *bar kushádan.* To open, remove.

P. بر کشودن *bar kashúdan.* To open, unloose.

P. برگشتن *bargashtan.* To invert; to return; to retreat.

P. بر کندن *bar kandan.* To tear up, eradicate, uproot.

P. برگ ونوا *barg u nawá.* Subsistence, provision.

P. برم *baram.* I may bear (fr. بردن *burdan*).

P. برماه *barmáh.* An auger or gimlet.

P. بر می اید *bar mí áyad.* It comes out, arises.

A. برمیل *barmíl.* A barrel.

P. برمیو *barmiyú.* The strangury.

P. برنا *barná* or *burná.* A youth.

A. برناساء *barnásá.* Men.

P. برنج *birínj.* Rice.

P. برنج *burinj.* Brass.

P. برنجن *baranjan.* A bracelet, anklet.

P. برنده *barenda.* A carrier, bearer.

P. برنده *burenda.* Sharp, cutting.

P. بر نشستن *bar nishastan.* To mount on.

P. بر نشاندن *bar nishándan.* To cause to sit on.

P. بر نیارد *bar nayárad.* It bears not (fr. بر اوردن *bar áwardan*).

P. بروت *burút.* Whiskers, mustachios.

A. بروج *burúj.* Towers; signs of the zodiac.

P. A. بر وجهی *bar wajhí.* In such a manner.

A. بزودت *burúdat.* Coldness.

A. بروز *burúz.* Going forth; appearing.

P. برومند *barúmand.* Fortunate, happy.

P. برون *birún.* Without, abroad.

P. بر وی *bar vai.* On him.

P. بره *bara.* A lamb, kid.

A. برهان *burhán,* Demonstration, proof.

A. برهة *burhat.* A space of time.

P. بر هیختن *bar híkhtan.* To extract, to draw; to educate, to teach.

P. برهم *barham.* Confused; displeased.

P. برهم زدن *barham zadan.* To strike together, slam.

A. برهمن *Brahman.* A Brahmin.

A. P. برهمنان *barahminán.* Brahmins.

P. برهنگی *barahnagí.* Nakedness.

P. برهنه *barahna.* Naked.

A. بریء *barí'.* Exempted from, free, clear.

A. بریء الذمه *barí' uz zimmah.* Innocent of the charge.

A. بری *barrí.* Wild.

P. بریان *biryán.* Fried, broiled.

P. بریدن *burídan.* To cut, fell, cleave.

P. بریشم *barísham.* Silk.

P. برین *barín.* High, superior.

P. برین *bar-ín.* i. q. براین. On this.

P. بز *buz.* A goat.

A. بز *bazz.* Fine linen.

A. بزاز *bazzáz.* A linen-draper.

P. بزاق *buzák.* Spittle.

P. بزباز *bazbáz.* Mace.

A. بزر *bizr.* Seed.

A. بزر الکتان *bizr ul kettán.* Linseed.

P. بزرجمهر *Buzurjmihr.* Name of the Prime Minister of Naushírwán, King of Persia.

P. بزرگ *buzurg.* Great, elder, chief.

P. بزرگان *buzurgán.* Nobles, philosophers.

P. بزرگانه *buzurgána.* Nobly.

P. بزرگر *bizrgar.* A husbandman.

P. بزرگ زاده *buzurg-záda.* Of noble race.

P. بزرگ سال *buzurg-sál.* Old, aged.

P. بزرگ وار *buzurg-wár.* Illustrious.

P. بزرگواری *buzurgwárí.* Magnificence.

P. بزرگی *buzurgí.* Greatness, eminence.

P. A. بزرگ همت *buzurg-himmat.* Magnanimous.

P. بزشك *bizishk.* A physician; a horse-doctor.

P. بزغاله *buz-ghála.* A kid, a calf.

P. بزله *bazla.* Pleasantry, jest.

P. بزله گو *bazla-gú.* A wit.

P. بزم *bazm.* A banquet; assembly.

P. بزمگاه *bazm-gáh.* A banqueting house.

A. بزور *buzúr.* Seeds.

P. بزور *bazúr.* By force.

P. بزه *baza.* A sin, crime.

P. بزه کار *baza-kár.* A sinner.

P. بس *bas.* Enough; many.

P. بس کردن *bas kerdan.* To finish, stop.

P. بسا *basá.* Many, much.

A. بساط *bisáṭ.* A bed; carpet.

A. بسالت *basálat.* Intrepidity.

P. بسان *basán.* Like, resembling.

A. بسباسه *basbása.* Mace.

P. بست *bist.* Twenty.

P. بستان *bustán.* A garden.

P. بستان *bistán* or *bisitán.* Take thou! fr. ستاندن.

P. بستر *bistar.* A bed, mattress.

P. بستم *bistam.* Twentieth.

P. بستن *bastan.* To bind. نعل بستن *na'l bastan.* To shoe a horse.

P. بستگی *bastagí.* A ligature.

P. بسته *basta.* Bound; a bale.

P. بسد *bussad* or *bissad.* Coral.

P. بسر بردن *basar burdan.* To effect; to complete; to harmonize.

P. بسر شدن *basar shudan.* To be finished.

A. بسط *basṭ.* Diffusiveness, extension.

A. بسم الله *bismillah.* In the name of God.

A. P. بسمل کردن *bismil kerdan.* To sacrifice.

P. بسنده *basenda.* Sufficient.

HIND. بسوه *biswa.* The twentieth part of an acre of land.

P. بسوی *basúi.* In the direction of.

P. بسیار *bisyár.* Many.

P. بسیار خسپ *bisyár-khasp.* A great sleeper, drowsy.

P. بسیار خوار *bisyár-kh'ur.* A great eater, a glutton.

P. بسیاری *bisyárí.* Abundance.

P. بسی *basí.* Many, much.

P. بسیج *besíj.* An enterprise; march; preparation; outfit.

A. بسیط *basíṭ.* Simple, uncompounded; plane.

A. بسیم *basím.* Affable, smiling.

A. بشارت *bishárat.* Glad tidings.

A. بشاشت *basháshat.* Joviality, mirth.

A. بشر *bashar.* Man, mankind.

A. بشرة *bashurat.* The cuticle, or outer skin.

A. بشریت *bashariyet.* Human nature, humanity.

P. بشکیر *bashgír.* A towel.

A. بشير *bashír.* A messenger of good news.

A. بصارت *baṣárat.* The sight, vision.

A. بصره *Baṣrah.* Basora, a city of Arabian 'Irák.

A. بصل *baṣal.* An onion.

A. بصير *baṣír.* Seeing, discerning.

A. بصيرت *baṣírat.* The sight, vision.

A. بضاعت *biẓá'at.* Capital, stock.

A. بط *baṭṭ.* A goose, a duck.

A. بطال *baṭṭál.* An idle talker, vain.

A. بطالت *baṭálat.* Absurdity; falsity; vanity.

A. بطانت *biṭánat.* The lining of a garment.

A. بطر *baṭar.* Petulance.

A. بطش *baṭsh.* Power; severity, violence.

A. P. بطك *baṭak.* A duckling.

A. بطل *baṭal.* A brave man, a champion.

A. بطلان *buṭlán.* Falsity, vanity.

A. بطن *baṭn.* The belly; the interior.

A. بطیء *baṭí'.* Slow, dull.

A. بعاد *bi'ád.* Distance.

A. بعث *ba's.* Rousing; sending.

A. بعثت *bi'sat.* Mission, embassy.

A. بعد *ba'd.* After, afterwards.

A. بعد *bu'd.* Distance.

A. بعده *ba'dahu.* Afterwards.

A. بعزة *ba'izzat.* In high estimation.

A. بعض *ba'ẓ.* Some, certain.

A. بعضی *ba'ẓí.* A few, some.

A. بعضی‌جمع *ba'ẓí-jam'.* Sundry impositions or taxes, forming a total of revenue.

A. P. بعضی خرج *ba'ẓí-kharch.* Petty charges.

A. بعل *ba'l.* Lord, husband.

A. بعلبك *Ba'lbekk.* Baalbekk.

A. بعيد *ba'íd.* Distant, far.

A. بعينه *bi'ainihi.* Exactly, the very same.

A. بغال *bighál.* Mules. (pl. of بغل *baghl.*)

A. بغاوت *bagháwat.* Rebellion.

A. بغايت *bi-gháyet.* Extremely, exceedingly.

A. بغتة *bughtatan.* Suddenly.

P. بغچه *bughcha.* A bundle.

A. بغداد *Baghdád.* The city of Bagdad.

A. بغض *bughẓ.* Hatred.

P. بغل *baghal.* The armpit.

A. بغل *baghl.* A mule.

A. بغی *baghy.* Rebellion, revolt.

A. بغير *bighair.* Excepting, besides.

P. بفت *baft.* Wrought, woven.

A. بقاء *baḳá'.* Eternity; permanency.

A. بقاع *biḳá'.* Places; lowlying tracts of land.

A. بقال *bakkál.* A green-grocer.

P. بقاول *bakáwal.* Overseer of the kitchens.

A. بقاءى *bakáí.* Endurance.

A. بقايا *bakáyá.* Balances, remainders. (pl. of بقيه *bakíyeh.*)

P. بقچه *bukcha.* A knapsack, wallet.

A. بقسومات *buksumát.* Biscuits.

A. بقعه *buk'ah.* A low-lying tract of land; a valley; a mausoleum, burial-place of a saint.

A. بقل *bakl.* Herbage, pot-herbs.

A. بقله *baklah.* A pot-herb.

A. بقيتى *bakíyatí.* Some remnants.

A. بقيه *bakíyeh.* The remainder, balance.

P. بيك or بك *beg* or *beig.* A lord, a Mogul title; a noble.

A. بكاء *buká.* Weeping, crying.

P. بكار امدن *bakár ámadan.* To be of use.

A. بكارت *bakárat.* Virginity.

P. بكاول *bakáwal.* A taster, a head cook.

P. بكتر *baktar.* A coat of mail, cuirass.

A. بكر *bikr.* A virgin; first-born.

P. بكزاده *beg-záda.* Son of a Bey; a non-commissioned officer (see فوج).

A. بكم *bukm.* Dumb.

A. بل *bal.* But, yet, however.

A. بلاء *balá.* A calamity, evil.

A. بلا *bilá.* Without.

A. بلاد *biládd.* Countries, cities. (pl. of بلده.)

A. بلاغ *balágh.* Transmitting, delivering a message.

A. بلاغت *balághat.* Eloquence.

A. بلاهت *baláhat.* Stupidity.

P. بلبل *bulbul.* The nightingale.

P. بلخ *Balkh.* A town of Khorassan.

P. بلخى *Balkhí.* A native of Balkh.

A. بلد *belad.* A city.

P. بلد *belad.* A guide.

A. بلدان *buldán.* Cities. (pl. of *belad.*)

A. بلده *beldah.* A city, a town.

P. بلست *bilist.* A span.

P. بلسن *bulsun.* A lentil, pulse.

A. بلع *bal'.* Swallowing.

A. P. بلعيدن *bal'ídan.* To swallow.

T. P. بلغم *balgham.* Phlegm.

A. بلغاء *bulaghá.* Eloquent men.

A. P. بلكه *balki.* But, however.

P. بلكه *balga.* Stolen goods by the possession of which the thief is traced.

A. بلقيس *Balkís.* Name of

the queen of Sheba, wife of Solomon.

P. بلما *balmá.* Thick, gross.

P. بلند *baland* and *buland.* High.

P. بلند اواز *baland-áwáz.* Loud-toned.

P. بلند بالا *baland-bálá.* Of high stature.

P. بلند بانك *baland báng.* Loud-sounding.

P. بلندبين *baland-bín.* Aspiring.

P. بلندى *balandí.* Height, sublimity.

P. بلوا *balwá.* Disturbance, confusion.

P. بلوچستان *Beluchistán.* A province in the south of Persia.

A. بلور *billaur* (or *ballúr*). Crystal.

A. P. بلورين *billaurín.* Made of crystal.

A. بلوط *ballúṭ.* An oak, an acorn.

A. بلوع *balúʿ.* Open wide (the mouth of a pot).

A. بلوغ *bulúgh.* Puberty.

A. بله *balah.* Ignorant, stupid.

P. بلى *balí.* Yes, indeed, certainly.

A. بلية *balíyet.* A misfortune.

A. بليد *balíd.* A dunce, a dolt.

A. بليغ *balígh.* Eloquent.

P. بليله *balíla.* Belleric, myrobalan.

A. بليات *balíyát.* Misfortunes (pl. of بلية *balíyeh*).

P. بم *bam.* The bass in music.

P. A. بمثل *ba masal.* For example.

P. بمبلى *bambulí.* A harlequin.

P. A. بمجرد *bamujarrad.* Instantly.

A. بن *'bn.* A son; (used for ابن when it occurs between two proper names).

P. بن *bun.* A root. سروبن *sar u bun.* Beginning and end.

A. بناء *biná.* A building, fabric.

A. P. بناء كردن *biná kerdan.* To build, construct.

A. بنات *benát.* Daughters.

P. بنابر *biná bar.* Because of.

بنابران *biná bar án.* Therefore.

A. بنادر *banádir.* Ports, harbours. (pl. of بندر *bandar.*)

P. بنا گوش *biná-gúsh.* The cavity or lower part of the ear.

A. بنان *banán.* Finger-tips.

A. بنائى *bináï.* Foundation.

A. بنت *bint.* A daughter, a girl.

A. بنت الجبل *bint ul jebel.* The echo.

A. بنج *banj.* Henbane.

P. بنچاق *bencháḳ.* See قباله.

P. بند *band.* A bandage

confinement; a bond; art; a scheme; a trick.

P. بند فرمودن *band farmúdan.* To send or order into confinement.

P. بند انگشت *band i angusht.* A knuckle.

P. بندر *bandar.* A port, harbour; emporium.

P. بندگان *bandagán.* Slaves, servants.

P. بندگی *bandagí.* Servitude, service.

P. بندن *bandan.* To bind; to design.

P. بندوبست *band u bast.* Settlement, arrangement.

P. بندور *bundúr.* Packthread.

A. بندوق *bandúḳ.* A musket.

A. بندوقچی *bandúḳchí.* A musketeer.

P. بنده *banda.* A servant, slave.

P. بندی *bandí.* Captivity, a captive.

P. بندیدن *bandídan.* To bind, confine.

A. بنصر *binṣir.* The ring-finger.

P. بنفشه *bunafsha.* A violet.

P. بنگ *bang.* An inebriating draught; *ḥashísh.*

P. بنگاه *bun-gáh.* Baggage, the rear of an army, a store-house.

P. A. بنوعی *ba-nau'í.* In such a manner.

P. بنه *buna.* Baggage, furniture.

A. بنی *bení.* Sons, children. (pl. of ابن *ibn.*)

P. بنیاد *bunyád.* Foundation origin.

A. بنی آدم *bení ádam.* The sons of Adam, the human race.

A. بنی‌عم *bení 'amm.* Nephews.

A. بنیان *bunyán.* Construction.

A. بنیه *bunya.* The structure of the human body.

P. بو *bú.* Smell, odour.

A. بواب *bawwáb.* A door-keeper, porter.

A. P. بواجبی *bawájibí.* Suitable.

A. بواسیر *bawásír.* The hemorrhoids, or piles.

A. بواطن *bawáṭin.* Interior parts, bellies.

A. بواعث *bawá'is.* Causes, motives. (pl. of باعث *bá'is.*)

A. بوالعجب *bu'l'ajab.* Wonderful thing.

A. بوالفضول *bu'lfuẓúl.* An idle talker.

A. بوالهوسی *bú'l hawasí.* Sensuality.

A. بیوت *buyút.* Houses.

P. بوته *búta.* A crucible.

P. بوتیمار *bú tímár.* A heron.

P. بودار *bú-dár.* Scented; a kind of leather.

P. بود باش *búd-básh.* Residence, dwelling.

P. بودن *búdan.* To be, to exist.

P. بودنی *búdaní.* Existence.

A. بورق *búraḳ.* } Borax;
P. بوره *búra.* } nitre.
P. بوری *búrí.* A trumpet.
P. بوریا *búriyá.* A rush-mat.
P. بوریاباف *búriyábáf.* A weaver of mats.
P. بوز *búz.* A roan horse.
P. بوزنه *búzina.* A monkey.
P. بوزه *búza.* A kind of beer.
P. بوزه‌خانه *búza-khána.* A beer-shop.
P. بوس *bús.* A kiss.
A. بوءس *bu's.* Distress, misfortune.
P. بوستان *bústán.* A garden.
P. بوس وکنار *bús u kenár.* Kissing and hugging.
P. بوسه *búsa.* A kiss.
P. بوسیدن *búsídan.* To kiss; to rot.
P. بوسیده *búsída.* Rotten.
P. بوشقاب *búshekáb.* A plate.
P. بوغره *búghra.* A dish made of boiled meat, flour, &c.
P. بوغچه *búghcha.* Bag, wrapper.
A. بوق *búḳ.* A trumpet.
A. بوقلمون *bú ḳalamún.* A chameleon; variegated.
A. بول *baul.* Urine.
A. بوم *búm.* An owl.
P. بوم *búm.* A country.
P. بوی *búy.* Odour, smell.
P. بوی *ba vai.* To him.
P. بویا *búyá.* Fragrant.
P. بوئیدن *bú-ídan.* To smell.
P. بویه *búya.* Hope, desire.

P. بهی *bihi.* Well; a quince.
P. به *ba.* With, to, in; i.q. ب.
P. به *bih.* A quince.
P. بها *bahá.* Price, value.
A. بها *bihá.* In, with, by, &c.; it.
P. به از *bih az.* Better than.
P. بهادر *bahádur.* Valiant, brave, bold, (see فوج).
P. بهادری *bahádurí.* Bravery.
P. بهار *bahár.* The spring.
P. بهاری *bahárí.* Vernal.
P. بهانه *bahána.* Pretence, excuse, pretext.
A. بهائم *baháïm.* Cattle, beasts. (pl. of بهیمه *bahíma.*)
P. بهبخت *bih-bakht.* Gaiety.
P. بهبود *bih-búd.* Welfare.
A. بهتان *buhtán.* A calumny, lie.
P. بهتر *bihtar.* Better.
P. بهترین *bihtarín.* Best.
A. بهجت *bahjat.* Joy, beauty.
P. بهر *ba har.* At, by, or to every or each.
P. بهر *bahr.* For, because of.
P. بهرام *Bahrám.* The planet Mars. Name of several kings of Persia.
P. بهرام گور *Bahrám-Gúr.* Bahrám of the Wild Ass, the 6th of that name, a king of the Sassanian dynasty.
P. A. بهرحال *ba har ḥál.* By all means; in any case.
P. A. بهر کیف *ba har kaif.* Anyhow.

P. بهره *bahra.* Part, portion; profit.

P. بهره مند *bahra-mand.* Fortunate; participating in.

P. بهست *bihast.* It is better.

P. بهشت *bihisht.* Paradise.

P. بهشت *ba-hisht.* He left, from هشتن.

P. بهشتی *bihishtí.* Paradisiacal; (in Hindustani, a water-carrier).

P. بهل *bihil.* Absolution; give over! let alone! (imp. of هلیدن).

P. بهم *baham.* Together; anger.

P. بهم برآمدن *baham bar ámadan.* To be displeased, discomposed.

P. بهم برزدن *baham bar zadan.* To convulse.

P. بهم بر کردن *baham bar kerdan.* To displease; upset.

P. بهم رسانیدن *baham rasánídan.* To procure.

P. بهی *bihí.* Goodness; a quince.

A. بهیمه *bahíma.* A beast.

A. بهیمی *bahímí.* Brutish.

P. بهین *bihín.* Better, best.

P. بی *bí.* Without, besides.

P. بیابان *biyábán.* A desert.

P. بیابان نشین *biyábán-nishín.* Dwelling in the desert.

P. بیابانی *biyábání.* Wild, savage.

P. بی آبرو *bí-ábrú.* Dishonourable.

A. بیاض *baiyáz.* Whiteness; an album or note-book; a fair copy of any document.

A. بیان *bayán.* Explanation.

P. A. بی اختیار *bí-ikhtiyár.* Without choice.

P. A. بی ادب *bí-adab.* Rude, impolite.

P. بی آزار *bí-ázár.* Without trouble.

P. A. بی اعتبار *bí-i'tebár.* Not respected.

P. بی اندازه *bí-andáza.* Without measure.

P. A. بی انصاف *bí-inṣáf.* Unjust.

P. A. بی باق *bí-báḳ.* Completely.

P. بی باك *bí-bák.* Fearless.

P. بی بر *bí-bar.* Fruitless.

P. بی پروا *bí-parwá.* Without care.

P. بی پیر *bí-pír.* Vicious.

A. بیت *bait.* A house; a distich.

P. بی تاب *bí-táb.* Faint, restless.

A. بیت المقدس *Bait al Muḳaddas.* Jerusalem.

P. A. بی تحاشا *bí-taḥáshá.* Rash, precipitate.

P. A. بی تدبیر *bí-tadbír.* Without deliberation.

P. A. بی تکلف *bí-takalluf* Without ceremony.

P. A. بی تمیز *bí-tamíz.* Without discernment.

P. بی توزگانه *bí-túzagána.* Irregular.

P. بی توشه *bí-túsha.* Without provisions.

P. A. بی توفیق *bí-taufíḳ.* Without grace.

P. بیجا *bí-já.* Improper; out of place.

P. بی جان *bi-ján.* Lifeless.

P. A. بی جواب *bí jawáb.* Irre futable; having no answer.

P. بیچاره *bí-chára.* Helpless.

P. بیچوبا *bí-chúba.* A kind of tent pitched without a pole.

P. بیچراغ *bí-chirágh.* Lampless; desolated; childless.

P. بیچون *bí-chún.* Incomparable. بیچون و چرا *bí-chún o cherá.* God (as not subject to the laws of cause and effect).

P. A. بی حاصل *bí-ḥáṣil.* Unprofitable.

P. A. بی حد *bí-ḥadd.* Without limit.

P. A. بی حساب *bí-ḥisáb.* Countless.

P. A. بیحضور *bí-ḥuẓúr.* Absent, inattentive.

P. A. بیحمیت *bí-ḥamíyet.* Spiritless, dastardly.

P. بیخ *bíkh.* A root, origin.

A. P. بی خبر *bí-khabar.* Uninformed.

P. بیختن *bíkhtan.* To sift.

P. بی خوابی *bí-kh'ábí.* Sleeplessness.

P. بیخود *bí-khud.* Beside one's self, senseless.

P. بیخودی *bí-khudí.* Rapture.

P. بید *bíd.* The willow.

P. A. بید مجنون *bíd i majnún.* The weeping willow.

P. بید مشك *bíd mushk.* The musk-willow.

A. بیدا *baidá.* A desert.

P. بیداد *bí-dád.* Unjust, lawless.

P. بیدار *bídár.* Waking, attentive.

P. بیداری *bídárí.* Wakefulness, vigilance.

P. بید انجیر *bíd-anjír.* The palma Christi.

P. بی دانش *bí-dánish.* Unwise.

P. بیدانه *bí-dána.* Seedless; a pomegranate.

A. بیدای *baidáï.* A desert.

P. A. بیدخل *bí-dakhl.* Dispossessed, excluded.

P. بیدرمان *bí-darmán.* Without remedy.

P. بیدرنگ *bí-dirang.* Without delay.

P. بیدریغ *bí-dirígh.* Undeniable; merciless.

A. بیدق *baidaḳ* (or بیذق *baiẓaḳ*). A pawn at chess. See also بیراق.

P. بی دل *bí-dil.* Heartless.

P. A. بی دین *bí-dín.* Irreligious.

A. بئر *bi'r.* A well.

P. بیراه *bí-ráh.* Unprincipled; astray.

A. بیراق *bairáḳ.* A flag, banner.

P. A. بی رسمی *bí-rasmí.* Irregularity.

P. بیروزی *bí-rúzí.* Destitute.

P. بيرون *bírún.* Without, exterior.

P. بيريا *bí-riyá.* Without guile.

P. بيزار *bí-zár.* Indifferent; affected with *ennui.*

P. بيزبان *bí-zabán.* Dumb, speechless.

P. بى زر *bí-zar.* Without money.

P. بيست *bíst.* Twenty.

P. بى سروپا *bí-sar u pá.* Destitute; without method.

P. A. بى سليقه *bí-salíka.* Inexpert; without method.

P. بيش *bísh.* More, much.

P. A. بيشائبه *bí-sháíba.* Doubtless.

P. بيشتر *bíshtar.* For the most part.

P. بى شرم *bí-sharm.* Shameless.

P. بيشمار *bí-shumár.* Innumerable.

P. A. بى شك *bí-shakk.* Doubtless.

P. بيشه *bísha.* A forest, desert.

P. بيشى *bíshí.* Excess.

P. A. بيصبر *bí-ṣabr.* Impatient.

A. بيض *baiz.* Eggs.

A. بيضاء *baizá.* White; the sun.

A. بيضوى *baizawí.* Oval.

A. بيضه *baiza.* An egg.

A. بيطار *baiṭár.* A horse-doctor.

P. A. بى طاقت *bí-ṭáḳat.* Without power.

A. بيع *bai'.* Sale.

A. P. بيعانه *bai'ána.* Earnest money.

A. بيعت *bai'at.* Homage, fealty; inauguration.

A. P. بيعنامه *bai'-náma.* A bill of sale.

P. A. بيعنايت *bí-'ináyet.* Unkind; rude.

P. بيغل وغش *bí-ghill u ghashsh.* Without deceit.

P. A. بى غم *bí-ghamm.* Without sorrow; unconcerned.

P. A. بيغيرت *bí-ghairat.* Spiritless, infamous; without jealousy.

P. A. بى فائده *bí-fáida.* Useless.

P. A. بيقرار *bí-ḳarár.* Uneasy, restless.

P. A. بيقياس *bí-ḳiyás.* Incalculable.

P. بيك *baig.* A lord; a Mogul title.

P. بيكار *bí-kár.* Unemployed.

P. بيكارى *bí-kárí.* Idleness.

P. بيگانگى *bígánagí.* Foreignness.

P. بيگانه *bígána.* A stranger.

P. بيگاه *bí-gáh.* Untimely.

P. بيكبار *ba-yek-bar.* Suddenly, all at once.

P. بيكران *bí-girán.* Immense, infinite.

P. بيكس *bí-kas.* Destitute, friendless.

P. بى كفش *bí-kafsh.* Shoeless.

P. بيكل *bi-kal.* Restless, out of order.

P. بیگم *baigam.* A lady.

P. بی گمان *bí-gumán.* Without doubt.

P. بی گناه *bí-gunáh.* Innocent.

P. بیل *bíl.* A spade.

P. بیلا *bílá.* Money to be distributed in charity.

P. بیلدار *bíldár.* A sapper, digger.

A. بیلقان *Bailḳán.* A city in Armenia near the Caspian Sea.

P. بیم *bím.* Fear.

P. A. بیمحابا *bí-muḥábá.* Dauntless; disrespectful.

P. بیمار *bímár.* Sick, infirm.

P. بیمارستان *bímáristán.* An hospital.

P. بیماری *bímárí.* Disease.

P. بیمانند *bí mánand.* Incomparable.

P. بیمایگی *bí-máyagí.* Indigence.

P. A. بیمروت *bí-murúwat.* Unkind, inhuman.

P. بیمزه *bí-maza.* Tasteless, insipid.

P. A. بیمعنی *bí-ma'ní.* Foolish, unmeaning.

P. بی مغز *bí-maghz.* Marrowless.

P. بیمه *bíma.* Insurance. بیمه کردن *bíma kerdan,* to insure.

A. بین *bain.* Between; an interval.

A. بین *baiyin.* Clear, evident, plain.

P. بین *bín.* See thou! (from دیدن).

P. بینا *bíná.* Seeing; a spectator.

P. بینائی *bínáí.* Light.

P. بینش *bínish.* Light, penetration.

P. بی نشان *bí-nishán.* With out sign; inscrutable.

P. A. بی نظیر *bí-naẓír.* Incomparable.

P. بی نمك *bí-namak.* Insipid, saltless, tasteless.

P. بینوا *bí-nawá.* Helpless.

P. بینی *biní.* The nose; thou seest. نمی بینی *namí bíní.* Dost thou not see? (from دیدن).

P. بی نیاز *bí-niyáz.* Content; without prayer.

P. A. بی واسطه *bí-wásiṭa.* Causeless.

P. A. بی وجود *bí-wujúd.* Without existence; low, mean.

P. A. بیوفا *bí-wafá.* Faithless, ungrateful.

P. A. بیوفای *bí-wafá-í.* Ingratitude.

P. A. بیوقت *bí-waḳt.* Untimely.

P. A. بیوقوف *bí-wuḳúf.* Stupid.

P. بیوه *bíva.* A widow.

P. بی همتا *bí-hamtá.* Incomparable.

P. بی هنر *bí-hunar.* Without ingenuity; lazy.

P. بی هنگام *bí-hangám.* Ill-timed, untimely.

P. بیهوده *baihúda.* Vain, absurd.

P. بیهوش *bí-húsh.* Faint, senseless.

P. بیهوشی *bí-húshí.* Deprivation of sense.

پ

پ *pá* or *pé*. The third letter of the Persian alphabet. It does not occur in Arabic; the letter ف being substituted for it, in Persian words adopted into Arabic. Even in Persian it sometimes interchanges with ف as سپید and سفید; and with ب as پادشاه and بادشاه.

P. پا *pá*. The leg, foot.

P. پا انداز *pá andáz*. A carpet spread at the entrance of a room.

P. پا برنجن *pá-baranjan*. An anklet.

P. پا بند *pá-band*. A rope with which the fore feet of a horse are tied.

P. پا بوس *pá-bús*. Kissing the foot, worshipping.

P. پا بوسی *pá-búsí*. Reverence.

P. پاپوش *pá-púsh*. A slipper, shoe.

P. پا پی *pá-pai*. Persecution.

P. پاتابه *pátába*. A sock.

P. پاجامه *pá-jáma*. Trousers.

P. پاجی *pájí*. Mean; a scoundrel.

P. پاچك *páchak*. Dried cows-dung used for fuel.

P. پاچه *pácha*. A paw.

P. پاداش *pádásh*. Retaliation; recompence.

P. پادزهر *pád-zahr*. The bezoar stone.

P. پادشاه *pádsháh*. A king.

P. پادشاهی *pádsháhí*. Empire, reign.

P. پار *pár*. Over, across.

P. پارچه *párcha*. A fragment, strip; cloth.

P. پاردم *pár-dum*. The crupper of a saddle.

P. پارس *Párs*. Persia.

P. پارسا *pársá*. Chaste; pious.

P. پارسال *pár-sál*. The last year.

P. پارسائی *pársáï*. Holiness; asceticism.

P. پارسی *Pársí*. A Persian.

P. پاره *pára*. A piece, portion; bribe.

P. پاره‌دوز *páradúz*. A patcher.

P. پارو *párú*. A broom, a shovel.

P. پارینه *párína*. Old, ancient.

P. پاس *pás*. Watch, guard, defence.

P. پاسبان *pás-bán*. A sentinel.

P. پاسبانی *pás-bání*. Keeping watch.

P. پاستان *pástán*. Former.

P. پاسخ *pásukh*. An answer.

P. A. پاسخاطر *pás-kháṭir*. For the sake of, in deference to.

P. پاسداری *pás-dárí*. Guardianship; partiality.

P. پاسنگ *pásang*. A makeweight.

P. پاش *pásh*. Sprinkling.

P. پاشا *páshá*. A Turkish title.

P. پاشته *páshta*. The heel.

P. پاشیدن *páshídan.* To sprinkle.
P. پاک *pák.* Pure, clean.
P. پاکباز *pák-báz.* Fair dealing.
P. پاک بردن *pák burdan.* To carry clean off.
P. پاکی *pákí.* Purity, chastity.
P. پاکیزه *pákíza.* Clean, chaste, neat.
P. پالان *pálán.* A pack-saddle.
P. پالودن *pálúdan.* To strain, press; drain (this verb is seldom used except in the past participle پالوده, e. g. پالودهٔ سیب *palúda i seib.* Extract of apples.)
P. پالهنگ *pál-hang.* A halter.
P. پالیز *páliz.* A kitchen-garden, melon-bed, &c.
P. پامال *pámál.* Ruin, devastation.
P. پانزده *pánzda.* Fifteen.
P. پانصد *pánṣad.* Five-hundred.
P. پای *pái.* The foot.
P. پایاب *páyáb.* A shallow, ford.
P. پایان *páyán.* Extremity, end.
P. پای بند *pái-band.* A fetter; tied, fettered.
P. پای پوش *pái-púsh.* Shoe, slipper.
P. پایتابه *pái-tába.* Socks.
P. پایتخت *pái-takht.* The pital, metropolis.
P. پایخانه *pái-khána.* A privy.
P. پایدار *pái-dár.* Firm, durable, permanent.
P. پائیدن *pá-ídan.* To stand firm or still; to hesitate.
P. پازیب *pá-zíb.* Anklets.
P. پاییز *páyiz.* Autumn.
P. پایستن *páyistan.* To expect; to be firm.
P. پایگاه *páï-gáh.* Dignity, rank.
P. پایمال *pái-mál.* Ruin, devastation.
P. پایمزد *pái-muzd.* Hire of a messenger, &c.
P. پایه *páya.* Step, degree, dignity, basis, &c.
P. پائین *páïn.* Beneath, down.
P. پتک *putk.* A smith's hammer
P. پتیل *patíl.* A match for a lamp, a linstock.
P. پختن *pukhtan.* To cook; ripen.
P. پخته *pukhta.* Cooked; ripe.
P. پدر *pidar.* A father.
P. پدرانه *pidarána.* Fatherly.
P. پدروار *pidr-wár.* Like a father.
P. پدرود *padrúd.* Farewell, leave.
P. پدری *pidrí.* Paternal.
P. پدنه *puduna.* Mint (herb).
P. پدید *padíd.* Evident, visible.
P. پدیدار *padídár.* Appearing.
P. پذیر *pazír.* Accepting; susceptible of.

P. پذیرای *pazírí.* Acceptance.

P. پذیرفتن *pazíraftan.* To accept, admit, be susceptible of.

P. پذیره *pazíra.* Acceptable, agreeable.

P. پر *pur.* Full, loaded.

P. پر *par.* A feather, a quill, wing.

P. پراسال *parásál.* The year before last.

P. پراکندگی *parágandagi.* Dispersion.

P. پراکندن *parágandan.* To disperse, to scatter.

P. پراکنده *paraganda.* Dispersed, scattered.

P. پران *parán.* Flying.

P. پرانیدن *paránídan.* To cause to fly.

P. پرتاب *partáb.* A bowshot; brilliancy.

P. پرتو *partav.* A ray, beam.

P. پرحذر *pur ḥażar.* Full of caution.

P. پرخاش *purkhásh.* War, battle.

P. پرداخت *pardákht.* Completion, relinquishment.

P. پرداختن *pardákhtan.* To accomplish; to attend to; to quit, leave.

P. پردگی *pardagí.* Concealment; a chaste woman.

P. پرده *parda.* A veil, curtain; a musical key or mode.

P. پردهٔ الحان *parda i ilḥán.* The musical scale or gamut.

P. پردهٔ بینی *parda i bíní.* The cartilage of the nose.

P. پرده بر انداز *parda-barandáz.* Revealing a secret.

P. پرده پوش *parda-púsh.* Keeping a secret.

P. پرده دار *parda-dár.* Holding the veil; a chamberlain.

P. پرده عنکبوت *parda i 'ankabút.* A cobweb.

P. پرده نشین *parda-nishín.* Remaining behind the veil; modest.

P. پرزه *purza.* A scrap, bit.

P. پرست *parast.* A worshipper.

P. پرستار *parastár.* A servant; a worshipper.

P. پرستش *parastish.* Worship.

P. پرستك *piristuk.* A swallow. Vulg. پرستو *piristú.*

P. پرستنده *parastenda.* A worshipper.

P. پرستیدن *parastídan.* To worship.

P. پرسش *pursish.* A question.

P. پرسنده *pursenda.* An interrogator.

P. پرسیدن *pursídan.* To ask, interrogate.

P. پرسیدنی *pursídaní.* A subject for inquiry.

P. پرك *Parak.* Canopus (star).

P. پرگار *pargár.* A pair of compasses.

P. پرکار *pur-kár.* Skilful; close; well made.

P. پرکاله *parkála.* A spark.

P. پرنده *parenda.* Flying; a bird.

P. پرنیان *parniyán.* Painted Chinese silk.

P. پروا *parwá.* Care, fear.

P. پرواری *parwárí.* Fatted, stall-fed.

P. پرواز *parwáz.* Flight.

P. پروانگی *parwánagí.* Permission.

P. پروانه *parwána.* A moth; a mandate.

P. پر و بال *par u bál.* Feathers and wings. بی پر و بال *bí-par u bál.* Destitute; impotent.

P. پرور *parwar.* Nourisher, patron.

P. پروردگار *Parwardagár.* Providence.

P. پروردن *parwardan.* To nourish; educate.

P. پرورش *parvarish.* Protection, nurture.

P. پرورنده *parvarenda.* Protector, patron.

P. پروریدن *parvarıdan.* To bring up, nourish.

P. پرویزن *parvízan.* A sieve.

P. پروین *Parvín.* The Pleiades.

P. پره *parra.* Side, border.

P. پره ٔ بینی *parra i bíní.* The nostrils.

P. پرهیز *parhíz.* Abstinence, continence.

P. پرهیزگار *parhíz-gár.* Continent, chaste.

P. پرهیزیدن *parhízídan.* To abstain, to avoid.

P. پری *parí.* A fairy.

P. پری *purí.* Fulness.

P. پریدن *parídan.* To fly.

P. پری روز *parí-rúz.* The day before yesterday.

P. پریشان *paríshán.* Afflicted, distracted.

P. پریشانی *paríshání.* Distress, destitution.

P. پریشب *parí-shab.* The night before last.

P. پزشک *pizishk.* A physician.

P. پزشکی *pizishkí.* The art of physic.

P. پژمان *pazhmán.* Withered.

P. پژمردن *pazhmurdan.* To wither.

P. پژمرده *pazhmurda.* Decayed, withered.

P. پژوهش *pizhúhish.* Inquiry.

P. پزیدن *pazídan.* To cook.

P. پس *pas.* After, behind; then, therefore, consequently.

P. پس انداز *pas-andáz.* Clear profit; savings.

P. پست *past.* Low, abject.

P. پستان *pistán.* The breast, nipple.

P. پسته *pista.* A pistachio nut.

P. پستی *pastí.* Inferiority, lowness.

P. پس خور *pas-kh'ur.* The leavings of a meal.

P. پس دادن *pas dádan.* To render.

P. پسر *pisar.* A son, boy.

P. پسر امجد *pisar i amjed.* Eldest son.

P. پسر خوانده *pisar-kh'ánda.* An adopted son.

P. پس فردا *pas-fardá.* The day after to-morrow.

P. پسکله *paskulla.* The bolt of a door.

P. پس گرفتن *pas-giriftan.* To take back.

P. پسند *pasand.* Approbation. پسند امدن *pasand ámadan.* To be approved.

P. پسندیدن *pasandídan.* To approve.

P. پسندیده *pasandída.* Commendable, agreeable.

P. پس و پیش *pas u písh.* Demur, hesitation.

P. پسیچ *pasích.* March; preparation.

P. پسین *pasín.* The last, posterior.

P. پشت *pusht.* The back. پشت پا *pusht i pá.* The instep.

P. پشتاره *pushtára.* A load, a pack.

P. پشت دادن *pusht dádan.* To retreat.

P. پشت پناه *pusht-panáh.* Patron, supporter.

P. پشته *pushta.* A bundle, load; a hillock; a quay.

P. پشتی *pushtí.* Support.

P. پشتیبان *pushtíbán.* A prop, buttress.

P. پشکل *pishkil.* Dung of a sheep.

P. پشم *pashm.* Wool; hair on the privities. این پشم است *ín pashm ast.* Stuff and non sense!

P. پشمینه *pashmína.* Woollen.

P. پشه *pashsha.* A gnat.

P. پشیز *pishíz.* A small piece of money.

P. پشیمان *pashímán.* Penitent.

P. پشیمانی *pashímání.* Repentance.

P. پگاه *pagáh.* The dawn.

P. پل *pul.* A bridge.

P. پلاس *palás.* Coarse cloth, sackcloth.

P. پلاو *piláv* and پلو *pilav.* A dish made of rice and meat.

P. پلپل *pulpul.* Pepper.

P. پلبندی *pul-bandí.* Embankment.

P. پلك *palak.* An eyelash.

P. پلنگ *palang.* A tiger, leopard.

P. پله *pala* or *pilla.* The bason of a balance; step of a ladder.

P. پله کردن *pilla kardan.* To importune.

P. پلیته *palíta.* The wick of a candle or lamp.

P. پلید *palíd.* Impure.

P. پناه *panáh.* Refuge, protection.

P. پناباد pron. *penábat.* A small silver coin worth about 6*d*.

P. پنبه *pamba.* Cotton.

P. پنبه دوز *pamba-dúz.* A carder of cotton.

P. پنج *panj.* Five.
P. پنجاه *panjáh.* Fifty.
P. پنجاهم *panjáham.* Fiftieth.
P. پنجره *panjara.* A cage; a lattice.
P. پنج گوشه *panj-gúsha.* A pentagon.
P. پنج شنبه *panj-shamba.* Thursday.
P. پنجه *panja.* A claw, the fist.
P. پنجم *panjam.* Fifth.
P. پند *pand.* Maxim; exhortation.
P. پندار *pindár.* Conceit; imagination.
P. پنداری *pindárí.* Self-conceit.
P. پنداشتن *pindáshtan.* To think, suppose.
P. پنهان *pinhán.* Concealed, secret.
P. پنهانی *pinhání.* Concealment.
P. پنیر *panír.* Cheese.
P. پنیر مایه *panír-máya.* Rennet.
P. پو *pú.* Search, inquiry.
P. پوچ *púch.* Injudicious, absurd.
P. پود *púd.* The warp, the web.
P. پودینه *púdína.* Garden mint.
P. پور *púr.* A son.
P. پوز *púz.* The parts round the mouth.
P. پوزش *púzish.* An excuse, apology.
P. پوزمال *púz-mál.* A farrier's twitch.
P. پوست *púst.* A skin, hide; bark of a tree.
P. پوست بر پوست *púst bar púst.* Coat upon coat (as an onion).
P. پوستین *pústín.* A fur-garment, a pelisse.
P. پوسیدن *púsídan.* To rot.
P. پوش *púsh.* A cover, lid.
P. پوشانیدن *púshánídan.* To cause to hide.
P. پوشاک *púshák.* Dress, clothes.
P. پوشش *púshish.* A Covering, dress.
P. پوشیدن *púshídan.* To hide; to dress.
P. پوشیده *púshída.* Hidden.
P. پوف کردن *púf kerdan.* To puff.
P. پول *púl.* Money. پول چکمه و شلوار *púl i chekma u shelwár.* Board wages: money given to servants to provide themselves with necessaries on a journey.
P. پولاد *púlád.* Steel.
P. پوی *púy.* Search, inquiry.
P. پویا *púyá.* } Seeking;
P. پویان *púyán.* } running.
P. پوئیدن *pú-ídan.* To search, to run.
P. پویه *púya.* A hand-gallop.
P. پهر *pahar.* A watch of the night.
P. پهره *pahra.* A guard.
P. پهلو *pahlú.* Side; quarter. پهلو بندی کردن *pahlú bandi kerdan.* To protect. پلو داشتن

pahlú dáshtan. To procure an advantage to any one.

P. پهلوان *pahluwán.* A hero, wrestler.

P. پهلوانی *Pahlaví.* The language of the ancient Persians.

P. پهن *pahn.*
P. پهن اوری *pahn-áwarí.* } Breadth, width.

P. پی *pai.* A foot; a tendon; behind.

P. پاپی *pay á pay.* Successively.

P. پیاده *piyáda.* A foot-soldier; pedestrian.

P. پیاز *piyáz.* An onion.

P. پیاله *piyála.* A cup.

P. پیام *paiyám.* A message.

P. پیامبر *paiyámbar.* A messenger; an apostle.

P. پیچ *pích.* A screw; twist.

P. پیچ خوردن *pích-khurdan.* To have the colic.

P. پیچ خور *pích-khur.* Pliant.

P. پیچش *píchish.* Contortion.

P. پیچك *píchak.* A skein of thread.

P. پیچیدن *píchídan.* To twist; to fold.

P. پیختن *píkhtan.* To twist.

P. پیدا *paidá.* Production; evident.

P. پیدایش *paidáyish.* Produce; birth.

P. پی در پی *pai dar pai.* Successively.

P. پیر *pír.* An old man; a saint.

P. پیر طریقت *pír i taríkat.* A spiritual guide; superior of a religious order.

P. پیرا *pairá.* Decorating (in comp.).

P. پیراستن *pairástan.* To adorn.

P. پیرامن *pírámun.*
P. پیرامون *pírámún.* } Environs; about.

P. پیرانه *pírána.* Like an old man.

P. پیراهن *píráhan.* A shirt.

P. پیراهن شاهی *píráhan i sháhí.* Calico.

P. پیرایش *pairáyish.* Embellishment.

P. پیرایه *pairáyah.* An ornament.

P. پیر زال *pír-zál.* A decrepit old man or woman.

P. پیرسال *pír-sál.* Stricken in years.

P. پیر مغان *pír i mughán.* Chief priest of the Magi.

P. پیرو *pai-rav.* A follower, a dependant.

P. پیروی *pai-raví.* Following; prosecution; imitation.

P. پیروز *pírúz.* Victorious; conqueror.

P. پیروزه *pírúza.* A turquoise.

P. پیروزی *pírúzí.* Victory, conquest.

P. پیرهن *pírahan.* See پیراهن.

P. پیری *pírí.* Old age.

P. پیش *písh.* Before, in front, forward.

P. پیشاب *písháb.* Urine.

P. پیش آمدن *písh ámadan.* To come before; to occur.

P. پیشانی *písháni.* The forehead.

P. پیشتر *píshtar.* Before, prior.

P. پیشخانه *písh-khána.* Camp-equipage sent on before.

P. پیشخور *písh-khur.* Receiving pay in advance.

P. پیشداد *písh-dád.* A law-giver; name of the earliest dynasty of Persian Kings.

P. پیشدستی *písh-dastí.* Aggression.

P. پیشدید *pish-díd.* In view.

P. پیشرفت *pish-raft.* Efficacacious.

P. پیش قبضه *pish-ḳabẓa.* A dagger.

P. پیش رو *pish-rav.* A chief, leader.

P. پیش کار *písh-kár.* A manager, agent, deputy.

P. پیشکاری *písh-kárí.* Deputyship.

P. پیشکش *pish-kesh.* A present; offerings.

P. پیشگاه *písh-gáh.* A portico.

P. پیشگرفتن *písh-giriftan.* To propose; to adopt; to embrace.

P. پیش مزد *písh-muzd.* Handsell.

P. پیش نماز *písh-namáz.* A priest; presiding at prayers.

P. پیش نهاد *písh-nihád.* Intention.

P. پیشوا *píshwá.* A leader.

P. پیشواز *písh-wáz.* Going out to meet a person of distinction.

P. پیشوائی *píshwáï.* Guidance, the office of Imám.

P. پیشه *písha.* An art, profession.

P. پیشه ور *píshawar.* An artizan.

P. پیشی *píshí.* Superiority, precedence.

P. پیشیاب *písh-yáb.* Foresighted.

P. پیشین *píshín.* Former; primitive.

P. پیشینه *píshína.* Formerly.

P. پیشینان *píshínán.* The ancients.

P. پیغام *paighám.* A message.

P. پیغامبر *paighámbar.* A messenger; prophet.

P. پیغم *paigham.* A message.

P. پیغمبر *paighamber.* A prophet.

P. پیغوله *paighúla.* A corner, angle.

P. پیک *paik.* A courier, messenger.

P. پیکر *paikar.* Form, figure.

P. پیکان *paikán.* The head of a spear, &c.

P. پیگار *paigár.* Combat, battle.

P. پیگو *Pigú.* The kingdom of Pegu.

P. پیل *píl.* An elephant.

P. پیلبان *píl-bán.* An elephant-keeper.

P. پیلپای *píl-pái.* A pillar; prop; a pillar-post.

P. پیلتن *píl-tan.* Bulky, burly.

P. پلور *pílawar.* A pedlar.

P. پله *píla.* A silkworm's cocoon.

P. پیم *paiyam.* A message.

P. پیما *paimá.* A measurer, a weigher.

P. پیمان *paímán.* A promise; treaty.

P. پیمانه *paimána.* A measure; a goblet.

P. پیمایش *paimáyish.* Measure, dimensions.

P. پیمبر *paiyambar.* A messenger; prophet.

P. پیمودن *paimúdan.* To measure.

P. پینه *pína.* A patch (of cloth).

P. پیوسته *paivasta.* Continually, successively.

P. پیوستن *paivastan.* To join.

P. پیوند *paivand.* Conjunction; joint; kindred.

P. پیه *píya.* Fat, grease.

P. پی‌هم *pai-ham.* Successively.

ت

ت The third letter of the Arabic and fourth of the Persian alphabet. At the end of a word it represents the pronoun of the second person singular.

P. تا *tá.* To, until, so far, as long as, that, in order that, while. It is generally added to the numerals, e. g. دو تا کتاب *dú tá kitáb.* Two books.

P. تاب *táb.* Heat, light; power, endurance.

P. تابان *tábán.* Shining, bright.

P. تابدان *tábdán.* A skylight; a stove.

P. تابستان *tábistán.* Summer, hot weather.

P. تابش *tábish.* Brilliancy; heat.

A. تابع *tábi'.* A dependant, follower.

P. تابناك *tábnák.* Bright, burning.

A. تابوت *tábút.* A coffin; an ark.

P. تابه *tába.* A frying-pan.

A. تأبید *ta'bíd.* Perpetuation.

P. تابیدن *tábídan.* To shine; to twist.

P. تاتار *Tátár.* A Tartar.

A. تأثیر *ta'sír.* Impression, effect.

A. P. تاج *táj.* A crown, a crest.

A. P. تاج خروس *táj i khurús.* A cock's comb.

A. P. تاجدار *táj-dár.* A crowned head.

A. تاجر *tájir.* A merchant.

A. P. تاجور *tájwar.* A prince, a king.

P. تاخت *tákht.* Attack, assault.

P. تاختن *tákhtan.* To attack; to gallop.

A. تأخیر *ta'khír.* Delay.

A. تأديب *ta'díb.* Chastisement; discipline.

P. تار *tár.* A thread; wire; dark.

P. A. تار برقى *tár i barkí.* The electric telegraph.

P. تاراج *táráj.* Spoil, plunder.

P. تارك *tárak.* The top; crown of the head.

P. تاركش *tár-kesh.* A wire-drawer.

P. تارومار *tár u már.* Topsy-turvy.

P. تاروپود *tár u púd.* The warp and woof of a cloth.

A. تاريخ *táríkh.* The date of a letter; an event, era, epoch; a history, chronicle.

P. تاريك *tárík.* Dark, obscure.

P. تاريكى *taríkí.* Darkness, obscurity.

P. تاز *táz.* An attack; a race.

P. تازگى *tázagí.* Freshness.

P. تازنده *tázanda.* Galloping.

P. تازه *táza.* Fresh, new.

P. تازى *Tází.* Arabian; Arabic.

P. تازيانه *táziyána.* A scourge, whip.

P. تازيدن *tázídan.* To attack; to gallop.

A. تاسع *tási'.* The ninth.

A. تأسف *ta'assuf.* Grief, regret.

A. تأسيس *ta'sís.* Founding.

P. تاش *tásh.* A master; partner. خواجه تاش *kh'ája-tásh.* A schoolfellow.

P. تافتن *táftan.* To twist, to spin; to turn away; to shine.

P. تافته *táfta.* Twisted, woven.

P. تاك *ták.* A vine, tendril.

P. تاكى *tá kai.* How long?

P. تاكجا *tá kujá.* How far?

A. تأكيد *ta'kíd.* Injunction.

P. تالاب *táláb.* A pond, a tank.

A. تألف *ta'alluf.* Affection.

A. تألم *ta'allum.* Grief, pain.

A. تأليف *ta'líf.* Compilation of a book.

A. تام *támm.* Complete, entire.

A. تأمل *ta'ammul.* Consideration, thought.

A. تأنى *ta'anní.* Delay, hesitation.

A. تأنيث *ta'nís.* Feminine.

P. تاو *táv.* Heat; strength.

P. تاوان *táwán.* Fine, mulct; recompense.

A. تأويل *ta'wíl.* Interpretation.

A. تأهل *ta'ahhul.* Marrying.

A. تأييد *ta'yíd.* Aid; corroboration.

P. تاى *táy.* Like, resembling (in comp.).

A. تائب *tá'ib.* Repenting, penitent.

P. تپ *tap.* A fever.

P. تبار *tabár.* Family, race.

P. تباه *tabáh.* Wicked, abject, ruined.

P. تباهی *tabáhí.* Depravity; ruin.

A. تبجیل *tabjíl.* Honouring; glorification.

A. تبحر *tabaḥḥur.* Profound learning.

A. تبختر *tabakhtur.* Walking jauntily.

A. تبخر *tabakhkhur.* Perfuming one's self.

A. تبخیر *tabkhír.* Perfuming, scenting.

A. تبدد *tabaddud.* Dispersion.

A. تبدل *tabaddul.* Change.

A. تبدیل *tabdíl.* Alteration; substitution.

A. تبذیر *tabźír.* Prodigality.

P. تبر *tabar.* A hatchet, axe.

A. تبر *tibr.* Gold.

P. تبرزین *tabar-zín.* A small hatchet borne by the Shah's body-guard.

P. A. تپ ربع *tap i rub'.* A quartain fever.

P. A. تپ دق *tap i dikk.* A hectic fever.

A. تبرك *tabarruk.* Benediction; relic.

A. تبرید *tabríd.* Cooling.

P. تبریز *Tabríz.* Tebríz. The chief town of the province of Azerbaiján.

A. تبسم *tabassum.* Smiling.

P. تپش *tapish.* A swoon; palpitation.

A. تبعیت *tab'iyet.* Obedience.

A. تبعید *tab'íd.* Removing to a distance.

P. A. تپ غب *tap i ghibb.* A tertian fever.

P. تپ لرزه *tap i larza.* An ague.

A. تبلیغ *tablígh.* Causing to arrive; despatching (letters, &c.).

P. A. تپ محرق *tap i muḥrik.* An ardent fever.

A. تبن *tibn.* Straw.

P. A. تپ نوبت *tapi naubat.* An intermittent fever.

P. تبه *tabah.* Corruption; ruin.

P. تبه کار *tabah-kar.* An evildoer.

A. تبیین *tabyín.* Explaining.

A. تبیان *tibyán.* Explanation.

P. تپیدن *tapídan.* To palpitate.

A. تتبع *tattabu'.* Imitation, following up.

P. تتر *tatar.* A Tartar.

P. تتری *tatari.* Tartarian.

P. تتق *tutuk.* A curtain, a veil.

A. تتمه *tatimma.* Supplement, appendix; balance (of an account).

A. تتمیم *tatmím.* Completing.

A. تثنیة *taśníyet.* The dual, doubling.

A. تجار *tujjár.* Merchants (pl. of تاجر *tájir.*).

A. تجارب *tajárib.* Experiments, trials.

A. تجارت *tijárat.* Trade, traffic.

A. تجاسر *tajásur.* Presumption, boldness.

A. تجاور *tajáwur.* Vicinity.

A. تجاوز *tajáwuz.* Transgression.

A. تجاهد *tajáhud.* Labouring hard.

A. تجاهل *tajáhul.* Feigned ignorance.

A. تجديد *tajdíd.* Renewal.

A. تجربة *tajribat.* Experience, proof, experiment.

A. P. تجربه كار *tajriba-kár.* Experienced in business.

A. تجرد *tajarrud.* Solitude; celibacy.

A. P. تجرد گزين *tajarrud-guzín.* A recluse.

A. تجريب *tajríb.* Testing.

A. تجريد *tajríd.* Separation, solitude.

A. تجسس *tajassus.* Search, spying.

A. تجلى *tajallí.* Brilliancy.

A. تجمل *tajammul.* Pomp, retinue.

A. تجنب *tajannub.* Avoiding.

A. تجنيس *tajnís.* Analogy, resemblance; a pun.

A. تجوير *tajwír.* Accusing of injustice.

A. تجويز *tajwíz.* Investigation; permitting; deciding.

A. تجهيز *tajhíz.* Furnishing (a funeral).

A. تحائف *taḥáïf.* Rarities; choice gifts (pl. of تحفه *tuḥfat*).

A. تحبير *taḥbír.* Speaking or writing elegantly.

A. تحت *taḥt.* Under, below.

A. تحذير *taḥẕír.* Threatening, warning.

A. تحرك *taḥarruk.* Motion.

A. تحرير *taḥrír.* Writing.

A. تحريص *taḥrís.* Instigating.

A. تحريف *taḥríf.* Inversion, transposition (of letters).

A. تحريق *taḥríḳ.* Burning, setting on fire.

A. تحريك *taḥrík.* Agitating; movement.

A. تحريم *taḥrím.* Interdicting, prohibiting.

A. تحزين *taḥzín.* Afflicting.

A. تحسر *taḥassur.* Regret.

A. تحسين *taḥsín.* Approbation.

A. تحصيل *taḥsíl.* Acquisition.

A. تحصيلدار *taḥsíldár.* A collector of revenue.

A. تحف *tuḥaf.* Presents (pl. of تحفه *tuḥfat*).

A. P. تحفگى *tuḥfagí.* Rarity; elegance.

A. تحفة *tuḥfat.* A present; rarity.

A. تحفجات *tuḥfaját.* Rarities.

A. تحقير *taḥḳír.* Contempt.

A. تحقيق *taḥḳíḳ.* Certainty; truth; investigation.

A. تحكم *taḥakkum.* Command, sway.

A. تحليف *taḥlíf.* Exacting an oath.

A. تحليل *taḥlíl.* Making lawful; dissolving; digesting.

A. تحمل *taḥammul.* Endurance.

A. تحمید *taḥmíd.* Praising God.

A. تحور *taḥawwur.* Precipitation.

A. تحویل *taḥwíl.* Changing.

A. P. تحویلدار *taḥwíldár.* A treasurer.

A. تحیة *taḥíyat.* Salutation. pl. تحیات *taḥíyát.*

A. تحیر *taḥaiyur.* Astonishment.

A. تخالف *takháluf.* Opposition, enmity.

A. تخبیر *takhbír.* Information.

P. تخت *takht.* A throne.

P. تخت روان *takht-rawán.* A litter.

P. تخت گاه *takht-gáh.* The seat of government.

P. تخته *takhta.* A board, plank.

P. تخته بندی *takhta-bandí.* Boarding.

P. تختی *takhtí.* A tablet.

A. تخریب *takhríb.* Devastation.

A. تخصیص *takhṣíṣ.* Appropriation, attributing.

A. تخفیف *takhfíf.* Abatement.

A. تخلص *takhalluṣ.* The nom-de-plume assumed by poets.

A. تخلیص *takhlíṣ.* Deliverance.

P. تخم *tukhm.* Seed; an egg.

P. تخمه *tukhma.* Indigestion.

A. تخمین *takhmín.* Conjecture, guess.

A. تخمیناً *takhmínan.* By conjecture; nearly, about.

A. تخویف *takhwíf.* Inspiring fear.

A. تدابیر *tadábír.* Deliberations.

A. تدارك *tadáruk.* Precaution; reparation.

A. تدبیر *tadbír.* Deliberation, control.

A. تدریج *tadríj.* Gradation.

A. تدریس *tadrís.* Teaching.

A. تدفین *tadfín.* Burying.

A. تدقیق *tadḳíḳ.* Scrutinizing.

P. تذرو *tażarv.* A pheasant, the jungle-cock.

A. تذکره *tażkera.* A memoir, memorandum, a passport.

A. تذکیر *tażkír.* Masculine gender.

P. تر *tar.* Moist, fresh; the sign of the comparative.

A. تراب *turáb.* Ground, earth.

A. تراخی *tarákhí.* Remissness.

A. ترادف *taráduf.* A series.

P. ترازو *tarázú.* A balance, scales; the sign Libra.

P. تراش *tarásh.* Cutting, shaving. (in comp.)

P. تراشه *tarásha.* A chip, paring, shaving.

P. تراشیدن *taráshídan.* To cut.

A. تراضی *taráẓí.* Mutual satisfaction

A. تراکم *tarákum.* A crowd, throng.

A. تراکیب *tarákíb.* Compounds. pl. of ترکیب *tarkíb.*

P. ترانه *taràna.* Melody.

P. تراوش *taráwish.* Exudation, oozing.

P. تراویدن *taráwídan.* To exude, to leak.

P. ترب *turb.* A radish.

A. تربت *turbat.* A grave, tomb.

P. تربد *turbud.* Turbith root.

P. تربز *tarbuz.* A watermelon.

A. تربیت *tarbíyet.* Education.

A. تربیع *tarbí'.* Dividing into four.

A. ترتیب *tartíb.* Arrangement, order.

A. ترتیل *tartíl.* Intoning, chanting.

A. ترجمان *tarjumán.* An interpreter, a translator (dragoman), also (colloquially) a fine. اورا ترجمان کردند *úrá tarjumán kerdand.* They fined him.

A. ترجمه *tarjuma.* Interpretation, translation.

A. ترجیح *tarjíḥ.* Preference.

A. P. ترجیح داشتن *tarjíḥ dáshten,* to be preferred.

A. ترحم *taraḥḥum.* Pity.

A. تردد *taraddud.* Hesitation; a going to and fro; application, labour.

P. تر دامن *tar-dáman.* A sinner.

P. تر زبان *tar-zaban.* Eloquent.

P. ترس *tars.* Fear, terror.

P. ترسا *tarsá.* A Christian.

P. ترسانیدن *tarsánídan.* To terrify, frighten.

P. ترسنده *tarsenda.* Timid, fearful.

P. ترسو *tarsú.* Fearful.

P. ترسیدن *tarsídan.* To fear.

A. ترسیل *tarsíl.* Sending, despatching.

P. ترش *tursh.* Sour, acid.

A. ترشح *tarashshuḥ.* Exudation, sprinkling.

P. ترشرو *tursh-rú.* Austere.

P. ترشك *turshek.* Sorrel.

P. ترشه *tursha.* Wild sorrel.

P. ترشی *turshí.* Acidity.

A. ترصد *taraṣṣud.* Hope, expectation.

A. ترغیب *targhíb.* Incitement.

A. ترفیع *tarfí'.* Elevation.

A. ترفیه *tarfíyeh.* Quieting, composing.

A. ترقب *t arakḳub.* Expectation.

A. ترقی *taraḳḳí.* Augmentation, promotion.

P. ترقیدن *tarḳídan.* To burst, split.

A. ترقیم *tarḳím.* Writing.

A. ترك *tark.* Relinquishing. abandoning.

P. ترك بستن *tark bastan.* To

put anything on the back of a beast of burden.

A. P. ترك *Turk.* A Turk.

A. تركات *tarikát.* Legacies, bequests.

P. تركانه *Turkána.* Turk-like.

P. تركتازى *turk-tází.* Depredation.

P. تركش *tarkash.* A quiver.

A. تركة *tarikah.* A legacy.

A. P. تركى *Turkí.* Turkish.

A. تركيب *tarkíb.* Compounding.

P. تركيدن *tarkídan.* To burst.

A. ترمس *tarmus.* The Turkish lupine.

P. ترنج *turunj.* A citron, an orange.

A. P. ترنجبين *taranjubín.* Manna.

A. ترنم *tarannum.* Intoning.

P. تروتازه *tar u táza.* Moist and fresh.

P. تر و خشك *tar u khushk.* Moist and dry.

A. ترويج *tarwíj.* Giving currency.

P. تره *tarra.* Pot-herbs.

P. ترى *tarí.* Freshness, moisture.

A. ترياق *tiriyáḳ.* An antidote; treacle.

A. تزايد *tazáyud.* Augmentation, increase.

A. تزكية *tazkiyat.* Purity, sanctity.

A. تزلزل *tazalzul.* Commotion; earthquake.

A. تزوير *tazwír.* Hypocrisy, fraud.

A. تزين *tazayyun.* Ornament. Adorning oneself.

A. تساوى *tasáwí.* Equality.

A. تسبيح *tasbíḥ.* Praising God; a rosary.

A. تسبيك *tasbík.* Melting.

A. تسخر *taskhar.* Ridicule.

A. تسخير *taskhír.* Subduing; conquest.

A. تسخين *taskhín.* Heating water.

A. تسطير *tasṭír.* Writing, delineating.

A. تسعير *tas'ír.* Taxation.

A. تسكين *taskín.* Pacifying, calming.

A. تسلسل *tasalsul.* Series, succession.

A. تسلط *tasalluṭ.* Dominion.

A. تسلى *tasallí.* Consolation, comfort.

A. تسليم *taslím.* Consignment, surrender. Salutation.

P. تسمه *tasma.* A thong of undressed leather.

A. تسمية *tasmíyet.* Nomination.

A. تسويد *taswíd.* Writing a rough draft or copy.

A. تسويل *taswíl.* Trickery.

A. تسوية *taswíyet.* Equality.

A. تشابه *tashábih.* Resemblances. (pl. of تشبيه *teshbíh.*)

A. تشارك *tasháruk.* Association.

A. تشبیه *tashbíh.* A likeness, simile.

A. تشتت *tashattut.* Dispersion.

A. تشخص *tashakkhus.* Being distinguished.

A. تشخیص *tashkhís.* Ascertaining, estimating, diagnosis.

A. تشدید *tashdíd.* Corroboration; the mark ـّ.

A. تشریح *tashríḥ.* Explanation; anatomy.

A. تشریف *tashríf.* Ennobling; visiting. تشریف اوردن to come (on a visit). تشریف بردن to go (on a visit).

A. تشفی *tashaffí.* Consolation; placidity.

A. تشکر *tashakkur.* Gratitude.

A. تشکک *tashakkuk.* Doubting.

A. تشنج *tashannuj.* Spasm; puckering.

P. تشنگی *tishnagí.* Thirst; temptation.

P. تشنه *tishna.* Thirsty.

A. تشنیع *tashní'.* Reproaching, taunting.

A. تشوش *tashawwush.* Disquietude.

A. تشویر *tashwír.* Anguish. Causing another to feel ashamed.

A. تشویش *tashwísh.* Confusion, distraction, anxiety.

A. تشویق *tashwík.* Inspiring with desire.

A. تشهد *tashahhud.* Pronouncing the formula. اشهد ان لا اله الا الله. I attest that there is no God but God.

A. تشهیر *tash-hír.* Proclaiming, publishing.

A. تشیخ *tashayyukh.* Boasting.

A. تشید *tashyíd.* Raising, erecting, plastering; reinforcement.

A. تشییع *tashyí'.* Accompanying, escorting.

A. تصاحب *taṣáḥub.* Taking legal possession of anything.

A. تصاریف *taṣáríf.* Revolutions, changes, inflections.

A. تصاعد *taṣá'ud.* Ascent, climbing.

A. تصانیف *taṣáníf.* Literary compositions.

A. تصاویر *taṣáwír.* Pictures. (pl. of تصویر.)

A. تصحیح *taṣḥíḥ.* Correction.

A. تصحیف *taṣḥíf.* Writing; making an error in writing.

A. تصدق *taṣadduk.* Almsgiving.

A. تصدی *taṣaddí.* Presumption.

A. تصدیع *taṣdí'.* Vexation.

A. تصدیق *taṣdík.* Verifying, attesting. A certificate.

A. تصرف *taṣarruf.* Possession; use; expenditure; embezzlement.

A. تصرفات *taṣarrufát.* Possessions, usages.

A. تصریح *taṣríḥ.* Setting forth clearly.

A. تصریف *taṣríf.* Change, inflection.

A. تصغیر *taṣghír.* Diminution; a diminutive.

A. تصفیه *taṣfíyeh.* Purification; reconciliation.

A. تصلیب *taṣlíb.* Crucifixion.

A. تصمیم *taṣmím.* Resolving, determining.

A. تصنع *taṣannuʿ.* Speciousness.

A. تصنیف *taṣníf.* Literary composition, writing a book.

A. تصور *taṣawwur.* Imagination.

A. تصوف *taṣawwuf.* The doctrine and profession of a Súfí or Mystic.

A. تصویر *taṣwír.* A picture.

A. P. تصویر کشیدن *taṣwír keshíden.* To paint.

A. تضاعف *tażáʿuf.* Double.

A. تضحك *tażaḥḥuk.* Mocking, ridicule.

A. تضرع *tażarruʿ.* Supplication.

A. تضمین *tażmín.* Indemnification; including.

A. تضییع *tażyíʿ.* Wasting.

A. تطابق *taṭábuḳ.* Analogy, conformity.

A. تطاول *taṭáwul.* Tyranny.

A. تطبیق *taṭbíḳ.* Conformity, comparison.

A. تطلیق *taṭlíḳ.* Repudiation.

A. تطویل *taṭwíl.* Extending.

A. تطهیر *taṭhír.* Purification.

A. تظالم *tażálum.* Oppressing. Pretending to be a victim.

A. تظلم *tażallum.* Oppression, injustice.

A. تعارض *taʿáruż.* Opposition.

A. تعاقب *taʿáḳub.* Persecution.

A. تعالی *Taʿála.* The Most High.

A. تعاون *taʿáwun.* Mutual assistance.

A. تعاهد *taʿáhud.* Making a mutual compact.

A. تعاویذ *taʿáwíż.* Amulets.

A. تعب *taʿb.* Fatigue.

A. تعبد *taʿabbud.* Adoration.

A. تعبیه *taʿbíyeh.* Insertion, inlaying.

A. تعبیر *taʿbír.* Interpretation (of dreams).

A. تعتب *taʿattub.* Reproaching.

A. تعثر *taʿaṡṡur.* Stammering, hesitating.

A. تعجب *taʿajjub.* Wondering.

A. تعجیب *taʿjíb.* Causing wonder.

A. تعجیز *taʿjíz.* Impotence.

A. تعجیل *taʿjíl.* Haste.

A. تعداد *taʿdád.* Number, account.

A. تعدد *taʿaddud.* Multitude, number.

A. تعدی *taʿaddí.* Invasion, transgression, transitive (a verb).

A. تعدید *ta'díd.* Enumeration.

A. تعدیل *ta'díl.* Equalising.

A. تعذر *taaźźur.* Difficulty; excuse.

A. تعذیب *ta'źíb.* Tormenting, punishment.

A. تعذیر *ta'źír.* Reprimand.

A. تعرض *ta'arruẓ.* Opposition; an obstacle; also تعرض کردن *ta'arruẓ kerdan.* To lay a case before any one.

A. تعرف *ta'arruf.* Knowledge of God.

A. تعریض *ta'ríẓ.* Allusion.

A. تعریف *ta'ríf.* Description; praise.

A. تعریق *ta'rík.* Causing perspiration.

A. تعزیه *ta'ziyeh.* Mourning.

A. P. تعزیه داشتن *ta'ziyeh dáshtan.* To perform the passion-play representing the death of Ḥasan and Ḥosein.

A. P. تعزیت پرسی *ta'ziyet pursí.* Condolence.

A. تعسر *ta'assur.* Difficulty.

A. تعشق *ta'ashshuk.* Falling in love.

A. تعشی *ta'ashshí.* Supping.

A. تعصب *ta'aṣṣub.* Bigotry.

A. تعطل *ta'aṭṭul.* Being unemployed, idleness.

A. تعطیل *ta'ṭíl.* Rendering useless; a holiday. ایام تعطیل *aiyám i ta'ṭíl.* The vacation.

A. تعظم *ta'aẓẓum.* Pride, grandeur.

A. تعظیم *ta'ẓím.* Reverence.

A. تعفن *ta'affun.* Becoming putrid or fetid.

A. تعقل *ta'akkul.* Understanding.

A. تعلق *ta'alluk.* Dependance, connexion.

A. تعلقه *taallukah.* Landed property; connexion. pl. *ta'allukát.*

A. تعلل *ta'allul.* Procrastination.

A. تعلیق *ta'lík.* Suspension; the Persian style of handwriting.

A. تعلیل *ta'líl.* Soothing, diverting.

A. تعلیقه *ta'líkah.* An order or passport signed by the prime minister. An inventory.

A. تعلیم *ta'lím.* Instruction.

A. تعلیمی *ta'límí.* A martingale.

A. تعمید *ta'míd* or غسل تعمید *ghusl i ta'míd.* Baptism.

A. تعمیر *ta'mír.* Building, repairing.

A. تعنت *ta'annat.* Finding fault, taunting.

A. تعویذ *ta'wíź.* An amulet.

A. تعویض *ta'wíẓ.* Substitution.

A. تعویق *ta'wík.* Suspense, delay.

A. تعهد *ta'ahhud.* Engagement, compact.

A. تعییب *ta'yíb.*
A. تعییر *ta'yír.* } Blame.

A. تعین *ta'aiyun.* Appointment.

A. تعيين ta'yín. Appointing, specifying.

A. تعينات ta'yínát. Appointments.

A. تعيناتى ta'yínátí. The duty of an office.

A. تغابن taghábun. Mutual deception.

A. تغار taghár. A bucket; a provision bag slung on a horse.

A. تغافل tagháful. Wilful negligence.

A. تغالب taghálub. Being victorious.

A. تغاير taghâyur. Difference.

A. تغذيه taghzíyeh. Diet.

A. تغريب taghríb. Exiling.

A. تغريق taghríḳ. Immersion, drowning.

A. تغلب taghallub. Dominance; imposition.

A. تغمه tughmeh. A medal.

A. تغير taghaiyur. Change.

A. تغيير taghyír. Changing, dismissing from office.

P. تف tuff. Spittle.

P. تف taf. Vapour.

A. تفاح tufáḥ. An apple.

A. تفاخر tafákhur. Boasting.

A. تفاريق tafáríḳ. Intervals, divisions.

A. تفاسير tafásír. Commentaries.

A. تفاصيل tafáṣíl. Details.

A. تفاوت tafáwut. Distance, difference.

A. تفاول tafáwul. Taking a good omen.

P. تفت taft. Warmth, heat.

P. تفته tafta. Warm.

A. تفتيح taftíḥ. Opening.

A. تفتيش taftísh. Inquiry, search.

A. تفحص tafakhuṣ. Strict inquiry.

A. تفخر tafakhrur. Inordinate boasting.

A. تفرج tafarruj. Amusement; taking a walk.

A. P. تفرجگاه tafarruj-gáh. A theatre; a place of recreation.

A. تفرد tafarrud. Separation; solitude.

A. تفرس tafarrus. Discernment.

A. تفرق tafarruḳ. Dispersion.

A. تفرقه tafriḳah. Separation, disjunction.

A. تفريح tafríḥ. Exhilaration.

A. تفريد tafríd. Isolation.

A. تفريط tafríṭ. Excess.

A. تفريق tafríḳ. Separation, partition.

P. تفسيدن tafsídan. To grow warm.

A. تفسير tafsír. A commentary.

A. تفصيل tafṣíl. Detail.

A. تفضل tafaẓẓul. Favour, kindness.

A. تفضيح tafẓíḥ. Disgrace.

A. تفقد tafaḳḳud. Inquiry, kindness.

A. تفكر tafakkur. Thought.

P. تفنگ *tufang.* A musket.

P. تفنگچی *tufangchí.* A matchlock-man.

A. تفنن *tafannun.* Diversion.

P. تفو *tafú.* Fy! for shame!

A. تفویض *tafwíẓ.* Consignment, entrusting to.

A. تفه *tafih.* Tasteless, insipid.

A. تفهم *tafahhum.* Understanding.

P. تفیدن *tafídan.* To warm.

A. تقابل *taḳábul.* Encounter.

A. تقادیر *taḳádír.* Divine decrees.

A. تقارب *taḳárub.* Approaching one another.

A. تقاریر *taḳárír.* Recitals, speeches.

A. تقاضی *taḳáẓí.* Urgency; importunity.

A. تقاعد *taḳáʿud.* Backwardness.

A. تقاطر *taḳáṭur.* Distilling, drop by drop.

A. تقالیب *taḳálíb.* Resolutions.

A. تقاوت *taḳawat.* Piety.

A. تقاول *taḳáwul.* Conversation.

A. تقاوی *taḳáwí.* Advancing money to a tenant to purchase seed.

A. تقاویم *taḳáwím.* Calendars.

A. تقدس *taḳaddus.* Being holy.

A. تقدم *taḳaddum.* Priority.

A. تقدیر *taḳdír.* Fate, predestination, purport, supposition.

A. تقدیس *taḳdís.* Sanctifying, consecration.

A. تقدیم *taḳdím.* Priority; presenting.

A. تقرب *taḳarrub.* Approximation, access.

A. تقرر *taḳarrur.* Confirmation.

A. تقریب *taḳríb.* Giving access; recommendation. Pretence, motive.

A. تقریبا *taḳríban.* Nearly; about.

A. تقریر *taḳrír.* A speech, or recitation.

A. تقسیم *taḳsím.* Division, distribution.

A. تقصیر *taḳṣír.* Fault, deficiency.

A. تقصیروار *taḳṣír-wár.* Culpable.

A. تقطیر *taḳṭír.* Distilling, dropping.

A. تقطیع *taḳṭíʿ.* Scanning (verse).

A. تقلب *taḳallub.* Writhing, rolling.

A. تقلص *taḳalluṣ.* Contracting, shrinking.

A. تقلیب *taḳlíb.* Inversion.

A. تقلید *taḳlíd.* Imitation, counterfeiting. تقلید در اوردن *taḳlíd dar áwardan.* To mimic any one.

A. تقلیدی *taḳlídí.* Counterfeit.

A. تقلیل *taḳlíl.* Diminishing.

A. تقوی *taḳwá.* Piety.

A. تقویه *taḳwíyet.* Strength.

A. تقویم *taḳwím.* An almanac.

A. تقی *taḳí.* Pious.

A. تقید *taḳayyud.* Diligence.

P. تك *tag.* The bottom; a race or heat.

P. تكاپو *takápú.* Search, inquiry.

A. تكاسل *takásul.* Indolence.

A. تكالیف *takálíf.* Exactions, impositions.

P. تكانیدن *takánídan.* To shake off.

A. تكاور *tak-áwur.* An ambling horse.

A. تكاهل *takáhul.* Negligence.

A. تكبر *takabbur.* Arrogance.

A. تكبیر *takbír.* Saying الله اكبر *Allâhu akbar.* God is greatest.

T. تكتك *tektek.* Isolated; separately.

A. تكثیر *takšír.* Augmentation.

A. تكدر *takaddur.* Being turbid.

P. تكدو *tag-dav.* Inquiry, search.

A. تكذیب *takẕíb.* Accusing of imposture or lying.

A. تكرار *takrár.* Altercation, repetition.

P. تكرك *tagarg.* Hail.

تكرك باریدن *tagarg báridan.* To hail.

A. تكریم *takrím.* Respect, honour.

A. تكسر *takassur.* Being broken.

A. تكسیب *taksíb.* Gaining, acquiring.

A. تكسیر *taksír.* Breaking in pieces.

A. تكفل *takafful.* Taking security or bail.

A. تكفیر *takfír.* Covering; expiation.

A. تكفین *takfín.* Enshrouding, "laying out" the dead.

A. تكلف *takalluf.* Ceremony; extravagance.

A. تكلم *takallum.* Speech.

A. تكلیف *taklíf.* Ceremony, trouble.

A. تكلیل *taklíl.* Crowning.

P. تكمه *takma.* A button.

A. تكمید *takmíd.* Fomentation.

A. تكمیل *takmíl.* Perfecting.

P. تكوپو *tagupú.* Search, inquiry.

A. تكیه *takyeh.* A pillow; a place of repose; reliance. A Dervish College.

A. P. تكیه زدن *takyeh zadan.* To lean; to rely.

A. P. تكیه گاه *takyeh-gáh.* A resting-place; a sofa.

A. تل *tell.* A hill.

P. تلاش *talásh.* Search, inquiry.

A. تلاطم *taláṭum.* Dashing (of the waves).

A. تلافی *taláfí.* Compensation, amends.

A. تلاقی *taláḳí.* Meeting, interview.

A. تلامیذ *talámíż.* } Disciples,
A. تلامذه *talámiżah.* } scholars.

A. تلاوت *tiláwat.* Reading (the Ḳorán).

A. تلبیس *talbís.* Fraud; imposture.

A. تلجیج *taljíj.* Going out to sea (a ship).

A. P. تلخ *talkh.* Bitter, pungent.

P. تلخ کام *talkh-kám.* Bitter tasting.

P. تلخی *talkhí.* Bitterness.

A. تلطف *talaṭṭuf.* Affability, kindness.

A. تلف *talaf.* Waste; loss.

A. تلفظ *talaffuz.* Expression; pronunciation.

A. P. تلفکار *talaf-kár.* A prodigal.

A. تلفیق *talfíḳ.* Stitching together.

A. تلقین *talḳín.* Instructing; dictating the words of a prayer.

A. تلمیذ *talmíż.* A scholar.

P. تلو *talv.* Contained in (a letter).

P. تلواسا *talwásá.* Grief; restlessness.

A. تلون *talawwun.* Fickleness.

A. تلین *talayyun.* Being softened.

A. تم *tamma.* Finis.

A. تماثیل *tamásíl.* Resemblances, images.

A. تمادی *tamádí.* Protraction.

P. تماشا *tumásha.* A show, spectacle.

P. تماشگاه *tumásha-gáh.* A theatre.

P. تماشائی *tumashái.* A spectator.

A. تمام *tamám.* The whole; finish; exactly.

A. P. تمامتر *tamámter.* Entirely.

A. تمامی *tamámí.* Completion.

A. تمتع *tamattu'.* Enjoyment.

A. تمثال *timsál.* Resemblance; an image.

A. تمثیل *tamsíl.* An example, simile.

A. تمجید *tamjíd.* Glorifying God.

A. تمدد *tamaddud.* Extension.

A. تمر *tamar.* A date.

A. تمرد *tamarrud.* Being refractory.

A. P. تمر هندی *tamar i hindí.* A tamarind.

A. تمریخ *tamríkh.* Anointing with oil.

A. تمساح *timsáḥ.* A crocodile.

A. تمسخر *tamaskhur.* Buffoonery.

A. تمسك *tamassuk.* A bond, note of hand.

P. تمغا *tamghá.* An official stamp.

A. تمکن *tamakkun.* Residence.

A. تمکنة *tamkinat.* Dignity.

A. تمکین *tamkín.* Dignity, authority.

A. تملق *tamalluḳ.* Flattery, coaxing.

P. تمن *tuman.* Ten thousand.

A. تمنا *tamanná.* Wish, desire.

A. تموج *tamawwuj.* Billowing (waves).

A. تموز *tammúz.* A Syrian month (July).

A. تمول *tamawwul.* Opulence.

A. تمهد *tamahhud.* To engage, occupy oneself in.

A. تمهید *tamhíd.* Arrangement, preamble.

A. تمیز *tamíz.* Discrimination.

T. تمیز *temíz.* Neat, clean.

P. تن *tan.* The body, person.

P. تن دادن *tan dadan.* To engage in; to yield.

A. تنازل *tanázul.* Descent.

A. تنازع *tanázuʿ.* Litigation, wrangling.

P. تن آسانی *tan ásání.* Ease.

A. تناسب *tanásub.* Symmetry.

A. تناسخ *tanásukh.* Metempsychosis.

A. تناسل *tanásul.* Succession, descent.

A. تناقض *tanáḳuẓ.* Disagreement.

P. تن آور *tan-ávar.* Corpulent.

A تناول *tanáwul.* Taking (a meal).

A. تناهی *tanáhí.* Finishing.

P. تنباکو *tambáku.* Tobacco.

P. تنبل *tambal.* Lazy.

A. تنبل *timbal.* A dwarf.

P. تنبول *tambúl.* Betel-leaf.

A. تنبیه *tambíh.* Admonition.

A. تنجس *tanajjus.* To be soiled.

A. تنجم *tanájjum.* Observation of the stars.

A. تنخواه *tan-kh'áh.* An assignment, draft; salary.

P. تن پرور *tan-parvar.* Voluptuous; a Sybarite.

P. تند *tund.* Swift, sharp, violent.

P. تندباد *tund-bád.* A tempest.

P. تندخو *tund-khú.* Hasty.

P. تندر *tundar.* Thunder.

P. تندرست *tan - durust.* Healthy.

P. تندرستی *tan-durustí.* Good health.

P. تندهی *tan-dihí.* Diligence, exertion.

P. تندی *tundí.* Swiftness, violence, vehemence.

A. تنزل *tanazzul.* Declination.

A. تنزيل *tanzíl.* Revelation (of the Korān).

A. تنزيه *tanzíh.* Purifying. Declaring God to be free from human attributes.

A. تنسل *tanassul.* Pedigree.

A. تنسم *tanassum.* Exhaling, sniffing.

A. تنصيف *tanṣíf.* Halving.

A. تنظيم *tanzím.* Composing (verses).

A. تنعم *tana"um.* Affluence.

A. تنعيش *tan'ísh.* Exalting.

A. تنفر *tanaffur.* Aversion.

A. تنفس *tanaffus.* Respiration, sighing.

A. تنقص *tanakkus.* Detriment, deficiency, loss.

A. تنقل *tanakkul.* Eating dessert.

A. تنقى *tanakkí.* Purity.

A. تنقيح *tankíḥ.* Investigation.

A. تنقيه *tankíh.* Purgation.

P. تنك *tunuk.* Brittle, slender, shallow.

P. تنك *tang.* Narrow, tight; a girth.

P. تنك‌اب *tang-āb.* Shallow water.

P. تنك‌جاى *tang-jái.* Tightness, closeness.

P. تنكار *tangár.* Borax.

P. تنك چشم *tang-chashm.* Covetous; insatiate.

P. تنك دست *tang dast.* Indigent, parsimonious.

P. تنك دستى *tang-dastí.* Indigence, parsimony.

P. تنك دل *tang-dil.* Narrow minded.

P. تنك روزى *tang-rúzí.* Being straitened in means.

T. تنكرى *Tangrí.* God.

P. تنك سال *tang-sál.* A season of scarcity.

P. تنك ناى *tang-náy.* A difficulty; a defile.

P. تنكه *tanga.* A small coin; cash. Tin.

P. تنكى *tangí.* Narrowness, distress.

A. تنور *tannúr.* An oven, a stove.

P. تنومند *tanúmand.* Robust, vigorous.

A. تنوين *tanwín.* Doubling a vowel (in Arabic) which then takes the sound of *n.*

P. تنومندى *tanúmandí.* Robustness, vigour.

P. تنه *tana.* The trunk of a tree; a web.

P. تنها *tanhá.* Alone, only.

P. تنهاى *tanhái.* Solitude.

P. تنى چند *taní chand.* A few people.

P. تنيدن *tanídan.* To twist, spin.

P. تو *tú.* Thou.

P. تو *tav.* A fold, plait.

A. توابع *tawábi'.* Followers. (pl. of تابع.)

A. تواتر *tawátur.* Succession.

A. توارد *tawárud.* Arriving at the same time. Coincidence.

A. تواریخ *tawárikh.* Histories, annals; dates.

A. تواضع *tawáẓu'.* Humility.

A. P. تواضع سمرقندی *tawáẓu' i Samarḳandí.* False politeness.

A. توافر *tawáfur.* Abundance.

A. توافق *tawáfuḳ.* Concord.

A. توالد *tawálud.* Generation, succession.

A. توالی *tawálí.* Continuation, succession.

A. توءام *taw'ám.* A twin.

A. توءامان *taw'ámán.* Twins.

P. توان *tawán.* Power, strength. It is possible, one can: e.g. توان گفت *tawán guft.* One may say.

P. توانا *tawáná.* Powerful, strong.

P. توانائی *tawánáí.* Power, ability.

P. توانستن *tawánistan.* To be able.

P. توانگر *tawángar.* Rich.

P. تونگری *tawángarí.* Opulence.

P. توپ *tóp.* A cannon, artillery.

P. توپ انداز *top andáz.* A gunner.

P. توبتو *tú ba tú.* In folds.

P. توپخانه *topkhána.* A train of artillery.

P. توپ خالدار *top-i-kháldár.* A rifled cannon.

P. توپ زدن *top zadan.* To cannonade.

P. توپك *topak.* A musket.

A. توبه *taubah.* Penitence.

A. توبیخ *taubíkh.* Reproach.

A. توت *tút.* A mulberry.

P. توتن *tútan.* Tobacco.

P. توتی *tútí.* A parrot.

P. توتیا *tútiyá.* Tutty; sulphate of zinc for the eyes.

A. توجه *tawajjuh.* Favour, condescension; going in the direction of any place.

A. توحید *tauḥíd.* Unitarianism; professing belief in God's unity.

P. توختن *túkhtan.* To desire.

A. تودد *tawaddud.* Friendship.

P. تودری *túdarí.* The seeds of the mallow.

P. توده *túda.* A heap, stack.

A. تودیع *taudí'.* Bidding adieu; depositing.

A. تورع *tawarru'.* Asceticism, abstinence.

P. توره *tora.* Law, regulation.

A. توریت *taurít.* The Pentateuch.

A. تورید *tauríd.* Blossoming (a tree); painting the cheeks rose-colour.

P. توز *toz.* Plundering; bark used to ornament bows.

P. توزك *túzak.* Institute, regulation.

P. توزیدن *tuzídan.* To plunder.

A. توزیع *tauzí'.* Distribution; dealing out.

A. توس *tús.* Nature; origin.

A. توسط *tawassuṭ.* Mediation; adopting a medium course.

A. توسع *tawassuʿ.* Amplitude.

A. توسل *tawassul.* Means, intervention.

P. توسن *tausan.* A horse.

A. توسیع *tausíʿ.* Extension, amplification.

P. توشدان *tush-dán.* A cartridge-box.

P. توشك *túshak.* A quilt, mattress.

P. توشك خانه *túshak-khana.* A wardrobe.

P. توشه *túsha.* Provision for a journey.

A. توصیه *tauṣíyeh.* Recommendation.

A. توصیف *tauṣíf.* Description, praise.

A. توضوء *tawaẓẓúʾ.* Ablution.

A. توضیح *tauẓíḥ.* Publication.

A. توطن *tawaṭṭun.* Fixing one's residence; naturalization.

A. توطیه *tauṭíyeh.* Trick, dissimulation.

A. توعیر *tauʿír.* Preventing, embarrassing.

A. توغل *tawagghul.* Deep research.

A. توفق *tawaffuḳ.* Conformity.

A. توفیر *taufír.* Increase, multiplication.

A. توفیق *taufíḳ.* The grace (of God).

A. توقر *tuwaḳḳur.* Respect, being sedate.

A. توقع *tawaḳḳuʿ.* Hope, expectation.

A. توقیر *tauḳír.* Honour, respect.

A. توقف *tawaḳḳuf.* Delay, persevering.

A. توکل *tawakkul.* Trust in God.

A. توکید *taukíd.* Positive injunction.

A. توکیل *taukíl.* Committing to the custody of anyone.

A. تولی *tawallí.* Forming a friendship.

A. تولد *tawallud.* Birth.

P. توله *tuleh.* A puppy, a whelp.

H. توله *tola.* A weight of 2½ miskáls.

P. تومان *túmán.* A gold coin worth about 10*s.*

P. تونگر *tawangar.* Wealthy.

P. تونگری *tawangarí.* Riches, wealth.

P. توه *túh.* A fold, plait.

A. توهم *tawahhum.* Suspicion, imagination.

P. توی *túy.* Inside. توی شهر *túy shahr.* In town. توی این قوتی *túy ín ḳútí.* In this box.

P. ته *tah.* A fold, plait; the bottom of anything.

P. تهٔ *tih.* Empty.

A. تهاون *taháwun.* Neglecting, slighting.

A. تهتك *tahattuk.* Disgrace; dissipation.

A. P. ته خانه *tah-khána.* A cellar.

P. ته دل *tah i dil.* The bottom of the heart.

A. تهديد *tahdíd.* A threat.

A. تهذيب *tahzíb.* Amending, amelioration.

A. تهطر *tahattur.* Perdition, ruin.

A. تهلكه *tahlikah.* Perishing.

A. تهليك *tahlík.* Destruction.

A. تهليل *tahlíl.* Praising God.

A. تهمت *tuhmat.* Accusation, calumny.

P. A. ته ناف *tah i náf.* The abdomen.

P. ته نشين *tah-nishín.* Sediment, dregs.

A. تهنيئت *tahní-et.* Congratulations.

P. ته و بالا *tah u bálá.* Topsy-turvy.

A. تهور *tahawwur.* Fury, temerity.

P. تهي *tihí.* Empty.

P. تهيدست *tihí-dast.* Empty-handed, indigent.

P. تهي گاه *tihí-gáh.* The hypochondria; the slender part of the body under the short ribs.

P. تهي مغز *tihí-maghz.* Empty-brained, ignorant.

A. تهية *tahíyeh.* Readiness, preparation.

P. تيار *taiyár.* Ready, prepared.

P. تياري *taiyárí.* Readiness, preparation.

P. تير *tír.* An arrow; the planet Mercury. (Colloquially) the best of anything; as تير كن *tír kun.* Choose the best.

P. تير انداز *tír andáz.* An archer.

P. تير بندوق *tír i bandúk.* A musket-ball.

P. تير دان *tír dán.* A quiver.

P. تير گر *tír-gar.* An arrow-maker.

P. تير كشتي *tír i kishtí.* The mast of a ship.

P. تيرگي *tíragí.* Obscurity; being turbid.

P. تير ماه *tír-máh.* The first summer-month of the Persian year.

P. تيره *tíra.* Dark; turbid.

P. تيره بخت *tíra-bakht.*
P. تيره روزگار *tíra-rúzgár.*
Unfortunate.

P. A. تيره راي *tíra-rái.* Dark-minded; having cloudy ideas.

P. تيره كردن *tíra-kerdan.* To tarnish.

P. تيز *tíz.* Sharp, acrid, swift.

P. تيز اب *tíz-áb.* Aquafortis.

P. تيز چنگي *tíz-changí.* Having sharp claws, rapacity.

P. تيز دست *tíz-dast.* Diligent.

P. تيز رو *tíz-rav.* Swift.

P. تيزك *tízak.* Cresses.

P. تیزی *tízí*. Sharpness, pungency, swiftness.

A. تیسر *tayassur*. Facility.

P. تیشه *tísha*. An axe, hatchet.

P. تیغ *tígh*. A sword, scimitar.

P. تیغا *tíghá*. A short, broad scimitar.

P. تیماج *tímáj*. Calf's skin.

P. تیمار *tímár*. Care; attendance on the sick; grooming a horse.

P. تیمار خانه *tímár-kháneh*. A hospital.

P. تیمار داری *tímár-dárí*. Care of the sick.

A. تیمم *tayammum*. Purifying before prayer with sand or dust, when water cannot be had.

A. تیمن *tayammun*. Taking a good omen.

A. تین *tín*. A fig.

A. تیه *tíh*. A desert. بادیة التیه *Bádiet et Tíh*. The wilderness of the forty years' wandering.

P. تیهو *tíhú*. A small partridge; a quail.

ث

ث *sá* or *se*. Ṡ. The fourth letter of the Arabic alphabet. It is never used in words of Persian origin.

A. ثابت *sábit*. Firm, fixed, proof.

A. ثابت قدم *sábit-ḳadam*. Steady.

A. ثابت کردن *sábit kerdan*. To conform; to prove.

A. ثابته *sábitah*. A fixed star.

A. ثاقب *sáḳib*. Glittering; penetrating.

A. ثالث *sális*. The third; an arbitrator.

A. ثالثی *salisí*. Arbitration.

A. ثآلیل *sa'álíl*. Warts. (pl. of ثوءلول.)

A. ثامن *sámin*. The eighth.

A. ثانی *sání*. The second.

A. ثبات *sabát*. Stability.

A. ثبت کردن *sabt kerdan*. To fix; to inscribe.

A. ثبوت *subút*. Proof by evidence.

A. ثدی *sady*. The breasts.

A. ثراء *sará*. Opulence.

A. ثروت *sarwat*. Wealth.

A. ثری *sará*. The ground.

A. ثری *saríy*. Rich, moist.

A. ثریا *suraiyá*. The Pleiades.

A. ثعبان *sa'bán*. A large serpent.

A. ثعلب *sa'leb*. A fox.

A. ثعلب مصری *sa'leb i miṣrí*. Salep (a medicinal root).

A. ثغور *sughúr* (pl. of ثغر). Ridges, frontiers.

A. ثقات *siḳát*. Trusty friends.

A. ثقالت *saḳálat*. Heaviness, weight.

A. ثقب *saḳb*. Perforation.

A. ثقبة *suḳbat*. A hole.

A. ثقل *siḳl*. Heaviness.

A. ثقة *sikat.* A trusty friend.

A. ثقوب *sukúb.* Holes.

A. ثقيل *sakíl.* Heavy.

A. ثلاث *salás.* Three. ثلاث *sulás.* In threes.

A. ثلاثى *sulásí.* Triple, triliteral.

A. ثلث *suls.* A third.

A. ثلثاء *salásá'.* Tuesday.

A. ثلج *silj.* Snow.

A. ثم *summa.* Then.

A. ثمر *samar.* Fruit.

A. ثمرة *samarat.* Fruit, advantage.

A. ثمن *saman.* Price, value.

A. ثمن *sumn.* An eighth.

A. ثمين *samín.* Valuable; precious.

A. ثناء *saná'.* Praise, applause.

A. ثناءى *saná'í.* The act of praising.

A. ثنية *saníyet.* A front tooth.

A. ثواب *sawáb.* A good work; reward.

A. ثوابت *sawábit.* Fixtures; fixed stars.

A. ثوب *saub.* Clothes, dress.

A. ثور *saur.* A bull; the sign Taurus.

A. ثوءلول *sú'lúl.* A wart; a nipple.

A. ثوم *súm.* Garlic.

A. ثياب *siyáb.* Clothes, garments.

ج

ج *jím.* J. The sixth letter of the Arabic and Persian alphabets.

P. جا *já.* Place.

P. جا بجا *já ba já.* Here and there; from place to place.

P. جاجم *jájim.* A kind of carpet.

P. جا داد *já-dád.* A place, station, service.

A. جادل *jádil.* A wrangler.

P. جادو *jádú.* Magic.

P. جادو كر *jádú-gar.* A magician.

P. جاده *jáda.* A high-road.

A. جاذب *jázib.* Attractive, absorbent.

A. جار *jár.* A neighbour.

A. جار و بالجار *jár u bi'ljár.* Neighbours and dependants.

P. جارو *járú.* A broom, a brush.

A. جارور *járúr.* A river, a stream.

A. جارى *járí.* Current, running, flowing.

A. جارية *járiyet.* A female slave.

A. جازم *jázim.* Resolving; conclusive.

A. جاسوس *jásús.* A spy.

A. جاسوسى *jásúsí.* Spying.

P. جاكوج *jákúj.* A sledge-hammer. (also چاكوچ *chákúch.*)

P. جاكير *jágír.* A grant of lands; pension.

P. جاگیر دار *jágír-dár.* The holder of a *jágír.*

A. جالس *jális.* Sitting.

P. جام *jám.* A cup, a goblet.

A. جامد *jámid.* Rigid, concrete.

A. جامع *jámiʿ.* The great mosque of a city; a collector; all, the whole.

A. جامعیت *jámiʿíyet.* Universality.

A. جاموس *jámús.* A buffalo.

A. جامقیه { *jámikíyeh* }
P. جامگی { or *jámagí.* }
A salary, stipend.

P. جامه *jáma.* A garment; cloth.

P. جامه خانه *jáma-kháneh.* A wardrobe.

P. جامه دان *jáma-dán.* A knapsack, portmanteau.

P. جامه وار *jáma-wár.* A flowered piece of *shawl;* chintz.

P. جان *ján.* The soul, life, spirit, mind.

P. جان ازاری *ján-ázárí.* Cruelty.

P. جانان *jánán.* A sweetheart; (pl. of جان) Dear ones.

A. جانب *jánib.* A side, part, quarter.

P. جانباز *ján-báz.* Risking one's life.

P. جانبازی *ján-bází.* Intrepidity.

P. A. جانبداری *jánib-dárí.* Partiality.

A. جانبین *jánibain.* Both sides; mutual.

P. A. جاننثار *ján-nis̤ár.* Devoted.

P. جاندار *ján-dár.* A living creature.

P. جانربا *ján-rubá.* Captivating the soul.

P. جانستان *ján-sitán.* Life-taking; deadly.

P. جانسوز *ján-súz.* Inflaming the mind.

P. جا نشین *já-nishín.* A locum-tenens.

P. جان فرسا *ján-farsá.* Wearing out the life.

P. جان کندن *ján-kandan.* To harrow the soul.

P. جان کاه *ján-káh.* Weakening the animal spirits.

P. جان گذار *ján-guẕár.* Heart-breaking; penetrating the soul.

P. جانگزا *ján-gazá.* Injuring life.

P. جانور *jánvar.* An animal.

P. جانی *jání.* A lover, a friend.

P. جاودان *jávidán.* Eternal, always.

P. جاودانی *jávidání.* Eternity.

P. جاوید *jávíd.* Eternal, always.

P. جاه *jáh.* Pomp, dignity.

A. جاهد *jáhid.* Industrious.

A. جاهل *jáhil.* Ignorant.

A. جاهلیت *jáhilíyet.* Ignorance; the Arabs before Mohammed's time.

P. جای *jáy*. A place.

P. جایداد *jáy-dád*. Assets.

A. جائر *jáir*. Tyrannical.

A. جائز *já'iz*. Permitted.

A. جائزه *já'izah*. Examination, trial.

P. جایگاه *jáy-gáh*. Station, place.

P. جایگیر *jáy-gír*. Efficacious.

A. جبار *jabbár*. Omnipotent; a tyrant.

A. جبال *jibál*. Mountains.

A. جبر *jabr*. Power, violence; restoration, setting a bone; reducing fractions to integers in Arithmetic.

A. الجبر و المقابلة *aljabr wa'lmukábalah*. Algebra.

A. جبراً *jabran*. Perforce.

A. جبروت *jubrút*. Omnipotence; عالم جبروت *'Alam i júbrút*. The Empyrean heaven.

A. جبرائیل *Jabrá'íl*. The Angel Gabriel.

A. جبل *jebel*. A mountain.

A. جبلت *jibillat*. Nature, disposition.

A. جبلی *jibillí*. Natural, innate.

A. جبن *jubn*. Cowardice. Cheese.

P. جبه *juba*. An over-coat.

A. جبهة *jubhah*. The forehead.

A. جبین *jabín*. The temple, the brow. Pusillanimous.

A. جثة *juṣṣah*. The body.

A. P. جثه داری *juṣṣa-dárí*. Corpulence.

A. جد *jadd*. Grandfather, ancestor.

A. جد *jidd*. Effort.

A. جدا *jiddan*. Strenuous.

P. جدا *judá*. Separate.

P. جدا جدا *judá-judá*. Separately.

A. جدار *jidár*. A wall.

P. جداگانه *judágána*. Separately.

A. جدال *jidál*. Dispute; wrangling.

A. جداول *jadáwil*. Columns; astronomical tables. (pl. of جدول *jadwal*.)

A. جداءی *judáí*. Separation.

A. جدری *jadaríy*. The small-pox.

A. جد صحیح *jadd i ṣaḥíḥ*. Paternal grandfather.

A. جدل *jadal*. Altercation.

A. P. جدوار *jadwár*. Zedoary, a root.

A. جدول *jadwal*. A column; astronomical table.

A. جده، صحیحه *jaddah i ṣaḥíḥah*. Paternal grandmother.

A. جدی *jidy*. The sign Capricorn.

A. جدی *jaddí*. Ancestral.

A. جدید *jadíd*. New, modern.

A. جذام *juẓám*. Elephantiasis.

A. جذب *jaẓb*. Absorption, attraction.

A. جذبة *jaẓbat*. Strong desire.

A. جذر *jażr.* The square root in arithmetic.

A. جر *jarr.* Drawing or dragging along; the genitive case.

P. جرابه *jarábah.* A sock.

A. جرأت *jará'at.* Boldness, audacity. کم جرأت *kam-jará'at.* Timid.

A. جراح *jarráḥ.* A surgeon.

A. جراحت *jiráḥat.* A wound.

A. P. جراحی *jarráḥí.* Surgery.

A. جراد *jarád.* A locust.

A. جرادالبحر *jarádu 'l baḥr.* A shrimp (sea-locust).

A. جرار *jarrár.* Brave, valiant. (said of an army.)

A. جرائد *jará'id.* Registers, books.

A. جرائم *jará'im.* Crimes, faults.

A. جرب *jarab.* The itch, scab.

A. جرح *jarḥ.* A wound.

P. جرس *jaras.* A bell.

A. جرسام *jirsám.* The pleurisy.

P. جرشفت *jarshaft.* A lampoon, pasquinade.

A. جرعه *jur'ah.* A draught of liquor.

A. جرم *jirm.* A (celestial) body.

A. جرم *jurm.* A crime, fault.

P. جرنغار *jaranghár.* The left wing of an army.

A. جریء *jarí'.* Bold, brave.

P. جریان *jarayán.* Flowing, running; a flux.

A. P. جریان شکم *jarayán i shikam.* Dysentery.

A. جریب *jaríb.* A land-measure.

A. جریح *jaríḥ.* Wounded.

A. جرید *jaríd.* A lance, spear.

A. جریده *jarídah.* A register.

A. P. جریمانه *jarímána.* } A fine, penalty.
A. جریمه *jaríma.* }

P. جز *juz.* Besides, except.

A. جزء *juz'.* A part; particle; section of the Korăn. جزء کلام *juz' e kelám.* In short, to sum up.

A. جزاء *jazá.* Compensation, reward.

A. جزاك الله *jazáka 'lláh.* May God reward you; bravo!

A. جزائر *jazá'ir.* Islands.

A. جزائل *jazá'il.* Dignities; abundancies.

A. P. جزدان *juz-dán.* A portfolio.

A. جزر *jazr.* The ebb tide; a carrot.

A. P. جز رسی *juz-rasí.* Knowledge, experience.

A. جزم *jazm.* Deciding; the orthographical character *jazm;* cutting. عزم بالجزم *'azm bi'l jazm.* A determined resolution.

A. P. جزوی *juzví.* A part, a little, few.

A. جزیره *jazírah.* An island.

A. جزيل *jazíl.* Great, dignified.

A. جزيه *jizyeh.* The capitation tax for dissenters (from the Mohammedan religion).

A. جسارت *jasárat.* Intrepidity.

A. جسامت *jasámat.* Corpulence.

P. جستن *jastan.* To leap, to spring, jump.

P. جستن *justan.* To search.

P. جست و جو *just u jú.* Strict search.

A. جسد *jasad.* The body.

A. جسر *jisr.* A bridge.

A. جسم *jism.* The body.

A. جسمانى *jismání.* Corporeal.

A. جسمانيت *jismáníyet.* Materiality.

A. جسور *jasúr.* Bold, audacious.

A. جسيم *jasím.* Corpulent. Majestic.

A. جشاء *jushá'.* Eructation.

P. جشن *jashn.* A feast, festival.

A. جعبة *ja'bah.* A quiver.

A. جعد *ja'd.* A crisp or curly lock of hair.

A. جعفر *ja'fer.* A little stream; a proper name.

A. P. جعفرى *ja'ferí.* The finest kind of gold; parsley.

A. جعل *ja'l.* Forgery, counterfeit.

A. جعلى *ja'lí.* Forged, false.

P. جغ *jugh.* A yoke for oxen.

P. جغرات *jughrát.* Curdled milk.

A. جفاء *jafá.* Violence, molestation. Coquetry.

A. P. جفاكار *jafá-kár.* } An
A. P. جفاگر *jafa-gar.* } oppressor.

P. جفت *juft.* A pair, couple, brace. جفت كرفتن to take a partner, to marry.

P. جفتى *juftí.* Pairing (of birds).

A. جفن *jafn.* The eyelid.

P. جفنك *jafnak.* Futile, frivolous.

P. جكر *jigar.* The liver.

P. جقه *jikka.* Crest, tuft (in a diadem, &c.).

P. جكر بند *jigar-band.* The intestines; a son.

P. جكر كوشه *jigar-gúshah.* Corner of the liver; a beloved object.

A. جل جلاله *jalla jaláluhu.* May His Majesty be glorified! (said of God).

A. جل *jull.* A housing, horse-cloth.

A. جل *jall or jull.* The sail of a ship.

A. جلا *jalá.* Brightness, polish. جلا دادن *jalá-dádan.* To polish.

A. جلاء *jalá'.* Emigration.

A. P. جلاب *julláb.* Any purgative, jalap; (from كل اب.)

A. جلاجل *jalájil.* Small spherical bells for cattle, drums, &c.

A. جلاد *jallád.* An executioner.

A. جلادت *jaládat.* Intrepidity.

A. P. جلا گر *jalá-gar.* A polisher; cutler.

A. جلال *jalál.* Majesty.

A. جلالت *jalálat.* Majesty, glory, splendour.

A. جلالی *jeláli.* The new Persian era of *Jelál ud dín, Malik Sháh,* in whose reign the Persian Calendar was reformed, A.H. 465.

A. P. جلا، وطن } *jalá i watan.*
A. P. جلا ی وطن } Emigration, expatriation.

A. جلب *jalab.* Attraction, allurement.

A. جلباب *jilbáb.* A screen, a veil.

P. جلد *jald.* Quick, speedy.

A. جلد *jild.* The skin, leather; a volume.

A. P. جلد گر *jild-gar.* A bookbinder.

P. جلدی *jaldí.* Speed, haste.

A. جلساء *julusá.* Companions, convives, members of an assembly. (pl. of جليس.)

A. جلسه *jalsa.* Meeting of a society; *séance.*

A. جلنار *jullanár.* A pomegranate-flower.

P. جلو *jalav.* A bridle.

P. جلو ريز *jalav-ríz.* Full speed.

P. جلو دار *jalav dár.* Head groom.

A. جلود *julúd.* Skins, volumes.

A. جلوس *julús.* Accession to the throne.

A. جلوه *jilvah.* Splendour; a bridal trousseau.

A. P. جلوه گر *jilva-gar.* Splendid, gracing.

A. جلی *jalíy.* Clear; plain.

A. جليس *jalís.* A companion.

A. جليل *jalíl.* Great, glorious.

A. جماد *jamád.* A fossil; anything inorganic.

A. جمادات *jamádát.* Minerals.

A. جمادی *jamádíy.* Inorganic.

A. جمادى الاولى *jumádá'l awwel.* The 5th month of the Arabian year.

A. جمادى الثانی *jumádá 'ssáni.* The 6th month of the Arabian year.

A. جماع *jimá'.* Copulation.

A. جماعت *jamá'at.* Congregation.

A. جمال *jamál.* Elegance, beauty.

A. جماهير *jamáhír.* Republics.

A. جمجمه *jumjuma.* A skull.

A. جمد *jamd.* Congealing; freezing.

A. جمرة *jamrat.* An ember.

P. جمشيد *Jemshíd.* A mythical hero, King of Persia.

A. جمع *jam'.* A collection; the plural; rental.

A. جمعه *juma'h.* Friday.

A. جمعيت *jam'iyet.* Collection.

A. P. جمعيت خاطر *jam'iyet i khâṭir.* Composure of mind.

A. جمل *jamal.* A camel.

A. جمل *jumal.* Sums, totals.

A. P. جملگی *jumlagí.* Totality.

A. جمله *jamla.* Sum, total, whole. فى الجملة *fil-jumla,* on the whole.

A. جمود *jumúd.* Congelation, freezing.

A. جمهور *jamhúr.* A republic; the masses.

A. جميع *jamí'.* All, universal.

A. جميعا *jamí'an.* Altogether.

A. جميل *jamíl.* Beautiful.

A. جن *jinn.* A genius, demon.

A. جناب *janáb.* Presence, excellency, lordship.

A. جنابت *janábat.* Ceremonial pollution.

A. P. جناب عالى *janáb i 'álí.* Your excellency; your highness!

A. جنات *jannát.* Paradises.

A. جناح *janáḥ.* A wing, fin, pinion.

A. جنازه *jenáza.* A funeral. تشييع جنازه كردن *tashyí'i jenáza kardan.* To act as bearer at a funeral.

A. جنان *jinán.* Paradise.

A. جنائب *janá'ib.* Led horses.

A. جنايت *jináyet.* A crime.

A. جنب *jamb.* A side; by the side of....

P. جنبان *jumbán.* Shaking, trembling.

P. جنبانيدن *jumbánídan.* To put in motion.

P. جنبش *jumbish.* Motion, agitation.

P. جنبيدن *jumbídan.* To move, stir.

A. جنت *jannat.* Paradise.

A. جنتى *jannatí.* Heavenly.

A. جند *jund.* An army; troops.

A. جندبيدست *jundbídast.* Castor; the testicles of a beaver.

A. جنس *jins.* Kind, sort, genus, race, goods.

A. جنسيت *jinsíyet.* Correspondence of species; a generic state.

LAT. جنطيانه *jinṭiyána.* Gentian.

P. جنگ *jang.* War, battle.

P. جنگ آوردن *jang áwardan.* To wage war.

P. جنگ آزموده *jang ázmúda.* Skilled in war.

P. جنگجو *jang-jú.* Quarrelsome.

P. جنگل *jangal.* A forest, wood.

P. جنگلى *jangalí.* Savage, wild.

P. جنگى *jangí.* Warlike.

P. جنگيدن *jangídan.* To fight.

A. جنوب *janúb.* The south.

A. جنوبی *janúbí.* Southern.

A. جنود *junúd.* Troops.

A. جنون *junún.* Insanity; demoniacal possession.

A. جنونی *junúní.* Insane, mad.

A. جنین *janín.* An embryo; a fœtus.

P. جو *jav.* Barley; a grain of silver. جو جو *jav-jav.* Grain by grain.

P. جو سیم *jav i sím.* A grain of silver.

P. جو *jú.* A stream; seek thou.

A. جواب *jawáb.* An answer.

A. P. جواب صاف *jawáb i ṣáf.* A positive answer.

A. جواد *jawwád.* Liberal, beneficent.

A. P. جواد مطلق *jawwád i muṭlaḳ.* The universal benefactor (God).

A. جواذب *jawázib.* Attractive qualities.

A. جوار *jiwár.* Neighbourhood.

A. جوارح *jawáriḥ.* The limbs; beasts of prey.

A. جوارش *jawárish.* Condiments; stomachics.

A. جواری *jawárí.* Female slaves. (pl. of جارية.)

A. جواز *jawáz.* Lawful, permitted. A custom-house permit (see گمرك).

A. جواسس *jawásís.* Spies. (pl. of جاسوس.)

P. جوال *juwál.* A sack, a bag.

P. جوال دوز *juwál-dúz.* One who sews sacks; a packing-needle.

P. جوال دوزی *juwál-dúzí.* Sack-making.

A. جوامع *jawámi'.* Comprehensive; mosques.

P. جوان *jawán.* Young; a youth.

A. جوانب *jawánib.* Sides, quarters, parts. (pl. of جانب.)

P. جوان بخت *jawán-bakht.* A promising youth.

P. جوان مرد *jawán-mard.* Generous, brave, a hero, a gentleman.

P. جوان مردی *jawán-mardí.* Generosity, manliness.

P. جوانی *jawání.* Youth.

A. جواهر *jawáhir.* Gems, jewels. (pl. of جوهر.)

A. جوائز *jawá'iz.* Gifts, benefits, rewards. (sing. جائزة.)

P. جوجه *júja.* A fowl.

A. جود *júd.* Liberality, munificence.

A. جودت *júdat.* Ingenuity.

A. جور *jaur.* Violence, tyranny.

A. P. جور پیشه *jaur-písha.* A tyrant.

A. جوز *jauz.* A nut.

A. جوزا *jauzá.* The sign Gemini. الجوزا *el jauzá.* Orion.

P. جوز بویا *jauz i búyá.* A nutmeg.

P. جوز رومی *jauz i rúmí.* A walnut.

P. جوز هندی *jauz i hindí.* A cocoa-nut.

P. جوز بر گنبد *jauz bar gambad.* A walnut on a cupola, i.e. lost labour.

P. جوزغه *jauzagha.* } A cotton-pod.
A. جوزق *jauzak.* }

A. جوزهر *jauzahr.* The dragon's head and tail (the nodes).

P. جوسه *jausa.* } A lofty building.
A. جوسق *jausak.* }
a villa; kiosk.

P. جوش *júsh.* Ebullition; heat.

P. جوش خوردن *júsh khurdan.* To solder.

P. جوشاندن *júshándan.* } To cause to boil.
P. جوشانیدن *júshánídan.* }

P. جوشش *júshish.* Ebullition; strong desire.

P. جوشن *jaushan.* A cuirass.

P. جوشن خای *jaushan-kháy.* Piercing the cuirass.

P. جوشیدن *júshídan.* To boil, ferment.

A. جوع *jau'.* Hunger.

A. جوف *jauf.* Cavity; the belly; inside (of a letter, &c.)

A. جوق *jauk.* A troop.

P. جولان *jaulán.* Galloping; careering to and fro.

P. جولان گاه *jaulán-gáh.* A plain for exercising or galloping horses.

P. جولاه *júláh.* A weaver. A spider.

A. جوهر *jauhar.* A gem, a pearl; essence, substance.

A. جوهری *jauharí.* A jeweller; the trade of a jeweller.

P. جوی *júy.* A river, a brook.

P. جویا *júyá.* Search.

P. جوی اب *júy áb.* A river.

P. جویان *júyán.* Searching; wishing.

P. جویای *júyáí.* Searching, inquiry.

P. جویبار *júy-bár.* A large river receiving many streams.

P. جوئیدن *jú'ídan.* To seek.

P. جوین *jú'ín.* Made of barley.

A. جهات *jihát.* Directions, sides.

A. جهاد *jihád.* A holy war.

A. جهاز *jaház.* Paraphernalia; trousseau; a ship.

A. جهال *juhhál.* Ignorant men.

A. جهالت *jahálat.* Ignorance.

P. جهان *jahán.* The world.

P. جهان *jihán.* Leaping.

P. جهان ارا *jahán-árá.* Adorning the world.

P. جهان افرین *jahán-áfrín.* The Creator of the world.

P. جهان بان *jahán-bán.* Protector of the world.

P. جهان بانی *jahán-bání.* Government of the world.

P. جهان پناه *jahán-panáh.* Asylum of the world; your majesty!

P. جہان بین *jahán-bín.* Seeing, comprehending the whole world.

P. جہان تاب *jahán táb.* Illuminating the world.

P. جہان جہان *jahán-jahán.* Much, many, very.

P. جہان دار *jahán-dár.* Possessor of the world, a king.

P. جہانداری *jahán-dárí.* Sovereignty.

P. جہان دیده *jahán-dída.* Experienced; a traveller.

P. جہان روای *jahán rawáï.* Government of the world.

P. جہان ستان *jahán-setán.* A conqueror.

P. جہان کشا *jahán - kushá.* Conqueror of the world.

P. جہان گرد *jahán-gard.* A traveller.

P. جہان گیر *jahán gír.* Conquering the world; name of an emperor of Hindustan.

P. جہان گیری *jahán gírí.* Conquest.

P. A. جہان مطاع *jahán-muṭá'.* Obeyed by the world.

P. جہان نما *jahán-numá.* Index or mirror of the world.

P. جہان نورد *jahán-naward.* A traveller.

P. جہانیان *jaháníyán.* People; creatures.

P. جہانیدن *jihánídan.* To cause to leap or spring.

A. جہت *jihat.* Cause; side; direction. از ین جہت *az ín jihat.* For this reason. جہت اینکه *jihat i ínki.* Inasmuch as. بہر جہت *ba har jihat.* Anyhow, in any respect.

A. جہد *jahd.* Effort, diligence.

A. جہرا *jahran.* Aloud, public.

A. جہل *jahl.* Ignorance.

A. جہلاء *juhalá.* Ignorant man.

A. جہنم *jehannum.* Hell.

P. جہودی *jahúdí.* A Jew; Jewish.

A. جہول *jahúl.* Very ignorant.

P. جہیدن *jihídan.* To spring, bound, leap.

A. جہیز *jahíz.* Paraphernalia; dowry.

A. جیب *jaib.* The collar or breast of a garment, a pocket.

A. جیحون *jaiḥún.* The river Oxus.

A. جید *jaiyid.* Elegant, excellent.

A. جیران *jírán.* Neighbours.

A. جیش *jaish.* Troops, an army.

P. جیغه *jígha.* i. q. جقه *jikka.*

A. جیفه *jífa.* A carcase.

A. جیل *jíl.* A generation, a race.

A. جیوس *juyúsh.* Armies.

P. جیوه *jívah.* Quicksilver.

چ

چ *chím* or *che*. Ch. The sixth letter of the Persian alphabet. It does not occur in Arabic words.

P. چابك *chábuk*. Alert; a whip.

P. چابکخرام *chábuk-khirám*. Swift-paced.

P. چابکدست *chábuk-dast*. Expert.

P. چابکسوار *chabuk-sawár*. A horse-breaker, a jockey.

P. چابکی *chabukí*. Activity.

P. چاپار *chápár*. Courier, the post.

P. چاپ کردن *cháp kardan*. To print.

P. چاپلوس *cháplús*. A flatterer.

P. چاپلوسی *cháplúsí*. Flattery.

P. چادر *chádar*. A sheet; a pavilion.

P. چار *chár*. Four.

P. چار بالش *char-bálish*. A throne; the four elements.

P. چار پایه *char-páya*. A quadruped.

P. چارپاءی *charpá'í*. A bedstead.

P. چارپر *chárpar*. A wine-bottle.

P. چار تکبیر برو زد *char takbír bar ú zad*. He repeated four *takbírs* over him (as they do over a corpse); i.e. abandoned him as dead.

P. چار چشم *chár-chashm*. Meeting, interview.

P. چارت زدن *chárt zadan*. To take a siesta.

P. چارده *chárdeh*. Fourteen

P. چار دیوار *chár-dívár*. Four walls; the elements.

P. چار سو *chár-sú*. Four roads meeting; a market.

P. چار طاق *chár-ṭák*. Four-arched; a tent with four doors.

P. چار گوشه *chár-gúsha*. Square, quadrangle.

P. چار مغز *chár-maghz*. A walnut.

P. چار نا چار *char ná chár*. Inevitable.

P. چاروا *chárvá*. A quadruped; a pony.

P. چاروا دار *chárvá-dár*. A muleteer.

P. چاره *chára*. A remedy, cure, help.

P. چاره پذیر *chára-pażír*. Curable.

P. چاره گر *chára-gar*. A knave, cheat.

P. چاشت *chásht*. Breakfast; the hours between sunrise and noon.

P. چاشنی *cháshní*. Taste, trial.

P. چاشنی گیر *cháshní-gír*. An assayer of metals; a taster.

P. چاق *cháḳ*. Vigorous, healthy, active.

P. چاك *chák*. A fissure, rent.

P. چاکر *chákar*. A servant.

P. چاکری *chákarí*. Service.

P. { چاکو cháḱú. } A pen-
P. { or چاقو cháḳú. } knife.

P. چاکوچ chákúch. A sledge-hammer.

P. چالاك chálák. Expert, active.

P. چالاکی chálákí. Activity.

P. چالش chálish. Graceful motion; war.

P. چانه chána. The jaw-bone.

P. چانه زدن chána-zadan. To jaw, to talk long and much.

T. چاءوش chá'ush. A sergeant, mace-bearer.

P. چاه cháh. A well, a pit.

P. چاهچور cháh-chúr. Ladies' trowsers for out-door wear.

P. چاه زنخ cháh i zanukh. The pit or dimple of the chin.

P. چاه کن cháh-kan. A well-digger.

P. چبان chabán. An ulcer, abscess.

P. چاءی chá'í. Tea.

T. چبوق chibúḳ. A pipe.

P. T. چوب چبوق chúb i chibúḳ. A pipe-stem.

P. چپ chap. The left hand.

P. چتر chatar. An umbrella.

P. چخین chikhín. Filthy.

P. چتر مار chatar i már. A mushroom.

P. چچك chichak. Small-pox.

P. چدن chadan. Cast iron.

P. چرا cherá. Why? wherefore? why not?

P. چراغ chirágh. A lamp.

P. چراغ پا chirágh-pá. Rearing (a horse).

P. چراغدان chirágh-dán. Stand for a lamp.

P. چراغ گرفتن chirágh-giriftan. To snuff the candle.

P. چراغ کشتن chirágh-kushtan. To put out the light.

P. چرا گاه chará-gáh. A pasture; meadow.

P. چرانیدن charánídan. To cause to graze.

P. چرب charb. Fat, greasy.

P. چرب زبان charb-zabán. Glib-tongued.

P. چربه charba. Oiled paper.

P. چربی charbí. Grease, fat.

P. چرخ charkh. A sphere, a wheel. The sky.

P. چرخ انداز charkh-andáz. A cross-bow man.

P. چرخ زدن charkh-zadan. To turn, to spin.

P. چرخه charkha. A wheel, reel.

P. چرخی charkhí. Celestial, spherical. Voluble; a pulley.

P. چرز charz. A kind of bustard.

P. چرغ chargh. A species of hawk.

P. چرغد chirghad. A cricket.

P. چرك chirk. Filth, dirt.

P. چرك را گرفتن chirk-rá giriftan. To clean off dirt.

P. چرك گوش chirk i. gúsh. Ear-wax.

P. چرگین chirgín. Filthy, nasty; dung.

P. چرم *charm.* Leather, skin, hide.

P. {چرم ساز *charm-sáz.*
P. {or چرم گر *charm-gar.*}
A currier, tanner.

P. چرمینه *charmína.* Leathern, leather.

P. چرنده *charenda.* Grazing; a ruminant animal.

P. چریدن *charídan.* To graze.

P. چسپانیدن *chaspánídan.*
P. or چسپاندن *chaspándan.*}
To cause to adhere.

P. چسپنده *chaspenda.* Adhesive.

P. چسپیدگی *chaspídagí.* Tenacity.

P. چسپیدن *chaspídan.* To adhere, to stick.

P. چسپیده *chaspída.* Inclined, attached, addicted to.

P. چست *chust.* Active, alert, brisk.

P. چسته *chusta.* Rennet.

P. چستی *chustí.* Activity.

P. چشانیدن *chashánídan.* To cause to taste.

P. چشم *chashm.* An eye; hope. چشم داشتن *chasm dáshtan.* To hope. چشم زدن *chashm zadan.* To injure by the evil eye; to wink. بچشم *ba chashm.* "On my eye," i.e. with pleasure, certainly. سیاه چشم *siyáhi chasm.* The apple of the eye. چشم سفید *chashm i safíd.* A white-blind eye.

P. چشم بد *chashm i bad.* The evil eye. چشم بد دور *chasm i bad dúr.* May the evil eye be averted! = bravo!

P. چشم پوشی *chashm-púshí.* Connivance.

P. چشمخانه *chashm-khána.* The socket of the eye.

P. چشمداشت *chashm-dásht.* Hope.

P. چشمدرد *chashm-dard.* Ophthalmia.

P. چشمه *chashma.* A fountain.

P. A. چشمهٔ حیوان *chashma e ḥaiwán.* The fountain of life or immortality.

P. چشمهٔ هور *chashma i hor.* The sun.

P. چشیدن *chashídan.* To taste

P. چغد *chughd.* An owl.

P. چغل *chughul.*
P. چغل خور *chughul khur.*}
A tale-bearer.

P. چغلی *chughulí.*
P. چغل خوری *chughul khurí.*}
Backbiting, informing.

P. چغندر *chughunder.* Beet-root.

P. چق *chiḳ.* A screen made of split bamboos; a venetian blind.

P. چقماق *chaḳmáḳ.* A flint.

P. چقماقی *chaḳmáḳí.* A fire-lock.

P. چقندر *chuḳundar.* Beet-root.

P. چکان *chakán.* Dropping, distilling. (in comp.)

P. چکاندن *chakándan.* To distil.

P. چکاوک *chakáwak.* A lark.

P. چکس *chakas.* A perch or roost.

P. چکش *chukush.* A hammer.

T. چکمه *chekma.* A boot.

P. چکله *chakla.* A district.

P. چکن *chakin.* Needlework, embroidery.

P. چکن دوز *chakin-dúz.* An embroiderer.

P. چکونگی *chigúnagí.* Manner.

P. چکونهٔ *chigúna'í.* How art thou?

P. چکیدن *chakídan.* To drop, to distil.

P. چل *chil.* Forty.

P. چلپاسا *chalpásá.* A small venomous lizard.

P. چلغوزه *chilghúza.* A pine-cone.

P. چلك *chilk.* A ladle; a cask, a tun.

P. چله *chilla.* A bowstring; fast of forty days.

P. چلیپا *chalípá.* A cross; a crucifix.

P. چم *cham.* An easy or graceful air.

P. { چمچه *chamcha* }
P. { or چمچم *chamcham.* }
A spoon, ladle.

P. چمن *chaman.* A pasture, orchard, flower-garden.

P. چمن زار *chaman-zár.* Garden-ground.

P. چمیدن *chamídan.* To walk gracefully.

P. چنار *chenár.* A plane-tree.

P. چنان *chunán.* Such.

P. چنانچه *chunánchi.* Such as; so that; inasmuch as; according to what.

P. چنانکه *chunánki.* As; as for example; since; so much that, &c.

P. چنبر *chambar.* A circle; a hoop.

P. چند *chand.* How many; some, few. تنی چند *taní-chand.* A few persons. روزی چند *rúzí chand.* A few days.

P. چندان *chandán.* As much; so much.

P. چندانکه *chandánki.* Insomuch as; notwithstanding.

T. چنداول *chandáwul.* The rear of an army, camp-followers.

P. چندن *chandan.* Sandal-wood.

P. چندگاه *chandgáh.* Sometime.

P. چندی *chandí.* A few, some.

P. چندین *chandín.* So much; some.

P. چنگ *chang.* A lute; fingers; claws.

P. چنگال *changál.* } Talons,
P. چنگل *changul.* } claws.
A hook, a fork.

P. چو *chu.* When; then; like; since.

P. چوال *chuwál.* A sack.

P. چوب *chúb.* Wood, timber.

P. چوبان *chúbán.* } A shep-
P. چوپان *chúpán.* } herd.

P. چوبدار *chúb-dár*. A mace-bearer.

P. چوبدستی *chúb-dastí*. A walking-stick.

P. چوبشکاف *chúb-shígáf*. A wedge.

P. چوبك *chúbak*. A drum-stick.

P. چوبك زن *chúbak-zan*. A drummer.

P. چوبین *chúbín*. Wooden.

P. چوخا *chúkhá*. A sort of tunic.

T. چورك *chúrek*. Bread.

P. چوز *chúz*. Pudenda mulieris.

P. چوزه *chúza*. A chicken.

P. چوگان *chaugán*. The club, or bat used in the game of "polo." Name of the game itself.

P. چون *chun*. When; because; like.

P. چون و چرا *chun u cherá*. When and wherefore?

P. چونی *chuní*. How do you do?

P. چه *chi*. What? how?

P. چها *chihá*. What? (pl. of چه.)

P. چهار *chehár*. Four.

P. چهار پایه *chehár-páya*. A quadruped.

P. چهار دانك *chehár-dáng*. The four quarters of the world.

P. چهارده *chehárdeh*. Fourteen.

P. چهاردهم *chehardahum*. Fourteenth.

P. چهار سو *chehár-sú*. A square or market-place.

P. چهار سواره *chehár-suwára*. A place where four roads meet.

P. چهار شنبه *chehár-shemba*. Wednesday.

P. چهار گانه *chehár-gána*. Fourfold.

P. چهارم *chehárum*. Fourth.

P. چهار یار *chehár yár*. The four friends (i.e. *Abubek*, *'Omar*, *'Osmán*, and *'Alí*).

P. چهار یك *chehár yek*. One of four; a fourth.

P. چهبچه *chebacha*. A cistern, a vat.

P. چهره *chihra*. Face, countenance.

P. A. چهره، حال *chihra i hál*. State, circumstance.

P. چهره کشای *chihra-kushái*. Displaying the face; coquetting.

P. چه قدر *chi kadar*. How much?

P. چهل *chihal*. Forty.

P. چهل منار *chihal minár*. The forty minarets, i.e. the ruins of Persepolis.

P. چهلم *chihlum*. Fortieth.

P. چیچك *chíchak*. The small-pox.

P. چیدن *chídan*. To gather, pluck, to select.

P. چیده *chída*. Select, picked.

P. چیره *chíra*. Bold, valiant; impudent.

P. چیره دست *chíra-dast*. Expert, active.

P. چره دستی *chíra-dastí.* Expertness; victory.

P. چیز *chíz.* A thing.

P. چیزی *chízí.* Something; a little, few.

P. چیست *chíst,* What is it?

P. چیستان *chístán.* A riddle, an enigma; quality, essence.

P. چین *chín.* A fold, wrinkle.

P. چینه *chína.* Grain used as a bait or food for birds; grain in general.

P. چینه دان *chína-dán.* The crop of a bird.

P. چینی *chíní.* Chinese; porcelain.

ح

ح *ḥá.* H. The sixth letter of the Arabic Alphabet: it does not occur in pure Persian words.

A. حاتم طائی *Ḥátim Táí.* A name of an Arab chief celebrated for his generosity.

A. حاجب *ḥájib.* A chamberlain; a veil; the eyebrow.

A. حاجت *ḥájat.* Want, necessity. (pl. حاجات.)

A. حاجت مند *ḥájat-mand.* Necessitous, indigent.

A. حاجز *ḥájiz.* Hindering, preventing.

A. حاج *ḥájj.* } A pilgrim
A. P. حاجی *ḥájjí.* } to Mecca.

A. حاجی لك لك *ḥáji lak-lak.* A stork.

A. حاد *ḥádd.* Sharp.

A. حادث *ḥádis.* New, recent; casual.

A. حادثه *ḥádisa.* An event, accident, novelty.

A. حاذق *ḥáziḳ.* Skilful, expert.

A. حارث *ḥáris.* A husbandman.

A. حارس *ḥáris.* A sentinel, guard.

A. حارص *ḥáriṣ.* Greedy.

A. حازم *ḥázim.* Wise, provident.

A. حاسد *ḥasid.* Envious.

A. حاسه *ḥássa.* One of the five senses.

A. حاشا *ḥáshá.* God forbid.

A. حاشیه *ḥáshiyeh.* Margin, border, brink, edge; foot-notes.

A. حاصل *ḥáṣil.* Produce, advantage, duty.

A. P. حاصل کردن *ḥáṣil kerdan.* To acquire.

A. حاصلات *ḥáṣilát.* Products.

A. حاضر *ḥáẓir.* Present, ready.

A. حاضری *ḥáẓirí.* Attendance; (in India) breakfast.

A. حافظ *ḥáfiẓ.* A guardian; one who has learnt the Korán by heart. The celebrated Persian lyric poet.

A. حافظه *ḥáfiẓah.* A retentive memory (the word قوت *ḳúwat* being understood).

A. حاکم *ḥákim.* A magistrate, ruler, governor.

A. حال *ḥál.* Condition; the present time, or tense.

A. حالا *ḥálá.* Now, at present.

A. حالة *ḥálat.* pl. حالات *ḥálát.* Quality, condition, state.

A. حالى *ḥálí.* Modern; at present.

A. حاليا *ḥáliyan.* Now, at present.

A. حامل *ḥámil.* A carrier, bearer.

A. حاملة *ḥámila.* Pregnant.

A. حامى *ḥámí.* A defender, protector.

A. حاوى *ḥáwí.* Comprehending.

A. حائط *ḥáit.* A wall.

A. حايل *ḥáyil.* Intervening; a screen.

A. حب *ḥabb.* } A grain,
A. حبه *ḥabbah.* } berry, pill.

A. حب *ḥubb.* Love.

A. حباب *ḥubáb.* A bubble of water.

A. حبات *ḥabbát.* Corn, grain, pulse.

A. حبال *ḥibál.* Ropes.

A. حبّال *habbál.* A rope-maker.

A. حبذا *ḥabbazá.* Bravo! Excellent!

A. حبر *ḥibr.* A learned (especially Jewish) doctor.

A. حبس *ḥabs.* Retention, confinement.

A حبشى *Ḥabashí.* An Abyssinian, a negro.

A. حبل *ḥabl.* A rope.

A. حبل الوريد *ḥabl ul warid.* The jugular vein.

A. حبلى *ḥablá.* A pregnant woman.

A. حبوب *ḥubúb.* Grains, berries.

A. حبيب *ḥabíb.* A friend, a beloved one.

A. حتى *ḥattá.* Until; so that.

A. حتى الوسع *ḥatta 'l was'.* To the utmost extent.

A. حتم *ḥatm.* Necessary. Determination.

A. حج *ḥajj.* The pilgrimage to Mecca.

A. حجاب *ḥijáb.* Modesty, shame; a veil, curtain.

A. P. حجاب بر داشتن *ḥijáb bar dáshtan.* To unmask.

A. حجاج *ḥujjáj.* Pilgrims to Mecca.

A. حجارة *ḥijárat.* Stones.

A. حجار *ḥajjár.* A lapidary.

A. حجاز *Ḥijáz.* Mecca and its territory.

A. حجام *ḥajjám.* A cupper, barber.

A. حجامت *ḥajámat.* Cupping, shaving.

A. حجة *ḥujjat.* Proof, argument.

A. حجر *ḥajar.* A stone (pl. حجار *ḥijár*).

A. حجره *ḥujrah.* A chamber, closet; magazine.

A. حجله *ḥajalah.* A bridal chamber.

A. حجم *ḥajm.* Thickness, size.

A. حد *ḥadd.* A limit; boundary.

A. حداثة *ḥadásat.* Novelty; tender age.

A. حداد *ḥaddád.* A blacksmith; a farrier.

A. حداقت *ḥadákat.* Ingenuity, skill.

A. حدایق *ḥadáik.* Gardens, orchards.

A. حدت *ḥiddat.* Sharpness, vehemence.

A. حدث *ḥadas.* Novelty.

A. حدس *ḥads.* Thinking, conjecturing.

A. حدقة *ḥadakah.* The pupil of the eye.

A. حدوث *ḥudús.* Novelty, invention.

A. حدود *ḥudúd.* Boundaries, limits.

A. حدیث *ḥadís.* A traditionary saying of the Prophet.

A. حدید *ḥadíd.* Iron.

A. حدیقة *ḥadíkah.* A garden.

A. حذاقت *ḥizákat.* Ingenuity.

A. حذر *ḥazar.* Caution, prudence.

A. حذف *ḥazf.* Apocopation.

A. حر *ḥarr.* Heat, ardour.

A. حر *ḥurr.* Free-born.

A. حراث *ḥurrás.* Agriculturists.

A. حراثت *ḥirásat.* Agriculture.

A. حرارت *ḥarárat.* Heat.

A. حراست *ḥirásat.* Watching, guarding.

A. حرام *ḥarám.* Unlawful, illegitimate.

A. P. حرام زاده *ḥarám-záda.* Base-born; a rascal.

A. P. حرام خور *ḥarám-khur.* Iniquitous; ill-living.

A. P. حرام مغز *ḥarám-maghz.* The spinal marrow.

A. حرامی *ḥarámiy.* A robber.

A. حرب *ḥarb.* War, battle.

A. حرباء *ḥirbá'.* A chameleon.

A. حربه *ḥarbah.* A spear.

A. حرث *ḥars.* Agriculture.

A. حرج *ḥirj.* A sin.

A. حرز *ḥirz.* An amulet.

A. حرص *ḥirṣ.* Avidity.

A. حرف *ḥarf.* A letter; particle.

A. P. حرف زدن *ḥarf zadan.* To speak, to talk. با من که حرف ندارد *bá man ki ḥarf na dárad.* It has nothing to do with me. حرفی در مقابل ندارد *ḥarfí dar mukábil na dárad.* There is nothing against it. حرف مفت زدن *ḥarf i muft zadan.* To talk nonsense. شما حرف فارسی می زنید *shumá ḥarf i fársí mí zaníd.* Do you talk Persian?

A. حرفا عن حرف *ḥarfan 'an-ḥarf.* Letter by letter.

A. حرف گیر *ḥarf-gír.* A caviller, critic.

A. حرفة *ḥurfat.* Occupation, trade, skill.

A. حرق *ḥarḳ.* Burning.

A. حرقت *ḥurḳat.* Heat, burning.

A. حرکت *ḥarakat.* Motion; a vowel-point; a bad action. (pl. حرکات.)

A. حرکات و سکنات *ḥarakát wa sakanát.* Proceedings; vowels and consonants.

A. حرم *ḥaram.* Sacred; a wife; women's apartments. The sacred enclosure at Mecca or Jerusalem.

A. حرمان *ḥirmán.* Exclusion, disappointment.

A. حرمة *ḥurmat.* Reputation, character, honour.

A. P. حرم سرا *ḥaram-sará.* A seraglio.

A. حروب *ḥurúb.* Wars, battles.

A. حرور *ḥurúr.* Heat.

A. حروف *ḥurúf.* Letters. (pl. of حرف.)

A. حرة *ḥurrah.* A free woman.

A. حریت *ḥurríyet.* Freedom, liberty.

A. حریر *ḥarír.* Silk.

A. حریص *ḥariṣ.* Covetous; greedy.

A. حریف *ḥaríf.* A rival; messmate, companion.

A. حریق *ḥaríḳ.* Burnt, fired.

A. حریم *ḥarím.* A sanctuary, women's apartments.

A. حزب *ḥizb.* A troop, crew, gang.

A. حزم *ḥazm.* Vigilance.

A. حزن *ḥuzn.* Grief, affliction.

A. حزین *ḥazín.* Grieved.

A. حس *ḥiss.* Sense, feelings.

A. حساب *ḥisáb.* Account, reckoning.

A. حسام *ḥuṣám.* A sword.

A. حسب *ḥasb.* According to; a sufficiency.

A. حسد *ḥasad.* Envy, malevolence.

A. حسرت *ḥasrat.* Regret.

A. حس مشترك *ḥiss i mushtarek.* Common sense.

A. حسن *ḥusn.* Beauty; goodness.

A. حسن خلق *ḥusn i khulḳ.* Good nature, good manners.

A. حسن ظن *ḥusn i ẓann.* Good opinion.

A. حسن *Ḥasan.* Son of the Caliph 'Alí and brother of Ḥusein.

A. حسنات *ḥasanát.* Good works. (sing. حسنة.)

A. حسود *ḥasúd.* Envious, malignant.

A. حسی *ḥissí.* Belonging to the senses.

A. حسین *ḥasín.* Good, beautiful.

A. حسین *Ḥusein.* See حسن.

A. حشر *ḥashar.* Gathering. The resurrection.

A. حشرات *ḥasharát.* Reptiles, creeping things.

A. حشم *ḥashm.* Train, retinue, suite.

A. حشمت *ḥashmat.* Pomp, equipage.

A. حشو *ḥashw.* The stuffing of a pillow, &c.

A. حشيش *ḥashísh.* Dry herbage, hay; an intoxicating preparation of *cannabis indica.*

A. حصى *ḥeṣá.* Gravel, pebbles.

A. حصاة *ḥeṣat.* Stone in the bladder.

A. حصاد *ḥiṣád,* or *ḥaṣád.* Reaping; harvest.

A. حصاد *ḥaṣṣád.* A reaper.

A. حصار *ḥiṣár.* A fence; fortress.

A. حصباء *ḥaṣbá'.* Gravel, pebbles.

A. حصبة *ḥaṣbat.* The measles.

A. حصر *ḥaṣr.* Restriction; blockading.

A. حصص *ḥiṣṣaṣ.* Shares. (pl. of حصه.)

A. حصن *ḥiṣn.* A fort. (pl. حصون.)

A. حصول *ḥuṣúl.* Produce, profit.

A. حصه *ḥiṣṣah.* A share, lot, part.

A. حصير *ḥaṣír.* A mat.

A. حصين *ḥaṣín.* Strong, well fortified.

A. حضار *ḥuẓẓár.* Spectators; attendants.

A. حضرة *ḥaẓrat.* Presence; majesty. (pl. حضرات.)

A. حضور *ḥuẓúr.* Presence.

A. حضيض *ḥaẓíẓ.* Bottom, lower extremity. Nadir (opposite of Zenith).

A. حطام *ḥuṭám.* Rubbish, trash. حطام الدنيا *ḥuṭám ud dunyá.* Worldly considerations; covetousness.

A. حطب *ḥaṭab.* Firewood.

A. حظ *ḥaẓẓ.* Pleasure, delight. حظ كردن *ḥaẓẓ kerdan.* To enjoy.

A. حفاظت *ḥifáẓat.* Custody, care.

A. حفر *ḥafr.* Digging, excavation; engraving.

A. حفظ *ḥifẓ.* Memory; protection.

A. حفيظ *ḥafíẓ.* A guardian.

A. حق *ḥaḳḳ.* Just, right, true. An attribute of God. (pl. حقوق *ḥuḳúḳ.* Rights, dues.) حق داشتن *ḥaḳḳ dáshtan.* To have a right. در حق *dar ḥaḳḳ.* Respecting, concerning.

A. حقا *ḥaḳḳan.* In truth.

A. حقارت *ḥaḳárat.* Contempt, meanness.

A. حقانى *ḥaḳḳání.* True, sincere.

A. حقانيت *ḥaḳḳáníyet.* Truth, sincerity.

A. حقايق *ḥaḳáyiḳ.* Narrations; truths.

A. P. حق پرست *ḥaḳḳ-parast.* Addicted to the truth.

A. P. حق پرستى *ḥaḳḳ-parastí.* Addiction to truth.

A. P. حق بين *ḥaḳḳ-bín.* Observant of justice.

A. حق تعالى *ḥaḳḳ-ta'álá.* God Most High.

A. P. حق جو *ḥaḳḳ-jú.* Seeking truth.

A. P. حق دار *ḥaḳḳ-dár*. Rightful owner.

A. P. حق شناش *ḥaḳḳ-shinás*. Knowing one's duty; grateful.

A. P. حق كذار *ḥaḳḳ-guzár*. Administering justice; upright.

A. P. حق كزين *ḥaḳḳ guzín*. Approving justice.

A. P. حق نا حق *ḥaḳḳ ná ḥaḳḳ*. Right or wrong.

A. P. حق نا شناس *ḥaḳḳ ná shinás*. Ungrateful.

A. حقنه *ḥuḳna*. A clyster, an enema.

A. حقوق *ḥuḳúḳ*. Rights. See حق.

A. حقه *ḥuḳḳa*. A casket; a pipe for smoking.

A. P. حقه باز *ḥuḳḳa-báz*. A juggler, thimble-rigger.

A. P. حقه بازى *ḥuḳḳa bází*. Thimble-rig.

A. P. حقه بردار *ḥuḳḳa bardár*. A pipe-bearer.

A. حقية *ḥaḳḳíyet*. Reality, right; real property.

A. حقير *ḥaḳír*. Mean, contemptible.

A. حقيقت *ḥaḳíḳat*. Explanation, account, truth, fact.

A. حقيقى *ḥaḳíḳí*. Intrinsic, real; own.

A. حك *ḥakk*. Scratching.

A. حكاك *ḥakkák*. A cutter and polisher of precious stones.

A. حكام *ḥukkám*. Rulers.

A. حكايت *ḥikáyat*. A tale.

A. حكم *ḥakam*. An arbitrator.

A. حكم *ḥukm*. Command, order, sentence; law. بحكم انكه *ba ḥukm i ánki*. Inasmuch as.

A. P. حكم انداز *ḥukm-andáz*. Obedient to orders; hitting the mark (an archer).

A. حكماء *ḥukamá*. Philosophers, doctors, sages. (pl. of حكيم.)

A. حكمت *ḥikmat*. Wisdom; metaphysics; science; mystery; a device.

A. حكمة الهى *ḥikmat i Iláhí*. Divine mystery.

A. P. حكم رانى *ḥukm-ráni*. Rule, dominion.

A. حكومت *ḥukúmat*. Government.

A. حكة *ḥikkat*. The itch.

A. حكيم *ḥakím*. A doctor (of any faculty, but especially a physician).

A. حل *ḥall*. Solution, loosing.

A. حلاق *ḥallák*. A barber.

A. حلال *ḥalál*. Legal, legitimate, lawful.

A. حلاوت *ḥaláwat*. Sweetness.

A. حلب *ḥalab*. Aleppo.

A. حلبه *ḥulba*. Fennigreek.

A. حلتيت *ḥiltít*. Asafœtida.

A. حلف *ḥalf*. An oath.

A. حلف *ḥilf*. An alliance.

A. حلق *ḥalḳ*. The throat.

A. حلقه *ḥalḳah*. A ring, circle; knocker of a door.

A. P. حلقه بكوش *ḥulḳah ba-gúsh*. Wearing ear-rings; (a slave).

A. حلقوم *ḥulḳúm.* The gullet, the windpipe.

A. حلقى *ḥalḳíy.* Guttural.

A. حلل *ḥulal.* Striped Arabian garments.

A. حلم *ḥilm.* Mildness, clemency. *ḥulm.* Dreaming, nocturnal pollution.

A. حلو *ḥulúw.* Sweet.

A. حلواء *ḥalwá'.* A sweetmeat.

A. حلوائى *ḥalwáï.* A confectioner.

A. حل و عقد *ḥall u 'aḳd,*
A. or حل و ربط *ḥall u rabṭ.*
Loosing and binding; absolute power.

A. حلول *ḥulúl.* Alighting, resting on a place.

A. حلة *ḥullat.* Garment, dress.

A. حلى *ḥulá.* Jewels, female ornaments.

A. حليت *ḥillíyet.* Lawfulness.

A. حليم *ḥalím.* Mild, affable.

A. حليه *ḥilyat.* The external form.

A. حمى *ḥumá.* A fever.

A. حمار *ḥimár.* An ass.

A. حماض *ḥumáẓ.* Sorrel.

A. حماقت *ḥimáḳat.* Folly, stupidity.

A. حمال *ḥammál.* A porter, carrier.

A. حمام *ḥammám.* A bath.

A. حمام *ḥamám.* A pigeon.

A. حمامى *ḥammámí,*
A. T. or حمامچى *ḥammámchí.*
A bath-keeper.

A. حمايت *ḥimáyet.* Protection, aid.

A. حمائد *ḥamáïd.* Laudable actions.

A. حمايل *ḥimáyil.* A sword-belt; a small Korân suspended round the neck as an amulet. The "grand cordon" of an order of Knighthood, &c.

A. حمد *ḥamd.* Praise, thanksgiving.

A. الحمد لله *el ḥamdu lilláh.* Praise be to God.

A. حمر *ḥumr.* Red. (pl. of احمر.)

A. حمرت *ḥumrat.* Redness; the erysipelas.

A. حمض *ḥamẓ.* Sour.

A. حمق *ḥumḳ.* Stupidity.

A. حمقاء *ḥumaḳá'.* Blockheads.

A. حمل *ḥamal.* The ram (sign of the Zodiac).

A. حمل *ḥaml.* A burthen; pregnancy. حمل كردن *ḥaml kerdan.* To impute, describe.

A. حمله *ḥamlah.* An attack, an assault.

A. حموضة *ḥumúẓat.* Acidity.

A. حمول *ḥamúl.* Patient, enduring.

A. حمى *ḥimá.* Forbidden ground; game-preserves.

A. حميت *ḥamíyet.* Ardour; a nice sense of honour.

A. حميد *ḥamíd.* Laudable.

A. حمير *ḥamír.* Asses. (pl. of حمار.)

A. حميم *ḥamím.* Hot water.

A. حناء *ḥinná'.* A plant (*Lawsonia inermis*) used to tinge the skin red.

A. حنجره *ḥanjarah.* The windpipe.

A. حنطه *ḥinṭah.* Wheat.

A. حنظل *ḥanẓal.* A colocynth gourd.

A. حنك *ḥanak.* The palate.

A. حوا *ḥawwá.* Eve, the mother of mankind.

A. حواجب *ḥawájib.* Brows. (pl. of حاجب.)

A. حوادث *ḥawádis̱.* Accidents, events. (pl. of حادثه.)

A. حوادث زده *ḥawádis̱-zadah.* Unfortunate.

A. حوارى *ḥawáríy.* One of the disciples or apostles of our Lord.

A. حواس *ḥawáss.* Sense, perception.

A. حواس خمسه *ḥawáṣṣ i khamsa.* The five senses.

A. حواشى *ḥawáshí.* Margins; attendants.

A. حواصل *ḥawáṣil.* A pelican; the crops of birds.

A. حوالات *ḥawálát.* Things given in charge, trusts.

A. P. حوالدار *ḥawáldár.* A military officer; "havildar," quartermaster sergeant.

A. حواله *ḥawálah.* Custody, consignment, care.

A. P. حواله كردن *ḥawála kerdan.* To entrust, consign.

A. حوالى *ḥawálí.* Environs, parts adjacent.

A. حوالىء شهر *ḥawáli e shehr.* The suburbs of a city.

A. حوائج *ḥawáij.* Necessaries; affairs.

A. حوت *ḥút.* A large fish; the sign Pisces.

A. حور *ḥúr.* Lustrous-eyed maidens; virgins of paradise; "houris." (pl. of حوراء.)

A. حوز *ḥauz.* Space, country.

A. حوصلة *ḥausalah.* The crop of a bird, &c.; ambition.

A. حوشية *ḥúshíyet.* Misanthropy, savageness.

A. حوض *ḥauẓ.* A reservoir, cistern.

A. حول *ḥaul.* Changing; power.

A. حويلى *ḥawílí.* A house; dwelling.

A. حى *ḥaiy.* Alive.

A. حياء *ḥayá'.* Modesty, shame.

A. حيوات or A. حيات *ḥaiyát.* Life.

A. حيثيت *ḥais̱íyet.* Capacity, ability.

A. حيدر *ḥaidar.* A lion; حيدر الله *Haider u 'llah.* A name of 'Alí.

A. حيران *ḥairán.* Amazed, bewildered.

A. حيرانى *ḥairání,* or A. حيرت *ḥairat.* Astonishment, perplexity.

A. حيز *ḥíz.* A side, part, place.

A. حيض *ḥaiẓ.* Menses.

A. حيطه *ḥiṭah.* An enclosure.

بحيطهء تصرف اوردن *ba ḥíta i taṣarruf áwardan.* To appropriate.

A. حيف *ḥaif.* Tyranny; alas!

حیف و میل کردن *ḥaif u mail kardan.* To appropriate unjustly.

A. حیله *ḥílat.* (pl. حیل *ḥiyal.*) Artifice, stratagem, ruse.

A. حیله ساز *ḥílah-sáz,* } A
A. or حیله کار *ḥílah-kár.* } cheat, a trickster, a cunning fellow.

A. حین *ḥín.* Time. حین رفتن *ḥín i raftan.* At the moment of departure.

A. حین حیات *ḥín i ḥaiyát.* Life-time.

A. حیوان *ḥaiwán.* (pl. حیوانات.) An animal, living creature.

A. حیوانی *ḥaiwání.* Animal, brutal.

خ

خ *Khá.* Kh. The seventh letter of the Arabic and Persian alphabet.

A. خاتم *khátam.* A seal, a signet.

A. خاتمه *khátimah.* A conclusion, finis.

P. خاتون *khátún.* A lady.

P. خاج *kháj.* The Christian cross.

A. خادع *khádiʻ.* A deceiver.

A. خادم *khádim.* A servant.

P. خاده *kháda.* An oar.

P. خار *khár.* A thorn.

P. خارا or خاره } *khára.* A hard stone.

P. خاربست *khár-bast.* A hedge of thorns.

P. خارپشت *khár-pusht.* A porcupine, hedgehog.

P. خاربن *khár-bun.* Roots of brambles.

A. خارج *khárij.* External.

A. خارجه *khárijah.* A catchword.

A. خارجی *khárijíy.* External; a heretic.

P. خار چینه *khár-chína.* Tweezers.

P. خار خار *khár-khár.* Anguish.

P. خار دار *khár-dár.* Thorny.

P. خار راه *khár i ráh.* Impediments in the road.

P. خارش *khárish.* The itch, the scab, the mange; a scratch.

P. خارشت *khárisht.* The itch.

A. خارق *khárik.* Splitting, tearing.

P. A. خارق عادت *khárik i ʻádat.* A miracle; contrary to experience.

P. خارکش *khár-kush.* Slippers worn over the boots.

P. خارکش *khár-kash.* A poor man who is obliged for the want of an ass to carry thorn-faggots.

P. خارکن *khár-kan.* A rooter up of thorns.

P. خار و خس *khár u khas.* Rubbish.

P. خاریدن *kharídan.* To scratch, to itch.

A. خازن *kházin.* Treasurer, cashkeeper.

P. خازنه *kházana.* A wife's sister.

P. خاستگی *khástagí.* An insurrection.

P. خاستن *khástan.* To rise up; to happen.

A. خاسر *khásir.* Disappointed.

P. خاشاك *khášhák.* Rubbish.

A. خاشع *kháshi'.* Humble, suppliant.

A. خاشی *kháshí.* Timid, fearful.

A. خاص *kháṣṣ.* Particular, special.

A. P. خاصان *kháṣṣan.* Persons of distinction.

A. خاصره *kháṣirah.* The abdomen.

A. P. خاصگی *kháṣṣagí.* Peculiarity, speciality.

A. خاص و عام *kháṣṣ u 'ámm.* Noble and plebeian, every body.

A. خاصیت *khaṣṣíyet.* Property, quality.

A. خاضع *khaẓi'.* Humble, submissive.

A. خاطر *kháṭir.* The mind, heart.

A. خاطر جمع *kháṭir-jam'.* Collected, composed in mind.

A. خاطر جمعی *kháṭir-jam'i.* Mental composure, ease of mind.

A. P. خاطر خواه *kháṭir-kh'áh.* According to wish.

A. P. خاطر داری *kháṭir-dárí.* Encouragement, comfort.

A. P. خاطر نشین *kháṭir-nishín.* Impressed on the mind; learnt by heart.

A. خاطیء *kháṭí'.* An offender; deviating.

A. خافق *kháfiḳ.* Palpitating. The horizon.

A. خافقین *kháfiḳain.* The two horizons; east and west.

P. خاقان *kháḳán.* An emperor, king.

P. خاقانی *kháḳání.* Imperial, royal.

P. خاك *khák.* Earth, dust.

P. خاك بیز *khák-bíz.* A large sieve for sifting gravel, &c.

P. خاك توده *khák-túda.* A butt for archers.

P. خاك دان *khák-dán.* A place for rubbish, a dust-bin; this world.

P. خاك زاد *khák-zád.* Earth-born.

P. خاکسار *khák-sár.* Humble.

P. خاکساری *kháksárí.* Humility.

P. خاکستر *khákister.* Ashes.

P. خاك كردن *khák kerdan.* To bury.

P. خاکروب *khák-rúb.* A sweeper.

P. خاکشی *khákshí.* A small seed used in preparing eye-salve.

P. A. خاك صفت *khák-ṣifat.* Earthlike, humble.

P. خاك كش *khák-kesh.* A harrow.

P. خاك مرده *khák i murda.* The ashes of a dead person.

P. خاکنشین *khák-níshín.* Sitting on the ground; humble.

P. خاکه *kháka.* A sketch.

P. خاکی *khákí.* Earthly.

P. خاك نهاد *khak-nihád.* Earth-born, humble.

P. خاکینه *khágína.* A fried egg; an omelette.

A. P. خال *khál.* A mole; a mother's brother.

A. خالد *khálid.* Eternal.

P. خالری *khálari.* Salt-works.

A. خالص *khális̤.* Pure, unmixed.

A. خالصه *khális̤ah.* Crown property, the exchequer.

A. خالف *khálif.* A successor.

A. خالق *khálik̤.* The Creator.

P. خالو *khálú.* Maternal uncle.

A. خاله *khála.* Maternal aunt.

A. خالی *khálí.* Empty, vacant.

P. خام *khám.* Raw, unripe, inexperienced.

P. A. خام طمع *khám-tamʿ.* Hoping vainly.

P. خام کار *khám-kár.* Unskilful, inexperienced.

P. خاموش *khámúsh.* Silent, اتش خاموش شده است *átish khámúsh shuda ast.* The fire has gone out.

P. خاموشیدن *khámúshídan.* To be silent.

P. خامه *kháma.* A pen.

P. خامه زن *kháma-zan.* A piece of wood for nibbing pens upon.

P. خامی *khámí.* Rawness, immaturity.

P. خان *khán.* Lord, prince, (a title).

P. خان خانان *khán i khánán.* Lord of lords.

P. خاندان *khándán.* Family, domestics.

P. خانسامان *khánsámán.* Steward of the household.

P. خانقاه *khánk̤áh.* A monastery.

P. خانگی *khánagí.* Domestic, belonging to the house.

P. خانمان *khán-mán,*
P. or خان و مان *khán u mán.*
Household furniture: real and personal property.

P. خانواده *khánaváda.* A family, house.

P. خانه *khána.* A house, dwelling.

P. اشپز خانه *ásh-paz khána.* A kitchen.

P. خانه بدوش *khána ba-dúsh.* A snail; a tramp. Having one's house on one's shoulders.

P. خانه پردازی *khána-pardází.* Domestic economy.

P. خانه دار *khána-dár.* A householder.

P. خانه داری *khána-dárí.* Housekeeping.

P. خانه زاد *khána-zád.* A slave born in the house.

P. خانه سوز *khána súz.* Disgracing one's family.

P. خانهٔ کمان *khána i kamán.* The curved parts of a bow.

P. خانی *khání.* The title of *Khán.*

P. خاو *kháv.* The pile of velvet, &c.

P. خاور *kháwar.* The east, also the west; the sun.

P. خاوند *khávand.* Lord, master, husband.

A. خاوی البطن *kháwí 'l baṭan.* Empty-bellied.

A. خایب *kháïb.* Unsuccessful.

P. خایسک *kháyisk.* A smith's hammer; malleable.

A. خایض *kháïz.* Exploring, diving into.

A. خایف *kháïf.* Timid, pusillanimous.

A. خاین *kháïn.* A deceiver, traitor.

P. خایه *kháya.* A testicle; an egg.

P. خائیدن *khá'ídan.* To chew, gnaw.

A. خباثت *khabáṡat.* Wickedness, depravity.

A. خبث *khubṡ.* The dross of metal.

A. خبر *khabar.* (pl. اخبار). News, intelligence.

A. خبرت *khubrat.* Experience, proof, trial.

A. خباز *khabbáz.* A baker.

A. خبائث *khabáïṡ.* Vices, depravities.

A. P. خبر دار *khabar-dár.* Cautious, vigilant. Take care!

A. P. خبر داری *khabar dárí.* Cautiousness.

A. P. خبر گیر *khabar-gír.* A spy, an informer; a patron.

A. P. خبر گیری *khabar-gírí.* Spying; aiding.

A. خبز *khubz.* Bread.

A. خبط *khabṭ.* Madness, infatuation.

P. خبه *khaba.* Strangulation.

A. خبیث *khabíṡ.* Wicked, impure.

A. خبیر *khabír.* Informed, skilful.

P. خیره *khabíra.* Sum total; winding, twisting.

P. خیره شدن *khabíra shudan.* To arm oneself, to muster.

A. ختام *khatám.* Finis.

A. ختم *khatm.* Conclusion, end. قرآن را ختم کردن *Kurăn-rá khatam kerdan.* To read the Ḳorăn through (after a funeral). ختم را بر چیدن *khatam-rá bar chídan.* To complete the obsequies of a dead person.

A. P. ختن *khutan.* Chinese Tartary, Cathay.

A. ختنه *khatna.* Circumcision.

A. خجالت *khijálat.* Blushing, bashfulness, shame.

P. خجسته *khujista.* Happy, fortunate, blest.

P. خجسته پی *khujista-pai.* Happy arrival.

P. خجسته فرجام *khujista-farjám.* Ending well.

A. خجل *khajil.* Blushing, modest, bashful.

A. خجلت *khajlat.* See خجالت.

A. خد *khadd.* A cheek.

P. خدا *khudá.* God. از خدا می خواهم *az khudá mí kh'áham.* I hope to God = I wish for nothing better.

P. خدا افرین *khudá-áfrín.* God the Creator.

P. خدا اگاه *khudá-ágáh.* Knowing God.

P. خدا پرستی *khudá-parastí.* Divine worship.

P. خدا ترس *khudá-tars.* God-fearing.

P. A. خدا حافظ *khudá ḥáfiz.* God preserve you; adieu.

P. خدارا *khudá-rá.* For God's sake.

P. خدا شناس *khudá-shinás.* Knowing God, righteous.

A. خداع *khaddá'.* A deceiver, impostor.

A. خدام *khuddám.* Servants, domestics.

P. A. خدا مشرب *khudá mashrab.* Religious, pious.

P. خداوند *khudáwand.* Lord, master, husband.

P. خداوندگار *khudáwandigár.* God.

P. A. خداوند نعمت *khudáwand i ni'mat.* A generous master, patron.

P. خداوندے *khudáwandí.* Lordship, sovereignty.

P. خدائی *khudá'í.* Divinity.

P. خدایا *khudáyá.* O God.

P. خدایرا *khudáërá.* For God's sake.

P. A. خدای تعالی *khudáï-ta'álá.* God most high.

A. خدائع *khadáï'.* Frauds, impostures.

P. خدائگان *khudáïgán.* Lords, masters.

A. خدر *khadar.* Torpor.

A. خدش *khadish.* Alarm.

A. خدعة *khud'at,* or خدع *khad'.* } Fraud, deceit.

A. خدم *khadam.* Servant, retinue.

A. خدمات *khidamát.* Services.

A. خدمت *khidmat.* Service; employment. In presence of.

A. P. خدمتگار *khidmat-gár.*
A. P. خدمتگذار *khidmat-guzár.* } A servant.

P. خدنگ *khadang.* An arrow made of white poplar.

A. خديعت *khadí'at.* Fraud, imposture.

P. خديو *khidív.* A king, mighty monarch.

P. A. خديوى *khidéwí.* The Viceroy of Egypt.

A. خذل *khazl.* Failing any one in an emergency.

A. خذلان *khizlán.* Weakness, feebleness.

A. خذله *khuzalah.* One who leaves another in the lurch.

P. خر *khar.* An ass.

A. خرء *khar'.* The dung (of birds, &c.).

A. خراب *kharáb.* Desolate, depraved, ruined, lost.

P. خرابات *kharábát.* A tavern, a brothel.

P. خراباتی *kharábátí.* A haunter of taverns, a debauchee.

A. خرابه *kharába.* A desolate place, a ruin.

A. P. خرابی *kharábí.* Ruin, desolation.

A. خراج *kharáj.* Tribute, tax, revenue.

A. P. خراج گذار *kharáj-guzár.* A tributary.

P. خراخر زدن *kharákhar zadan.* To snore.

A. خراد *kharád.* A turning lathe. See خراط.

A. خرادی *kharádí.* A turner.

P. خراسان *khurásán.* Khurássán, a province of Persia.

P. خراس *kharásh.* Scratching, itching.

A. خراشة *khuráshah.* Scales or filings.

P. خراشیدن *kharashídan.* To scratch.

A. خراط *kharráṭ.* A turner.

A. خراطت *kharaṭat.* The art of turning.

A. خراطیم *kharáṭím.* Probosces. (pl. of خرطوم.)

A. خراطین *kharáṭín.* Earthworms.

A. خرافات *khuráfát.* Idle stories. (pl. of خرافه *khuráfeh.*)

P. خرام *kharam.* Graceful in walking (in composition).

P. خرامان *kharámán.* Walking gracefully, strutting.

P. خرامیدن *kharámídan.* To walk gracefully.

P. خر انبار *khar-ambár.* A crowd.

P. خر بان *khar-bán.* An ass-driver or keeper.

P. خر پشته *khar-pushta.* A high-pitched roof.

P. خر پشه *khar-pasha.* A gadfly.

P. خربق *kharbuḳ.* Hellebore.

P. خربوزه *kharbúza,* or P. خربزه *kharbuza.* A melon.

P. خربزه زار *kharbuza-zár.* A cucumber- or melon-ground.

A. P. خرج *kharch.* Expense, expenditure.

P. خر چنك *khar-chang.* A crab.

P. خرچه *kharcha.* The costs of a lawsuit.

P. خرجین *khurjín.* Saddle-bags.

P. خرخر *khar-khar.* Purring.

P. خرخرا *kharkhará.* Snoring.

P. خرخره *kharkhara.* A curry-comb.

P. خرخشه *kharkhisha.* A tumult, a riot.

P. خرد *khurd.* Minute, small, young.

P. خرد *khirad.* Wisdom.

P. خرداد *khur-dád.* The third Persian month.

P. خرد پسند *khirad-pasand.* Commendable.

P. خرد پیشه *khirad-písha.* Practising wisdom.

P. خرد خان *khurd-khán.* Dispersed, dissipated.

P. خر دشتی *khar i dashtí.* The wild ass.

A. خردق *kharduḳ.* Broth, soup.

A. خردل *khardal.* Mustard-seed.

P. A. خرد مشرب *khirad-mashrab.* Practising wisdom.

P. خردمند *khiradmand.* Wise, intelligent.

P. خردمندانه *khiradmandána.* Wisely, prudently.

P. خردمندی *khiradmandí.* Wisdom, prudence.

P. خرد منشی *khirad-manishí.* Prudence.

P. خردوات *khurdawát.* Trifles.

P. خرده *khurda.* A particle, small.

P. خردها *khurdahá.* Fractions, fragments.

P. خرده بینی *khurda-bíní.* Subtilty of genius; cavilling.

P. خردی *khurdí.* Smallness; infancy.

A. P. خرز *kharaz.* Glass beads, &c.

P. خر زهره *khar-zahra.* Colocynth.

P. خرس *khirs.* A bear.

P. خرسک *khirsak.* A boys' game, leap-frog or blind man's buff.

P. خرسند *khursand.* Content, satisfied.

P. خرسندی *khursandí.* Contentment.

P. خرسنگ *kharsang.* A large stone; a rival.

P. خرشید *khursheid.* The sun. نشان شیر خرشید *nishán i shír khursheid.* The Order of the Lion and the Sun.

A. خرط *kharṭ.* The art of turning.

A. خرطوم *kharṭúm.* The trunk of an elephant.

A. خرف *kharif.* A decrepit old man.

P. خرفه *khurfa.* Purslain.

A. P. خرق عادت *khirḳ i 'ádat.* A miracle.

A. خرقه *khirḳa.* A religious habit. A short pelisse worn in the house in winter-time.

P. خرگاه *khargáh.* The royal tent, pavilion.

P. خرک *kharak.* A little ass.

P. خرگوش *khar-gúsh.* A rabbit, a hare. من حافظهٔ خرگوشی دارم *man ḥáfiẓa e khargúshí dáram.* I have a wretchedly bad memory.

P. خرم *khurram.* Cheerful, pleasant.

P. خرما *khurmá.* A date. هم خرما و هم ثواب است *ham khurmá wa ham s̤awáb ast.* It is both a duty and a pleasure; a saying derived from the practice of fasting, i.e. to break one's fast with only a date is both grateful to the palate and a meritorious action.

P. خرمست *khar-mast.* Obstinate, stupid.

P. خر مگس *khar-magas.* The gadfly.

P. خرمن *khirman*. A barn or threshingfloor.

P. خرمهره *khar-muhra*. A small shell or kowrie.

P. خرّمی *khurramí*. Gladness, cheerfulness.

P. خر نفسه *khar-nafsa*. Magnum penem habens.

P. خروار *khar-wár*. An ass's load.

A. خروار *kharvár*, pronounced *halvár*. A measure of about 700 lbs.

A. خروج *khurúj*. Sallying forth; rebelling.

P. خروس *khurús*. A dunghill-cock.

P. خروش *khurúsh*. Clamour, cry.

P. خروشیدن *khurúshídan*. To cry out, to exclaim.

A. خروق *khurúḳ*. Fissures, cracks.

P. خریدار *kharídár*. A buyer, purchaser.

P. خریدن *kharídan*. To buy.

P. خریده *kharída*. Purchased.

A. خریطه *kharíṭah*. A bag, purse, packet.

A. خریف *kharíf*. The autumn.

A. خریفی *kharífí*. Grown in harvest.

A. خز *khaz*. Raw silk.

A. خزاف *khazzáf*. A potter.

P. خزان *khizán*. The autumn.

A. T. خزانچی *khezánchí*. Treasurer, cashkeeper.

A. خزانه *khizána*. Treasury, granary.

A. P. خزانه عامره *khizána i 'ámirah*. The imperial treasury.

A. خزائن *khazáin*. Treasures.

A. خزز *khazaz*. The former inhabitants of the shores of the Caspian (بحرالخزز).

A. خزف *khazf*. An earthen vessel.

P. خزف ریزه *khazf-ríza*. A potsherd.

P. خزفی *khazafí*. A potter.

P. خزیدن *khazídan*. To creep, crawl.

A. خزیز *khazíz*. Brambles, fences to walls.

A. خزینه *khazína*. A treasury.

A. P. خزینه دار *khazínah dár*. A treasurer.

P. خس *khas*. A weed; rubbish, trash; a mean person.

P. خس *khus*. A lettuce.

A. خسار *khasár*, or A. خسارت *khasárat*. Damage, loss.

A. خساست *khasásat*. Vileness; being mean or abject.

P. خسان *khasán*. Mean persons.

P. خساندن *khasándan*. To grind, triturate.

P. خسانده *khasánda*. An infusion.

P. خسپانیدن *khuspánídan*. To cause to sleep.

P. خس پوش *khas-púsh*. Covered with weeds.

P. خسپیدن *khuspídan*. To sleep.

A. خست *khissat.* Meanness.

P. خستگی *khastagí.* Wounding, distress, fatigue.

P. خستن *khastan.* To wound.

P. خستو *khastú.* The stone of fruit.

P. خستوانه *khastuwána.* A woollen garment worn by Dervishes.

P. خسته *khasta.* Wounded, hurt, tired; the stone of fruit.

P. خسته بند *khasta-band.* A bandage.

A. خسر *khasr.* Damages; loss; fraud.

P. خسر *khusur.* A father-in-law.

A. خسران *khusrán.* Damage, injury; perfidy.

P. خسر پوره *khusar-púra.* Wife's brother.

P. خسرو *khusrav.* A king; a royal surname.

P. خسروی *khusraví.* Royal, kingly.

P. خسروانه *khusruwána.* Like a king.

P. خس و خاشاك *khas u kháshák.* Rubbish.

P. خسوردن *khasúrdan.* To reap.

A. خسوف *khusúf.* An eclipse of the moon.

P. خسیدن *khasídan.* To chew.

A. خسیر *khasír.* Damaged, injured.

A. خسیس *khasís.* Mean, base, miserly.

P. خش *khash* or *khush.* A mother-in-law.

P. خشانیدن *khashánídan.* To bite, lacerate.

P. خشاده *khusháda.* Cultivated fields.

A. خشب *khashab.* Wood, timber.

P. خشت *khisht.* A brick or tile.

P. خشت پیروزه *khisht i pírúza.* Turquoise-coloured bricks.

P. خشت پز *khisht-paz.* A brickmaker.

P. خشت زر *khisht i zar.* An ingot of gold.

P. خشخاش *khaskhásh.* A poppy.

A. خشاب *khashsháb.* A seller of wood.

A. خشاف *khushsháf.* A bat.

A. خشع *khash'.* Humility.

P. خشك *khushk.* Dry, withered.

P. خشکار *khushkár.* Coarse bread or flour.

P. خشك رودی *khushk-rúdí.* A dried-up stream.

P. خشك سالی *khushk-sálí.* Drought, famine.

P. خشك مغز *khushk-maghz.* Crazy.

P. خشکه *khushka.* Boiled rice without butter.

P. خشکی *khushkí.* Dryness, dry land.

P. خشکیدن *khushkídan.* To dry.

P. خشم *khashm.* Anger, rage, fury.

P. خشم آلوده *khashm álúda.* Sullied with anger.

P. خشمگین *khashm-gín.* Angry, enraged.

P. خشمناك *khashm-nák.* Passionate, angry.

A. خشن *khushn.* Rough, severe.

P. خشنود *khushnúd.* Contented, happy.

P. خشنودى *khushnúdí.* Contentment, pleasure.

P. خشو *khushú.* A mother-in-law.

P. خشودن *khashúdan.* To prune.

A. خشوع *khushú'.* Humility.

A. خشونت *khushúnat.* Asperity, disdain.

A. خشى *khashíy.* Timid; a dried herb.

P. خشيج *khashíj.* The contrary; opposite, opposed.

A. خصاف *khaṣṣáf.* A shoemaker.

A. خصال *khiṣál.* Manners, qualities. (pl. of خصلة.)

A. خصائص *khaṣáiṣ.* Properties, qualities.

A. خصايل *khaṣáil.* Dispositions, qualities.

A. خصلة *khaṣlat.* Quality, habit, mode.

A. خصم *khaṣam.* An enemy.

A. P. خصمانه *khaṣmána.* Inimically.

A. خصوص *khuṣúṣ.* Particularity, speciality.

P. A. در خصوص *dar khuṣúṣ.* Concerning.

A. خصوصا *khuṣúṣan.* Especially.

A. خصوصيات *khuṣúṣíyát.* Particularities. (pl. of خصوصية.)

A. خصوم *khuṣúm.* Antagonists, rivals.

A. خصومات *khuṣúmát.* Disputes.

A. خصومت *khuṣúmat.* Litigation, enmity.

A. خصى *khaṣíy.* A castrated animal.

A. خصيتان *khuṣyatáni.* The testicles.

A. خصيم *khaṣím.* An antagonist.

A. خصين *khaṣín.* A small axe.

A. خصية *khuṣyat.* A testicle.

A. خضاب *khiẓáb.* Hair-dye.

A. خضب *khaẓb.* Dyeing the hair or tinging the nails.

A. خضر *Khiẓir.* The prophet Khizir or Elias.

A. خضراء *khaẓrá'.* Green, fresh. (fem. of اخضر.)

A. خضرت *khuẓrat.* Greenness.

A. خضل *khaẓl.* A pure pearl.

A. خضوع *khuẓú'.* Submission.

A. خضيب *khaẓíb.* Stained, dyed.

A. خط *khaṭṭ.* A line, a letter, an incipient beard.

A. خطاء *khaṭá'.* A sin, error, mistake.

P. خطای *khaṭáy.* Scythia, Cathay.

A. خطاب *khiṭáb.* A title; conversation; address.

A. P. خطا بخش *khaṭá-bakhsh.* Forgiver of sins.

A. P. خط استوا *khaṭṭ i istiwá* or خط اعتدال اللیل و النهار *khaṭṭ i i'tidál ullail wa nnahár.* The equator.

A. خطاط *khaṭṭáṭ.* Calligraphist.

A. خطام *khiṭám.* A halter, a bridle.

A. خطایا *khaṭáyá.* Sins.

A. خطب *khuṭab.* Orations, sermons.

A. خطب *khaṭb.* Marrying, betrothing.

A. خطبه *khuṭba.* The sermon or bidding-prayer recited every Friday in the mosque. Prayer for the sovereign. An oration.

A. خطة *khiṭṭat.* A country, region.

A. خطر *khaṭar.* Danger, risk; occurring (to the mind).

A. P. خطر ناك *khaṭar-nák.* Perilous, full of danger.

A. خطره *khaṭra.* Danger, fear, risk.

A. P. خط سبز *khaṭṭ i sabz.* An incipient beard; a black line.

A. P. خط عمود *khaṭṭ i 'amúd.* A perpendicular line.

A. P. خط فاصل *khaṭṭ i fáṣil.* Line of demarcation.

A. P. خط کش *khaṭṭ-kesh.* A ruler for drawing lines.

A. خطل *khaṭal.* Levity of speech, obscenity.

A. P. خط متوازی *khaṭṭ i mutawází.* A parallel line.

A. P. خط مستدیر *khaṭṭ i mustadír.* A circular line.

A. P. خط مستقیم *khaṭṭ í musta ḳím.* A right line.

A. P. خط منحنی *khaṭṭ i munḥaní.* A curved line.

A. P. خط محور *khaṭṭ i miḥwar.* Ecliptic line.

A. خطمی *khaṭmíy.* Marshmallows.

A. P. خط نصف نهار *khaṭṭ i niṣf i nahár.* A meridional line.

A. خطوات *khaṭawát.* Paces, steps.

A. خطور *khuṭúr.* Occurring to the mind.

A. خطوط *khuṭúṭ.* Lines, lette

A. خطوة *khaṭwat.* A step, pace.

A. P. خط همایون *khaṭṭ i hamáyún.* The Shah's autograph.

A. خطیب *khaṭíb.* A preacher; a notary.

A. خطیر *khaṭír.* Great, important; dangerous.

A. خطئة *khaṭi-at.* A crime, fault.

A. خظاو *khuẓúw.* Firmness; compactness.

A. خف *khuff.* A boot.

A. خف *khiff.* Light (of weight or conduct).

A. خفاء *khafá'*. Concealment, secret.

P. خفاچه *khafácha*. Arab banditti.

A. خفاش *khuffásh*. The bat.

A. خفاجل *khufájil*. Tongue-tied.

A. خفايا *khafáyá*. Secrets.

A. خفت *khiffat*. Levity of conduct; affront; disgrace.

P. خفت *khuft*. Sleep, a nap.

P. خفتان *khuftán*. A vest worn under armour.

P. خفتن *khuftan*. To sleep.

P. خفچه *khafcha*. An ingot of gold or silver.

A. خفر *khafr*. Protection.

A. خفس *khafs*. Derision, ridicule.

A. خفقان *khafakán*. Palpitation of the heart; waving of a flag.

A. خفقانی *khafakání*. Subject to palpitation.

P. خفگی *khafagí*. Suffocation. (In India) anger.

P. خفه *khafa*. Suffocation; strangling; a sneeze. (In India) anger.

A. خفی *khafíy*. Clandestine, concealed, latent.

A. خفیه *khufya*. A secret. در خفیه *dar khufya*. In secret.

A. خفیات *khafíyát*. Secrets.

A. خفیة *khafíyah* (*khafíyat*). Hidden, latent, (fem. of خفی).

P. خفیدن *khafídan*. To sneeze; to be strangled.

A. خفیف *khafíf*. Light (of weight), undignified.

A. خل *khall*. Vinegar.

A. خلاء *khalá'*. Vacancy.

P. خلاب *khaláb*. Mud, mire.

P. خلاشه *khalásha*. Rubbish.

A. خلاص *khalás*. Free, liberated.

A. خلاصة *khulásat*. Essence; abstract.

A. P. خلاصی *khalásí*. Freedom, liberation.

A. خلاع *khilá'*. Dresses of honour.

A. خلاف *khiláf*. Contradiction; opposition.

A. خلافت *khiláfat*. The office of Caliph; monarchy.

A. خلاق *khallák*. The Creator.

A. خلال *khilál*. A toothpick.

A. خلالت *khilálat*. Sincere friendship.

A. خلا ملا *khalá-malá*. Unfeigned friendship.

A. خلان *khullán*. Intimate friends. (pl. of خل *khill*.)

P. خلانیدن *khalánídan*. To prick, to insert.

A. خلائف *khaláïf*. Successors; caliphs.

A. خلائق *khaláïk*. Men, people, creatures.

A. خلت *khullat*. Friendship.

P. خلجان *khalaján*. Disquietude.

A. P. خلخال *khalkhál*. An anklet; a bangle.

A. خلد *khuld*. Eternity.

A. P. خلد برین *khuld i. barín.* The sublime paradise.

P. خلش *khalish.* Disquietude, anxiety.

A. خلص *khilṣ.* A sincere friend.

A. خلط *khalṭ.* Mixture.

A. خلط *khilṭ.* A humour.

A. خلطة *khulṭat.* An association, partnership.

A. خلع *khalʿ.* Removal from office.

A. خلعت *khilʿat.* A dress of honour.

A. خلف *khalf.* A successor, an heir, a son.

A. خلفاء *khulafá.* Caliphs, emperors.

A. P. خلفاء راشدین *khulafái ráshidín.* The four orthodox (i. e. the first four) caliphs.

A. خلق *khalḳ.* The creation; creatures.

A. P. خلق ازار *khalḳ ázár.* Tormenting or injuring mankind.

A. خلق الله *khalḳ ulláh.* God's creatures.

A. خلق *khulḳ.* Good nature; quality.

A. خلقان *khulḳán.* Tattered garments. (pl. of خلق *khalaḳ.*)

A. خلقة *khilḳat.* The creation.

A. خلقی *khalḳiy.* Natural.

A. خلل *khalal.* Disturbance, confusion, disorder; a leak, flaw, &c.

A. P. خلل رسانیدن *khalal rasánídan.* To damage.

A. خلو *khalw.* Vacuity.

A. خلوت *khalwat.* Retirement. سرکار شمارا در خلوت خواهم دید *sarkár i shumá-rá dar khalwat kh'áham díd.* I will see you privately.

A. P. خلوت خانه *khalwat khána.* A private apartment.

A. P. خلوت نشین *khalwatnishín.*
A. خلوتی *khalwatí.*
A recluse.

A خلود *khulúd.* Eternity.

A. خلوص *khulúṣ.* Purity, sincerity.

P. خلیته *khalíta.* A bag, purse.

P. خلیدگی *khalídagí.* Puncture.

P. خلیدن *khalídan.* To prick, pierce.

A. خلیفه *khalífah.* A caliph.

A. P. خلیفه کتاب *khalífa i kuttáb.* The monitor of a school.

A. خلیق *khalíḳ.* Humane, polite.

A. خلیل *khalíl.* A friend.

A. خلیل الله *khalíl ulláh.* The friend of God, Abraham.

P. خم *kham.* Crooked, bent; a ringlet, coil, noose.

P. خم کمند *kham-kamand.* A noose.

P. خم *khum.* A jar, alembic.

A. خمار *khumár.* The effects felt after drinking; crop-sickness, "hot coppers."

A. خماره *khammára.* A tavern.

A. خماسی *khumásí.* A word of five letters.

P. خمان *khumán.* Bent, curved; a bow.

P. خمان *khumán.* The elder-tree; a bow.

P. خمانیدن *khamánídan.* To bend; to grimace, to mimic.

P. خمخانه *khum-kháná.* A tavern, a wine-vault, inn.

A. خمر *khamr.* Wine; any alcoholic or fermented liquor.

A. خمس *khams.* Five (fem.).

A. خمسه *khamsa.* Five (masc.).

A. خمسین *khamsín.* Fifty.

P. خمش *khamush,* } Si-
A. or خموش *khamúsh.* } lent, see خاموش.

P. خم و چم *kham u cham.* Coquetry.

A. خمور *khumúr.* Wines.

A. خمول *khumúl.* Being or rendering oneself of no repute.

A. P. خمولستان *khumúlistán.* The land of oblivion; the grave.

P. خمی *khamí.* Crookedness, curvatnre.

P. خمیازه *khamyáza.* Gaping, yawning.

P. خمیدن *khamídan.* To be bent, crooked, curved or vaulted.

A. خمیر *khamír.* Dough, leaven.

A. خمیس *khamís.* The fifth; Thursday.

A. خناث *khinás.* Hermaphrodites.

A. خنادیق *khanádík.* Trenches, ditches.

A. خنازیر *khanázír.* Swine, pigs.

A. خناس *khannás.* A demon, devil.

A. خناسی *khannásíy.* Devilish.

A. خناق *khinák.* A rope for strangling.

A. خناق *khannák.* A strangler, hangman.

A. خناق *khunák.* The quinsy.

P. خنبیدن *khumbídan.* To beat time.

A. خنثی *khunsá.* A hermaphrodite.

P. خنج *khanj.* Profit, gain; delight. Lost.

P. خنجر *khanjar.* A dagger.

P. خنجری *khanjarí.* A small tambourine.

P. خندان *khandán.* Laughing, merry.

P. خندانیدن *khandánídan.* To cause to laugh.

A. خندق *khandak.* A foss, moat, trench, ditch.

P. خنده *khanda.* Laughing, a laugh.

P. خندگی *khandagí.* Laughter.

P. خنده رو *khanda-rú.* A smiling countenance.

P. خندیدن *khandídan.* To laugh.

A. خنزیر *khinzír.* A pig.

A. خنصر *khinsar.* The little finger.

A. خنق *khanik.* Suffocating, strangling.

P. خنك *khunuk.* Cool, temperate. Happy.

P. خنكار *khunkár.* An emperor.

P. خنكى *khunukí.* Coolness, temperature.

P. خنگ *khing.* White or gray (horse).

P. خنگا *khingá.* Ablebodied.

A. خنو *khanw.* Obscenity of speech.

P. خنيا *khunyá.* Singing, melody.

P. خنيا گر *khunyá-gar.* A minstrel, musician.

P. خو *khú.* Habit, disposition.

P. خواب *kh'áb.* Sleep; a dream.

P. خواب آلوده *kh'áb álúda.* Sleepy, drowsy.

P. خوابانيدن *kh'ábánídan,*
P. or خواباندن *kh'ábándan.*
To cause to sleep; to make a beast of burden lie down.

P. خواب ديدن *kh'áb dídan.* To dream.

P. خواب رفتن *kh'áb raftan.* To go to sleep.

P. خواب كردن *kh'áb kerdan.* To sleep.

P. خوابستان *kh'ábistán,*
P. or خوابگاه *kh'ábgáh.* A dormitory, bed-room.

P. A. خواب و خيال *kh'áb u khayál.* Illusion; fancy.

P. خواباناك *kh'áb-nák.* Sleepy, drowsy.

P. خوابيدگى *kh'ábídagí.* Negligence.

P. خوابيدن *kh'ábídan.* To sleep.

A. خواتم *khawátim.* Seals; conclusions.

P. خواجگان *kh'ójagán.* Masters.

P. خواجه *kh'ájah.* A rich merchant, a gentleman.

P. خواجه تاش *kh'ája-tásh.* Fellow-servants, schoolfellows.

A. خواجه سرا *kh'ája-sará.* An eunuch.

A. خوار *khuwár.* The lowing or bleating of cattle.

P. خوار *kh'ár.* Poor, ruined.

P. خوار گرفتن, كردن, شمردن, داشتن *kh'ár giriftan, kerdan, shumurdan,* or *dáshtan.* To despise.

P. خوار *kh'ár.* (In comp.) eating, or drinking, as شير خوار *shír-kh'ár.* A suckling. مردم خوار *mardum kh'ár.* A cannibal.

A. خوارج *khawárij.* Schismatics.

P. خوارزم *kh'árezm.* Chorasmia, the country on the banks of the river Oxus.

A. خوارق *khawárik.* Miracles.

P. خوار و زار *kh'ár u zár.* Abject and distressed.

P. خوارى *kh'árí.* Abjectness, distress.

P. خواست *kh'ást.* Wish, request, desire.

P. خواستگار *kh'ástgár.* Wanting; a petitioner.

P. خواستکاری *kh'ástgárí.* Request; asking in marriage.

P. خواستن *kh'ástan.* To want, to wish, to desire.

A. خواص *khawáṣṣ.* Domestics; qualities.

A. خواصی *khawáṣṣí.* The back seat on an elephant.

A. خواطر *khawáṭir.* Thoughts; the mind.

A. خوافق *khawáfiḳ.* The four cardinal points.

A. خواقین *khawáḳín.* Emperors, kings.

P. خوال *khuwál.* Lampblack.

P. خواه مخواه *kh'áh makh'áh.* Right or wrong, *nolens volens.*

P. خوان *kh'án.* A tray; (in composition) reading, singing.

P. خوان پوش *kh'án-púsh.* Cover of a tray.

P. خوانچه *kh'áncha.* A small tray.

P. خواندگی *kh'ándagí.* Reading; calling; adoption.

P. خوندن *kh'ándan.* To read; to call; to invite.

P. خوان سالار *khán-sálár.* A table-decker; a cook.

P. خوانسامان *kh'ánsámán.* A house-steward.

P. خواندگان *khándagán.* Readers, singers.

A. خوانین *khawánín.* Lords, nobles.

P. خواه *kh'áh.* Wishing, desiring.

P. خواهر *kh'áher.* A sister.

P. خواهش *kh'áhash.* Wish, desire.

P. خواهل *kh'áhil.* Crooked, curved.

P. خواهنخواه *kh'áh na kh'áh.* *Nolens volens.*

P. خواهنده *kh'áhenda.* Wishing, a petitioner.

P. خوب *khúb.* Good, well, fine.

P. خوبان *khúbán.* The fair sex; the good.

P. خوبانی *khúbání.* Apricots stuffed with almonds.

P. خوبتر *khúbtar.* More excellent.

P. خوبترین *khúbtarín.* Most excellent, best.

P. خوبرو *khúb-rú.* Beautiful in face.

P. خوبصورت *khúb-ṣúrat.* Beautiful in form.

P. خوب منظر *khúb-manẓar.* Of beautiful aspect.

P. خوبی *khúbí.* Goodness, beauty.

P. خوجه *khojah.* An eunuch.

A. خوخ *khaukh.* A peach; the water-melon.

P. خود *khud.* Self.

P. خود *khúd.* A helmet, a crest.

P. خود ارا *khud-árá.* Self-praise.

P. خود بخود *khud ba khud.* Voluntarily, spontaneously.

P. A. خود بدولت *khud ba daulat.* Your excellency in council.

P. خود پرست *khud-parast.* Self-conceited.

P. خود پسند *khud-pasand.* Self-complacent.

P. خود بین *khud-bín.* Ostentatious, vain.

P. A. خود ثنا *khud-saná.* A boaster, an egotist.

P. خود خواه *khud-kh'áh.* Selfish.

P. A. خود راى *khud-ráï.* Opinionated, selfwilled, capricious.

P. خود رو *khud-rau.* Wild (vegetables).

P. خود سر *khud-sar.* Obstinate, vain, voluntarily. این امر را خود سر نکردم بمن حکم شد *Ín amr rá khud-sar na kerdam, baman hukm shud.* I did not do this of my own accord, I was ordered.

P. A. خود غرض *khud-gharz.* Self-interested.

P. خود فروش *khud-farúsh.* Boasting, proud.

P. خودى *khudí.* Self-conceit; egotism.

P. خور *khur.* Food; the sun; (in comp.) eating.

P. خوراك *khurák.* Food, victuals.

P. خوراكى *khurákí.* Daily food.

P. خوراندن *khurándan.* To cause to feed.

P. خورچين *khurchín.* A leather wallet.

P. خورد *khurd.* Small, young.

P. خوردن *khurdan.* To eat.

P خوردنى *khurdaní.* Provisions, food.

P. خورده *khurda.* Eaten; minute, small.

P. خوردهٔ انبان *khurda i ambán.* Crumbs in a wallet.

P. خورده دان *khurda-dán.* A minute investigator.

P. خوردى *khurdí.* Smallness, infancy.

P. خورسند *khursand.* Contented; happy.

P. خورش *khurish.* Victuals.

P. خورشيد *khursheid.* The sun.

P. خورم *khurram.* Joyful, pleasant.

P. خورنده *khurenda.* An eater.

P. خور و پوش *khur u púsh.* Food and raiment.

P. خوره *khwara.* Anything that corrodes, as gangrene; the leprosy, &c.

P. خوزستان *khúzistán.* A province of Persia, the ancient Suziana.

P. خوش *khush.* Happy, pleasant, good.

P. خوشا *khushá.* Well! very well!

P. خوش امدى *khush ámadí.* Flattery. خوش امديد *khush ámadíd.* You are welcome.

P. خوش امدن *khush ámadan.* To please.

P. خوشانیدن *khushánídan.* To cause to dry up.

P. خوش اینده *khush-áyenda.* Pleasant, flattering.

P. خوش اواز *khush-áwáz.* Having a sweet voice.

P. خوش باش *khush-básh.* Independent, well off.

P. خوش بو *khush-bú.* Fragrance, perfume.

P. خوش بو دار *khush-bú-dár.* Fragrant, aromatic.

P. خوش تر *khushtar.* Sweeter, pleasanter.

P. A. خوش تقریر *khush-taḳrír.* Eloquent.

P. A. خوش حال *khush-ḥál.* Happy, glad.

P. خوش خبر *khush-khabar.* Glad tidings.

P. خوش خرید *khush-kharíd.* Ready-money purchase.

P. A. خوش خط *khush-khaṭṭ.* Fine writing.

P. خوش خو *khush-khú.* Good-natured.

P. خوش خوان *khush-kh'án.* Having a sweet voice.

P. خوشدامن *khush-dáman.* A mother-in-law.

P. خوش دماغ *khush-dimágh.* Pleasant, merry.

P. خوش ذائقه *khush-żáïḳah.* Savour, pleasant to the taste.

P. خوش طبع *khush-ṭab'.* Well-disposed.

P. خوش گام *khush-gám.* Quick-paced.

P. خوش گفتار *khush-guftár.* Eloquence.

P. خوشکل *khush-kal.* Pretty, pleasing.

P. خوش گوار *khush-guwár.* Wholesome, digestible.

P. خوش مزه *khush-maza.* Delicious.

P. A. خوش معامله *khush-mu'ámilah.* Dealing fairly.

P. A. خوش منظر *khush-manẓar.* Of good aspect.

P. خوش نما *khush-numá.* Beautiful, neat, pretty.

P. خوشنود *khushnúd.* Contented, happy.

P. خوش نویس *khush-nawís.* A calligraphist.

P. خوش وقت *khush-waḳt.* Happy, pleased.

P. خوشه *khúsha.* A cluster, bunch, an ear of corn. The constellation Virgo.

P. خوشی *khushí.* Gladness, pleasure.

P. خوشیدن *khúshídan.* To be parched, shrivelled.

A. خوض *khauẓ.* Mature consideration.

A. خوف *khauf.* Fear, dread.

A. P. خوفناك *khauf-nák.* Dreadful, tremendous.

P. خوك *khúk.* A hog, a sow, a pig.

P. خوك دریا *khúk-i-daryá.* A porpoise (sea-hog).

P. خوگر *khúgar.* Accustomed to.

P. خوگیر *khú-gír.* A pad, stuffing of a saddle.

P. خولنجان *khúlinján.* The herb gallingale.

P. خون *khún.* Blood.

P. خوناب *khúnáb.* Bloody water, a torrent of blood; vermilion.

P. خون اشام *khún ásham.* Blood-thirsty.

P. خون بار *khún-bár.* Shedding or raining blood.

P. خون بها *khún-bahá.* The fine paid for murder.

P. خون جگر خوردن *khún i jigar khurdan.* Deep anxiety or study, lit. to consume the blood of one's liver. The idea being that the heart supplies the liver and the liver the brain.

P. خونخوار *khún - kh'ár.* Sanguinary, cruel.

P. خونخواری *khún - kh'árí.* Bloodshed.

P. خون ريز *khún-ríz.* Shedding blood.

P. خون گرفته *khún-girifta.* Charged with murder.

P. خونكار *khún-kár.* The title given in Persia to the Sultan of Turkey as having the power of life and death.

P. خونی *khúní.* A murderer, a homicide.

P. خونين *khúnín.* Bloody.

P. خوی *khúy.* Temper; sweat.

P. خويد *khawíd.* Unripe or green corn.

P. خويدن *khawídan.* To chew the cud.

P. خويش *kh'ísh.* Own, self; kinsman, son-in-law.

P. خويشان *kh'íshán.* Relations, kindred.

P. خويشاوند *kh'ísáwend.* A kinsman.

P. خويشتن *kh'íshtan.* He, himself.

P. خويشی *kh'íshí.* Relationship.

P. خويدن *kh'aydan.* To perspire.

P. خه *khah.* Ridicule, derision.

P. خی *khí.* A skin for holding water.

P. خيابان *khiyábán.* A parterre, an avenue.

A. خيار *khiyár.* Election; a cucumber.

A. خياری *khayárí.* A kind of violet.

P. خيار چنبر *khiyár i chambar.* Cassia fistularis.

A. خياشيم *khayáshím.* The cartilages of the nose.

A. خياط *khayyáṭ.* A tailor.

A. خياط *khiyáṭ.* A needle.

A. خياطت *khiyáṭat.* Sewing.

A. خيال *khayál.* Imagination, fancy.

A. خيالات *khayálát.* Imaginations, phantoms.

A. P. خيال پرست *khayál-parast.* A visionary.

A. P. خیال خام *khayál i khám.* Vain imagination.

A. خیالی *khayálí.* Fanciful, imaginary.

A. P. خیال بستن *khayál bastan.* To fancy.

A. خیام *khiyám.* Tents, pavilions. (pl. of خیمة.)

A. T. خیام باشی *khiyám báshí.* Inspector general of tents.

A. خیام *khayyám.* A tent-maker.

A. خیانت *khiyánat.* Perfidy, treason, dishonesty, embezzlement.

A. خیر *khair.* Good, goodness; well.

A. خیرة *khairat.* Good-nature.

A. خیرات *khairát.* Good things, alms, charity.

A. P. خیر باد *khair bád.* Farewell!

A. P. خیر خواه *khair-kh'áh.* Well-wisher.

P. خیرگی *khíragí.* Malignancy; obscurity.

P. خیرو *khírú.* The flower of the mallow.

A. خیر و عافیت *khair u 'áfiyat.* Health and welfare.

P. خیره *khíra.* Malignant, wicked; dark.

P. A. خیره رای *khíra-ráï.* Of mean intelligence; grovelling.

A. خیریت *khairiyat.* Welfare; safety.

P. خیز *khíz.* (In comp.) Raising; a leap.

P. خیزاب *khíz-áb.* A wave, billow.

A. خیزران *khaizurán.* A cane, rod, wand.

P. خیزیدن *khízídan.* To rise up.

P. خیسانده *khísánda.* A cold infusion.

P. خسیدن *khísídan.* To moisten, to infuse.

A. خیشوم *khaishúm.* The bridge of the nose.

A. خیطه *khaiṭah.* Sewing thread.

P. خیك *khík.* A skin for carrying water.

A. خیل *khail.* A body of men, a troop; cavalry.

A. P. خیلتاش *khail-tásh.* Fellow-soldier, comrade.

P. خیلی *khailí.* Many, too much; very, exceedingly.

P. خیلی خوب *khailí khúb.* Very well! all right!

A. خیم *khiyam.* Tents.

A. خیمه *khaima.* A tent.

A. P. خیمه زدن *khaima zadan.* To pitch a tent.

A. P. خیمه گاه *khaimah-gáh.* A camp.

P. خیو *khív.* Saliva.

A. خیول *khuyúl.* Horses, troops, tribes.

د

د *dál.* D. The eighth letter of the Arabic and Persian alphabets.

A. داء *dá'.* Disease, infirmity.

A. دأب *da'b.* Custom, institution.

A. دابة *dábbah.* Beast, quadruped.

A. داج *dáj.* Darkness.

A. داجن *dájin.* Tame, domestic (animal).

A. داخل *dákhil.* Arrival, entrance; the interior part.

A. داخله *dákhila.* A receipt, entry in an account.

P. داد *dád.* Justice; a gift.

P. دادار *dádár.* The distributor of justice (God).

P. داد خواه *dád-kh'áh.* A plaintiff.

P. داد دل *dád i dil.* The heart's desire.

P. داد دهش *dád-dihish.* Munificence.

P. داد رس *dád-ras.* Administering justice.

P. داد ستد *dád-sitad.* Give and take, traffic.

P. داد سخن دادن *dád i sukhan dádan.* To write or speak with a nice appreciation of the beauties of the language.

P. داد کر *dád-gar.* An administrator of justice.

P. دادکری *dád-garí.* Administration of justice.

P. دادن *dádan.* To give.

P. دادنی *dádaní.* Fit to be given; advance of money on account.

A. دار *dár.* A house, dwelling.

P. دار *dár.* A gibbet, scaffold.

P. دار *dár.* (In composition) possessing, having.

P. دارا *dárá.* A sovereign, Darius.

P. داراءی *darái.* Sovereignty.

A. دار الا خرت *dár ul ákhirat.* The last home; future life.

A. دار الارشاد *dár ul irshad.* Ardebil.

A. دار الامان *dár ul amán.* The mansion of safety, the towns of Koum or Kirman.

A. دار البقا *dár ul baká.* Eternal life.

A. دار البوار *dár ul bawár.* The mansion of perdition, hell.

A. دار الحرب *dár ul harb.* An enemy's country.

A. دار الخلافت *dár ul khiláfat.* The metropolis, Teheran.

A. دار السرور *dár us surúr.* Tiflis.

A. دار السلام *dár us salám.* The mansion of peace, Bagdad.

A. دار السلطنت *dár us saltanat.* The seat of empire, capital. Tebriz, Kazwin and Isfahán.

A. دار الشفا *dár us shefá.* An hospital, infirmary

A. دار الضرب *dár uz zarb.* The mint.

A. دار العبادة *dár ul 'ibádat.* Yezd.

A. دار الفنا *dár ul faná.* The house of transience, this world.

A. دار القضاء *dar ul kazá.* The tribunal of justice.

A. دار الملك *dár ul mulk.* The capital.

A. دار النشاط *dár un nishát.* Ourmiah.

P. دار بار *dár-bár.* A rope-dancer.

P. دار چینی *dár-chíní.* Cinnamon.

A. دارع *dári'.* Armed with a coat of mail.

P. دار فلفل *dár-filfil.* Long pepper.

P. دارنده *dárenda.* Having, possessing.

P. دارو *dárú.* Medicine, any remedy.

P. داروغه *dárúgha.* A superintendent; an overseer.

P. دارو فروش *dárú-farúsh.* A druggist.

P. دار و گیر *dár u gír.* Tumult, conflict.

A. دارین *daraín.* The two abodes, i.e. the present and future life.

P. داس *dás.* A sickle, a scythe.

P. داستان *dástán.* Tale, history, fable.

P. داشتن *dáshtan.* To have, to hold, to keep.

A. داعی *dá'í.* A claimant, pretender, petitioner.

A. داعیه *dá'iyeh.* Petition, demand, wish.

P. داغ *dágh.* Mark, scar, stain.

P. داغ دار *dágh-dár.* Scarred, stained.

P. داغی *dághí.* Spotted, damaged.

A. دافع *dáfi'.* Repulsing, averting.

P. دال *dál.* An eagle; a great fish.

A. دال *dáll.* Indicating, denoting.

P. دالان *dálán.* A vestibule.

P. دالان دار *dálán-dár.* The porter at a caravanserai.

P. دام *dám.* A net, snare.

A. دام *dáma.* May it be perpetual! دام اقباله *dama ikbáluhu.* May his prosperity continue!

P. داماد *dámád.* A son-in-law.

P. دامان *dámán.* The skirt, hem, &c.

A. دامع *dámi'.* Shedding tears, tearful.

A. دامغه *dámigha.* A wound or concussion of the brain.

P. دامن *dáman.* The skirt of a garment.

P. دامن or دامنه *dámaneh.* The foot of a mountain.

P. دامن گیر *dáman-gír.* Attaching one's self to a patron; a client.

P. دان *dán.* (In composition) knowing; as زبان دان *zabán-dán.* A linguist. Having, holding; as شمعدان *sham'dán,* a candlestick.

P. دانا *dáná.* Learned, wise.

P. داناى *dánáí.* Wisdom, knowledge.

P. دانستگی *dánistagí.* Knowledge.

P. دانستن *dánistan.* To know, acknowledge.

P. دانش *dánish.* Science, knowledge.

P. دانشمند *dánishmand.* Wise, learned.

P. دانشور *dánishwar.* Wise, intelligent.

P. دانشورى *dánishwarí.* Wisdom, science.

A. دانق *dánaḳ,* } The sixth
P. or دانك *dának.* } part of a dram, &c.; a small silver coin.

P. دانك *dánk.* The fourth part of a dirhem.

P. داننده *dánenda.* Knowing, intelligent.

P. دانه *dána.* A grain; a berry; a pimple. يك دانه سيب *yak dána i seib.* One apple. دو دانا در *dú dana i durr.* Three pearls.

P. داو *dáv.* A stroke at play; a bet.

A. داؤد *dá'úd.* David.

P. داور *dávar.* God; a sovereign.

P. داورى *dávarí.* Sovereignty.

P. داه *dáh.* A maid-servant.

A. داهيت *dáhiyat.* A calamity.

P. داهيم *dáhím.* Dominion, a diadem.

A. داير *dáïr.* Revolving; circling.

A. داير و ساير *dáïr u sáïr.* Going in the assize circuit (a judge).

P. دائره *dáïrah.* A circle; circumference, circuit, orbit. دائرهٔ استواء *dáïra i istiwá.* The equator. دائرهٔ افق *dáïra i ufḳ.* The horizon. تربيع الدائرة *tarbí' ud dáïrah.* Squaring the circle.

A. دائم *dáïm.* Perpetual, enduring.

A. دائماً *dáïman.* Always; for ever.

A. دايمى *dáïmí.* Perpetuity; eternal.

A. دايه *dáya.* A nurse; midwife.

A. دب *dubb.* A bear.

A. دب اكبر *dubb i akbar.* The great bear (constellation).

A. دب اصغر *dubb i aṣghar.* The lesser bear.

A. دبار *dabár.* Destruction.

A. دباغ *dabbágh.* A currier, tanner.

A. دباغت *dibághat.* The art of tanning or dyeing.

P. دبدبه *dabdaba.* Pomp.

A. دبر *dubr.* The back side.

P. دبستان *dabistán.* A school.

A. دبق *dibḳ.* Birdlime.

A. دبيقى *dabíḳí.* Gold tissue manufactured at Dabíḳ in Egypt.

A. دبوس *dabús.* A club, cudgel or mace.

P. دبه *daba.* Ruptured, a rupture.

P. دبه *dabba.* An oil-flask or butter-cooler.

A. دبيب *dabíb.* Creeping; crawling.

A. دبير *dabír.* A writer, a secretary, editor.

A. دجال *dajjál.* Antichrist (usually described as having only one eye and riding upon an ass).

A. دجاج *dajáj.* } A fowl,
A. دجاجه *dajájah.* } hen.

A. دجله *Dijlah* or *Dajlah.* The river Tigris.

A. دخان *dukhán.* Smoke.

P. دخت *dukht.* A daughter.

P. دختر *dukhtar.* A daughter, girl, virgin.

P. دخترك *dukhtarak.* A little girl.

P. دختندر *dukhtandar.* Daughter-in-law.

A. دخل *dakhl.* Entrance, possession, occupancy; rent; income. بمن دخلی ندارد *ba man dakhlí na dárad.* It has nothing to do with me.

A. دخل و خرج *dakhl u kharch.* Receipt and disbursement.

P. دخمه *dakhma.* A "tower of silence;" building used by Parsees for the disposal of their dead.

A. دخول *dukhúl.* Entrance, access.

A. دخيل *dakhíl.* Admitted; one who implores the protection of another.

A. P. دخيل كار *dakhíl-kár.* Admitted, possessed.

P. دد *dad.* A beast of prey.

P. در *dar.* In; a door.

P. در پيش كردن *dar písh kerdan.* To shut the door.

P. در وا كردن *dar wá kerdan.* To open the door.

A. در *durr.* A pearl.

P. در ا *der á.* Enter thou; *dará*, a bell.

A. دراج *durráj.* A kind of partridge.

P. دراز *daráz.* Long.

P. دراز دستی *daráz-dastí.* Tyranny, oppression.

P. A. دراز قد *daráz-ḳadd.* Tall of stature.

P. دراز گوش *daráz-gúsh.* Having long ears (the ass).

P. A. دراز نفسی *daráz-nafasí.* Being long-winded or prolix.

A. دراست *dirásat.* Study, instruction, lesson.

P. در آشفتن *dar áshuftan.* To be disturbed, thunderstruck.

A. دراعه *durráʿah.* An upper garment of cotton.

A. درام *darrám.* A hedgehog.

P. در آمد بر آمد *dar ámad bar ámad.* Ingress and egress; receipt and disbursement.

P. در آمدن *dar ámadan.* To enter, to arrive.

P. در آموختن *dar ámúkhtan.* To teach.

P. در انداختن *dar andákhtan.* To hurl, cast.

P. در آوردن *dar áwardan.* To produce.

P. در آویختن *dar áwíkhtan.* To suspend, to hang up.

A. دراهم *daráhim.* Dirhems, drams.

A. درایت *diráyet.* Apprehension, sagacity.

P. A. با درایت *bá diráyet.* Judicious.

P. A. در باب *dar báb.* With regard to; respecting.

P. در باختن *dar-bákhtan.* To trifle, to play, to gamble, to lose at play.

P. در بار *dar-bár.* A prince's court, a levee.

P. در باره *dar-bára.* In behalf of; respecting.

P. در بان *dar-bán.* A porter, doorkeeper.

P. در بدر *dar badar.* From door to door, a vagabond.

P. در بدر شدن *dar ba dar shudan.* To be reduced to beggary.

P. در بند *dar-band.* A difficult pass; confined. A town of the Caucasus.

P. در پی *dar-pai.* At the heels; in the track of.

P. در پیش *dar-písh.* Before, under consideration.

P. در پیوستن *dar paivastan.* To be engaged in; to join.

A. درج *durj.* A casket.

A. درج *darj.* Enfolding; comprising.

A. درجات *daraját.* Steps, degrees.

A. درجه *darjah.* A degree, rank; step of a ladder.

P. A. در حال *dar ḥál.* Instantly, immediately.

P. A. در حضور *dar ḥuẓúr.* Ready, at hand.

P. A. در حق *dar ḥaḳḳ.* Concerning; on behalf of.

P. A. در حقیقت *dar ḥaḳíḳat.* In reality.

P. در خانه *dar-khána.* The Imperial Court.

P. درخت *dirakht.* A tree.

P. درخش *duruksh.* Splendour, brightness.

P. درخشان *durukhshán* and
P. درخشنده *durukhshenda.*
Shining, flashing.

P. درخشیدن *durukhshídan.* To shine, to flash.

P. در خواست *dar-kh'ást.* Request, petition, wish.

P. در خواستن *dar-kh'ástan.* To request, to desire.

P. در خور *dar-khur.* Suitable, proper, convenient.

P. درد *dard.* Pain.

P. درد *durd.* Dregs, lees.

P. دردا *dardá.* Alas! Oh!

P. درد آلود *dard álúd.* Painful.

P. در دختن *dar dukhtan.* To sew; accuse

P. در ربودن *dar rabúdan.* To seize, snatch away; to rescue.

P. در رسانیدن *dar rasánídan.* To bring in.

P. درد سر *dard i sar.* The headache.

P. در دم *dar dam.* Instantly.

P. درد مند *dard-mand.* Compassionate, sympathetic.

P. دردمندی *dardmandí.* Sympathy.

P. درد ناك *dard-nák.* Afflicted.

A. درر *durar.* Pearls. (pl. of درة *durrat.*)

P. در ساختن *dar sákhtan.* To do with; to agree with.

P. درز *darz.* A salvage, suture, seam.

P. در زمان *dar zamán.* Instantly.

P. درزی *darzí.* A tailor.

A. درس *dars.* Lecture, lesson, teaching.

A. P. درس دادن - گفتن - خواندن *dars dádan, guftan* or *kh'ándan.* To teach.

P. A. در ساعت *dar sá'at.* Instantly.

P. درست *durust.* Right, true.

P. درست کردن *durust kerdan.* To amend, to set right, to attend to.

P. درستی *durustí.* Propriety, amendment, reform. بدرستی *badurustí.* Verily.

P. درشت *durusht.* Harsh, stiff, severe, rough.

P. درشتی *durushtí.* Severity, harshness.

P. در شدن *dar shudan.* To enter, penetrate.

A. درع *dir'.* Armour; a coat of mail.

P. A. در عقب *dar 'aḳab.* Behind, after.

P. درفش *dirafsh.* An awl; a flag.

P. درفشان *dirafshán.* Shining, splendid; trembling.

P. درفشیدن *dirafshídan.* To shine; to tremble.

A. درق *daraḳ.* Leathern bucklers. (pl. of درقه *darḳah.*)

T. درك *dirak.* A beam.

A. درك *dark.* Knowledge, perception.

A. درکات *darakát.* Descending steps; lowest degree.

P. در کار *dar-kár.* Necessary, requisite.

P. درگاه *dar-gáh.* A place, court, threshold, door; a mosque.

P. در گذشتن *dar guzashtan.* to decline, to leave off.

P. در گذاشتن *dar-guzáshtan.* To mix, confuse; to pass by or over.

P. در گرفتن *dar giriftan.* To take effect, make an impression on.

A. درم *diram,* } A direm,
A. or درهم *dirham.* } money.

P. درمان *darmán.* Remedy, medicine.

P. در ماندگی *dar-mándagí.* Distress, want.

P. در ماندن *dar-mándan.* To be fatigued or helpless.

P. درمانده *dar-mánda.* Distressed, helpless.

P. درمن *darman.* Drugs, remedy,

P. درمنه *dirmana.* Wormwood.

P. در میان *dar miyán.* Between, in the midst; the interior; under consideration.

P. درنده *darenda.* Rending, tearing; ravenous, fierce.

P. درنگ *dirang.* Slow, dilatory; tardiness.

P. در نوردن *dar navardan.* To travel.

P. در نوردیدن *dar navardídan.* To fold, wrap together; to obliterate.

P. درو *dirav.* The harvest; reaping.

P. دروازه *dar-wáza.* A door, gate.

P. A. در واقع *dar wáki'.* In fact, verily.

A. دروب *dárúb.* Obsequious; tractable.

P. درود *durúd.* Blessing, salutation. Timber; a plank.

P. درودگر *durúdgar.* A carpenter.

P. درودن *durúdan.* To reap, mow.

A. دروز *durúz.* Joints, seams, sutures. (pl. of درز *darz.*)

A. دروس *durús.* Obliterating; lectures.

P. دروغ *durúgh.* A lie, falsehood.

P. دروغ گو *durúgh-gú.* A liar.

P. درون *darún.* In, within; interior; heart.

P. درونده *diravenda.* A reaper, a mower.

P. درونی *darúní.* Internal, intrinsic.

P. درویدن *diravídan.* To reap.

P. دروبزه *darwíza.* Beggary.

P. درویش *darvísh.* Poor, indigent; a dervish, monk.

P. درویشی *darvíshí.* Poverty; being or becoming a dervish.

P. دره *dara.* A valley or pass between two mountains.

P. درهم *dar-ham.* Intricate, confused. درهم افتاده *dar-ham uftáda.* Fallen into confusion.

P. روی درهم کشیدن *rúy dar-ham keshídan.* To frown.

A. درهم *dirham.* A direm, money.

P. دری *darí.* The Persian language.

P. دریا *daryá.* A river, sea.

P. بالا امدن دریا *bálá ámadan i daryá.* The flow of the tide.

P. فرو امدن دریا *farau ámadan i daryá.* The ebb of the tide.

P. A. دریای محیط *darya i muhít.* The ocean.

P. در یاب *dar yáb.* Know thou; knowing. (from دریافتن.)

P. دریا بار *daryá-bár.* Abounding in rivers.

P. دریا بند *daryá-band.* A port, haven.

P. دریابنده *dar-yábanda.* Intelligent.

P. دریاچه *daryáche.* A rivulet.

P. دریا دل *daryá-dil.* A heart bountiful as the sea.

P. دریافت *dar-yáft.* Perception, understanding.

P. دریافتن *dar-yáftan.* To perceive.

P. دریا کش *daryá kesh.* An insatiable drunkard.

P. دریا گوش *daryá-gúsh.* Sea-ears, a kind of shell.

P. دریا نورد *daryá-navard.* A traveller by sea.

P. دریای *daryáï.* Marine.

P. دریای شور *daryáï shúr.* The salt sea.

P. A. در یتیم *durr i yatím.* A unique pearl.

P. دریچه *daríche.* A window, a wicket.

P. دریدن *darídan.* To tear.

P. دریده *darída.* Torn, rent.

P. دریغ *darígh.* A sigh, sorrow; refusal, grudging. Ah!

P. دریغا *darígha.* Ah! alas!

P. درین *darín.* In this.

P. دریوزه *daryúza.* Beggary.

P. دژ *dazh.* A fortress, castle.

P. دزد *duzd.* A thief, robber.

P. دژدار *dazh-dár.* Governor of a fort.

P. دزد ریگ *duzd-ríg.* A quicksand.

P. دزدی *duzdi.* Theft, robbery.

P. دزدیدن *duzdídan.* To rob, to steal.

P. دزغاله *dizghála.* A citadel, a tower.

P. دژم *dizham.* Melancholy, cropsick.

A. دسام *disám.* A plug, spigot, bung.

A. دساتیر *dasátír.* A common-place book; copies, exemplars.

P. دست *dast.* The hand; superiority.

P. دستار *dastár.* A turban.

P. دستار خوان *dastár-kh'án.* A table-cloth.

P. دست افراز *dast-afráz.* A tool, implement.

P. دست آمدن *dast ámadan.* To be fluxed.

P. دست آموز *dast-ámúz.* Trained by the hand.

P. دستان *dastán.* A tale.

P. دست آویز *dast áwíz.* Motive, argument.

P. دستان سرای *dastán saráï.* A reciter of stories.

P. دستانه *dastána.* A glove.

P. دستاویز *dast áwíz.* A certificate, voucher; bond.

P. دست بدست *dast ba dast.* From hand to hand.

P. دست برد *dast burd.* Superiority, victory.

P. دست بر داشتن *dast bar dáshtan.* To withdraw the hand, to leave alone.

P. دست بر فشاندن *dast bar fishándan.* To rub the hands together for joy.

P. دست برنجن *dast-baranjan.* A bracelet.

P. دست بوسی *dast-búsí.* Kissing or shaking hands.

P. دست پیمان *dast-paimán.* An agreement ratified by shaking hands; a marriage portion.

P. دست تنگ *dast-tang.* Indigent, poor.

P. دست چپ *dast i chap.* The left hand.

P. A. دستخط *dast-khaṭṭ,*
P. A. or دسخط *das-khaṭṭ.*
Signature, sign, manual.

P. A. دسخط خاص *daskhaṭṭ i kháṣṣ.* Royal signature; to give the hand.

P. دست دادن *dast-dádan.* To promise; to strike a bargain.

P. دست درازی *dast-darází.* Tyranny, oppression.

P. دست راست *dast i rást.* The right hand.

P. دست رس *dast-ras.* Power, means.

P. دست رنج *dast-ranj.* Hire, pay.

P. دست شستن *dast shustan.* To wash the hand; relinquish.

P. دست شکن *dast-shikan.* Bruising the hand; a curling lock.

P. دست شوی *dast-shúy.* A wash-hand bason.

P. دست فال *dast-fál.* Handsel.

P. دستک *dastak.* Clapping the hands; the hands of a watch.

P. دستکار *dast-kár.* An artificer.

P. دستکاری *dast-kárí.* Handicraft.

P. دستگاه *dast-gáh.* Power, strength.

P. دستک زدن *dastak-zadan.* To clap the hands.

P. دست کش *dast-kesh.* A glove.

P. دست کشادن *dast-kushádan.* To open the hand; to give alms.

P. دستگیر *dast-gír.* A patron; a captive.

P. دستگیری *dast-gírí.* Patronage, protection.

P. دستمال *dast-mál.* A napkin, handkerchief.

P. دست مایه *dast-máya.* Stock-in-trade.

P. دست مزد *dast-muzd.* Wages, hire.

P. دستنبویه *dastambúya.* A perfume.

P. دستوانه *dast-wána.* A gauntlet.

P. دستور *dastúr.* Custom, usage, fee. A prime minister.

A. دستور العمل *dastúr ul 'amal.* Regulation, rule of conduct.

P. دستوری *dastúrí.* Leave, permission.

P. دسته *dasta.* A handle; pestle; a quire of paper (see also فوج).

P. دسته گل *dasta i gul.* A nosegay.

P. دستی *dastí.* Whatever can be held in the hand.

P. دستیاب *dást-yáb.* Procurable, ready to hand.

P. دستیار *dast-yár.* An assistant, coadjutor.

P. دستیاری *dast-yárí.* Assistance, succour.

P. دست یافتن *dast-yáftan.* To acquire, to conquer.

A. دسم *dasim.* Greasy.

P. دشت *dasht.* A desert, a plain.

P. دشتی *dashtí.* Wild, savage.

P. دشخوار *dushk'ár.* Difficult.

P. دشخواری *dushkh'árí.* Difficulty, trouble.

P. دشمن *dushman.* An enemy.

P. دشمنی *dushmaní.* Enmity, hostility.

P. دشنام *dushnám.* Reproach, abuse.

P. دشنه *dashna.* A dagger.

P. دشوار *dushwár.* Difficult, arduous, painful.

P. دشواری *dushwárí.* Difficulty, trouble.

A. دعاء *du'á.* Invocation, prayer.

A. P. دعا گوی *du'á-gúí.* One who prays.

A. دعات *du'át.* Invocations, prayers.

A. دعام *di'ám.* Pillars; a column.

A. P. دعاء خیر *du'ái kheir.* A benediction.

A. دعوی *da'wá.* Claim, pretension, plaint.

A. دعوت *da'wat.* A benediction; an invitation.

P. دغا *daghá.* Imposture; deceit.

P. دغاباز *daghá-báz.* A cheat, impostor.

P. دغابازی *daghá-bází.* Fraud, villainy.

P. دغدغه *daghdagha.* Tumult, alarm; titillation.

A. دغر *daghr.* Strangling, choking.

P. دغل *daghal.* False, base, spurious.

P. دغلی *daghalí.* Treacherous, treachery.

P. دف *daf.* A small tambourine.

P. دفاتر *dafátir.* Volumes, registers. (pl. of دفتر.)

A. دفائن *dafáïn.* Hidden treasures.

P. A. دفتر *daftar.* A book, register.

P. دفتر خانه *daftar khána.* An office, counting-house, exchequer.

P. دفتر نویس *daftar-navís.* A clerk, register.

P. دفتری *daftarí.* An office-keeper.

A. دفتین *daffatain.* Pasteboard; the two covers of a book.

A. دفع *daf'.* Repulsion; time.

A. P. دفع انداختن *daf' andákhtan.* To defer, refuse, postpone.

A. دفعات *dafa'át.* Times.

A. دفعدار *daf' - dár.* An officer of cavalry.

A. دفعه *daf'ah.* One time, once. یك دفع *yek daf'ah.* One time, once.

A. دفن *dafn.* Burying, interment.

A. دفینه *dafínah.* Buried or hidden treasure.

A. دق *dakk.* Beating, bruising.

A. دق *dikk.* Vexation; a hectic fever.

A. دقائق *dakáik.* Subtilties; minutes.

A. دقت *dikkat.* Uneasiness; abstruseness.

P. دق و لق *dak u lak.* An extensive uncultivated plain.

A. دقیق *dakík.* Abstruse; subtle; minute.

A. دقیقه *dakíkah.* A minute; a subtlety.

A. P. دقیقه یاب *dakíkah-yáb.* Discovery, subtilties.

A. دکاکین *dakákín.* Shops.

A. P. دکان *dukán.* A shop, a workshop.

P. دکانچه *dukánche.* A small shop.

P. دگانه *dugána.* See دوگانه.

P. دگر *digar.* Another, again, anew.

P. دگر بار *digar bár.* Another time.

P. دگر گون *digar gún.* Of another colour.

T. دکمه *dukmeh.* A button.

P. دل *dil.* The heart, the mind.

P. دل ارام *dil-árám.* A mistress, sweetheart.

P. دل ازار *dil-ázár.* A sweetheart; cruel.

P. دل ازرده *dil-ázurda.* Displeased, provoked.

P. دلاسا *dil-ásá.* Comfort, soothing.

A. دلاك *dallák.* A waiter at baths; a barber.

A. دلال *dallál.* A broker.

A. دلالت *dalálat.* Indication.

A. دلاله *dallálah.* A procuress.

A. دلالی *dalláli.* Brokerage.

P. دلاور *diláwer.* Brave, intrepid.

P. دلاوری *dilávarí.* Intrepidity.

P. دل اویخته *dil-áwíkhta.* Enamoured, loved.

P. دلاویز *dil-áwíz.* Heart-ravishing.

A. دلائل *daláil.* Demonstrations.

P. دلبازی *dil-bází.* Rashness.

P. دلپذیر *dil-pazír.* Heart's desire, amiable.

P. دلبر *dil-bar.* A ravisher of hearts; a sweetheart.

P. دلبری *dil-barí.* Captivating hearts.

P. دل بستگی *dil-bastagí.* Attachment; anguish.

P. دل بسته *dil-basta.* Attached; addicted.

P. دل پسند *dil-pasand.* Agreeable, plausible.

P. دل بند *dil-band.* The bowels; lovely.

P. دلتنگ *dil-tang.* Sad, distressed.

P. دل جو *dil-jú.* Striving to please.

P. دل خراش *dil-kharásh.* Excruciating.

P. دل خسته *dil-khasta.* Afflicted mind.

P. دل خواه *dil-kh'áh.* Beloved, desired object.

P. دلخوش *dil-khush.* Contented, cheerful.

P. دلداده *dil-dáda.* One who has given his heart, a lover.

P. دلدار *dil-dár.* A lover, a mistress.

P. دلدل *Duldul.* The famous mule of 'Alí.

P. دلداری کردن *dil-dárí kerdan.* To console.

P. دلدوز *dil-dúz.* Piercing the heart.

P. دلربا *dil-rubá.* Seizing the heart.

P. دلریش *dil-rísh.* Heart-wounded.

P. دل ساز *dil-sáz.* Pleasing the heart.

P. دل ستان *dil-sitán.* Heart-stealing.

P. دل سرد *dil-sard.* Cold-hearted.

P. دل سوز *dil-súz.* Compassionate.

P. دل سوزی *dil-súzí.* Compassion.

P. دل شب *dil i shab.* Midnight.

P. دل شده *dil-shuda.* Heart-bereft.

P. دل شکسته *dil-shikesta.* Broken-hearted.

P. دل شکفته *dil shigufta.* Heart-expanded.

P. دل فروز *dil-ferúz.* Enlightening the heart.

P. دل فریب *dil-faríb.* Ensnaring the heart.

P. دل فگار *dil-figár.* With heart rent; a lover.

P. A. دلفین *dulfín.* A dolphin.

A. دلق *dalaḳ.* A dervish's habit.

P. A. دل قوی *dil-ḳawí.* Confidence.

A. دلك *dalk.* Friction.

P. دل گداز *dil-gudáz.* Melting the heart.

P. دل گران *dil-gerán.* Displeased.

P. دل گرانی *dil-gerání.* Displeasure.

P. دل کش *dil-kesh.* Heart-attracting.

P. دل کشا *dil-kushá.* Heart-expanding, exhilarating.

P. دل گیر *dil-gír.* Sad, sorrowful, annoyed.

P. دل نشین *dil-nishín.* Satisfying the heart.

P. دل نگرانی *dil-nigarání.* Sorrow.

P. دل نواز *dil-nawáz.* Soothing the mind, conciliating.

P. دل نهاد *dil-nihád.* Attention.

A. دلو *dalw.* A bucket; the sign Aquarius.

T. دلی *delí.* Foolish, mad.

P. دلیر *dilír.* Brave, intrepid.

P. دلیرانه *dilírána.* Boldly, heroically.

P. دلیری *dilírí.* Intrepidity.

A. دلیل *dalíl.* An argument, proof, indication.

A. P. دلیل قاطع *dalíl i ḳáti'.* A decisive proof.

P. دم *dam.* The breath, life; boasting; a moment. دم بر اوردن *dam bar áwardan.* To draw a breath. دم زدن *dam zadan.* To breathe; to proceed; to boast.

A. دم *dam.* Blood.

P. دم *dum.* A tail.

P. دما *dama.* The asthma.

P. دمادم *damádam.* Continually, always.

A. P. دمار *damár.* Ruin, destruction; the root of a tree, &c.

P. A. دمار بر اوردن از *damár bar áwardan az.* To annihilate, exterminate.

A. P. دماغ *dimágh.* The brain; conceit, pride, fancy.

A. دم الاخوین *dam ul akhawaín.* Dragon's blood.

P. دمامه *damáma.* A small drum, a trumpet.

P. دمان *damán.* Fierce, strong, swift.

A. دمامیل *damámíl.* Boils.

P. دماوند *Demávend.* Name of a mountain near Teheran.

P. دمبدم *dam ba dam.* Incessantly.

A. دمث *damiś.* A soft, sandy place.

P. دمدار *dum-dár.* Having a tail.

P. دم در کشیدن *dam dar keshídan.* To cease to breathe, to be silent, hold one's breath.

P. دمدمه *damdama.* A raised battery.

P. دم ساز *dam-sáz.* A confidant, friend.

P. دم سازی *dam-sází.* Intimacy, confidence.

A. دمسق *Demeshḳ,* or A. دمشق الشام *Demeshḳ ush-shám.* } Damascus.

A. دمع *dam'.* A tear.

P. دمگاه *dam-gáh.* A forge.

A. دمل *dumal.* A boil, a swelling.

A. دموع *dumú'.* Tears. (pl. of دمع *dam'.*)

A. دموی *damawíy.* Plethoric, bloody.

P. دمه *dama.* A pair of bellows.

P. دمی *damí.* Inflated, puffy, windy.

P. دمی چند *damí chand.* A few minutes.

A. دمياطی *Dimyáṭíy.* Dimity.

P. دمیدن *damídan.* To blow; to grow up; to appear.

P. دمیده *damída.* Blown, budded, shot up.

A. دناءت *danáát.* Baseness, meanness.

A. دنانیر *danánír.* Dinars, coins. (pl. of دینار *dínár.*)

P. دنبال *dumbál.* A tail; hinder part, after. A rudder.

P. دنبل *dumbul.* A boil, bubo.

P. دنبه *dumba.* The fat of a sheep's tail.

P. دندان *dandán.* A tooth.

P. دندانه *dandána.* The teeth of a saw; the wards of a lock.

P. دنده *danda.* A rib, the side of the body. دنده اش نرم شود *danda ash niram shawad.* Let him try it.

P. دنگل *dangil.* A cuckold.

A. دنی *daníy.* A worthless man.

A. دنیا *dunyá.* The world.

A. P. دنیا پرست *dunyá-parast.* Worldly-minded.

A. P. دنیا دار *dunyá-dár.* A wealthy man, worldling.

A. P. دنیا داری *danyá-dárí.* Economy; mammon.

A. دنیوی *dunyawíy.* Belonging to this world.

P. دو *dav.* Running; a race.

P. دو *dú.* Two.

A. دوا *dawá.* Medicine, a remedy.

A. دواب *dawább.* Quadrupeds, beasts, cattle.

A. دوات *dawát.* An inkstand.

A. دوار *dawwár.* Revolving.

A. دوار *duwár.* Giddiness, the vertigo.

P. دوازده *duwázda.* Twelve.

P. دوازدهم *duwázdahum.* The twelfth.

P. دواسبه *dú-aspa.* A trooper who has two horses; a messenger.

A. دواعی *dawá'í.* Pretensions; claims.

P. دوال *duwál.* A leathern strap, a belt.

P. دوالی *duwálí.* A cheat, juggler, prestidigitator.

A. دوالیب *dawálíb.* Water-wheels. (pl. of دولاب.)

A. دوام *dawám.* Perpetuity.

P. دوان *daván.* Running fast.

P. دوانیدن *davánídan.* To cause to run.

A. دواوین *dawáwín.* Díwáns, collected odes. (pl. of دیوان q. v.)

A. دوایر *dawáir.* Circles. (pl. of دایرة.)

P. دو باره *dú-bára.* Double, double-distilled.

P. دو بالا *dú-bálá.* Excessive.

P. دو پیازه *dú-piyáza.* A fricassee of butter, onions, &c.

P. دو تا *dú-tá.* Twice, double; bent. Colloquially the particle تا is used after all numerals as دوتا *dú-tá.* Two; سه تا *seh-tá.* Three.

P. دو چار *du-chár.* Meeting, interview; three or four.

P. دو چند *dú-chand.* Twice, double.

P. دو جہان *dú-jehán.* The present and future life.

A. دوحة *dauḥat.* An orchard, bower.

P. دوخت *dúkht.* A seam, suture.

P. دوختن *dúkhtan.* To sew, stitch.

A. دود *dúd.* A worm.

P. دود *dúd.* Smoke.

A. دود الحریر *dúd ul ḥarír.* A silkworm.

P. دود دل *dúd i dil.* A sigh.

P. دود کش *dúd-kesh.* A chimney.

P. دو دل *dú-dil.* Of two minds, irresolute.

P. دودمان *dúdmán.* An illustrious race.

P. دوده *dúda.* Soot.

P. دودهٔ چراغ *dúda i chirágh.* Lampblack.

A. دور *dawr.* Revolution; an age; around. دور گرفتن *dawr giriftan.* To surround.

P. دور *dúr.* Remote, far, distance.

P. دور افتاده *dúr uftáda.* Strayed away, gone afar off.

A. دوران *daurán.* Time, age.

P. دور اندیش *dúr-andísh.* Provident, foreseeing.

P. دور باش *dúr-básh.* Have a care! stand off!

P. دور بین *dúr-bín.* Fore-sighted; a telescope.

A. P. دور چرخ *daur i chirkh.* The revolutions of the heavens.

P. دور دست *dúr-dast.* Afar off, distant.

P. دو رنگ *dú-rang.* Of two colours; a hypocrite.

P. دو رنگی *dú-rangí.* Hypocrisy.

P. دو روی *dú-rúí.* Two-faced, a deceitful villain.

A. دوره *daurah.* A revolution, circuit.

P. دوری *dúrí.* Distance, separation.

P. دو ریشه *dú-rísha.* A handkerchief.

P. دوزخ *dúzakh.* Hell.

P. دوزخی *dúzakhí.* Hellish; a glutton.

P. دوست *dúst.* A friend.

P. دوستانه *dústána.* Friendly.

P. دوست کام *dúst i kám.* As one's friends could wish, prosperous.

P. دوستی *dústí.* Friendship.

P. دو سه *dú-seh.* Two or three.

P. دوسیدن *dusídan.* To cement, to plaster.

P. دوش *dúsh.* The shoulder; last night.

P. دوشا *dúshá.* Any animal giving milk.

P. دوشاب *dúsh-áb.* The expressed juice of dates, &c.

P. دو شاخه *dú-shákha.* The pillory; bifurcated.

T. دوشك *dúshek.* A mattress.

P. دو شنبه *dú-shamba.* Monday.

P. دوشنده *dushenda.* A milker; milking.

P. دوشنه *dúshana.* A milk-pail.

P. دوشیدن *dúshídan.* To milk, to draw.

P. دوشیزگی *dushízagí.* Virginity.

P. دوشیزه *dúshíza.* A virgin.

P. دوغ *dúgh.* Sour milk, curds, buttermilk.

P. دوغ زدن *dúgh zadan.* To churn.

P. دوك *dúk.* A spindle.

T. دوكمه *dúkmeh.* See دكمه.

P. دوكارد *dú-kárd.* A pair of scissors.

P. دوكان *dúkán.* A shop.

P. دوگان *dú-gán.* In twos, double.

P. دوكان دار *dúkán-dár.* A shopkeeper.

P. دوكانی *dúkání.* Shop-keeping.

P. دوگانه *dú-gána.* Double; a prayer in which two genuflections or inclinations of the body are made.

P. دوكدان *dúk-dán.* A spindle-case.

A. دول *dawal.* Riches. (pl. of دولة.)

P. دول *dúl.* A bucket; the sign Aquarius.

P. دولاب *dul-áb.* A wheel for raising water.

A. دولت *dawlat.* Fortune, wealth, dynasty, state; the government.

A. P. دولت بر انداز *dawlat-bar andáz.* Destroying the government.

P. دولت پناه *dawlat-panáh.* The asylum of empire.

P. دولت خانه *dawlat-khána.* A palace.

P. دولت خواه *dawlat-kh'áh.* A well-wisher.

A. P. دولت عظمی *dawlat i 'uzmá.* The mighty empire.

A. P. دولتمند *dawlat-mand.* Fortunate, rich.

P. دولچه *dúlche.* A small bucket.

P. دوم *duwum.* Second; inferior.

P. دو مغز *dú-maghz.* An almond.

A. دون *dún.* Mean, base, ignoble.

P. دونده *davenda.* A runner, running.

A. دونی *dúní.* Baseness, inferiority.

P. دو نیم *dú-ním.* Divided in two, two halves.

A. دوی *dawíy.* Disease; sick.

P. دوی *dúí.* Duality, duplicity.

P. دویدن *davídan.* To run; to spring up.

P. دویست *duwíst.* Two hundred.

P. دویل *duwíl.* Fraud; a kind of silk.

P. دویم *dúyum.* The second.

P. ده *dah.* Ten.

P. ده *dih.* A village; giver; give thou.

P. دهات *dihát.* The country.

P. دهاتی *diháti.* A villager.

A. دهاقین *dihákín.* Villagers. (pl. of دهقان.)

P. دهاك *dahák.* The place of the tens in arithmetic.

A. دهام *duhám.* Black; a stallion-camel.

P. دهان *dahán.* The mouth; orifice.

P. دهانه *dahána.* The bit of a bridle.

P. دهانیدن *dehánídan.* To cause to give.

P. دهاءی *daháí.* The tenth part.

P. T. ده باشی *dah-báshí.* A commander of ten men.

P. ده بست *dah-bist.* Ten or twenty.

P. ده خدا *dih-khudá.* The head-man of a village.

A. دهر *dahr.* Time; the world.

A. دهری *dahríy.* Worldly, temporal.

A. دهریا *dahriyá.* An atheist.

P. دهش *dihish.* A present.

A. دهشت *dahshat.* Fear.

P. دهقان *dihkán.* A villager, ploughman.

P. دهقانی *dihkání.* Husbandry.

P. دهل *duhul.* A drum.

P. دهلزن *duhul-zan.* A drummer.

P. دهلی *dehlí.* The city of Delhi.

A. P. دهلیز *dihlíz.* A portico.

P. دهم *dahum.* The tenth.

P. دهن *dahan.* The mouth; an orifice.

A. دهن *duhn.* Oil.

P. دهنده *dihenda.* A giver.

A. دهور *duhúr.* Ages, times. (pl. of دهر.)

P. دهیم *dihím.* The crown worn by Persian kings.

P. دی *dai.* Winter.

P. دی *dí.* Yester, as دیروز *dí-rúz.* Yesterday. دیشب *dí-shab.* Yesternight.

A. دیار *diyár.* Inhabited country, district. (pl. of دار *dár.*)

A. دیار بکر *Diyár Bekr.* Mesopotamia.

A. دیان *daiyán.* A judge, an umpire.

A. دیانت *diyánat.* Integrity, piety.

A. P. دیانت دار *diyánat-dár.* Honest, pious.

A. دیبا *díbá.* Brocade, cloth of gold.

P. دیباچه *díbáche.* Preface, exordium.

A. دیت *diyat.* The mulct or compensation for manslaughter.

A. دیثان *dísán.* The nightmare.

A. دیجور *daijúr.* Darkness, obscurity.

P. دیدار *dídár.* Interview; look, face.

A. دیدان *dídán.* Worms. (pl. of دود.)

P. دید بان *díd-bán.* A watch, a guard, one who keeps a look-out.

P. دیدن *dídan.* To see, to observe.

P. دیده *dída.* Seen; the eye, the sight.

P. دیده ور *dída-war.* Perspicacious.

A. دیر *dair.* A monastery · a tavern.

P. دیر *dír.* Delay; slow; late.

P. دیر پا *dír-pá.* Lasting, permanent.

P. دیر باز *dír-báz.* Long, long ago; the world.

P. دیر رنج *dír-ranj.* Long-suffering.

P. دیروز *dí-rúz.* Yesterday.

P. دیری *dírí.* Lateness, slowness.

P. دیریدن *díridan.* To break, rend asunder.

P. دیرینه *dírína.* Old, ancient.

P. دیشب *dí-shab.* Last night.

P. دیگ *díg.* A kettle, pot.

A. دیك *dík.* A cock.

P. دیگچه *dígche.* A small kettle.

P. دیگدان *díg-dán.* A stove, trivet.

P. دیگر *dígar.* Another.

P. دیگرانه *dígarána.* Secondly, otherwise.

P. دیم *dím.* Leather.

P. دیمك *dímek.* A white ant.

P. دیمی *dímí.* Land not needing artificial irrigation.

A. دین *dín.* Faith, religion. دین بدنیا فروختن *dín ba dunyá ferúkhtan.* To sell the next world for this.

A. دین *dain.* Debt.

A. دینار *dínár.* The name of a coin; a ducat, dinar.

A. P. دینار سرخ *dínár i surkh.* A gold coin.

A. P. دین پرور *dín-parwar.* Promoter of religion.

A. P. دین پناه *dín-panáh.* The asylum of religion.

A. P. دین دار *dín-dár.* Religious, faithful.

A. دینی *díní.* Belonging to religion.

P. دیو *dív.* A demon, devil.

P. دیوار *dívár.* A wall.

P. دیوالی *díválí.* Bankruptcy.

A. P. دیوان *díván.* A tribunal; a steward; a collection of odes arranged in alphabetical order of rhymes; the *Díván i Háfiz* is the most celebrated.

P. دیوان بلخ کردن *díván i balh kerdan.* A phrase used to express an unjust sentence.

P. T. دیوان بیگی *díván begí.* An officer of state.

P. دیوانگی *dívánagí.* Insanity.

P. دیوانه *dívána.* Insane.

P. دیوانی *dívání.* The office of dewan.

P. دیو باد *dív-bád.* The devil's wind, a whirlwind.

P. دیو دار *dív-dár*. A demoniac, a juniper-tree.

P. دیو ستان *dív-setán*. A demoniac.

P. دیوستان *dívistán*. A desert; a haunted spot.

P. دیوک *divak*. See دیهک.

P. دیو کردار *dív-kerdár*. An evildoer.

P. دیولاخ *dív-lákh*. A haunted spot, desert.

A. دیون *duyún*. Debts. (pl. of دین *dain*.)

P. دیوه *díva*. A silkworm; mushrooms.

P. دیهه *díha*. A village.

P. دیهبان *díhbán*. The chief of a village.

P. دیهور *díhúr*. Heaven.

P. دیهیم *díhím*. A crown or diadem.

ذ The ninth letter of the Arabic and Persian Alphabets.

A. ذا *żá*. Lord, master; endowed with.

A. ذابح *żábiḥ*. A sacrificer, a slaughterer.

A. ذات *żát*. The essence, nature; person; caste; fem. of ذو *żú* possessor.

A. ذات شریف *żat i sheríf*. A noble personage.

A. ذاتی *żátí*. Natural, essential.

A. ذاخر *żákhir*. Fat.

A. ذاکر *żákir*. Remembering; praising God.

A. ذانب *żánib*. A follower; coming behind.

A. ذاهب *żáhib*. Going, passing away.

A. ذاهل *żáhil*. Careless, forgetful.

A. ذائب *żáïb*. Liquid; melting.

A. ذائق *żáïḳ*. Tasting.

A. ذائقه *żáïḳah*. The sense of tasting, the palate.

A. ذباب *żubáb*. A fly; a bee.

A. ذبح *żabḥ*. A sacrifice, slaughter.

A. ذبول *żubúl*. Emaciating; languishing.

A. ذبیح *żabíḥ*. Sacrificed, slaughtered.

A. ذخر *żukhr*. Provisions, stores.

A. ذخیره *żakhíra*. Store, treasure. (pl. ذخایر.)

A. ذرات *żarrát*. Atoms, particles.

A. ذراری *żarárí*. Progenies, descendants.

A. ذراع *żirá'* (pl. ذرائع). A cubit; the fore-arm.

A. ذرع *żar'*. A cubit, two bright stars in the head of Gemini.

A. ذروه *żurwah*. The summit; pomp.

A. ذره *żarrah*. An atom, particle, little.

A. ذرية *żarríyet.* Progeny, race.

A. ذريعه *żarí'ah.* A cause, means; request addressed from an inferior to a superior.

A. ذقن *żaḳn.* The chin.

A. ذكاء *żaká.* Acuteness of intellect.

A. ذكاوت *żakáwat.* Brightness of genius.

A. ذكر *żakar.* Male, membrum virile.

A. ذكر *żikr.* Remembrance, commemoration. Reading the Coran through. A religious service performed by the Dervishes, during which the name of God is frequently repeated.

A. ذكور *żukúr.* Males.

A. ذكورت *żukúrat.* The male sex.

A. ذكى *żakíy.* Ingenious, acute.

A. ذل *żull.* Abjectness, baseness.

A. ذلالت *żalálat.* Baseness.

A. ذلة *żillat.* Disgrace, vileness.

A. ذلف *żulf.* Small or apenosed.

A. ذلق *żalḳ.* Quick, sharp, ready.

A. ذلك *żálik.* That.

A. ذليل *żalíl.* Mean, abject.

A. ذم *żamm.* Blame, reproach.

A. ذمائم *żamáïm.* Misdeeds. (pl. of ذميمة.)

A. ذمه *żimmah.* Trust, charge, responsibility.

A. ذمى *żimmíy.* A client; a person not being a Mohammedan who pays a capitation tax for permission to practise his religion.

A. ذميم *żamím.* Blameable.

A. ذنب *żanab.* A tail.

A. ذنب *żamb* (pl. ذنوب *żunúb*). A crime, sin, fault.

A. ذو *żú.* Lord, master; endowed with.

A. ذوات *żawát.* Fem. plural of ذو *żu*, as ذوات الاربع *żawát ul arba'.* Quadrupeds.

A. ذوالجلال *żu'l jelál.* The Lord of Glory.

A. ذوالحجة *żu'l ḥijjah.* The twelfth Arabian month.

A. ذوالفقار *żú'l faḳár.* Vertebrate; the two-edged sword of Ali.

A. ذوالقربى *żu'l ḳurbá.* A kinsman.

A. ذوالقعده *żu'l ḳa'dah.* The eleventh Arabian month.

A. ذو فنون *żu funún.* Cunning, skilful.

A. ذوق *żauḳ.* Taste, relish, delight.

A. ذوى *żawí.* Masters, possessors. (pl. of ذو.)

A. ذهاب *żiháb.* Departure.

A. ذهب *żahab.* Gold.

A. ذهن *żahan.* Genius; ability.

A. P. ذهن نشين *żahan-nishín.* Understood, remembered.

A. ذهول *żuhúl.* Oblivion.

A. ذهين *żahín.* Ingenious, sagacious.

A. ذی *żí.* A master; endowed with. (oblique case of ذو *żu.*)

A. ذیشان *żí-shán.* Endowed with dignity.

A. ذئب *żi'b.* A wolf.

A. ذئفان *żi'fán.* Venom, poison.

A. ذیت کیت *żait-kait.* So and so, thus.

A. ذیل *żail.* The skirt; supplementary part; margin.

A. از قرار تفصیل ذیل *az ḳerár i tefṣíl i żail.* As detailed below, in accordance with the following statement.

A. ذیول *żuyúl.* Skirts; appendices. (pl. of ذیل.)

ر

ر *Rá.* R. The tenth letter of the Arabic and Persian alphabets.

P. را *rá.* The sign of the oblique case.

A. رابح *rábiḥ.* Gainful, usurious.

A. رابط *rábiṭ.* A chain, ligature.

A. رابطه *rábiṭah.* A conjunction (in grammar); a catchword.

A. رابع *rábi'.* The fourth.

A. رابعا *rábi'an.* Fourthly.

A. راتب *rátib.* Daily bread, provision.

A. راتبه *rátiba.* Salary, pay.

A. راجح *rájiḥ.* Preferable; preponderating.

A. راجع *ráji'.* Returning; relative (in grammar).

A. راجل *rájil.* A pedestrian.

A. راجی *rájí.* Hoping; asking.

A. راح *ráḥ.* Wine.

A. راحت *ráḥat.* Repose, ease, tranquillity; the palm of the hand.

A. راحل *ráḥil.* A traveller.

A. راحله *ráḥilah.* A caravan.

A. راحم *ráḥim.* Pitying, pardoning.

A. رادع *rádi'.* Repelling, prohibiting.

A. رادف *rádif.* Coming after, sitting behind.

P. راز *ráz.* A secret, mystery; a mason.

P. راز دار *ráz-dár.* A confidant; private and confidential (a letter).

A. راز دان *ráz-dán.* Knowing a secret; a confidant.

A. رازق *rázik.* Providing; Providence.

P. رازیانه *ráziyána.* Aniseed.

A. راس *ra's.* The head, chief; top.

A. P. دو راس اسپ *dú rás i asp.* Two head of horses.

A. راس الجدی *rá's ul jidy.* The winter solstice.

A. راس السرطان *ra's us saraṭán.* The summer solstice.

A. راس المال *ra's ul mál,*
A. or راس مال *rás mál.*
Capital, stock in trade.

A. راسب *rásib.* Sediment.

P. راست *rást.* True, right; straight.

P. راست باز *rást-báz.* Faithful, just.

P. راستا *rástá.* A road.

P. راستاد *rástád.* A pension.

P. راست بین *rást-bín.* Impartial.

P. راست سخن *rást-sukhun.* Truthful.

P. راست کردار *rást-kerdár.* Fair dealing.

P. راست گو *rást-gú.* Truthful.

P. راست نما *rást-numá.* Appearing upright.

P. راستی *rástí.* Rectitude; truth.

P. راستی و درستی *rástí u durustí.* Honesty and fidelity.

A. راسخ *rásikh.* Firm, rooted; constant.

A. P. راسخ دم *rásikh-dam.* Firm in mind, constant.

P. راسو *rású.* A weasel.

A. راشد *ráshid.* Orthodox.

A. راشی *ráshí.* Receiving a bribe.

A. راصد *ráṣid.* An observer (of the stars).

A. راضی *rází.* Satisfied, content.

A. راطب *ráṭib.* Humid.

A. راعی *rá'í.* A shepherd; guardian.

P. راغ *rágh.* A meadow, a declivity.

A. راغب *rághib.* Wishing, desiring.

A. رافت *rá'fat.* Pity, tenderness.

A. رافض *ráfiẓ.* Refusing; abdicating.

A. رافضی *ráfiẓí.* A heretic.

A. رافع *ráfi'.* Raising; adducing.

P. رافه *ráfa.* A herb resembling garlic.

A. راقب *ráḳib.* An observer.

A. راقم *ráḳim.* A writer.

A. راقی *ráḳí.* An enchanter.

A. راکب *rákib.* A rider.

A. راکع *ráki'.* Performing inclinations of the body at prayers.

P. رام *rám.* Tame, obedient.

A. رامج *rámij.* A decoy-bird.

P. رامش *rámish.* Cheerfulness.

P. رامش گر *rámish-gar.* A musical performer.

A. رامی *rámí.* An archer.

P. ران *rán.* The thigh.

P. راندن *rándan.* To drive, banish.

P. رانی *rání.* Driving.

A. راوی *ráwí.* A historian, reciter.

P. راه *ráh.* A way, road. از چه راه *az chi ráh.* How?

P. خیلی راه *kheilí ráh.* A long way.

P. راه رفتن *ráh-raftan.* To walk.

P. راه اورد *ráh-áward.* A present, offering.

A. راهب *ráhib.* A monk.

P. راهبان *ráhbán.* A traveller; a sentinel.

P. راهبر *ráh-bar.* A road-guide.

P. راه بریدن *ráh burídan.* To travel.

P. راه دادن *ráh-dádan.* To admit.

P. راه دار *ráh-dár.* A road-patrol; collector of customs or excise duties.

P. راه داری *ráh-dárí.* A pass-port; customs or excise duties (see گمرك).

P. راه رو *rah-rav.* A traveller.

P. راه زن *rah-zan.* A highwayman.

P. راه گذار *ráh-guzár.* Passage.

A. راهن *ráhin.* Mortgager.

P. راه نبرده *ráh na-burda.* Untravelled.

P. راه نما *ráh-numá.* A guide.

P. راه نمونی *ráh namúní.* Guidance.

P. راهوار *ráh wár.* An ambler.

P. راهی *ráhí.* A traveller.

A. رای *rái.* Counsel, wisdom, opinion.

A. رایات *ráyát.* Standards.

A. رائب *ráïb.* Doubting.

A. رایت *ráyat.* A standard.

A. رایج *ráïj.* Usage, currency.

A. P. رای زدن *rái-dádan.* To give an opinion.

A. رایحه *ráïha.* Odour.

A. رایض *ráïẓ.* A horse-breaker.

A. رایق *ráïḳ.* Wonderful, beautiful.

P. رایگان *ráïgán.* Gratis.

A. رب *rabb.* The Lord.

A. رب *rubb.* Inspissated juice, syrup.

P. ربا *rubá.* (In comp.) seizing, robbing.

A. ربا *riba.* Usury.

A. P. رباب *rabáb.* A rebeck, a kind of guitar.

A. P. ربا خور *ribá-khur.* A usurer.

A. رباط *ribáṭ.* An inn; a monastery.

P. رباعی *rubá'íy.* A quatrain.

A. ربنا *rabbaná.* O our Lord!

A. ربانی *rabbání.* Divine.

P. ربانیدن *rubánídan.* To seize, rob.

P. رباننده *rubáninda.* Ravisher; rapacious.

P. ربائیدن *rubáïdan.* To seize, to rob.

A. ربح *ribḥ.* Profit, interest, usury.

A. ربط *rabṭ.* A tie, joining.

A. ربع *rub'.* A fourth.

A. ربع مسکون *rab' i maskún.* The inhabited quarter of the world.

A. ربعی *rib'íy.* Vernal; born in spring.

A. ربقه *ribka.* A collar; yoke.

A. ربوبیت *rabúbíyat.* Deity, divinity; dominion.

P. ربودن *rabúdan.* To seize, ravish.

A. ربیب *rabíb.* A step-son.

A. ربیبه *rabíba.* A step-daughter.

A. ربیع *rabí'.* The spring.

A. ربیع الاخر *rabí' ul ákhir.* The fourth Arabian month.

A. ربیع الاول *rabí' ul awwal.* The third Arabian month.

A. رتبة *rutbat.* Rank, degree.

A. رتق *ratk.* Repairing; reformation.

A. رتق و فتق *ratk u fatk.* Shutting and opening.

A. رج *rajj.* Moving, trembling.

A. رجاء *rijá'.* Hope.

A. رجاع *rija'.* Return.

A. رجال *rijál.* Men.

A. رجالی *rijálíy.* Footmen, infantry.

A. رجب *rejeb.* The seventh Arabian month.

A. رجز *rejez.* A species of verse.

A. رجس *rijs.* Uncleanness.

A. رجع *raj'.* Returning, repeating.

A. رجعة *raj'at.* Answering a letter.

A. رجف *rajf.* Tremour, emotion.

A. رجل *rajul.* A man.

A. رجل *rijl.* A foot.

A. رجم *rujum.* Shooting stars.

A. رجم *rajm.* Stoning to death.

A. رجوع *rujú'.* Return, repetition.

A. P. رجوع کردن *rujú' kerdan.* To refer, to appeal.

A. رجولیت *rujúlíyet.* Virility, manhood.

A. رحی *raha.* A hand-mill.

A. رحلت *rihlat.* Marching; death.

A. رحم *rahm.* Mercy, compassion.

A. رحم *rahim.* The womb.

A. رحمان *rahmán.* Merciful (God).

A. رحمت *rahmat.* Mercy.

A. رحیل *rahíl.* March, departure.

A. رحیم *rahím.* Merciful (God).

P. رخ *rukh.* The cheek; side.

A. رخام *rukhám.* Marble, alabaster.

A. رخاوت *rakháwat.* Being loose and flabby; laxity.

P. رخت *rakht.* Furniture.

P. رخت خواب *rakht i kh'áb.* Bed-clothes.

P. رخت زنانه *rakht i zanána.* Women's attire.

P. رخت کش *rakt-kesh.* A beast of burden.

P. رخسار *rukhsár.* } The
P. رخساره *rukhsára.* } cheek, face.

P. رخشان *rakhshán.* Shining.

P. رخشیدن *rakhshídan.* To shine, flash.

A. رخصت *rukhsat.* Permission to retire; leave.

P. رخنه *rakhna.* A fracture; a notch, crevice, hole.

A. رخوت *rikhwat.* Laxity.

A. رد *radd.* Repulsion, refutation.

A. رداء *ridá.* A cloak or mantle.

A. رداءت *radáat.* Depravity.

A. P. رد جواب *radd i jawáb.* A rejoinder.

A. P. رد کلام *radd i kalám.* Refutation.

P. رده *rada.* A line; rule; row.

A. ردی *radíy.* Wicked, depraved.

A. ردیف *radíf.* One who rides behind; auxiliary forces.

A. ردیم *radím.* A worn or torn habit.

A. رذیل *razíl.* Mean, base.

A. رذیلت *razílat.* Baseness, mean. (pl. رذایل.)

P. رز *raz.* A vineyard; a grape.

A. رز *ruzz.* Rice.

A. رزاز *razzáz.* A rice-seller.

A. رزاق *razzák.* Providence.

A. رزانت *razánat.* Firmness, strength.

A. رزایا *razáyá.* Afflictions, misfortunes.

P. رز بان *raz-bán.* The keeper of a vineyard.

A. رزق *rizk.* Subsistence, daily bread.

P. رزم *razm.* War, combat.

P. رزم *razam.* (From رزیدن) I stain.

P. رزمگاه *razm-gáh.* The field of battle.

P. رزیدن *razídan.* To dye, tinge, colour.

P. رزین *razín.* Strong (fort).

P. رس *ras.* (In comp.) arriving.

P. رسا *rasá.* Capable; arriving.

A. رسالت *risálat.* A legation; mission.

A. رساله *risála.* A treatise, letter; a troop of horse.

A. رسام *rassám.* A designer, describer.

P. رسان *rasán.* Bring thou. (In comp.) bringing.

P. رساندن *risándan.* } To
P. رسانیدن *risánídan.* } cause to arrive.

P. رسائی *rasáí.* Access.

A. رسائل *rasáïl.* Letters, treatises.

P. رست *rast.* Liberated, escaped.

P. رست *rust.* It grew; growing.

P. رستخیز *rastakhíz.* The resurrection.

P. رستخیز *rustakhíz.* Newly sprung up.

P. رستکار *rastakár.* Liberated, escaped.

P. رستم *rustam.* Rustam, the Persian Hercules.

P. رستن *rastan.* To escape.

P. رستن *rustan.* To grow.

P. رستن *ristan.* To twist, spin; to buzz.

P. رستنی *rustaní.* A vegetable.

P. رسد *rasad.* Supply of provisions.

A. رسغ *rusgh.* The wrist, fetlock.

A. رسل *rusul.* Prophets. (pl. of رسول.)

A. رسم *rasm.* A rule, custom. (pl. رسوم.)

A. رسم الخط *rasm ul khaṭṭ.* Prescribed form of writing.

A. رسماً *rasman.* Officially.

A. رسمی *rasmíy.* Customary.

A. رسمیات *rasmíyát.* Rules, usages.

A. P. رسن *rasan.* A rope, cord.

P. رسن گر *rasan-gar.* A rope-maker.

P. رسن لنگر *rasan i langar.* A ship's cable.

P. رسوا *ruswá.* Infamous, dishonoured.

P. رسوائی *ruswáí.* Infamy, disgrace.

A. رسوب *rusúb.* Sediments.

P. رسوخ *rusúkh.* Firmness, stability.

A. رسول *rasúl.* A messenger; a prophet.

A. رسوم *rusúm.* Customs, fees; diagrams.

P. رسیدن *rasídan.* To arrive.

P. رسید *rasíd.* A receipt; arrival.

P. رسیده *rasída.* Arrived; mature.

P. رسیدگی *rasídagí.* Maturity.

A. رش *rash.* Sprinkling, aspersion.

A. رشادت *rashádat.* Rectitude of conduct; bravery. نشان جلادت و رشادت *nishán i jeládat u rashádat.* Decorations for distinguished military service.

P. رشت *resht.* Very dry, friable, crumbling.

P. رشت *resht.* The capital of Ghílán.

P. رشتن *rishtan.* To spin, twist.

P. رشته *rishta.* A thread; relationship.

P. رشته دار *rishta-dár.* A relation.

A. رشح *rash.*
A. رشحه *rasḥah.* } Sprinkling, moistening.

A. رشد *rushd.* Rectitude; orthodoxy.

A. رشف *rashf.* A drop, sip.

P. رشك *rashk.* Jealousy, envy.

P. رشك خور *rashk-khur.* Envious.

A. رشوت *rishwat.* A bribe.

A. P. رشوت خوردن *rishwat khurdan.* To take a bribe.

A. رشید *rashíd.* Orthodox.

A. رصاد *raṣṣád.* An astronomical observer.

A. رصاص *raṣáṣ.* Lead; tin.

A. رصانت *raṣánat.* Solidity.

A. رصد *raṣad.* Observing (the stars).

A. P. رصد گاه *raṣad-gáh.* An observatory.

A. رصید *raṣíd.* Watching, observing.

A. رصین *raṣín.* Strong, solid.

A. رضا *riẓá.* Acquiescence, consent, leave.

A. P. رضا جوی *riẓá-júí.* Striving to please.

A. رضاع *reẓá'.* Suckling.

A. P. رضا مندی *riẓá-mandí.* Consent, permission; satisfaction.

A. رضیع *raẓí'.* A suckling infant.

A. رضیه *raẓíyeh.* Laudable.

A. رطب *raṭb.* Moist, tender, fresh.

A. رطوبت *ruṭúbat.* Moisture.

A. رعاف *ru'áf.* Bleeding at the nose.

A. رعایا *ra'áyá.* Subjects. (pl. of رعیة.)

A. رعایت *ri'áyat.* Care, attention, regard.

A. رعب *ra'b.* Terror, fear.

A. رعد *ra'd.* Thunder.

A. P. رعد صدا میکند *ra'd ṣadá mí kunad.* It thunders.

A. رعشه *ra'sha.* Tremour.

A. رعنا *ra'ná.* Beautiful, amiable.

A. رعونت *ru'únat.* Pride, haughtiness.

A. رعیت *ra'íyat.* A subject, peasant, ryot.

A. رغبت *raghbat.* Desire, avidity.

A. رغد *raghd.* Affluence.

A. رغم *raghm.* Abhorrence, contempt. علی رغم *'alá raghm.* In spite of.

A. رغوت *raghwat.* Froth (on milk).

A. رغیف *raghíf.* A thin cake.

A. رفاده *rifáda.* A bandage.

A. رفاقت *rifákat.* Society, companionship.

A. رفاهت *rafáhat,*
A. or رفاهیت *rafáhiyet.* } Comfort, tranquillity.

P. رفتار *raftár.* Walking; conduct.

P. رفتن *raftan.* To go, walk, proceed.

P. رفتن *ruftan.* To sweep.

P. رفته رفته *rafta rafta.* By degrees.

A. رفرف *rafraf.* A shelf; green cloth.

A. رفع *raf'.* Elevation; removing; decision.

A. رفعت *rif'at.* Sublimity, altitude.

A. رفق *rifḳ.* Benevolence.

A. رفقاء *rufaḳá'.* Companions.

A. رفقة *rafka.* A company of fellow-travellers; association, companionship.

P. رفو *rafú.* Sewing, darning.

P. رفو گر *rafú-gar.* A darner.

A. رفيع *rafí'.* High, elevated.

A. رفيق *rafík.* A friend, a companion.

A. رق *rakk.* Thin; parchment.

A. رق *rikk.* Servitude; thin.

A. رقاب *rikáb.* Guarding; necks. (pl. of رقبة *rakabat.*)

A. رقابت *rakábat.* Waiting, watching.

A. رقاص *rakkás.* A dancer.

A. رقاع *ruká'.* Short letters, notes. (pl. of رقعة.)

A. رقائق *rakáik.* Subtilties.

A. رقائم *rakáim.* Epistles, writings; sorts.

A. رقباء *rukabá'.* Watchers.

A. رقبه *rakbat.* The neck; a slave.

A. رقت *rikkat.* Pity; tenuity; delicacy.

A. رقص *raks.* A dance, dancing.

A. P. رقصيدن *ráksídan.* To dance.

A. رقعه *ruk'ah.* A short letter.

A. P. رقع بر رقع *ruk'ah bar ruk'ah.* Patch upon patch.

A. رقم *rakam.* Writing; a figure, notation; embroidery. An act (of a play). A letter written by a Prince of the blood Royal.

A. رقم پذير *rakam pazír.* Committed to writing.

A. P. رقم زدن *rakam zadan.* To write.

A. P. رقم زده *rakam zada.* Signed.

A. رقوم *rukúm.* Characters, inscriptions.

A. رقيب *rakíb.* A watcher, guardian; a rival, a competitor.

A. رقيه *rukyah.* Incantation, a spell.

A. رقيه *rikkíyat.* Slavery.

A. رقيق *rakík.* Thin, delicate.

A. رقيم *rakím.* A writing.

A. رقيمه *rakímah.* An epistle, writing.

A. ركاب *rikáb.* A stirrup.

P. ركاب *rikáb.* A dish, a plate.

A. P. ركابدار *rikáb-dár.* A butler; a stirrup-holder.

P. ركابي *rikábí.* A dish, plate.

A. ركاكت *rekákat.* Weakness, languor.

A. ركبة *rukbat.* The knee.

P. رگ *rag.* A vein.

P. رگ جان *rag i ján.* An artery.

P. رگ جهنده *rag i jihenda.* A pulsating artery.

P. رگ زدن *rag zadan.* To open a vein.

P. رگ زن *rag-zan*. A phlebotomist.

A. رکعه *ruk'ah*. An inclination of the body in prayer.

A. رکن *rukn*. A pillar; a foot (of verse).

A. رکن الدولة *rukn ud daulah*. Title given to Princes and other dignitaries in Persia.

A. رکوب *rukúb*. Riding.

A. رکوع *rukú'*. Performing a *rak'ah* q. v.

A. رکیدن *rakídan*. To mutter.

P. رکیک *rakík*. Thin, flimsy; weak, worthless.

P. رم *ram*. Elopement.

P. رم کردن *ram kerdan*. To run away (said of horses).

A. رماح *rimáḥ*. Spears.

A. رماد *ramád*. Ashes.

A. رمال *rammál*. A soothsayer, a fortune-teller; lit. one who practises *raml* or geomancy.

A. رمان *rummán*. A pomegranate.

P. رمان *ramán*. Timid, fugitive.

P. رمانیدن *ramánídan*. To terrify.

A. رمایت *rimáyet*. Shooting, archery.

A. رمائم *ramáim*. Rotten, corrupted things.

A. رمح *rumḥ*. A spear, a lance.

A. رمد *ramad*. Ophthalmia.

A. رمز *ramz*. A nod, signal; secret; cypher, cryptogram.

A. رمضان *ramaẓán*. The ninth Arabian month during which a fast is kept.

A. رمق *ramaḳ*. The last breath.

A. رمل *raml*. Sand.

A. رمل *ramal*. Geomancy.

A. رمنده *ramenda*. Timid, fugitive.

A. رموز *rumúz*. Signs, mysteries.

A. P. رموز دان *rumúz-dán*. Skilled in mysteries.

P. رمون *ramún*. Earnest money.

P. رمه *rama*. A herd, flock.

P. رمیدن *ramídan*. To be scared, to flee.

A. رمیز *ramíz*. Intelligent; moveable.

A. رمیم *ramím*. Putrid, carious.

P. رنج *ranj*. Distress, trouble.

P. رنجانیدن *ranjánídan*. To distress.

P. رنجش *ranjish*. Affliction, annoyance.

P. رنجش امیز *ranjish-ámíz*. Angry, annoyed.

P. رنجور *ranjúr*. Sick, afflicted.

P. رنجور دار *ranjúr-dár*. An attendant on the sick.

P. رنجه *ranja*. Trouble.

P. رنجیدن *ranjídan*. To be vexed.

P. رنجیده *ranjída*. Displeased, afflicted.

P. رند *rind*. A drunkard, debauchee.

P. رندش *randish.* Sawdust, shavings, filings, chips.

P. رنده *runda.* A joiner's plane.

P. رنگ *rang.* Colour, manner.

P. رنگا رنگ *rang-á-rang.* Of various sorts or kinds.

P. رنگ امیز *rang-ámíz.* Coloured, fickle.

P. رنگ امیزے *rang-ámízí.* Painting; stratagem.

P. رنگ پریدن *rang-parídan.* To grow pale.

P. رنگ ریز *rang-ríz.* A dyer.

P. رنگساز *rang-sáz.* A painter.

P. رنگ کردن *rang kerdan.* To paint.

P. رنگین *rangín.* Coloured, figurative; racy.

P. رو *rú.* The face, surface; motive, sake.

P. روا *ravá.* Allowable.

P. روا داشتن *ravá dáshtan.* To allow, sanction.

A. روابط *rawábiṭ.* Ligatures, conjunctions.

A. رواة *ruwát.* Historians, narrators. (pl. of راوی *ráwí.*)

A. رواج *rawáj.* Being current.

A. P. رواج داشتن *rawáj-dáshtan.* To be current.

A. رواحل *rawáḥil.* Caravans.

P. روا دار *ravá-dár.* Permitting.

P. روارو *ravá-rav.* Proceeding, travelling.

P. روارو *rú-á-rú.* Face to face.

A. روافض *rawáfiẓ.* Heretics.

A. رواق *riwáḳ.* A portico.

P. روان *raván.* The soul.

P. روان *raván.* Flowing, passing.

P. روان / روانه شدن *raván* or *ravána shudan.* To depart.

P. روان / روانه کردن *raván kerdan.* To send away.

P. روانه *ravána.* A passport.

P. روان اسا *raván-ásá.* Refreshing.

P. روانه کردن *ravána kerdan.* To despatch.

A. روایا *rawáyá.* Narrations, traditions.

A. روایت *riwáyat.* A tradition, relation. A various reading (in a manuscript).

A. روایح *rawáiḥ.* Odours.

P. روب *rúb.* Wipe or sweep thou, (in comp.) sweeping.

P. روبان *rúbán.* Sweeping.

P. روباه *rúbáh.* A fox.

P. روباه بازے *rúbáh-bází.* Craftiness.

P. رو برو *rú-ba-rú.* In presence of; face to face.

P. رو برو کردن *rú-ba-rú kerdan.* To confront.

P. رو بکار *rú-bakár.* Under consideration.

P. رو بکاری *rú-ba kárí.* Proceedings (of a lawsuit).

P. رو پوش *rú-púsh.* Absent, concealed.

P. روبه *rúbah*. See روباه.

P. روبهك *rúbahck*. A young fox, a cub.

P. رويدن *rúbídan*. To wipe, sweep.

H. روپيه *rúpiya*. A rupee.

A. روح *rúḥ*. The soul, spirit.

A. روحانى *rúḥání*. Spiritual.

A. روح الامين *rúḥ ul amín*. The faithful spirit, Gabriel.

A. روح القدس *rúḥ ul ḳuds*. The Holy Ghost.

A. روح الله *rúḥ ulláh*. The spirit of God; Jesus Christ.

A. P. روح حيوانى *rúḥ i ḥaiwání*. The animal spirit.

A. P. روح نباتى *ruḥ i nabátí*. The vegetable spirit.

P. رود *rúd*. A river.

P. رود *ravad*. He goes (from رفتن).

P. روداد *rú-dád*. A narrative; an event.

P. رو دادن *rú-dádan*. To happen.

P. رود بار *rúd-bár*. The bed of a river; abounding with rivers.

P. روده *rúda*. An intestine, a gut.

P. روز *rúz*. A day. در روز روشن *dar rúzi raushan*. By daylight. همه روز *hama rúz*. Every day, all day.

P. روز افزون *rúz-afzún*. Increasing daily.

P. روزانه *rúzána*. Daily.

P. روز بروز *rúz ba rúz*. Day after day.

P. روز پسين *rúz i pasín*. The last day.

P. روزبه *rúz-bih*. Improving daily.

P. روز داد *rúz i dád*. Day of retribution.

P. روز دار *rúz-dár*. A day-labourer.

P. روز كار *rúz-gár*. The world; service; time.

P. روز كار بردن *rúz-gar burdan*. To live, associate.

P. روز كور *rúz-kúr*. Purblind.

P. روز مره *rúz-marra*. Daily; common discourse.

P. روز مه *rúz i mah*. Day of the month, date.

P. روز ميدان *rúz i maidán*. The day of battle.

P. روزن *rauzan*. A window; chimney.

P. روز نامه *rúz-náma*.
P. روز نامچه *rúz námcha*.
A diary, a journal, an almanack.

P. روز نامه نويس *rúz-náma navís*. A government reporter.

P. رو نما *rú-numá*. A wedding present (from the bridegroom).

P. روزنه *rauzena*. A hole.

P. روزه *rúza*. Fasting.

P. روزه كرفتن *rúza giriftan*. To fast.

P. روزه خوردن *rúza khurdan*. To avoid fasting.

P. روزى *rúzí*. Daily; daily food.

P. روزے چند rúzí chand. Several days.

P. روزی خوار rúzí-kh'ár. An eater of daily bread, a living creature.

P. روزی دو سه ruzí dú sih. Two or three days.

P. روزی کناد rúzí kunád. May God prosper him!

P. روزينه rúzína. Daily allowance.

A. رءوس ru'ús. Heads.

A. روءسا rú'sá. Chiefs, leaders.

P. روسپی rúspí. A prostitute.

P. روستا rústá. } A village;
P. روستاءی rustáí. } a villager.

P. روستا زاده rústá-záda. Rustic, village-born.

P. روسیاه rú-siyáh. A sinner, criminal.

P. روش ravish. Mode, custom.

P. روشن raushan. Light, enlightened, manifest.

P. روشن کردن raushan kerdan. To light.

P. رو شناس rú-shinás. An acquaintance.

P. رو شناسی rú-shinásí. Acquaintance.

P. روشناءی rúshnáí. Light; ink.

P. روشندان raushan-dán. A sky-light.

P. روشن گهر raushan-guhar. Bright-souled, intelligent; sparkling like a gem.

P. روشنی raushaní. Light, splendour.

A. روضه rauzah. A garden.

P. روغن raughan. Oil, grease, varnish.

P. روغن تلخ raughan i talkh. Oil of mustard-seed.

P. روغن زرد raughan i zard. Melted or clarified butter.

P. روغن گرفتن raughan giriftan. To go into training (a horse); when trained it is called سوغانی sawagání.

P. روغنی rauganí. Oily, greasy.

A. رءوف ra'úf. Benign (God).

P. رءوفت ru'úfat. Benignity.

P. رو گردان rú-gardán. Disobedient.

P. رو گردانیدن rú-gardánídan. To desert, to abandon.

P. رو مال rú-mál. A handkerchief.

A. روم rúm. Greece, Asia Minor, Turkey.

A. رومی rúmí. Greek, Turkish.

P. رونده ravenda. A traveller; a passport.

A. رونق raunak. Splendour, elegance, beauty.

P. روئیده rú'ída. Growing, vegetating.

P. روئیدن rú'ídan. To grow, to vegetate.

P. روئین rú'ín. Brass.

P. روئین چنگ rú'ín-chang. Brazen-clawed.

P. رویندہ *rúyanda.* Growing.

P. روی *rúy.* The face, surface.

P. روِی *raví.* Thou goest (from رفتن).

P. از روی *az rú i.* By way of.

A. رویا *rúyá.* A dream.

A. رویت *rú'yat.* Sight, vision, opinion.

P. رویت *rúyat.* Thy face.

P. رویداد *rúydád.* State of facts.

P. روی زرد *rúy zard.* Pale-faced, ashamed.

P. رہ *rah.* A road.

P. رہا *rahá.* Liberated, escaped.

P. رہاندن *rahándan.* } To release.
P. رہا کردن *rahá kerdan.* }

P. رہاءی *rahái.* Liberation, escape.

A. رہبان *ruhbán.* Monks.

A. رہبانیت *ruhbániyet.* Monasticism, monkery.

P. رہبر *rah-bar.* A guide.

P. رہبردن *rah-burdan.* To find the way.

P. رہبرے *rah-barí.* Guidance.

P. رہدار *rah-dár.* See راہدار.

P. رہ رو *rah-rav.* A traveller.

P. رہ زن *rah-zan.* A highway-robber.

P. رہ کزر *rah guzar.* A high road.

A. رہن *rahn.* A pledge, pawn.

P. رہ نما *rah-numá.* A guide.

P. رہوار *rah-vár.* An ambling horse.

P. رہور *rah-var.* A traveller; a guide.

P. رہی *rahí.* A servant, a slave.

P. رہیدن *rahídan.* To escape, to be liberated.

A. رہین *rahín.* Pledged, pawned.

P. ری *rai.* Rai, the ancient Rhagis, the ruins of which are near Teheran.

A. رياء *riyá'.* Hypocrisy.

A. رياح *riyáḥ.* Winds; odours.

A. رياحين *riyáḥín.* Odoriferous herbs.

A. رياست *riyásat.* Government, sway.

A. رياض *riáẓ.* Gardens, meadows. (pl. of روضه.)

A. رياضت *riyáẓat.* Abstinence, austerity.

A. P. رياضت كش *riyáẓat kish.* Practising austerity.

A. رياضی *riyáẓí.* Mathematics.

A. P. ريا كار *riyá-kár.* A hypocrite.

P. ريال *riyál.* A dollar.

نيم ريال *ním-riyál.* A half-dollar.

A. ريان *raiyán.* Fresh.

A. ريب *raib.* Doubt, suspicion.

A. ريح *ríḥ.* Wind; odour.

A. ريحان *raiḥán.* Sweet basil, or any odoriferous herb.

P. ريختن *rikhtan.* To pour; to break in pieces.

A. ريخته *ríkhta.* Scattered, crumbled, spilt; mortar; the mixed dialect of Hindústání, also called Urdú.

P. ريدن *rídan.* *Stercorare.*

P. ريزان *rízán.* Pouring, scattering.

P. ريزش *rízish.* Effusion.

P. ريزه *ríza.* A fragment, chip. حساب ريزه *ḥisáb i ríza.* The items of an account.

P. ريزه خور *ríza-khur.* A gleaner.

P. ريستن *rístan.* To twist.

P. ريسمان *rísmán.* A rope, cord, thread.

P. ريسيدن *rísídan.* To twist, spin.

P. ريش *rísh.* A beard.

P. ريش *rísh.* A wound, a sore; (in comp.) wounded, sore.

P. ريشخند *rísh-khand.* Ridicule; flattery.

P. ريشم *rísham.* Silk.

P. ريشه *rísha.* Fibre; fringe.

P. ريعان *raiʿán.* The flower of youth; shining.

P. ريغ *rígh.* Hatred, malevolence.

A. ريق *rík.* Spittle, saliva. على ريق *ʿalá rík.* On an empty stomach, fasting.

P. ريك *ríg.* Sand.

P. ريكا *ríká.* A police-agent.

P. T. ريكا باشى *ríká-báshí.* Chief of the agents of police.

P. ريك دان *ríg-dán.* A sand- or pounce-box.

P. ريك زار *ríg-zár.* A sandy region.

P. ريم *rím.* Pus, matter.

P. ريو *rív.* Fraud, deceit.

P. ريوند *rívand.* Rhubarb.

P. ريوند چينى *rívand i chíní.* China rhubarb.

A. رئيس *raís.* A chief, leader, head.

A. رئيس دولت جمهور *raís i daulat i jamhúr.* President of the Republic.

A. P. رئيس مدرسه دار العلوم *raís i madrasa i dar ul ʿulúm.* The Rector of a University.

ز

ز *zain.* Z. The eleventh letter of the Arabic and thirteenth of the Persian alphabets.

ژ *zhá.* Zh. The fourteenth letter of the Persian alphabet.

P. ز *zi.* See از.

A. زابل *zábil.* Short, dwarfish.

P. زاج *záj.* Vitriol.

P. A. زاج ابيض *záj i abyaz.* Alum.

P. زاج سبز *záj i sabz.* Green vitriol.

P. زاج كبود *záj i kabúd.* Blue vitriol.

A. زاحف *záḥif.* Fatigued.

A. زاخر *zákhir.* Full; swelling (the sea).

A. زاد *zád.* Provisions for a journey.

P. زاد *zád.* (In comp.) born.

P. زاد بوم *zád-búm.* Native country.

P. A. زاد راه *zád i ráh.* Provision for a journey.

P. زادگی *zádagí.* Birth.

P. زادن *zádan.* To be born, to beget.

P. زاد و بود *zád u búd.* Goods and chattels.

P. زاده *záda.* Born; offspring.

P. زار *zár.* Lamentation; (in comp.) a place where anything grows, as لاله زار *lála-zár.* A tulip-bed.

P. زار زار *zár-zár.* Great lamentation.

P. زاری *zárí.* Lamentation.

P. زاریدن *zárídan.* To lament, to cry.

P. ژاژ *zházh.* Idle speech.

A. ژاژ خای *zházh-kháy.* A trifle, idle speaker.

P. زاغ *zágh.* A crow, a raven.

P. زاغر *zághar.* The crop of a bird.

P. زاگ *zág.* Vitriol.

P. زاگاب *zág-áb.* Water of vitriol.

P. زال *zál.* An old man, or woman; the father of the hero Rustam.

P. زالو *zálú.* A leech.

P. زالو انداختن *zálú an-dákhtan.* To apply leeches.

P. ژاله *zhála.* Hail, dew.

P. زان *zán.* From that.

P. زانکه *zánki.* From that time, since.

P. زانو *zánú.* The knee.

P. زانو زدن *zánú-zadan.* To sit on the hams, to kneel.

A. زانی *zání.* An adulterer.

A. زانیه *zániyeh.* An adulteress.

P. زاولانه *záwalána.* A fetter, a chain.

A. زاویه *záwiyeh.* An angle, corner.

A. P. زاویهٔ قائمه *záwiyeh i ḳáïmah.* A right angle.

A. P. زاویهٔ حاده *záwiyeh i ḥáddeh.* An acute angle.

A. P. زاویهٔ منفرجه *záwiyeh i munfarijah.* An obtuse angle.

A. زاهد *záhid.* A hermit, a devotee.

A. زاهدانه *záhidana.* Like a recluse.

A. زاهدی *záhidí.* The life of a recluse.

A. زاهر *záhir.* Shining, vivid, florid.

A. زاهری *záhirí.* Fragrance; clearness.

P. زائدگی *záïdagí.* Childbirth.

P. زائدن *záïdan.* To bring forth young, to be born.

P. زایچه *záiche.* Horoscope; one's natal star.

A. زائد *záïd.* Redundant, additional.

A. زاید الوصف *záïd ul waṣf.* Beyond description.

A. زایر *záïr.* A visitor; pilgrim.

A. زایل *záïl.* Transitory; exterminated.

P. زاینده *záyenda.* Bringing forth, productive. Unfailing (a spring or well).

P. زائیده *záïda.* Bringing forth, begotten.

A. زباد *zabád.* Civet.

P. زبان *zabán.* The tongue, language.

P. زبان آور *zabán-ávar.* Fluent in speech.

P. زبان بریده *zabán-burída.* Tongue-tied, silent.

P. زبان دادن *zabán-dádan.* To promise.

P. زبان دان *zabán-dán.* A linguist.

P. زبان دراز *zabán-daráz.* Abusive.

P. زبان رانی *zabán-rání.* Conversation.

P. زبان زده *zabán-zada.* Spoken of.

P. زبان کشادن *zabán-kushádan.* To speak, to open one's mouth.

P. زبان کوفتن *zabán-kúftan.* To stammer.

P. زبان گیر *zabán-gír.* A spy; a caviller; stammering.

P. زبانه *zabána.* A flame.

P. زبانی *zabání.* Verbal.

A. زبد *zabad.* Butter; froth.

A. زبده *zubdah.* Cream; the best part of anything.

P. زبر *zabar.* Above, superior; the vowel point *fatḥah* ´

P. زبر تنگ *zabar-tang.* A surcingle, girth.

P. زبرجد *zabarjad.* A topaz.

P. زبردست *zabar-dast.* Powerful, strong; overbearing.

P. زبر دستی *zabar-dastí.* Force, oppression.

P. زبرین *zabarín.* Superior, upper.

P. زبل *zibl.* Dung, manure.

A. زبور *zabúr.* The psalms of David.

P. زبون *zabún.* Bad, vile, ill.

P. زبونی *zabúní.* Badness.

A. زبیب *zabíb.* Raisins.

P. زپای در آوردن *zi páï dar áwardan.* To throw down.

P. زپس *zi pas.* After, behind.

A. زجاج *zujáj.* Glass.

A. زجاج *zajjaj.* A glass-blower.

A. زجاجه *zujájah.* A bit of glass, a wine-glass.

A. زجر *zajar* or *zajr.* Threatening, molesting.

P. زجه *zaja,* } A woman
P. زچه *zacha.* } in childbed.

A. زحل *zuḥal.* The planet Saturn.

A. زحمت *zaḥmat.* Disquietude.

A. زحمت دادن *zaḥmat dádan.* To give trouble.

A. زحمت كشيدن *zaḥmat keshí-dan.* To take trouble.

A. زحير *zaḥír.* Twisting of the guts, dysentery.

A. زخارف *zakhárif.* Ornaments, embellishments. (pl. of زخرف *zakhraf.*)

P. زخم *zakhm.* A wound, sore.

P. زخمه *zakhma.* The bow of a violin, &c.

P. زخمخورده *zakhm-khurda.*
P. زخم دار *zakhm-dár.*
P. زخم زده *zakhm-zada.*
P. زخمى *zakhmí.*
Wounded.

A. زخيخ *zakhíkh.* Flaring.

P. زد *zad.* Striking; a blow.

P. زدا *zidá.* Polishing; scouring.

P. زدن *zadan.* To strike, beat.

P. زد و خورد *zad u khurd.* Conflict, battle.

P. زودن *zúdan.* To polish; to erase.

P. زد و كوب *zad u kúb.* Beating, assault and battery.

P. زر *zar.* Gold, money.

P. A. زر اصل *zar i aṣal.* Principal sum.

A. زراعت *zirá'at.* Agriculture.

P. زراف *zaráf.* The camelopard.

P. زر اندودن *zar andúdan.* To gild; to acquire money.

P. زر بفت *zar-baft.* Cloth of gold:

P. A. زر جعفرى *zar i ja'farí.* The purest gold.

P. زرد *zard.* Yellow, pale, vivid.

P. زرد آب *zard-áb.* Gall, bile.

P. زرد آلو *zard-álú.* An apricot.

P. زرد چوب *zard-chúb.* Turmeric.

P. زرد رو *zard-rú.* Pale, bashful.

P. زرد فام *zard-fám.* Yellowish.

P. زردك *zardak.* A carrot.

P. زر دوز *zar-dúz.* Embroidered with gold.

P. زر دوزى *zar-dúzí.* Gold embroidery.

P. زرده دهى *zarda-dihí.* Pure gold.

P. زردى *zardí.* Yellowness.

P. زر سرخ *zar i surkh.* Red gold.

P. زرشك *zirishk.* Barberries.

P. زر شناس *zar-shinás.* A banker or goldsmith.

A. زرع *zar'.* A sown field.

P. ژرف *zharf.* Deep, steep.

P. ژرفا *zharfá.* Depth.

P. زرفان *zarfán.* A decrepit old man.

P. زرق *zarḳ.* Deceit.

P. A. زرق برق *zarḳ-barḳ.* Glittering, magnificence.

P. A. زر قلب *zar i ḳalb.* Base coin.

P. زرك *zarak.* Gold-dust.

P. زر کار *zar-kár.* Gilt.

P. زر گر *zar-gar.* A goldsmith.

P. زر گری *zar-garí.* The business of a goldsmith.

P. زر کش *zar-kash.* A gold-wire-drawer.

P. زر کوفت *zar-kúft.* Plated with gold.

P. زر مغربی *zar i maghribí.* Pure gold.

P. زرنك *zarank.* Magnificence; intelligent.

P. زر نگار *zar-nigár.* Inlaid with gold, gilded.

P. زرنیخ *zarníkh.* Orpiment; gold paint.

P. زره *zireh.* Armour, mail.

P. زرین *zarín.* Golden.

P. زستن *zistan.* To live.

P. زشت *zisht.* Ugly, bad.

P. زشت خوی *zisht-khúy.* Ill-tempered.

P. زشتی *zishtí.* Deformity, ugliness.

A. زعاف *zuʻáf.* Sudden death.

A. زعرور *zaʻrúr.* A medlar.

A. زعزع *zaʻzaʻ.* A hurricane.

A. زعفران *zaʻfarán.* Saffron.

A. زعم *zaʻm* or *zuʻm.* Opinion, arrogance.

P. زغال *zughál.* Live embers.

P. زغن *zaghan.* A kite.

P. زغند *zaghand.* A jump, leap.

A. زفاف *zifáf.* Matrimonial consummation.

A. زق *zikk.* A skin for holding any liquid.

A. زقوم *zakkúm.* A thorny tree.

A. زکاء *zaká.* Being pure, pious, just.

A. زکات *zakát.* Alms; purity.

A. زکام *zukám.* Defluxion. a catarrh.

A. زکاوت *zakáwat.* Ingenuity; purity.

A. زکوت *zakát.* Alms of a 40th part (see زکات).

P. زکور *zakúr.* A miser; a curling lock.

A. زکی *zakíy.* Ingenious, pure, pious.

P. زکیدن *zakídan.* To mutter in a rage.

P. زگیل *zigíl.* A wart.

A. زل *zall.* A slip, error. (pl. زلات *zallát.*)

A. زلازل *zalázil.* Trembling, earthquakes.

A. زلال *zulál.* Limpid water.

A. زلزال *zalzál.* Tremour, agitation.

A. زلزله *zilzilah.* An earthquake.

A. زلط *zalt.* A quick pace.

P. زلف *zulf.* A ringlet.

A. زلل *zalal.* Erring, blundering.

P. زلو *zalú.* A leech.

A. زلیخا *zuleikhá.* Potiphar's wife.

P. زم *zam.* Cold; a cheek, a jaw.

A. زمام *zimám.* A bridle, a rein. (pl. ازمة *azimmat.*)

A. زمان *zamán.* Time, an age; the world.

P. زمانه *zamána.* Time; fortune; calamity.

P. زمانه ساز *zamána-sáz.* A time-server.

P. زمانی *zamání.* Temporal, worldly.

P. زمانیان *zamániyán.* People of the world.

P. زمخک *zumukhk.* Astringent, styptic.

A. زمرد *zumurrud.* An emerald.

P. زمردین *zumurrudín.* Emerald-coloured.

A. زمرة *zumra.* A body of men.

A. زمزم *zemzem.* A famous well at Mecca.

A. زمزمه *zemzemeh.* Murmur; modulation.

P. زمستان *zamistán* The winter.

A. زمم *zamam.* Intention, design.

A. زمن *zaman.* Time.

P. زمیدن *zamídan.* To chew.

P. زمین *zamín.* The earth, soil.

A. زمین دار *zamín-dár.* A landholder.

P. زن *zan.* A woman.

A. زنا *ziná.* Adultery.

A. زنابیر *zanábír.* Wasps. (pl. of زنبور *zambúr.*)

A. زنادیق *zanádíḳ.* Pagans, heretics; pl. of *zindíḳ.*

A. زنار *zunnár.* The Brahminical thread; the guebre's belt.

A. P. زنار دار *zunnár dár.* One who wears the thread last mentioned.

A. P. زنا کار *ziná-kár.* An adulterer, a fornicator.

P. زنانه *zanána.* Womanly; a seraglio.

P. زن بار دار *zan i bár-dár.* A pregnant woman.

A. زنبور *zambúr.* A wasp, &c.

A. P. زنبور خانه *zambúr-khána.* A wasp's nest.

A. P. زنبور سرخ *zambúr i surkh.* A hornet.

A. زنبور عسل *zambúr i 'asal.* A bee.

T. P. زنبورك *zambúrak.* A small cannon carried on a camel's back.

P. زنبوره *zambúra.* A kind of guitar; a bee.

P. زنبیل *zambíl.* A basket.

A. زنجار *zinjár.* Verdigris.

A. زنجبیل *zanjabíl.* Dry ginger.

P. زنجرف *zinjarf.* Red lead, vermilion.

P. زنجف *zinjaf.* Lining for a fringe, edging.

P. زنچه *zanche.* A prostitute.

A. زنجیر *zinjír.* A smack of the fingers.

P. زنجیر *zanjír.* A chain.

P. زنجیره *zanjíra.* Lace.

P. زنخ *zanakh.* The chin.

P. زنخدان *zanakh-dán.* The pit or dimple in the chin.

P. زن خواستن *zan khástan.* To marry.

P. زند اوستا *zend-ávesta.* The book of Zoroaster.

P. زند *zend.* The book of Zoroaster; a steel (for striking fire with).

P. زندان *zindán.* A prison.

P. زندانیان *zindániyán.* Prisoners.

P. زند خوان *zend-khan.* A follower of the Zendavesta.

P. زندگانی *zindagání.* Life, living, subsistence.

P. زندگانی دوم *zindagání i duvam.* The next life.

P. زندگی *zindagí.* Life, existence.

P. زندوست *zan-dúst.* Addicted to women.

P. زنده *zinda.* Living, alive.

P. ژنده *zhanda.* Old, patched.

P. زنده گشتن *zinda gashtan.* To revive, to come to life.

P. زنده دل *zinda-dil.* A man of piety.

P. زنده کردن *zinda kerdan.* To animate, enliven.

P. زندیق *zindík.* A fire-worshipper; atheist.

A. P. زنقحبه *zan-kahbah.* One whose wife is disreputable.

P. زنگ *zang.* Rust; a small bell.

P. زنگ خورده *zang-khurda.* Corroded, rusted.

P. زن کردن *zan kerdan,*
P. زن گرفتن *zan giriftan.*
To marry.

P. زنگوله *zangúla.* A little bell, a rattle, a musical note.

P. زنگه *zangah* for زانگاه *zángáh.* From that time.

P. زنگی *zangí.* An Ethiopian, negro.

P. زننده *zanenda.* Striking, a striker.

P. زنهار *zinhár.* Protection. (An exclamation) Take care!

P. زو *zú.* From him.

A. زواجر *zawájir.* Admonitions.

A. زواد *zawád.* Provision.

A. زوار *zawwár.* Pilgrims.

A. زوال *zawál.* Decline, decadence.

P. زواله *zawála.* A globular mass of leaven.

A. زوان *zawán.* Darnel; tares; a flame.

A. زواهر *zawáhir.* Flowers, ornaments.

A. زوایا *zawáyá.* Corners, angles. (pl. of زاویة.)

A. زوائد *zawáid.* Superfluities. (pl. of زائدة.)

A. زوج *zauj.* A pair; a husband.

A. زوجه *zauja.* A wife.

P. زود *zúd.* Soon, quick, swift.

P. زودی *zúdí.* Haste, swiftness.

P. زور *zúr.* Strength; violence, power.

P. زور آزما *zúr ázmá.* An athlete, a wrestler.

P. زور آور *zúr-ávar.* Powerful, robust; violent.

P. زور آوری *zúr-ávarí.* Violence, strength.

P. زور خانه *zúr-khána.* A gymnasium.

P. زورق *zaurak.* A ship, vessel.

P. زورمند *zúr-mand.* Strong, powerful.

P. زور مندے *zúr-mandí.* Strength, violence.

P. زوره *zaura.* The backbone.

P. زولانه *zaulána.* A fetter.

P. ژولیدن *zhúlídan.* To be entangled or intricate.

P. ژولیده *zhúlída.* Intricate, entangled.

P. زه *zih.* A bow-string; brink of a well; excellence. Bravo!

A. زهاد *zuhád.* Recluses. (pl. of زاهد.)

A. زهادت *zahádat.* A religious life.

P. زهار *zahár.* The lower parts of the belly.

A. زهد *zuhd.* The life of a recluse.

P. زهدان *zihdán.* The womb.

P. زهر *zahr.* Poison, venom.

A. زهره *zahra.* A flower; beauty, grace.

P. زهر دار *zahr-dár.* Venomous, poisonous.

P. زهر دارو *zahr-dárú.* Bezoar; an antidote against poison.

P. زهر ناك *zahr-nák.* Poisoned, envenomed.

P. زهره *zahra.* The gall-bladder; bile; choler.

P. زهره *zuhra.* The planet Venus.

P. زهگیر *zih-gír.* A thumb-stall for archers.

A. زهور *zuhúr.* Shining (as a lamp, &c.)

P. زهی *zihí.* O excellent! bravo!

P. زهیدن *zihídan.* To bring forth young.

P. زی *zí.* Life.

P. زی *zí.* Limit, side.

A. زیاد *ziyád.* Augmentation, excess. لطف شما زیاد *lutf i shumá ziyád.* Thank you.

A. زیادت *ziyádat.* Increase, abundance.

A. زیاده *ziyáda.* More, much.

A. P. زیاده سری *ziyáda-sarí.* Vanity, conceit.

A. زیارت *ziyárat.* Pilgrimage, visiting.

P. زیان *ziyán.* Damage, loss.

P. ژیان *zhiyán.* Fierce, furious.

P. زیان کار *ziyán-kár.* Hurtful; a sinner.

P. زیب *zíb.* Ornament, elegance, beauty.

P. زیبا *zíba.* Beautiful, adorned.

P. زیبائے *zíbáí*. Beauty, gracefulness.

P. زیبق *zíbak*. Quicksilver.

P. زیبنده *zíbenda*. Adorning.

P. زیب و زینت *zíb u zínat*. Grace and beauty.

P. زیبیدن *zíbídan*. To adorn, to suit. این از برای شما می زیبد *ín az baráí shumá mí zíbad*. This suits you.

A. زیت *zeit*. Olive-oil.

A. زیتون *zeitún*. An olive.

P. زیچ *zích*. An ephemeris; a mason's rule.

A. زید *zeid*. A fictitious name employed in scholastic and legal treatises.

P. زیر *zír*. Under, below; the vowel point ِ.

P. زیرا *zírá*. Because.

P. زیراکه *zíráki*. Because that, since.

P. زیر بار *zír-bár*. In embarrassed circumstances, indebted.

P. زیر بند *zír-band*. A martingale.

P. زیر پوش *zír-púsh*. An under garment.

P. زیر جامه *zír-jáma*. Breeches, drawers.

P. زیر چوب *zír-chúb*. Under correction.

P. زیر دست *zír-dast*. A subject; under command.

P. زیر زمین *zír-zamín*. An underground cellar or cave.

P. زیرك *zírak*. Intelligent, sagacious.

P. زیرکی *zírakí*. Sagacity.

P. زیر و بالا *zír u bálá*,
P. زیر و زبر *zír u zabar*.
Topsy-turvy.

P. زیره *zíra*. Cummin-seed, aniseed.

P. زیرهٔ رومی *zíra i Rúmí*. Carraway-seed.

P. زیرین *zírín*. Inferior.

P. زیست *zíst*. Life, existence.

P. زیستن *zístan*. To live.

P. زیش *zísh*. A pipe; a little tube.

P. زیغال *zíghál*. A cup, a goblet.

P. زین *zín*. From this; a saddle.

P. زین پوش *zín-púsh*. A saddle-cloth.

A. زینب *zeinab*. A woman's name.

A. زینت *zínat*. Ornament; decoration.

P. زین ساز *zín-sáz*.
P. زین گر *zín-gár*.
A saddler.

P. زینهار *zínhár*. Care, caution, defence.

P. زینه *zína*. A ladder, stairs, steps.

P. زیو *zív*. A ship-worm; deceit.

P. زیور *zíwar*. Jewels, ornaments.

س

س *sín.* S. The twelfth letter of the Arabic, and fifteenth of the Persian alphabets.

P. سا *sá.* (In comp.) like, resembling.

P. سا *sá.* Tribute.

A. سابع *sábi'.* The seventh.

A. سابغ *sábigh.* Ample, full.

A. سابق *sábiḳ.* Preceding, former.

A. سابقا *sábiḳan.* Before this, formerly.

A. سابقه *sábiḳá.* The past. مسبوق بسابقه *masbúḳ ba sábiḳa.* Based on a precedent.

A. سابقين *sábiḳín.* Predecessors.

P. سابو دانه *sábú-dána.* Sago.

P. سابوره *sábúra.* A hermaphrodite, a sodomite.

A. ساتر *sátir.* Covering, hiding.

P. ساتكين *sát-gín.* A cup, a bumper.

P. ساج *sáj.* The teak-tree.

A. ساجد *sájid.* Prostrate, adoring.

A. ساجع *sáji'.* Speaking rhythmically.

A. ساحت *sáḥat.* An area, a plain.

A. ساحر *sáḥir.* A magician.

A. ساحق *sáḥiḳ.* One who brays, grinds or pounds.

A. ساحل *sáḥil.* The shore.

P. ساختن *sákhtan.* To make, to do.

P. ساخته *sákhta.* Made, artificial.

A. ساخر *sákhir.* A mocker.

A. سادات *sádát.* Princes. (pl. of سيد.)

P. سادج *sádij.* Indian spikenard.

A. سادس *sádis.* The sixth.

P. سادگی *sádagí.* Artlessness, plainness.

P. ساده *sáda.* Plain, simple, artless.

P. ساده دل *sáda-dil.* A simpleton. Sincere.

P. ساده رو *sáda-ru.* Beardless, smooth-faced.

P. سار *sár.* (In comp.) abounding in. A starling; a camel.

P. سارا *sárá.* Pure, excellent.

P. سار بان *sár-bán.* A camel-driver.

A. سارق *sárik.* A thief.

P. سارك *sárak.* A species of starling.

A. ساری *sárí.* Pervading; infecting.

P. ساز *sáz.* Apparatus, musical instrument. (In comp.) making, doing.

P. سازش *sázish.* Combination, collusion.

P. ساز كار *sáz-kár.* Salutary, proper, salubrious.

P. ساز كاری *sáz-kárí.* Concordance.

P. سازنده *sázenda.* A maker; a musician.

P. سازیدن *sázídan.* To make.

P. ساس *sás.* A bug, a louse.

A. ساطع *sáṭiʿ.* Shining, clear, evident.

A. ساطور *sáṭúr.* A butcher's knife.

A. ساعات *sáʿát.* Hours; a clock.

A. ساعت *sáʿat.* An hour; a space of time. A watch. چند ساعت است *chand sáʿaṭ ast.* What o'clock is it? یك ساعت *yek sáʿat.* One o'clock. یك ربع ساعت *yek rubʿ sáʿat.* A quarter of an hour. نیم ساعت *ním-sáʿat.* Half an hour. ساعت تند کار می کند *sáʿat tund-kár mí kunad.* The watch is fast. ساعت کند کار می کند *sáʿat kund-kár mí kunad.* The watch is too slow. ساعت را کوك کردن *sáʿat-rá kúk kerdan.* To wind up a watch.

A. ساعت بساعت *sáʿat ba sáʿat.* Hourly.

A. P. ساعت ساز *sáʿat-sáz.* A watch-maker.

A. ساعد *sáʿid.* The forearm.

A. ساعور *sáʿúr.* A furnace, a stove.

A. ساعی *sáʿiy.* Assiduous.

P. ساغر *sághir.* A cup, bowl, goblet.

A. سافر *sáfir.* A traveller.

A. سافل *sáfil.* The inferior part, mean.

A. ساق *sáḳ.* The leg, stem, stalk.

A. ساقط *sáḳiṭ.* Fallen.

A. ساقی *sáḳí.* A cup-bearer.

A. ساکب *sákib.* Flowing (blood or water).

A. ساکت *sákit.* Silent.

A. ساکن *sákin.* Quiescent (a letter); an inhabitant.

A. ساکوت *sákút.* A silent man.

A. سال *sál.* A year.

A. سالار *sálár.* A chief, leader.

A. سالانه *sálána.* Yearly.

A. سالب *sálib.* A plunderer, ravisher.

P. سال خورده *sal-khúrda.* Very old.

P. A. سال شمسی *sál i shamsíy.* A solar year.

A. سالف *sálif.* Preceding, predecessor.

P. A. سال قمری *sál i ḳamaríy.* A lunar year.

A. سالك *sálik.* A traveller, a disciple.

P. سالگی *salagí.* (In composition) age.

P. سالم *sálim.* Safe; entire, perfect.

P. سال ماه *sál-máh.* Date of the year and month. Continually.

P. سالوس *sálús.* Hypocritical, deceitful.

P. سالوس *sálús.* Deceit, hypocrisy.

P. سالوك *sálúk.* A highway robber; courteous.

P. ساله *sála.* The rear of an army; age, years.

P. سالها *sálhá.* Years.

P. سالی *sálí.* A year. سالی چند *sálí chand.* A few years.

P. سالیان *sáliyán.* Years; life.

P. سالیانه *sáliyána.* Salary.

A. سام *sám.* Shem, the son of Noah; gold.

P. سام *sám.* Sám, a Persian hero, grandfather of Rustam.

P. ساماخچه *sámákhche.* A bodice.

P. سامان *sámán.* Furniture, proportion.

A. سامح *sámiḥ.* Liberal; affable, gentle.

A. سامع *sámiʿ.* A hearer.

A. سامعه *sámiʿah.* The sense of hearing.

A. سامن *sámin.* Fat, plump.

A. سامی *sámí.* Sublime, exalted.

P. سان *sán.* A whetstone; (in comp.) mode, like, manner.

P. سان دادن *sán-dádan.* To review troops.

A. سانحه *sániḥah.* A casualty.

P. سای *sáy.* Filing, polishing, rubbing.

P. سایان } *sáyabán.* A canopy, a parasol.
P. سایه بان }

A. سایر *sáir.* Travelling; the whole; the remainder; tax, custom.

A. سایق *sáiḳ.* Driving; one who pursues another.

A. سایل *sáil.* Flowing; a question; a beggar.

P. سایه *sáya.* Shade, shadow; protection. سایه شما کم نشود *sáya i shumá kem nashawad.* May I never be deprived of your protection.

P. سایه پرورده *sáya-parvarda.* Brought up delicately.

P. سائیدن *sáidan.* To grind.

A. سائیس *sáis.* A groom.

A. سب *sabb.* Reviling; reproach.

P. سپا *sipá.* A trivet, a tripod.

A. سبابه *sabbába.* The forefinger.

P. سپارش *sipárish.* A recommendation.

P. سبار یدن *sabárídan.* To plough, break ground.

P. سپاریدن *sipárídan.* To give in charge; to recommend.

P. سپاس *sipás.* Thanksgiving.

A. سباسب *sabásob.* Deserts.

A. سباع *sibáʿ.* Beasts of prey. (pl. of سبع *sabuʿ.*)

A. سباك *sabbák.* A melter, a smelter.

P. سپاه *sipáh.* A soldier; an army.

P. سپاهگری *sipáhgarí.* Soldiership.

P. سپاهی *sipáhí.* A soldier.

A. سبب *sabab.* Cause, motive.

A. سبحان الله *subḥán Alláh.* Gracious God!

A. سبحه *subha.* A rosary for prayers.

P. سبد *sabad.* A basket.

P. سپر *sipar.* A shield.

P. سپر انداختن *sipar andákhtan.* To submit.

P. سپر باز *sipar-báz.* A skilful warrior.

P. سپرد *sipurd.* Trust.

P. سپردن *sipurdan.* To entrust, to consign.

P. سپردنی *sipurdaní.* Fit to be trusted.

P. سپرز *supurz.* The spleen.

P. سپری شدن *siparí shudan.* To be finished.

P. سبز *sabz.* Green.

P. سبزه *sabza.* Verdure.

P. سبزی *sabzí.* Greenness, verdure; greens.

P. سپس *sipas.* After, afterwards.

A. سبط *sabt.* A daughter's son; a tribe.

A. سبع *sab'.* Seven.

A. سبعین *sab'ín.* Seventy.

A. سبق *sabk.* Pre-eminence; a lesson.

A. P. سبق بردن *sabk burdan.* To surpass, overcome.

A. P. سبقت *sabkat.* Precedence.

A. P. سبقت گرفتن *sabkat giriftan.* To take precedence of, to anticipate.

P. سبك *sabuk.* Light, not heavy; unsteady.

P. سبك پا *sabuk-pá.* Swift-footed.

P. سبکبار *sabuk-bár.* Unencumbered.

P. سبك پر *sabuk-par.* Swift-winged.

P. سبك خیز *sabuk-khíz.* Vigilant.

P. سبك دست *sabuk-dast.* Expert.

P. سبك روح *sabuk-rúh.* Light-souled, merry, jovial.

P. سبك سار *sabuk-sár.* Light-headed; contemptible.

P. سبك سیر *sabuk-sír.* Soon satisfied.

P. سبکی *sabukí.* Levity; disgrace.

A. سبل *subul.* Ways. (pl. of سبیل.)

A. سبلت *sabalat.* Whiskers, mustachios.

A. سپنج *sipanj.* A loan.

P. سپنجی سرای *sipanjí saráy.* This world.

P. سبو *sabú.* A jar, a goblet.

P. سپوختن *sabúkhtan.* To pierce.

P. سبوس *sabús.* Bran.

P. سبوسه *sabúsa.* Scurf on the head.

P. سپه *sipah.* An army.

P. سپهبد *sipah-bad.* A general; an emperor.

P. سپهر *sipihr.* The sphere; time; a halting-place where one stays for a few days only.

P. سپه سالار *sipah-sálár.* Commander of an army.

P. سپه کش *sipah-kash.* A general.

P. سپید *sapeid.* White (see سفید).

P. سپید اب *sapeid-áb.* White-lead.

P. سپیده دم *sapeida-dam.* Day-break.

A. سبیل *sabíl.* A road; mode.

A. ست *sitt.* Six.

P. ستا *sitá.* (In comp.) one who praises.

P. ستادن *sitádan.* To stand; to carry away.

P. ستار *sitár.* A kind of guitar.

P. ستاره *sitára.* A star.

P. ستارهٔ دم دار *sitára ï dum-dár.* A comet.

P. ستان *sitán.* Seizing, captivating.

P. ستان *-stán.* A termination signifying place, country, &c., as گلستان *gulistán.* A rose-garden. هندوستان *Hindústán.* India.

P. ستاندن *sitándan.* To seize, to take.

P. ستائیدن *sitáïdan.* To praise.

P. ستایش *sitáyish.* Praise.

P. ستبر *sitabr.* Thick, coarse.

P. ستبری *sitabri.* Thickness, coarseness.

P. ستدن *sitadan.* To take, seize.

A. ستر *sitr.* A veil, a covering.

P. ستر *sutur.* Shaving; a razor.

P.ستردن *suturdan.* To shave, to scrape.

P. سترگ *suturg.* Bulky, big; brave.

P. ستم *sitam.* Oppression.

P. ستم دیده *sitam-dída.* Oppressed.

P. ستم کار *sitam-kár.* A tyrant.

P. ستودن *sitúdan.* To praise.

P. ستوده *sitúda.* Praised, laudable.

P. ستوده مال *sitúda-ma'ál.* Of happy issue.

P. ستور *sutúr.* An animal; cattle.

P. ستون *sutún.* A pillar.

P. ستوه *sutúh.* Tired, jaded, weary.

A. ستین *sittín.* Sixty.

A. ستة *sittah.* Six.

P. ستهیدن *sitihídan.* To contend.

P. ستیدن *sitídan.* To take, seize.

P. ستیزنده *sitízenda.* Quarrelsome.

P. ستیز *sitíz,* } Strife, contest.
P. ستیزه *sitíza.* }

P. ستیزه رو *sitíza-rú.* Ugly, contentious.

P. ستیزیدن *sitízídan.* To contend.

A. سجاده *sajjáda.* A prayer-carpet.

A. سجاف *sijáf.* The border of a garment.

A. سجایا *sajáyá.* Dispositions, natures.

A. سجحة *sajḥat.* Nature; symmetry.

A. سجدات *sijdát.* Prostrations.

A. سجدة *sijdah.* The act of prostration or adoration.

A. P. سجده كاه *sijdah-gáh.* A place of worship.

A. سجع *saj'.* Rhythm, cadence.

A. سجف *sajf.* A veil, a curtain.

A. سجل *sijil.* The record of a court; attestation of a copy.

A. P. سجل كردن *sijil kerdan.* To stamp or seal a document.

A. سجن *sijn.* A prison.

A. سجود *sujúd.* Adoration, prostration.

A. سجول *sujúl.* Registers, records. (pl. of سجل *sijil.*)

A. سجيه *sajíyeh.* Disposition, nature.

A. سحابة *saḥábat.* A cloud. (pl. سحاب *saḥáb.*)

A. سحار *saḥḥár.* A magician, an enchanter.

A. سحاق *saḥḥáḳ.* A grinder, rubber, &c.

A. سحر *saḥar.* The dawn.

A. سحر *siḥr.* Magic.

A. P. سحر اميز *siḥr-ámíz.* Fascinating.

A. P. سحر كاه *saḥar-gáh.* The dawn.

A. سحرے *saḥarí.* Matutinal.

A. سخاء *sakhá,* }
A. or سخاوت *sakháwat.* }
Liberality.

P. سخت *sakht.* Hard, strong, vehement.

P. سخت پى *sakht-pai.* Strong, muscular.

P. سختن *sakhtan.* To weigh.

P. سخته *sakhta.* Weighed.

P. سختى *sakhtí.* Hardness, difficulty.

P. سختى كشيده *sakhtí keshída.* One who has endured hardships.

A. سخره *sukhra.* Derision.

P. سخره *sukhra.* Pressed service.

P. سخن *sukhun.* A word, speech.

P. سخن ارائے *sukhun-árát.* Eloquence.

P. سخن پرور *sukhun-parwar.* A poet.

P. سخن پيوستن *sukhun-paiwastan.* To connect or draw out a discourse.

P. سخن چين *sukhun-chín.* A caviller, a tale-bearer.

P. سخن دان *sukhun-dán.* Eloquent; a poet.

P. سخن راندن *sukhun-rándan.* To discourse.

P. سخن سرا *sukhun-sará.* An orator.

P. سخن سنج *sukhun-sanj.* A poet.

P. سخن فروش *sukhun-farúsh.* A flatterer; a poet.

P. سخن گو *sukhun-gú.* An orator.

P. سخن گذار *sukhun-guzár.* One who delivers a message.

P. سخن کوتاه *sukhun-kotáh.* Summarily.

A. سخی *sakhíy.* Liberal; generous.

A. سخیف *sakhíf.* Weak in understanding; flimsy.

A. سد *sadd.* An obstruction.

A. سد راه *sadd i ráh.* A barrier.

A. سد رمق *sadd i ramaḳ.* Sufficient to preserve life.

A. سداب *suḏáb.* Rue.

A. سداد *sadád.* Rectitude; salvation.

A. سدس *suds.* The sixth part.

A. سدم *sadam.* Grief, repentance.

A. سده *saddah.* An obstruction.

A. سدید *sadíd.* Right, salutary.

P. سر *sar.* The head; tip, top, surface, summit, &c. بسر شما قسم است *ba sar i shumá ḳasm ast.* I swear to you, on my honour. بسر و چشم *ba sar u chashm.* With pleasure.

A. سر *sirr.* A secret.

P. سرا *sará.* A mansion.

A. سراء *sarrá.* A happy state (opposed to ضرا *ẓarrá*).

A. P. سراب *saráb.* The mirage.

P. سر بالا *sará-bálá.* Steep.

P. سر ا پا *sar-á-pá.* From head to foot, totally.

P. سرا پرده *sará-parda.* A large pavilion.

P. سرابستان *sarábistán.* The land of delusion, this world.

A. سرابیل *sarábíl.* Shirts, garments. (pl. of *sirbál.*)

P. سراج *siráj.* A lamp; the sun.

P. سراچه *saráché.* A small tent, a closet.

P. سر اخور *sar ákhur.* The best horse in a stable.

A. سرادق *surádiḳ.* A curtain, veil.

A. سراری *saráríy.* Concubines. (pl. of سریة.)

P. سراسر *sarásar.* From beginning to end.

P. سراسیمگی *sarásímagí.* Amazement.

P. سراسیمه *sarásíma.* Amazed, stupefied.

P. سر اشنائی *sar-áshnáí.* Intimacy.

P. سراغ *surágh.* Inquiry, clue, track. دزدرا سراغ کردند *duzd-rá surágh kerdand.* They found the thief.

P. سراغاز *sar-ágház.* A preamble.

P. سر افراز *sar-afráz.* Eminent, exalted.

P. سر افسار *sar-afsár.* The head of the reins, i.e. the part held in the hands.

P. سر افگند *sar-afgand.* Abashed, confused.

P. سر امد *sar-ámad.* Complete, chief.

P. سر امدن *sar-ámadan.* To accomplish.

P. سران *sarán.* Heads, chiefs.

P. سر انجام *sar-anjám.* Conclusion, end; apparatus.

P. سر انداز *sar-andáz.* One who risks his life in battle.

P. سر انگشت *sar-angusht.* The tip of the finger.

A. سراويل *saráwíl.* Breeches, drawers.

P. سراى *saráy.* A mansion; an inn.

A. سرايت *siráyat.* Contagion.

A. P. سرايت كردن *siráyat kerdan.* To penetrate, to communicate, to infect.

A. سراير *saráïr.* Secrets.

P. سرايچه *saráyché.* A tent, small habitation.

P. سرايدار *saráy-dár.* A warder.

P. سراينده *saráënda.* Singing, reciting.

P. سرائيدن *saráïdan.* To sing, to play on a musical instrument.

P. سرب *surb.* Lead.

P. سر باختن *sar-bakhtan.* To risk one's life.

P. سر بار *sar-bár.* A load carried on the head.

P. سرباز *sar-báz.* Brave, resolute; a soldier (see فوج *fauj*).

P. سر پاس *sar-pás.* A head watchman.

P. سر بالا *sar-bálá.* A hill, a mountain.

P. سر براه كردن *sar ba-ráh kerdan.* To accomplish.

P. سر براهى *sar ba-ráhí.* Accomplishment.

P. سر بر داشتن *sar bar-dáshtan.* To raise the head; to rebel.

P. سر بر زدن *sar bar zadan* To happen, occur.

P. سر پرست *sar-parast.* A body-servant.

P. سر بست *sar-bast.* Free, at liberty. Obscure, difficult.

P. سر بستن *sar-bastan.* To close; to form a scum (milk, &c.).

P. سر بسته *sar-basta.* Closed, kept secret; a contract.

P. سر بسر *sar-ba-sar.* Totally all.

P. سر بسر گذاشتن *sar-ba-sar guzáshtan.* To puzzle, tease, or deceive any one.

P. سر بلند *sar-baland.* Eminent.

P. سر بلندى *sar-balandí.* Eminence.

P. سر پوش *sar-púsh.* A cover, lid.

P. سر بها *sar-bahá.* The price of blood, ransom.

P. سر پنجه *sar-panja.* Nails, claws; the open hand.

P. سر پنجگى *sar-panjagí.* Strength, violence.

P. سر پیچ *sar-pích.* A jewel worn in the turban.

P. سر پیچیدن *sar-píchídan.* To disobey.

P. سر تابی *sar-tábí.* Disobedience.

P. سر تا پا *sar tá pá,* } From
P. سر تا سر *sar tá sar.* } head to foot, totally.

P. سر تراش *sar-tarásh.* A barber.

P. سرتیب *sartíb.* See فوج.

P. سر تیز *sar-tíz.* Irascible, sharp.

A. سرج *sarj.* A saddle.

A. سر جنك *sar-jang.* The leader of an army.

P. سر جوش *sar-júsh.* What is taken out of a pot for tasting; effervescence.

A. سرجین *sirjín.* Dung, ordure.

P. سر چشمه *sar i chasma.* A fountain.

A. P. سر حد *sar-ḥadd.* A boundary, a frontier.

P. سرخ *surkh.* Red.

P. سرخاب *surkh-áb.* A kind of water-fowl.

P. سرخچه *surkhicha.* The measles.

P. سرخرو *surkh-rú.* Pleased; acquitted.

P. سرخروی *surkh-rúí.* Honour, character.

P. سر خس *sar khas.* Laurel.

P. A. سر خط *sarkhaṭṭ.* A bill of sale; an agreement to hire a servant.

P. سرخك *surkhak.* The measles.

P. سر خواب *sar-kh'áb.* The first sleep.

P. سر خوش *sar-khush.* Exhilarated.

P. سرخی *surkhí.* Redness.

P. سر خیل *sar-khail.* The chief of a band.

P. سرد *sard.* Cold.

P. سرداب *sardáb,* } A grotto,
P. سردابه *sardába.* } ice-house, cavern.

P. سر دادن *sar dádan.* To let loose, to discharge.

P. سر دار *sar-dár.* A leader, chief.

P. سر داری *sar-dárí.* Command, authority.

P. سر دردی *sar-dardí.* Vexation.

P. سر در کشیدن *sar dar keshídan.* To disobey.

P. سر دست *sar-dast.* The tips of the fingers.

P. سرد سیر *sard-sír.* A cold climate; summer-quarters.

P. سر دفتر *sar-dafter.* Keeper of the records.

P. سردی *sardí.* Coldness.

P. سر راه *sar i ráh.* The high-road.

P. سر رشته *sar-rishta.* A thread; connexion.

P. سر زانو *sar i zánú.* The knee-pan.

P. سر زبان *sar i zabán.* The tip of the tongue.

P. سر زدن *sar-zadan.* To happen.

P. سر زمین *sar i zamín.* The face of the earth; upon the spot, the premises.

P. سر زنش *sar-zanish.* Reproof.

P. سر زیر *sar-zír.* Upside-down.

P. سر سال *sar i sál.* The beginning of the year.

P. سر سام *sar-sám.* Frenzy, delirium.

P. سر سبز *sar-sabz.* Verdant, flourishing.

P. سر سبزی *sar-sabzí.* Freshness, verdure.

P. سر سری *sar-sarí.* Inconsiderate, easy. Folly.

P. سر شار *sar-shár.* Intoxicated, brimful.

P. سرشت *sirisht.* Nature, temperament.

P. سرشتن *sirishtan.* To mix, to knead.

P. سر شدن *sar-shudan.* To happen.

P. سرشف *sarshaf.* Mustard-seed.

P. سرشك *sirishk.* A tear, a drop; a barberry.

P. سر شیر *sar-shír.* Cream.

A. سرط *saraṭ.* Swallowing (anything).

A. سرطان *saraṭán.* A crab, the sign Cancer.

A. سرعت *sur'at.* Haste, expedition.

P. A. سر عسکر *sar-'askar.* A commander in chief.

P. سرغنه *sarghana.* A chief.

P. سرغوت *sarghút.* Opulence; beneficence.

P. سرف *saraf.* Extravagance.

P. سر فراز *sar-faráz.* Eminent, exalted.

P. سر فرازی *sar-farází.* Eminence, exaltation.

P. سر فرو اوردن *sar farau-áverdan.* To submit.

P. سر فرو بردن *sar-farau burdan.* To be ashamed.

P. سرفه *surfa.* A cough.

A. سرقة *sarkat.* Theft, plagiarism.

P. سرکار *sarkár.* A king's court; an epithet applied to all persons of distinction, governments, &c., as سرکار ایلچی *sarkár i élchí.* H. E. the ambassador. سرکار دولت *sarkár i daulat.* The government.

P. سر گذشت *sar-guzasht.* An event, transaction.

P. سر گران *sar-girán.* Dissatisfied.

P. سر گرانی *sar-giráni.* Dissatisfaction.

P. سر گردان *sar-gardán.* Confounded, giddy.

P. سر گرده *sar-garda.* Astonished, stupefied.

P. سر کردن *sar-kerdan.* To let loose; to discharge a fire-arm.

P. سر گرم *sar-garm.* Zealous, ready.

P. سر گروه *sar-gurúh.* Chief.

P. سر کش *sar-kash.* Refractory.

P. سر کشاده *sar-kushâda.* Having the table-cloth spread.

P. سر گشته *sar-gashta.* Astonished, wandering.

P. سر کشی *sar-kashí.* Refractoriness.

P. سر کشیدن *sar-kashídan.* To rebel.

P. سر کوب *sar-kúb.* A molester.

P. سرکه *sirka.* Vinegar.

P. سرگین *sargín.* Dung.

P. سرما *sarmá.* Winter, cold.

P. سرمائی *sarmáí.* Wintry.

P. سر مایه *sar-máya.* Capital stock.

A. سرمد *sarmad.* Eternity; perpetual.

A. سرمدی *sarmadí.* Eternal.

P. سر مست *sar-mast.* Intoxicated.

P. سر مشق *sar-mashk.* A copy (for writing).

P. سر منزل *sar i manzil.* The end of a day's journey.

P. سرمه *surma.* Collyrium; antimony.

P. سر مو *sari-mú.* The point of a hair, a hair's-breadth.

P. سرنا *sarna.* A clarion, a hautbois.

P. سر نامه *sar-náma.* The address of a letter.

P. سرنج *sirinj.* Red lead.

P. سرند *sirind.* A swing. Ivy.

P. سر نگون *sar-nigún.* Topsy-turvy.

P. سر نو *sar i nau.* Over again, recommencement.

P. سر نوشت *sar-navisht.* Destiny.

P. سر نهادن *sar nihádan.* To obey, to lower the head.

P. سر نیزه *sar i níza.* The point of a spear.

P. سرو *sarv.* A cypress.

A. سروال *sirwál.* Trousers, breeches.

P. سر و برگ *sar u barg.* Means of subsistence.

P. سر و بن *sar u bun.* Root and branch, totally.

A. سروج *surúj.* Saddles.

P. سرود *surúd.* Melody, song.

P. سرودن *surúd.* To sing.

P. سرور *sarvar.* A chief, leader.

P. سرور *surúr.* Joy, delight.

P. سروری *sarvarí.* Chiefship.

P. سروش *surúsh.* An angel (especially Gabriel).

P. سر و شاخ *sar u shákh.* Root and branch, totally.

P. سر وقت *sar i wakt.* A convenient time.

P. سر و کار *sar u kár.* Connexion, relationship.

P. سره *sara.* Current (coin).

P. سرهنگ *sarhang.* A commander, chief, overseer. (See فوج.)

P. سرے *sarí.* Chiefship, government; desire, longing.

A. سریانی *suriyání.* Syrian.

P. سریچه *saríché.* A water-wagtail.

P. سریخه *saríkha.* A pelican.

P. سریدن *sarídan.* To sing.

A. سریر *sarír.* A throne, bedstead.

A. سریرت *sarírat.* Secrecy.

P. سریش *sirísh.* Glue.

A. سریع *sarí'.* Quick, nimble.

P. سرین *surín.* The buttocks.

A. سریه *surríyeh.* A concubine.

P. سزا *sazá.* Retribution, punishment.

P. سزاوار *sazávár.* Worthy, meriting.

P. سزاییدن *sazáídan.* } To
P. سزیدن *sazídan.* } be worthy, to suit.

P. سست *sust.* Loose, lazy, negligent.

P. سست رغبت *sust-rughbat.* With passions blunted.

P. A. سست عنان *sust-'inán.* Loose-reined, inactive.

P. سستی *sustí.* Languor, negligence, laziness.

P. سصد *sisad.* Three hundred.

P. ستبر *sitabr.* Thick, coarse.

A. سطح *sath.* A surface.

A. سطر *satr.* A row, line, series.

A. سطع *sat'.* Radiance, light.

A. سطوت *satwat.* Dominion, authority.

A. سطوح *sutúh.* Surfaces.

A. سطور *sutúr.* Lines.

A. سطوع *sutú'.* Being diffused (light or odours).

A. سعادت *sa'ádat.* Felicity.

A. P. سعادت مند *sa'ádat-mand.* Fortunate.

A. سعال *su'ál.* A cough.

A. سعایت *si'áget.* Calumny.

A. سعت *si'at.* Amplitude.

A. سعتر *sa'tar.* Marjoram, origany.

A. سعید *sa'd.* Felicity, prosperity, a fortunate aspect of the stars.

A. سعدے *sa'dí.* Sa'dí the celebrated poet and moralist, born at Shíráz, A. D. 1175.

A. سعدین *sa'dain.* The two fortunate stars, Jupiter and Venus.

A. سعود *su'úd.* Good fortune.

A. سعوط *sa'út.* Medicinal snuff.

A. سعی *sa'í.* Endeavour, effort.

A. سعید *sa'íd.* Fortunate, happy.

P. سغری *saghrí.* Shagreen, a kind of leather.

A. سفارت *sifárat.* An embassy.

P. سفارش *sifárish.* Recommendation.

P. سفاك *saffák.* A shedder of blood.

P. سفال *sufál.* Earthenware tiles.

P. سفالگر *sufálgar.* A potter.

A. سفاهت *safáhat.* Stupidity.

A. سفائن *safáin.* Ships, boats. (pl. of سفينه.)

P. سفت *suft.* A perforation; the eye of a needle.

P. سفت *sift.* Hard, stiff.

P. سفتگر *suft-gar.* A borer of pearls, &c.

P. سفتن *suftan.* To bore, perforate.

P. سفته *sufta.* Bored, pierced. در نا سفته *dur i ná sufta.* An unpierced pearl, a maiden.

P. سفته *sufta.* A bill of exchange.

A. سفر *safar.* A journey, voyage.

A. سفر *sifr.* A book, a register.

A. سفرجل *safarjal.* A quince. (pl. سفارج *safárij.*)

A. سفره *sufra.* A table-cloth, or tray.

A. T. سفرچی *sufra-chí.* A table-decker.

A. سفل *safl.* Meanness; ignoble, inferior.

P. سفله *sifla.* Mean, base.

A. سفلی *suflá.* Lower (fem. of اسفل). يد سفلی *yad i suflá.* The lower (i.e. receiving hand).

P. سفوف *sufúf.* Powder. A medicine taken unmixed (opposed to an electuary).

A. سفهاء *safahá.* Block-heads.

P. سفيد *safeid.* White.

P. سفيدا *safeidá.* White lead.

P. سفيدار *safeidar.* The white poplar, or aspen.

A. سفير *safír.* An ambassador.

A. سفينه *safína.* A ship, vessel.

A. سفينهٔ نوح *safína i núh.* Noah's ark.

A. سفيه *safíh.* Stupid; ignorant.

A. سقا *saḳḳá.* A water-carrier. مرغ سقا *murgh i saḳḳá.* A pelican.

A. P. سقاچی *saḳḳáchí.* A goldfinch.

A. سقام *saḳám.* Sickness, infirmity.

A. سقايت *saḳayet.* Water-supply, irrigation.

A. سقر *saḳar* Hell.

A. سقرلات *saḳirlát.* Broad-cloth.

A. سقط *saḳat.* A fall; death; abuse, bad language.

A. سقف *saḳf.* A roof.

A. سقم *suḳm* or *saḳam.* Sickness.

A. سقنقور *saḳunḳúr.* A species of lizard (said to be an aphrodisiac).

A. سقوط *suḳút.* Falling.

A. سقوف *suḳúf.* Roofs.

A. سقی *saḳy.* Watering, irrigating.

A. سقیم *saḳím.* Sick, infirm.

P. سگ *sag.* A dog.

P. سگ ابی *sag i ábí.* An otter.

A. سکین *sikkín.* A knife.

P. سکال *sikál* or *sigál.* Thought.

P. سکالیدن *sikálídan* or *sigálídan.* To think.

A. سکان *sukkán.* Inhabitants.

A. سکان *sukkán.* The helm or rudder of a ship.

A. سکبینج *sakbínaj.* Sagapenna (a medicinal herb).

P. سگ تازی *sag i tází.* A greyhound.

A. سکته *sakta.* The apoplexy.

P. سگ دندان *sag-dandán.* A canine tooth.

A. سکر *sukr.* Intoxication.

A. سکر *sakkar.* Sugar.

A. سکرات *sakarát.* Agony.

A. سکران *sukrán.* Intoxicated.

A. سکن *sakan.* A dwelling.

P. سکنج *sukunj.* Fetid breath.

A. سکنجبین *sikenjabín.* Oxymel.

P. سگلیدن *saglídan.* To sob; to belch.

A. سکناء *sukaná.* Inhabitants.

A. سکوت *sukút.* Silence.

P. سکوره *sukúra.* An earthenware dish.

A. سکون *sukún.* Quiescence. The mark *jezmah* ٥.

A. سکونت *sukúnat.* Residence, tranquillity.

A. سکة *sikkat.* A coining die; current.

A. P. سکه زدن *sikka zadan.* To strike coins.

A. سکیت *sikkít.* Very silent.

P. سگیت *sagíyet.* Naughtiness.

P. سکیزیدن *sikízídan.* To rear, to prance.

A. سکینه *sakína.* Tranquillity.

P. سل *sull.* The lungs; consumption.

A. سلاح *siláḥ.* Arms, weapons.

A. P. سلاح خانه *siláḥ-khána.* An arsenal.

A. P. سلاح شور *siláḥ-shúr.* A gladiator.

A. سلاست *salásat.* Facility.

A. سلاسل *salásil.* Chains. (pl. of سلسلة *silsila.*)

A. سلاطین *saláṭín.* Sultans, kings. (pl. of سلطان.)

A. سلام *salám.* A salutation, peace, safety.

A. سلامت *salámat.* Safety, peace.

A. سلالة *sulálat.* Progeny, race.

A. سلب *salb.* A negation in logic.

A. سلجم *saljam.* A turnip.

A. P. سلحدار *silaḥ-dar.* An armed man.

A. P. سلح شور *silaḥ shúr.* See سلاحشور.

A. سلخ *salkh.* The end of the month.

A. سلس *salis.* Easy, docile.

A. سلسال *salsál.* A pure limpid stream.

A. سلس البول *salas ul baul.* Diabetes.

A. سلسبيل *salsabíl.* A river in paradise.

A. سلسله *silsila.* A chain, concatenation.

A. سلطان *sulṭán.* A king, monarch.

P. سلطانى *sulṭání.* Royal, imperial.

A. سلطنت *salṭanat.* Empire, reign.

A. سلف *salaf.* Preceding, former time.

A. سلك *silk.* A thread on which beads, &c. are strung; a series.

A. سلم *silm.* Money paid in advance.

A. سلم *sullam.* A ladder.

A. سلنج *silunj.* A cracked or ulcerated lip.

A. سلوت *salwat.* Solace.

A. سلوق *sulúḳ.* Nature, genius.

A. سلوك *sulúk.* Way, road; proceeding, conduct.

P. سله *sila.* A box on the ears.

A. سليب *salíb.* Stripped, carried off.

A. سليخه *salíkha.* Benzoin.

A. سليس *salís.* Easy, plain.

A. سليقه *salíḳa.* Method, skill.

A. سليم *salím.* Pacific, mild, affable.

A. سم *samm.* Venom.

P. سم *sum.* A hoof, a foot.

A. سماء *samá.* Heaven, the sky.

A. سمات *simát.* Brands, marks.

A. سماجت *samájat.* Adulteration, turpitude.

A. سماحت *samáḥat.* Beneficence, liberality.

A. سماخ *simákh.* The orifice of the ear.

P. سماروغ *samárúgh.* A mushroom.

A. سماع *samá'.* Hearing. The song and dance of the Mevlevíyeh Dervishes. The place in which it is performed is called سماع خانه *samá' kháná.*

A. سماعت *samá'at.* Hearing, audience.

A. سماعى *samá'iy.* Traditional, oral. (In grammar) irregular, opposed to قياسى *ḳiyásiy.*

A. سم الفار *samm ul fár.* Ratsbane, arsenic.

A. سمان *sammán.* A seller of butter.

P. سمانى *samání.* Sky-coloured, azure.

A. سمانى *sumána.* A quail.

A. سماوات *samáwát.* The heavens.

A. سماوى *samáwí.* Heavenly; azure.

A. سمت *samt.* A road, way, quarter, direction.

A. سمج *samj.* Deformed, hideous.

A. سمر *samr.* An evening entertainment of dancing and story-telling.

A. سمسم *simsim.* Sesame.

A. سمط *simṭ.* A thread upon which pearls, &c. are strung.

A. سمع *sam'.* Hearing; the ear.

A. سمك *samak.* A fish.

P. سمند *samand.* A bay horse.

P. سمندر *samandar.* A salamander.

A. سمنیت *sumaníyet.* A sect professing the doctrine of metempsychosis.

A. سمو *samw.* High, sublime.

A. سموت *sumút.* Ways.

A. سمور *sammúr.* The sable.

A. سموم *samúm.* A hot pestilential wind.

A. سمی *samíy.* Namesake.

A. سمین *samín.* Fat, plump.

A. سنا *saná.* Senna. Light, radiance.

A. سنان *sinán.* A spear-head.

A. سنانیر *sanánír.* Cats. (pl. of سنور *sinnaur.*)

A. P. سنبل *sumbul.* The hyacinth; spikenard. An ear of corn.

A. سنبل الطیب *sumbul uṭ ṭíb.* Spikenard.

A. سنبلة *sumbulat.* The sign Virgo. An ear of corn.

P. سنبوسك *sambusak.* A pasty, a pie.

P. سنپدن *sumbídan.* To perforate.

A. سنه *sanna.* A year.

A. سنت *sunnat.* The traditional law based on the precepts of Mohammed.

A. سنت و جماعت *sunnat u jumá'at.* The followers of the four first *khalifs.*

P. سنج *sanj.* (In comp.) a weigher, examiner.

P. سنجاب *sinjáb.* The grey squirrel, ermine.

P. سنجابی *sinjábí.* Grey, russet.

P. سنجاف *sanjáf.* Edging, the border of a garment.

P. سنجه *sanjah.* A weight.

P. سنجیدگی *sanjídagí.* Gravity, weight.

P. سنجیدن *sanjídan.* To weigh.

P. سنجیده *sanjída.* Weighed.

A. سند *sanad.* A grant; proof; document.

A. سندان *sandán.* An anvil.

A. سندروس *sandarús.* Gum sandarach, red arsenic.

P. سندل *sandal.* A sandal; sandal-wood. A bum-boat.

P. سنگ *sang.* A stone.

P. سنگ اسیا *sang-ásyá.* A mill-stone.

P. سنگ انداز *sang-andáz.* A slinger.

P. سنگ پشت *sang-pusht.* A tortoise.

P. T. سنگ چاقماق *sang í chák-mák.* A flint for striking fire with.

P. سنگ خارا *sang i khárá.* A hard stone, marble.

P. سنگ خرده *sang-khurda.* A small piece of stone.

P. سنگدان *sang-dán.* The crop or gizzard of a bird.

P. سنگدل *sang-dil.* Hard-hearted.

P. سنگر *sangur.* An intrenchment.

P. سنگ راه *sang i ráh.* Impediment.

P. سنگ ریزه *sang-ríza.* Gravel, pebbles.

P. سنگ سار *sang-sár.* Stoning to death.

P. سنگستان *sangistán.* A stony country.

P. سنگ مثانه *sang i masána.* A stone in the bladder.

P. سنگی *sangí.* Stony, heavy.

A. سنن *sunan.* Rules, laws. (pl. of سنت *sunnat* q.v.)

A. سنین *sanín.*
A. سنوات *sanawát.*
A. سنون *sunún.* } Years.

A. سنوح *sunúh.* Happening, occurring.

A. سنور *sinnaur.* A cat.

T. سنور *sinúr* or *sinír.* Limit, frontier.

A. سنوی *sanawí.* Annual.

A. سنه *sanna.* A year.

A. سنی *sunní.* A Sunnite, a follower of the *sunnet* as opposed to a Shí'ah.

P. سو *sú.* Side, quarter; towards.

A سوء *sú'.* Evil; indisposition.

A. سوا
A. سوی } *síwá.* Equal, parallel.

A. سوی *síwá.* Besides, except.

A. سوابق *sawábik.* Past events.

A. سواد *sawád.* Blackness, blacking, soot, smoke; environs, a rough draught or copy, reading; ability.

A. سوار *sawár.* A bracelet.

P. سوار *suwár.* A rider, horseman.

P. سواره *suwára.* Horseman; sweepings.

P. سواری *suwárí.* Horsemanship; retinue.

P. سوال *su'ál.* A question, request.

A. سوالف *sawálif.* Past events.

A. سوانح *sawánih.* Accidents, occurrences.

A. سوای *siwáy.* Besides, except.

P. سوختگی *súkhtagí.* Burning, combustion.

P. سوختن *súkhtan.* To burn.

P. سود *súd.* Profit, interest.

A. P. سودا *saudá.* Melancholy; passion.

P. سودا *sauda.* Trade, traffic.

P. سوداگر *saudágar.* A merchant.

P. سوداگری *saudágarí.* Merchandise, traffic.

A. P. سوداوی *saudáwí.* Melancholic.

P. سود خور *súd-khur.* A usurer.

P. سود مند *súd-mand.* Profitable, useful.

P. سودن *súdan.* To wear, to rub.

P. سوده *súda.* Rubbed, obliterated.

A. سور *súr.* A wall, rampart.

P. سوراخ *surákh.* A hole, orifice, passage.

A. سورت *saurat.* Effervescence; despotic power.

A. سورت *súrat.* A chapter of the Koran.

P. سورنا *súrná.* } A trumpet.
P. سورنای *súrnáy.* }

P. سورنجان *súrinján.* Colchicum.

P. سوز *súz.* Burning; vexation; affection; a stanza of an elegiac poem.

P. سوزاك *súzak.* Gonorrhœa.

P. سوزان *súzán.* Burning, ardent.

P. سوزانيدن *súzánídan.* To set on fire, to kindle.

P. سوزش *súzish.* Inflammation, conflagration.

P. سوزن *súzan.* A needle.

P. سوز ناك *súz-nák.* Burning, ardent.

P. سوزنده *súzenda.* Kindling, burning.

P. سوزنی *suzení.* Quilting.

P. سوزيدن *súzídan.* To burn, to be burned.

P. سوسر *súsar.* A marten.

P. سوسك *súsak.* A beetle.

P. سوسمار *súsmár.* A species of lizard; an alligator; a porpoise.

A. سوسن *sausan.* } A lily.
P. سوسن *súsan.* }

A. سوط *sauṭ.* A scourge.

P. سوغات *saughát.* A rich present.

P. سوفار *súfár.* The notch of an arrow.

P. سوفته *súfta.* A weevil; fraud, deceit.

A. سوق *suḳ.* A market.

P. سوك *súg.* Grief, anguish.

P. سوگند *saugand.* An oath.

P. سوگند خوردن *saugand khurdan.* To take an oath.

P. سوگوار *sūg-vár.* Sorrowful, grievous.

P. سوگواری *súg-várí.* Grief, mourning.

P. سولاخ *sulákh.* See سوراخ.

SANSC. سولی *súlí.* An impaling stake.

P. سوم *siwum.* Third.

P. سوهان *súhán.* A file.

P. سوی *súy.* A side or part; towards.

A. سوی *sawíy.* Equal.

A. سويت *sawíyet.* Equality.

P. سه *sih.* Three.

A. سها *suhá.* An obscure star in the Lesser Bear.

A. سهام *sihám.* Arrows.

P. سه تار *sih-tár* or *sih-tára.* A three-stringed instrument, a guitar.

A. سهر *sahar.* Sleeplessness.

P. سه شش *sih-shash.* Three-sixes (a throw at dice).

P. سه شنبه *sih shamba.* Tuesday.

P. سهصد *sihṣad.* Three hundred.

P. سه گوشه *sih-gúsha.* A triangle.

A. سهل *sahl.* Easy.

A. P. سهل جو *sahl-jú.* Seeking the easiest course; peaceable.

A. سهم *sahm.* An arrow.

P. سهم *sahm.* Terror, fright.

P. سهمگین *sahm-gín.* Horrible, awful.

P. سهمیدن *sahmídan.* To dread.

... سهو *sahw.* An error, fault.

A. سهولت *suhúlat.* Facility, ease.

P. سهی *sahí.* Straight, erect.

P. سه یك *sih-yek.* Three aces (at dice).

P. سهیل *suheil.* The star Canopus.

P. سهیم *sahím.* A partner.

P. سی *sí.* Thirty.

A. سیئات *say'iyát.* Sins.

A. سیاج *siyáj.* A thorn-hedge, a fence.

A. سیاح *saiyáḥ.* A traveller, a pilgrim.

A. سیاحت *siyáḥat.* Travelling.

A. سیادت *siyádat.* Chieftainship; dominion. Descent from Mohammed, (such persons being called Saiyids).

A. سیار *saiyár.* Wandering, walking, revolving.

A. سیاره *saiyárah.* A planet; travellers.

A. سیاست *siyásat.* Government, punishment.

A. سیاف *saiyáf.* A swordsman.

A. سیاقت *siyáḳat.* Mode, style; topic. Numeration by the Arabic alphabet.

A. سیال *siyál.* A thorny acacia-tree.

A. سیال *saiyál.* Flowing; a current.

P. سیاوش *siyávush.* Name of the father of *Cyrus* the Great.

P. سیاه *siyáh.* Black.

P. سیاه چشم *siyáh-chashm.* Black-eyed, unkind.

P. سیاه رو *siyáh-rú.* Black-faced, a criminal.

P. سیاه فام *siyáh-fám.* Blackish, swarthy.

P. سیاه گوش *siyáh-gúsh.* A lynx.

P. سیاهی *siyáhí.* Blackness, ink.

P. سیاهه *siyáha.* A list, an invoice.

P. سیب *síb.* An apple.

P. سیچیدن *sichídan.* To prepare, to arrange.

P. سیخ *síkh.* A spit.

A. سید *saiyid.* A chief; one descended from Mohammed.

A. P. سید سامره *saiyid i Sámera.* A pseudo-Saiyid, holding a diploma from the Herald's College of Sámera (a town near Kerbelá, where such documents are forged).

P. سیر *sír.* Full, satisfied.

P. سیر *sír.* Garlic.

A. سیر *sair.* Walking, perambulating.

A. سیر *siyar.* Pl. of سیرت q.v.

P. سیر اب *sír-áb.* Moist; fresh, juicy.

A. سیرت *sírat.* Temperament, character.

P. سیری *sírí.* Satiety.

P. سیزده *sízhda.* Thirteen.

P. سیزدهم *sizhdahum.* Thirteenth.

A. سیف *saif.* A sword.

A. سیکران *saikerán.* Hyocyamus (a plant).

P. سیکی *síkí.* Wine boiled down to a third.

A. سیل *sail.* A torrent, flood.

P. سیلاب *sailáb.* An inundation, current.

A. سیلان *sayalán.* Flowing (a torrent).

P. سیلانچه *sílánché.* A cook.

P. سیلی *sílí.* A slap on the nape of the neck.

P. سیم *sím.* Silver; a telegraphic wire.

P. سیم *síyum.* Thirtieth.

P. سیما *símá.* Aspect, forehead.

P. سیم اب *sím-áb.* Quicksilver.

P. سیم بر *sím-bar.* White-bosomed.

P. سیم تن *sím-tan.* Silver-bodied.

P. سیمرغ *símurgh.* A fabulous bird, the griffin also called عنقا *'anká.*

P. سیم سیه *sím i siyah.* Bad silver, base coin.

A. سیمیا *símiyá.* Natural magic.

A. سیمین *símín.* Of silver; silvery.

P. سینه *sína.* The bosom, breast.

P. سینه بند *sína-band.* Bodice.

P. سینی *síní* or قهوه سینی *kahveh-síní.* A tea-tray.

P. سیور غال *suyúr-ghál.* A fief, feudal tenure.

A. سیوف *suyúf.* Swords.

P. سیوم *síwum.* The third.

P. سیومین *síwumín.* Thirdly.

P. سیه *siyah.* Black.

P. سیه چرده *siyah-charda.* A black complexion.

P. سیه درونی *siyah-dirúní.* Inward baseness.

P. سیه دل *siyah-dil.* Black-hearted, malevolent.

P. سیہ روز *siyah-rúz.* Unfortunate.

P. سیہ کار *siyah-kár.* A sinner.

P. سیہ نامہ *siyah-náma.* The black book; the record of one's misdeeds.

ش

ش *shín.* Sh. The thirteenth letter of the Arabic, and sixteenth of the Persian alphabets.

P. ش *ash.* (Pronominal termination) his, hers, its.

A. شاب *shább.* A young man.

P. شاباش *shábásh.* Bravo!

P. شاۃ *shá't.* A sheep, a wild ox.

P. شاخ *shákh.* A branch, a shoot; a horn.

P. شاخ اهو *shákh i áhú.* See برات.

P. شاخ شاخ *shákh-shákh.* In branches, in pieces.

P. شاخچه *shákhcha.* A twig.

P. شاخ در شاخ *shákh dar shákh.* Branching out.

P. شاخ زدن *shákh-zadan.* To butt with the horn.

P. شاخسار *shákh-sár.* Branchy, spreading.

P. شاخوره *shákhúra.* A brick-kiln.

P. شاد *shád.* Glad, pleased.

P. شاد اب *shád-áb.* Fresh, moist.

P. شادان *shádán.* Glad, happy.

P. شاد باش *shád-bash.* Bravo!

P. شاد کام *shád kám.* Exultant, happy.

P. شاد گونه *shád-gúna.* Bedding.

P. شامان *shámán.* Glad, happy.

P. شادمانی *shád-mání.* Gladness, happiness.

A. شادن *shádin.* A fawn.

P. شادنه *shádna.* Blood-stone.

P. شادی *shádí.* Festivity; marriage. (Arabic فرح.)

A. شاذ *sháżż.* Uncommon, irregular.

P. شار *shár.* A whirlpool, an eddy.

A. شارب *shárib.* Drinking, drinker.

A. شارح *shárih.* A commentator.

A. شارع *shári'.* A highway.

A. شارق *shárik.* Shining, rising (the sun).

P. شارك *shárik.* A talking bird.

P. شاریدن *sháridan.* To flow (as a river) with a great noise.

P. شاشدان *shásh-dán.* The bladder, a urinal.

P. شاشه *shásha.* Urine.

P. شاشیدن *sháshídan.* To make water.

A. شاطر *sháṭir.* Arch, cunning, clever.

A. شاعر *shá'ir.* A poet.

A. شاعری *shá'irí.* The art of poetry.

A. شاغل *shághil.* Occupied.

A. شافع *sháfi'.* An intercessor.

A. شافعی *sháfi'iy.* One of the four principal sects of the Mohammedan religion.

A. شافی *sháfí.* Healing.

A. شاق *shákḳ.* Difficult, toilsome.

A. شاکر *shákir.* Praising, thanking.

P. شاگرد *shágird.* A student, apprentice.

P. شاگرد پیشه *shágird písha.* A menial servant.

P. شاگردی *shágirdí.* Apprenticeship.

A. شاکی *shákí.* A complainer; armed.

P. شال *shál.* A shawl.

P. شال ترمه *shál i terma.* A cashmir shawl.

P. شال ترمه نما *shál i terma-numá.* An imitation cashmir shawl.

A. شام *shám.* Damascus.

P. شام *shám.* The evening.

A. شأمت *shá'mat.* Adversity.

P. شام گاه *shám-gáh.* Evening-time.

A. شامخ *shámikh.* High, exalted.

A. شامل *shámil.* United, included.

A. شامل حال *shámil i ḥál.* Including, comprehending.

A. شامه *shámmah.* The smell, smelling.

A. شامی *shámí.* A Syrian.

A. شأن *sha'n.* Thing, state, condition.

P. شان *shán.* Condition; state, dignity. صاحب عالی شان *ṣáḥib i 'álí shán.* A person of lofty dignity.

P. شان *-shán.* Affixed pronoun for ایشان. Them, their.

P. شانزده *shánzdah.* Sixteen.

P. شانزدهم *shánzdahum.* Sixteenth.

P. شانه *shána.* A comb; the shoulder-blade.

A. شانی *shání'.* One who hates.

P. شاه *sháh.* A king.

P. شاهانه *sháhána.* Royal.

P. شاه باز *sháh-báz.* A falcon.

P. شاه بلوط *sháh ballúṭ.* A chestnut.

A. شاهد *sháhid.* A witness.

P. شاهد *sháhid.* A mistress.

A. P. شاهدی *shahidí.* Insolence, airs and graces, testimony.

P. شاهراه *sháh-ráh.* A high-road.

P. شاهزاده *sháhzáda.* A prince.

P. A. شاه مات *sháh-mát.* Checkmate at chess.

P. شاه نامه *sháh-náma.* The book of kings, a celebrated history of Persia in Epic verse.

P. شاهنشاه *sháhansháh.* emperor.

P. شاه نشین *sháh-nishín.* A balcony.

P. شاهوار *sháh-vár.* Royal, king-like.

P. شاهول *sháhúl.* A plumb-line.

P. شاهی *sháhí.* Royalty, royal.

P. شاهین *sháhín.* A falcon.

P. شایان *sháyán.* Worthy.

A. شائبه *sháiba.* Suspicion, doubt; mixture.

P. شاید *sháyad.* Perhaps, it may be proper.

P. شایستن *sháyistan.* To suit.

P. شایستگی *sháyistagí.* Aptitude, propriety.

P. شایسته *sháyista.* Suitable, worthy.

A. شایع *sháyi'.* Promulgated, divulged.

A. شایق *sháik.* Exciting, longing. Desirable.

P. شایگان *sháigan.* Worthy, suitable.

A. شایدن *sháyidan.* To be worthy.

P. شب *shab.* Night.

A. شب *shabb.* Alum.

A. شباب *shebáb.* Youth.

P. شباشب *shabáshab.* Night after night.

A. شباط *shubát.* The Syro-Macedonian month, February.

P. شبان *shabán* or *shubán.* A shepherd.

P. شبانروز *shabánrúz.* Night and day, incessantly.

P. شبانگاه *shabángáh.* The night-time.

P. شبانه *shabána.* Stale, last night's leavings.

P. شبانی *shabání.* Pastoral care.

P. شب اهنك *shab-áhang.* The morning star.

P. A. شب برات *shab i barát.* The 14th night of *Sha'bán.*

P. شبت *shebit.* Fennel.

P. شب چراغ *shab-chirágh.* The glow-worm.

P. شب خانه *shab-khána.* A bed-chamber.

P. شب خون *shab-khún.* A night attack.

P. شب خیز *shab-khíz.* One who rises or watches in the night.

P. A. شب دیجور *shab i daijúr.* A dark night.

A. شبر *shibr.* A span.

P. شبخون *shab-khún.* A night-attack.

P. شب رنك *shab-rang.* Obscure, black.

P. شب رو *shab-rav.* Travelling in the night.

P. شب پره *shap-para.* A bat.

P. شب زنده دار *shab-zinda-dár.* Vigilant during night.

P. شبستان *shabistán.* A bed-chamber.

A. شبع *shab'.* Satiety.

A. شبق *shabak.* Lust.

P. A. شب قدر *shab i kadr.* The night of power, i.e. the 27th of Ramazán, on which the heavens are said to be opened for a second, and any one witnessing the phenomenon will have his wishes fulfilled.

P. شب گاه *shab-gáh.* The night-time.

P. شب گرد *shab-gard.* The night-watch, patrol.

P. شب کور *shab-kúr.* Purblind at night.

A. شبکه *shabakeh.* A net.

P. شبگیر *shab-gír.* Travelling before daybreak, a night-attack.

P. شبنم *shab-nam.* Dew.

P. شبو *shab-bú.* A flower that is fragrant at night (*polyanthus tuberosa*).

P. شبه *shaba.* A jet or glass-bead.

A. شبه *shubh.* Doubt, suspicion.

P. شب هنگام *shab-hangám.* The night-time.

P. شب یار *shab-yár.* A composing medicine.

P. شبینه *shabína.* State; last night's leavings.

A. شبیه *shabíh,* Alike, resembling; a picture.

A. شتی *shattá.* Various, distinct.

A. شتا *shitá.* Winter.

P. شتاب *shitáb.* Haste, quickness.

P. شتابان *shitábán.* Hastily.

P. شتابانیدن *shitábánídan.* To cause to make haste.

P. شتابزدگی *shitáb-zadagí.* Precipitancy.

P. شتابنده *shitábenda.* Making haste.

P. شتابی *shitábí.* Haste, speed.

P. شتابیدن *shitábídan.* } To make haste.
P. شتافتن *shitáftan.* }

P. شتالنگ *shitálang.* The ankle.

P. شتر *shutur.* A camel.

P. شترپا *shutur-pá.* The sunflower.

P. شتر بان *shutur-bán.* A camel-driver.

P. شتر بختی *shutur i bakhtí.* The Bactrian two-humped camel.

P. شتر دل *shutur-dil.* A coward.

P. شتر گاو پلنگ *shutur-gáv-palang.* A giraffe.

P. شترکینه *shutur-gína.* Malicious.

P. شتر مرغ *shutur-murgh.* An ostrich.

P. شتر نال *shutur-nál.* A swivel-gun.

P. شتلم *shutulum.* A quarrel.

A. شتم *shatm.* Abuse, contumely.

A. شجاع *shujá'.* Brave, intrepid.

A. شجاعة *shajá'at.* Intrepidity.

A. شجر *shajar.* A tree; a plant.

A. شجو *shajw.* Affliction, anguish.

A. شحّ *shaḥḥ.* Avaricious; avarice.

A. شحم *shaḥm.* Fat; pulp.

A. شحناء *shaḥná'.* Hatred.

P. شحنگی *shaḥnagí.* The police.

P. شحنه *shaḥna.* A superintendent of the police.

A. شخص *shakhṣ.* A person, body, individual.

A. P. شخصی *shakhṣí.* Some one, somebody.

A. شداد *shidád.* Violent, vehement. (pl. of شدید).

A. شدائد *shadáïd.* Adversities.

A. شدة *shiddat.* Vehemence, violence.

P. شدگان *shudagán.* People of former times.

P. شدن *shudan.* To be, to become, to go. چه شدی *chi shudí.* What would it have mattered?

P. شدنی *shudaní.* Possible, practicable, fit to live.

A. شدید *shadíd.* Vehement, violent.

A. شذا *shaza.* An injury; pungency of odour.

A. شر *sharr.* Wickedness, depravity.

A. شرا *shará.* Buying; selling.

A. شراب *sharáb.* Wine, liquor.

A. شراح *sharraḥ.* A commentator.

A. شرار *sharar.* Sparks.

A. شرارة {*sharárat.* Mischief. *sharára.* A spark of fire.

A. شرافت *sharáfat.* Grandeur, nobility.

A. شراكةً *sharákatan.* Jointly.

A. شر انگیز *sharr-angíz.* An incendiary.

A. شرائط *sharáit.* Conditions, stipulations.

A. شرائع *sharáï'.* Laws.

A. شرائف *sharáïf.* Nobles.

A. شرب *sharb.* Drinking.

A. شربت *sharbat.* Beverage, sherbet.

A. شرح *sharḥ.* Explanation, commentary.

A. شرح و بسط *sharḥ u bast.* Explicitly and openly.

A. شرذمه *shirzimah.* A band, a small troop.

A. شرر *sharar.* Sparks of fire. Malice. (pl. of شرره.)

P. شرزه *sharza.* Fierce, enraged.

A. شرشر *sharshar.* A dripping, buzzing, murmur, noise.

اب شرشر *áb i sharshar.* A cascade.

A. شرط *sharṭ.* Stipulation, condition; a wager.

A. شرط بستن *sharṭ-bastan.* To stipulate, to bet.

P. شرطه *shurṭa.* A fair wind.

A. شرطی *sharṭí.* Conditional.

A. شرع *shar'.* Law, equity; a highway.

A. شرعی *shar'iy.* Legal.

A. شرف *sharaf.* Nobility.

A. شرفاء *shurafá'.* Nobles.

P. شرفنج *sharfanj.* A rugged road.

A. شرفیت *sharfíyet.* Nobility.

A. شرق *shark.* The east; rising (the sun).

A. شرقی *sharkí.* Eastern, oriental.

A. شرك *shirk.* Partnership; polytheism.

A. شرکاء *shuraká'.* Partners.

A. شرکة *shirkat.* Partnership; a company.

P. شرم *sharm.* Modesty, shame.

P. شرمسار *sharm-sár.* Modest, ashamed.

P. شرمساری *sharm-sárí.* Modesty, bashfulness.

P. شرمگین *sharm-gín.*
P. شرمناك *sharm-nák.*
P. شرمنده *sharmenda.*
Bashful, modest, ashamed.

A. شروح *shurúh.* Commentaries.

A. شروع *shurú'.* Commencement, beginning.

A. شره *sharah.* Appetite, avidity. (In Persian) greedy.

A. شریان *sharyán.* An artery.

A. شریر *sharír.* Wicked.

A. شریط *sharít.* A rope for binding the load upon a beast of burden.

A. شریعت *sharí'at.* Law.

A. شریف *sharíf.* Noble, illustrious.

A. شریف و وضیع *sharíf u wazí'.* High and low.

A. شریك *sharík.* A partner, accomplice.

P. شست *shast.* An archer's thumb-stall.

P. شست *shist.* An aim.

P. شستگی *shustagí.* Washing, cleaning.

P. شستن *shustan.* To wash.

P. شست و شو *shust u shú.* Washing and cleansing.

P. شش *shash.* Six.

P. شش *shush.* The bosom, the lungs.

P. شش جهتی *shash-jihatí.* Hexagonal.

P. ششدر *shash-dar.* A cube, a dice. A point in the game of backgammon نرد, from which one cannot extricate oneself.

P. ششدر شدن *shashdar shudan.* To be "cornered", confounded.

P. ششصد *shash-sad.* Six hundred.

P. ششك *shusk.* Excrement of the eye.

P. شش گوشه *shash-gúshah.* A hexagon.

P. ششم *shashm.* Sixth.

P. شصت *shast.* Sixty.

P. شصتم *shastum.* Sixtieth.

A. شطء *shat'.* The bank of a river.

A. شطاح *shattáh.* Obscene.

P. شطرنج *shaṭranj*. The game of chess. The pieces are named شاه *shah*, King; فرزين *farzín*, Queen; فيل *fíl*, Bishop; اسپ *asp* or سوار *sawár*, Knight; رخ *rukh*, Castle; and پياده *piyáda*, Pawn.

P. شعار *shi'ár*. A habit, custom.

P. شعاع *shu'á'*. Light, splendour, rays.

A. شعب *sh'ib*. A mountain-path.

A. شعبان *sha'bán*. The eighth Arabian month.

A. شعبده *shu'bdah*. Sleight of hand.

A. P. شعبده باز *shu'bdah-báz*. A juggler.

A. P. شعبده بازى *shu'bdah-bází*. The art of juggling.

A. شعر *shá'r*. Hair.

A. شعر *shi'r*. Poetry, verse.

A. شعراء *shu'ará*. Poets, literati.

A. شعرى *shi'rá*. Sirius, the Dog-star.

A. شعله *shu'lah*. Flame.

A. شعور *shu'úr*. Knowledge, understanding.

A. شعير *sha'ír*. Barley.

P. شغال *shaghál*. A jackal.

A. شغب *shaghb*. A broil, tumult.

A. شغل *shughl*. Employment, study.

A. شفاء *shifá'*. Cure; convalescence.

A. شفاعت *shifá'at*. Intercession.

A. شفاف *shaffáf*. Transparent, clear.

P. شفتالو *shaftálú*. A peach.

A. شفة *shifat*. The lip.

A. شفة الصائم *shifat uṣ saïm*. The lip of one who fasts (flabby and withered).

A. شفق *shafaḳ*. The red glow of dawn or sunset.

A. شفقت *shafaḳat*. Clemency, compassion.

P. شفك *shafak*. A villain.

A. شفيع *shafí'*. An intercessor.

A. شفيق *shafíḳ*. Kind, compassionate.

A. شق *shaḳḳ*. A fissure, crack. A category, phrase, combination, &c. اين كار دو شق دارد *ín kár dú shaḳḳ dárad*. There are two sides to this question.

P. شقاقل *shaḳáḳul*. The wild carrot.

A. شقاوت *shaḳáwat*. Misery, disgrace, poverty.

A. شقائق *shaḳáïḳ*. An anemone, a tulip.

P. شقدار *shiḳ-dár*. A collector of revenue.

A. شقوق *shuḳúḳ*. Fissures.

A. شقه *shiḳḳah*. A letter; a royal order; cleaving in two, a mode of capital punishment.

A. شقى *shaḳíy*. Poor, miserable.

A. شقيقه *shaḳíḳ*. The temples, a pain in half the head.

A. شك *shakk.* Doubt, suspicion.

P. شكار *shikár.* Hunting, prey, game.

P. شكارى *shikárí.* Appertaining to hunting; a sportsman.

P. شكاف *shikáf.* A fissure, crack.

P. شكافتن *shikáftan.* To split, to cleave.

A. شكايت *shikáyet.* Complaint, accusation.

A. شكر *shukr.* Thanks, gratitude.

P. شكر *shakar.* Sugar, sweet.

A. شكران *shukrán.* Gratitude; grateful.

A. P. شكر ايزد *shukr i ízad.*
A. P. شكر خدا *shukr i khudá.*
Thank God.

P. شكر خنده *shakar-khanda.* A sweet smile.

P. شكرستان *shakaristán.* A sugar plantation.

P. شكرف *shigarf.* Wonder; rare, fine.

P. شكر قند *shakar-ḳand.* Sugar-candy.

A. P. شكر گذار *shukr-guzár.* Grateful.

P. شكر لب *shakar-lab.* Sweet-lipped.

A. شكر نعمت *shukr i ni'mat.* Gratitude.

P. شكست *shikast.* Broken; a defeat.

P. شكست دادن *shikast-dádan.* To defeat.

P. شكست خوردن *shikast-khurdan.* To be defeated.

P. شكستگى *shikastagí.* Defeat.

P. شكستن *shikastan.* To break, to defeat.

P. شكسته *shikasta.* Broken; the current Persian hand.

P. شكسته بال *shikasta-bál.* Broken-hearted.

P. شكفت *shiguft.* Astonishment.

P. شكفتن *shiguftan.* To blossom; to wonder.

P. شكفته *shigufta.* Blooming.

A. شكل *shakl.* Figure, form, shape.

P. شكم *shikam.* The belly.

P. شكم بنده *shikam-banda.*
P. شكم پرور *shikam-parvar.*
A glutton, sensualist.

P. شكم درد *shikam-dard.* Belly-ache.

P. شكن *shikan.* Breaking; a fold, wrinkle.

P. شكنبه *shikamba.* The tripe.

P. شكنج *shikanj.* A fold, a wrinkle.

P. شكنجه *shikanja.* The rack, torture; the stocks; a press.

P. شكنجيدن *shikanjídan.* To press.

A. شكور *shakúr.* Grateful.

P. شكوفه *shigúfa.* A blossom.

A. شكوے *shakwá.* Complaint.

P. شکوه *shikúh.* Pomp, majesty, dignity.

P. شکیب *shakíb.* Patience.

P. شکیبائی *shakíbáí.* Patience; patient.

P. شکیبیدن *shakíbídan.* To be patient.

P. شل *shal.* Paralytic.

P. شل *shul.* Of feeble character, &c.

A. شلاق *shalák.* Flagellation.

P. شلتاق *shilták.* Tumult, riot; an agitator.

P. شلغم *shalgham.* A turnip.

A. شلق *shalk.* A stroke with a scourge; the report of a gun.

P. شلوار *shalvár.* Trowsers, drawers.

A. شم *shamm.* The sense of smell.

P. شما *shumá.* You.

A. شماتت *shamátat.* Rejoicing at another's misfortunes.

P. شمار *shumár.* Reckoning, computation, number.

P. شماریدن *shumárídan.* To reckon, calculate.

A. شماع *shammá'.* A wax-chandler.

A. شمال *shimál* The North.

P. شمامه *shamáma.* A perfumed pastille.

P. شمایان *shumáyán.* You.

P. شمایل *shamáil.* Innate qualities.

A. P. شمایلی *shámaïlí.* Natural.

A. شمایم *shamáïm.* Perfumes, odours.

P. شمردن *shumurdan.* To reckon, count.

P. شمرده *shumurda.* Numbered.

A. شمس *shems.* The sun.

A. شمسیه *shamsíyeh.* A parasol.

P. شمشاد *shamshád.* The box-tree.

P. شمشیر *shamshír.* A sword.

A. شمع *sham'.* Wax; a wax-candle.

A. P. شمع دان *sham'-dán.* A candlestick.

A. شمول *shumúl.* Comprehending, containing.

A. P. شمه *shamma.* An atom, a pinch (of snuff), odour.

P. شمیدن *shamídan.* To be scared; to weep.

A. شمیم *shamím.* Smelling, scenting; perfume, odour.

P. شنا *shiná.* Swimming.

A. شناة *shunát.* (pl. of شانی.) Haters.

A. شناخ *shinákh.* A promontory.

P. شناخت *shinákht.* Acquaintance.

P. شناختن *shinákhtan.* To know.

P. شناس *shinás.* Intelligent, knowing (in comp.).

P. شناسائی *shinásáí.* Acquaintance, knowledge.

P. شناسیدن *shinásídan.* To know, perceive.

A. شناعت *shanáʿat.* Filthiness; being odious.

P. شنافتن *shináftan.* To hear, understand.

P. شنا کردن *shiná kerdan.* To swim.

P. سناور *shinávar.* A swimmer.

P. شناوری *shináverí.* Swimming.

P. شناه *shináh.* Swimming.

A. شنايع *shanáiʿ.* Vices, villainies.

P. شنبه *shambeh.* Saturday. يك شنبه *yek shambeh.* Sunday. دو شنبه *dú shambeh.* Monday. سه شنبه *sih shambeh.* Tuesday. چهار شنبه *chehár shambeh.* Wednesday. پنج شنبه *panj shambeh.* Thursday.

A. شنع *shaniʿ.* Abominable, villainous.

A. شنعة *shunʿat.* Baseness, villainy.

P. شنفتن *shiniftan.* To bear.

P. شنك *shang.* Fair; wanton.

P. شنكار *shingár.* Bugloss.

P. شنكرف *shangarf.* Cinnabar, vermilion.

P. شنو کردن *shinau kerdan.* To swim; to drown.

P. شنوا *shinavá.* A hearer.

P. شنوای *shinaváí.* Hearing.

P. شنودن *shunúdan.* To bear; to sniff.

P. شنونده *shinavenda.* A hearer.

P. شنيدن *shunídan.* To hear; to smell.

A. شنيع *shaníʿ.* Base, shameful, hateful.

A. شنيعت *shaníʿat.* Turpitude.

P. شو *shav.* Be, become. *shú.* Wash thou. *shú.* A husband.

A. شوات *shawát.* The skin of the head, the scalp.

A. شوارع *shawáriʿ.* Highways. (pl. of شارع.)

A. شوارق *shawárik.* Splendours, brightness. (pl. of شارق.)

A. شواعل *shawáʿil.* Flames. (pl. of شاعلة.)

A. شوال *shawwál.* The 10th Arabian month.

A. شواهد *shawáhid.* Witnesses. Verses or passages quoted by a commentator in illustration of the text.

A. شوائب *shawáïb.* Impurities. (pl. of شائبة.)

P. شوبا *shaubá.* Gruel; weaver's glue.

P. شوخ *shúkh.* Wanton, impudent.

P. شوخ چشمی *shúkh-chashmí.* Impudence.

P. شوخ ديده *shúkh-dída.* Impudent, wanton.

P. شوخی *shúkhí.* Jollity, mirth, impudence.

P. شور *shúr.* Salt, brackish; barren soil; tumult.

P. شور انكيز *shúr-angíz.* Seditious.

P. شورانيدن *shúránídan.* To cause to mix; to drive one crazy.

P. شوربا *shúrbá.* Broth, soup, gruel.

P. شور بخت *shúr-bakht.* Unfortunate.

P. شورستان *shúristán.* A salt-marsh.

P. شورش *shúrish.* Confusion, tumult.

P. شوره *shúra.* Saltpetre, nitre; barren ground.

P. شوری *shúrí.* A craze.

P. شوریدگی *shúrídagí.* Madness, love.

P. شوریدن *shúrídan.* To be perplexed, to grow mad.

P. شوریده *shúrída.* Confounded, crazy.

P. شوریده بخت *shúrída-bakht.* Unfortunate.

P. شوریده خاطر *shúrída-kháṭir.* Melancholy.

P. شوشه *shúsha.* An ingot of gold or silver; chips, rubbish; a particle, a part.

A. شوق *shauḳ.* Desire, longing, curiosity.

P. شوك *shauk.* A thorn, thistle.

A. شوکت *shaukat.* Pomp, dignity.

P. شوکران *shavkerán.* Hemlock, fennel.

P. شولوق *shúlúḳ.* Tumult, confusion, difficulty.

P. شولیدن *shúlídan.* To be distracted.

P. شولیده *shúlída.* Distracted; a stable.

A. شوم *shúm.* Unlucky; niggardly.

A. P. شومی *shúmí.* Misfortune, miserly conduct.

P. شومین *shúmín.* Spinage.

P. شوه *shava.* A gate; jet.

P. شوهر *shauhar.* A husband.

P. شوهیز *shauhíz.* Beholding, observation.

P. شوے *shúy.* Washing; glue, starch.

P. شویانیدن *shúyánídan.* To cause to wash.

P. شوییدن *shúídan.* To wash.

P. شه *shah.* A king.

P. شها *shahá.* O king!

A. شهاب *shiháb.* A falling star, a meteor. (Supposed to be brands with which the Angels pelt the genii who are caught eaves-dropping at the gates of heaven.)

A. شهادت *shahádat.* Testimony, martyrdom. Repeating the Mohammedan profession of faith.

A. شهامت *shahámat.* Ingenuity, bravery.

A. شهب *shahab.* Ash-coloured.

P. شهباز *shahbáz.* A falcon.

P. شهبد *shahbad.* The leader of an army.

P. شهپر *shah-par.* The longest feather in the wing.

A. P. شهبیت *shah-beit.* The last distich of an ode.

A. شهترج *shahtaraj.*
P. شهتره *shahtara.* } Frumenty.

P. شهتوت *shah-túť.* A blackberry.

A. شهد *shahd.* Honey.

A. شهداء *shuhadá.* Martyrs. (pl. of شهيد.)

A. P. شهد اب *shahd-áb.* Metheglin.

P. شهدانه *shah-dána.* The largest bead in a rosary.

P. شهديوار *shah-díwár.* A high wall surrounding a palace.

P. شهر *shahr.* A city.

A. شهر *shahr.* A month.

P. شهراه *shah-ráh.* The highway.

P. شهر بند *shahr-band.* City-walls.

P. شهر پناه *shahr-panáh.* Fortifications.

A. سهرة *shuhrat* or *shuhrah.* Report, fame, rumour.

P. شهر دار *shahr-dár.* A bird-catcher.

P. شهرستان *shahristán.* A large fortified city.

P. شهروا *shahravá.* Name of a tyrant who forced leathern money to pass current in his kingdom.

P. شهری *shahrí.* A citizen; belonging to a city.

P. شهريار *shahr-yár.* A king.

P. شهرير *shahrír.* The 8th Persian month (August).

P. شهنشاه *shahanshāh.* King of kings, an emperor.

P. شهنشاهی *shahanshāhí.* Imperial.

P. شه نشين *shah-nishín.* A royal seat; a balcony.

P. شهوار *shahvár.* Befitting a king, a precious pearl.

A. شهوت *shahwat.* Lust.

A. P. شهوت پرست *shahwat-parast.* A sensualist.

A. شهود *shuhúd.* Witnesses.

A. شهور *shuhúr.* Months.

P. شهی *shahí.* Royalty, royal.

A. شهيد *shahíd.* A witness, a martyr.

A. شهير *shahír.* Celebrated, famous.

A. شی *shai.* A thing.

P. شياد *shaiyád.* An impostor.

P. شياريدن *shiyárídan.* To plough.

A. شياطين *shayáṭín.* Devils. (pl. of شيطان.)

A. شياف *shiyáf.* Finely pulverized collyrium.

A. شيب *shaib.* Hoariness.

P. شيب *shaib.* A declivity; below, under.

P. شيپور *shaipúr.* A brazen trumpet.

A. شيخ *sheikh.* An elder, a chief.

A. P. شيخی *sheikhí.* Boasting, bragging.

P. شيد *shaid.* Trick, deceit, hypocrisy, folly.

P. شيد *shaid.* Bright, shining.

P. شیدا *shaidá.* Mad, frantic.

P. شیدائی *shaidáí.* Madness.

P. شیر *shír.* A lion, a tiger.

P. شیر *shír.* Milk.

P. شیرازه *shíráza.* The binding of a book.

P. شیراور *shír-áver.* Any animal that gives milk.

P. شیر بها *shír-bahá.* A present to a wet-nurse.

P. شیر خشت *shír-khisht.* Manna.

P. شیر خوارگی *shír-khváragí.* Suckling.

P. شیر خواره *shír-khára.* A babe, a suckling.

P. شیر دوغ *shír-dúgh.* Sour milk.

P. شیر ده *shír-dah.* A wet-nurse.

P. شیرزه *shírza.* }
P. شیر ژیان *shír i zhiyán.* }
A fierce, rapacious beast.

P. شیر مایه *shír-máya.* Rennet.

P. شیر مرد *shír-mard.* A brave man.

P. شیر مست *shír-mast.* A fattened lamb.

P. شیره *shíra.* The juice of fruit.

P. شیری *shírí.* Intrepidity.

P. شیرین *shírín.* Sweet.

P. شیرین گوار *shírín-guwár.* Of easy digestion.

P. شیرینی *shíríní.* Sweetness, a sweetmeat.

P. شیشه *shíshá.* Glass, a bottle.

P. شیشه گر *shísha-gar.* A glass-blower.

A. شیطان *shaitán.* Satan.

A. شیعه *shíʿah.* A follower of the sect of ʿAlí. (Opposed to سنی *sunní.*)

P. شیفتن *shíftan.* To be distracted with love.

P. شیفته *sheifta.* Mad, enamoured.

P. شیلان *shílán.* A royal entertainment.

A. شیمه *shímah.* Nature, disposition.

P. شیو *sheiv.* A declivity, a foundation.

A. شیوخ *shuyúkh.* Old men.

A. شیوع *shuyúʿ.* Publishing.

A. شیون *shívan.* Lamentation.

P. شیوه *shíva.* Custom, manner; gestures; coquetry.

P. شیهه *shíha.* The neighing of a horse.

ص

ص *ṣád.* Ṣ. The fourteenth letter of the Arabic and seventeenth of the Persian alphabet.

A. صابر *ṣábir.* Patient.

A. صابون *ṣábún.* Soap.

A. صاحب *ṣáḥib.* A master; possessor. Sir.

A. P. صاحبدل *ṣáḥib-dil.* A man of piety.

A. P. صاحب قران *ṣaḥib-ḳirán.* Lord of the conjunction; title given to a monarch who has reigned 40 years.

A. P. صاحب قراب pronounced *sábḳrán* or merely *ḳrán.* A silver coin value 1000 dínars. It is also called هزار دینار *hazár dínár* or هزار *hazár.*

A. صاحب نظر *ṣáḥib-nažar.* Clear-sighted.

A. صاحبه *ṣaḥiba.* A lady; madam.

A. صادر *ṣádir.* Happening, issuing.

A. صادق *ṣádiḳ.* Truthful.

A. صاعقه *ṣáʿiḳah.* Lightning, a thunderbolt.

A. P. صاف *ṣáf.* Clean, pure, sincere.

A. صافات صفّا *ṣáffát ṣaffan.* Adoring Angels (ranged in ranks).

A. صافن *ṣáfin.* The saphena vein.

A. صافی *ṣáfí.* Purity, cleanness.

A. صاقل *ṣaḳil.* A polisher.

A. صالح *sáliḥ.* A pious or honest man; name of a prophet.

A. صامت *ṣámit.* Silent; saturnine.

A. صانع *ṣániʿ.* Creator, maker.

A. صائب *ṣáïb.* Right, straight; hitting the mark.

A. صائل *ṣáïl.* Presumptuous; furious.

A. صائم *ṣáïm.* Thirsty; one who fasts.

A. صائم الدهر *ṣáïm ud dahr.* Continually fasting.

A. صب *ṣabb.* Effusion; a lover.

A. صبا *ṣabá.* The zephyr, a gentle gale.

A. صبابت *ṣabábat.* Love; a fog.

A. صباح *ṣabáḥ.* The morning, dawn.

A. صباحت *ṣabáḥat.* Beauty, grace.

A. صباغ *ṣabbágh.* A dyer.

A. صبح *ṣubḥ.* The morning, dawn.

A. P. صبح دم *ṣubḥ-dam.* At daybreak.

A. صبح صادق *ṣubḥ i ṣádiḳ.* The true dawn.

A. صبح كاذب *ṣubḥ i kážib.* Twilight.

A. صبر *ṣabr.* Patience.

A. صبر *ṣabir.* Aloes.

A. صبغ *ṣibagh.* Colour, tincture.

A. صبوح *ṣabúḥ.* A morning draught.

A. صبور *ṣabúr.* Patient.

A. صبوری *ṣabúrí.* Patience.

A. صبی *ṣabíy.* (pl. صبیان *ṣibyan.*) A boy.

A. صبیح *ṣabíḥ.* Beautiful; of a fine complexion.

A. صبیه *ṣabíyeh.* A girl, daughter.

A. صحاب *ṣiḥáb.* Companions.

A. صحابت *ṣaḥábat.* Society, company.

A. صحاراً *ṣiḥáran.* Publicly, openly.

A. صحارى *ṣaḥárá.* Deserts. (pl. of صحراء.)

A. صحاف *ṣaḥḥáf.* A book-seller, a bookbinder.

A. صحائف *ṣaḥáïf.* Leaves, pages.

A. صحب *ṣaḥb.* Companions.

A. صحبت *ṣuḥbat.* Society, company.

A. صحت *ṣiḥḥat.* Health.

A. صحراء *ṣaḥrá.* A desert-plain.

A. صحراءى *ṣaḥrát.* Wild.

A. صحف *ṣuḥuf* Books, ·aves, pages.

A. صحن *ṣaḥn.* A court, an ·rea.

A. صحو *ṣaḥw.* Becoming ·ober.

A. صحيح *ṣaḥíḥ.* Correct, exact; healthy.

A. صحيفه *ṣaḥífah.* A book, epistle.

A. صخره *ṣakhrah.* A rock. Name of an evil genius who stole Solomon's ring.

P. صد *ṣad.* A hundred.

A. صدا *ṣadá.* A sound, noise; an echo.

A. صدارت *ṣadárat.* The office of prime minister; precedence.

A. صداع *ṣudáʿ.* The head-ache.

A. صداق *ṣadáḳ.* A marriage-settlement.

A. صداقت *ṣadáḳat.* Sincerity, fidelity.

P. صد پا *ṣad-pá.* A centi-pede.

P. صد برگ *ṣad-barg.* Cent-foil.

A. صدح *ṣadḥ.* Raising the voice, singing.

P. صد چندان *ṣad chandán.* A hundred times as much.

A. صدر *ṣadr.* The front part; the breast.

A. صدر اعظم *ṣadr i aʿẓam.* Title given to the prime minister in Persia.

A. P. صدر نشين *ṣadr nishín.* A president.

A. صدف *ṣadaf.* A shell; mother-of-pearl.

A. صدق *ṣidḳ.* Veracity.

A. صدقه *ṣadaḳah.* Alms.

A. صدمه *ṣadmah.* A blow; collision; calamity.

A. صدور *ṣudúr.* Breasts; issuing.

A. صديق *ṣadíḳ.* A sincere friend.

A. صديق *ṣiddíḳ.* True, faith-ful.

P. صد يك *ṣad-yek.* One per cent.

A. صراحت *ṣaráḥat.* Clear-ness, perspicuity, purity, sin-cerity.

P. صراحى *ṣuráḥí.* A flask, bottle, flagon.

A. صراخ *ṣurákh.* A clamour, a scream.

A. صراط *ṣiráṭ.* A high-way.

A. صراف *ṣarráf.* A banker, money-changer.

A. صرة *ṣurrat.* A purse of money. The keeper of the privy purse.

A. صرصر *ṣarṣar.* A cold boisterous wind.

A. صرع *ṣarʻ.* Epilepsy.

A. صرف *ṣirf.* Pure; mere. Accidence (opposed to نحو *naḥw*, syntax).

P. صرفه *ṣarfa.* Surplus, gain.

A. صريح *ṣaríḥ.* Clear; evident.

A. صعاب *ṣiʻáb.* Difficulties.

A. صعب *ṣaʻb.* Hard, difficult.

A. صعلوك *ṣaʻlúk.* A robber, a mendicant.

A. صعوبت *ṣuʻúbat.* Difficulty.

A. صعود *ṣuʻúd.* Ascent.

A. صغار *ṣighár.* Small (things).

A. صغارت *ṣaghárat.* Smallness; infancy.

A. صغر *ṣughr.* Meanness.

A. صغر *ṣighar.* Smallness, infancy.

A. صغرى *ṣughrá.* The minor term of a syllogism.

A. صغير *ṣaghír.* Small.

A. صف *ṣaff.* A series, order, rank, file.

A. صفاء *ṣafá.* Purity, clearness, polish.

A. صفات *ṣifát.* Qualities.

A. صفاح *ṣifáḥ.* Tracts, sides.

A. صفت *ṣifat.* Quality, attribute, adjective, description.

A. صفحات *ṣafaḥát.* Pages.

A. صفحه *ṣafḥah.* Surface; page. من جستم از روى دو صفحه *man jastam az rúi dú ṣafḥa.* I skipped two pages.

A. P. صف در *ṣaff-dar.* Breaking the ranks, a hero.

A. صفر *ṣafar.* The second Arabian month.

A. صفر *ṣifr.* A cipher.

A. صفراء *ṣafrá.* The bile; yellow.

A. صفراوى *ṣafráwíy.* Bilious; choleric.

A. صفرت *ṣufrat.* Yellowness.

A. صفوت *ṣafwat.* Purity of heart.

A. صفوف *ṣufúf.* Ranks.

A. صفى *ṣafíy.* Pure, choice.

A. صفير *ṣafír.* Whistling, hissing.

P. صلا *ṣalá.* Proclamation.

A. صلابت *ṣalábat.* Firmness, hardness.

A. صلات or A. صلوت } *ṣalát.* Prayer, benediction.

A. صلاح *ṣaláḥ.* Rectitude; good advice.

A. P. صلاح ديد *ṣaláḥ-díd.* Advisable.

A. صلاح كار *ṣaláḥ-kár.* An adviser.

A. صلاحيت *ṣaláḥiyet.* Propriety.

A. صلب *ṣulb.* The backbone, loins; hard.

A. صلب *ṣulb.* Crucifixion.

A. صلبی *ṣulbíy.* Proceeding from the loins, lumbar.

A. صلح *ṣulḥ.* Peace, reconciliation.

A. صلحاء *ṣulaḥá.* Righteous men.

A. صلح نامه *ṣulḥ-náma.* A treaty, compromise.

A. صلد *ṣald.* Hard, solid.

A. صلعم *ṣal'am.* Abbreviation for صلی الله علیه و سلم *ṣall' alláh 'alaihi wa sallam.* God bless and preserve him (a formula used when the name of Mohammed is mentioned).

A. صلوات *ṣalawát.* Prayers.

A. صله *ṣilah.* A present, reward.

A. صلیب *ṣalíb.* A cross, crucifix.

A. صمم *ṣumm.* Deafness.

T. صمان *ṣamán.* Straw.

A. صمت *ṣamt.* Silence.

A. صمصام *ṣamṣám.* A sword that will not bend.

A. صمغ *ṣamagh.* Gum.

A. صمیم *ṣamím.* Pure, sincere.

A. صنادید *sanádíd.* Chiefs, leaders.

A. صناعت *ṣiná'at.* Art, trade.

A. صنائع *ṣaná'i.* Arts.

A. P. صندل *ṣandal.* Sandal-wood.

A. صندوق *ṣandúḳ.* A chest, box.

A. P. صندوقچه *ṣandúḳcha.* A little box.

A. P. صندوقخانه *ṣandúḳ-khána.* A wardrobe; place where the regalia are kept.

A. صنع *ṣan'.* Creation.

A. صنعت *ṣan'at.* Art, profession or trade.

A. صنعت کر *ṣan'at-gar.* An artizan.

A. صنف *ṣinf.* Sort, kind, species.

A. صنم *ṣanam.* An image, idol.

A. صنوبر *ṣanauber.* A fir, a pine.

A. صنوف *ṣunúf.* Different sorts. (pl. of صنف.)

A. ضواب *ṣawáb.* Rectitude, probity.

A. صواب دید *ṣawáb-díd.* Advisable.

A. صوارف *ṣawárif.* Vicissitudes. (pl. of صارفة.)

A. صواعق *ṣawá'iḳ.* Lightnings, thunderbolts. (pl. of صاعقه.)

A. صوامع *ṣawámi'.* Monasteries. (pl. of صومعه.)

A. صوب *ṣaub.* Side, direction.

A. صوبه *ṣúba.* A province.

A. صوت *ṣaut.* Sound, voice, noise.

A. صورت *ṣúrat.* (pl. صور *ṣuwar.*) Form, figure; a picture; a condition.

A. P. صورت کر *ṣúrat-gar.* A painter, sculptor.

A. صورے *ṣúrí.* Exterior, apparent; formal.

A. P. صوف *ṣúf.* Wool.

A. P. صوفی *ṣúfí.* *Ṣúfí*; a mystic.

A. صولت *ṣaulat.* Fury, onslaught.

A. صوم *ṣaum.* A fast, fasting.

A. صومعه *ṣúmi'ah.* A monastery, an oratory.

A. صهباء *ṣahbá'.* Red wine.

A. صهیل کردن *ṣahíl-kerdan.* To neigh.

A. صیاد *ṣaiyád.* A hunter, fowler.

A. صیانت *ṣiyánat.* Defence, guarding.

A. صیت *ṣít.* Fame, good reputation.

A. صید *ṣaid.* Game, prey.

A. P. صید گاه *ṣaid-gah.* A hunting-ground.

A. صیر *ṣair.* Being, becoming.

A. صیغه *ṣíghah.* (pl. صیغ *ṣiyagh.*) A mood, tense, formula.

A. صیف *ṣaif.* Summer.

A. صیقل *ṣaiḳal.* Polish, lustre; a polisher.

ض

ض *ẓád.* Ẓ. The fifteenth letter of the Arabic and eighteenth of the Persian alphabet.

A. ضابط *ẓábiṭ.* A ruler; one who holds firm.

A. ضابطه *ẓábiṭah.* Rule, custom.

A. ضاجع *ẓáji'.* Lying in bed.

A. ضاحك *ẓáḥik.* Laughing.

A. ضار *ẓárr.* Noxious, hurtful.

A. ضارب *ẓárib.* A striker, beater.

A. ضاری *ẓárí.* Trained to hunting, (a dog).

A. ضال *ẓáll.* Straying, erring.

A. ضامن *ẓámin.* A surety, security, bail.

A. P. ضامنی *ẓáminí.* Suretiship.

A. ضائع *ẓá'i.* Lost, ruined, injured.

A. ضبط *ẓabṭ.* Control, confiscation.

A. ضحی *ẓuḥá.* The forenoon.

A. ضحاك *ẓaḥḥák.* A laugher; name of a tyrannical king of Persia.

A. ضخامت *ẓakhámat.* Thickness, bulk.

A. ضد *ẓidd.* The contrary, opposite.

A. ضراء *ẓarrá'.* Adversity.

A. ضرب *ẓarb.* Striking; a blow; multiplication.

A. ضراب *ẓarráb.* A coiner.

A. ضراب خانه *ẓarráb-khána.* The mint.

A. ضرب المثل *ẓarb ul maśal.* Proverbial, a proverb.

A. ضرر *ẓarar.* Damage, injury.

A. ضرس *ẓirs.* A double-tooth, a grinder.

A. ضرور *zurúr*. Necessary, expedient.

A. ضرورت *zarúrat*. Necessity, compulsion.

A. ضرورے *zarúrí*. Necessary.

A. ضروریات *zarúriyát*. Necessaries.

A. ضریر *zarír*. Blind.

A. ضعف *zu'f*. Weakness, infirmity.

A. ضعفاء *zu'afá*. Feeble (persons).

A. ضعیف *za'íf*. Weak, infirm.

A. ضفدع *zefda'*. A frog.

A. ضل *zall*. } Error,
A. ضلالت *zalálat*. } losing one's way.

A. ضلع *zila'*. (pl. ضلوع *zulú'*.) Side, district; a rib.

A. ضلل *zalal*. An error.

A. ضلیل *zalíl*. Erring.

A. ضم *zamm*. Marking with the vowel-point ُ.

A. ضماد *zimád*. An embrocation, a poultice.

A. ضمائر *zamáïr*. Ideas; pronouns. (pl. of ضمیر.)

A. ضمائم *zamáïm*. Supplements. (pl. of ضمیمة).

A. ضمن *zamn*. Subject-matter; comprised.

A. ضمه *zammah*. The vowel-point ُ.

A. ضمیر *zamír*. The mind; a personal pronoun.

A. ضمران *zumrán*. Sweet basil.

A. ضمیم *zamím*. Annexed, included.

A. ضمیمه *zamímah*. Incorporation, supplement.

A. ضمین *zamín*. A sponsor, surety.

A. ضیاء *ziyá'*. Light, splendour.

A. ضیافت *ziyáfat*. An entertainment.

A. ضیغم *zaigham*. A lion.

A. ضیف *zaif*. A guest.

A. ضیق *zaik*. Tightness, anguish.

A. ضیق الصدر *zaik us sadr*. Asthma.

A. ضیمران *zaimurán*. An odoriferous herb.

ط

ط *tá*. T. The sixteenth letter of the Arabic and nineteenth of the Persian alphabet.

A. طاب *táb*. Being sweet, pure, excellent. طاب ثراه *tába sarahu*. May the earth lie light upon him, (said of a deceased Sheikh, &c).

T. طاپنچه *tápenché*. See طبنچه.

A. طاجن *tájin*. A frying-pan.

P. طارم *táram*. An arched roof.

A. طاری *ṭárí.* Happening suddenly, intervening.

P. A. طاس *ṭás.* A cup, goblet.

A. طاعت *ṭá'at.* (pl. طاعات *ṭaát.*) Obedience.

A. طاعن *ṭá'in.* One who taunts or reproaches.

A. طاعون *ṭá'ún.* A plague, pestilence.

A. طاغی *ṭághí.* A rebel.

A. P. طاق *ṭák.* An arch; unique, odd.

A. طاقت *ṭákat.* Power, strength.

A. P. طاقچه *ṭákcha.* A small arch, a niche.

A. طالب *ṭálib.* Asking, demanding, wanting.

A. طالب العلم *ṭálib ul 'ilm.* A student.

A. طالع *ṭáli'.* Fate, fortune, destiny.

A. طالعمند *ṭáli'-mand.* Fortunate.

P. طامات *ṭámát.* Incoherent speech.

A. طامع *ṭámi'.* Covetous.

A. طاءوس *ṭá'ús.* A peacock.

A. طاءوسی *ṭá'úsí.* Made of peacock's feathers; like a peacock.

A. طاهر *ṭáhir.* Pure, clean, chaste.

A. طایر *ṭáïr.* A bird; flying.

A. طایش *ṭáïsh.* Inconstant, volatile, light.

A. طائف *ṭáïf.* Surrounding, circumambulating.

A. طائفه *ṭáïfa.* A sect, a tribe.

A. طب *ṭibb.* The medical art.

A. طباخ *ṭabbákh.* A cook.

A. طباخت *ṭibákhat.* Cookery.

A. طباشیر *ṭabáshír.* Chalk, whiting.

A. طباع *ṭabbá'.* A printer.

A. طباعت *ṭibá'at.* Printing.

A. طبال *ṭabbál.* A drummer.

P. طبانچه *ṭapáncha.* A box, blow, slap.

P. طباندن *ṭapándan.* To stuff, to cram.

A. طبائع *ṭabá'i.* Natures, temperaments.

A. طبخ *ṭabkh.* Cooking.

P. طبرزد *ṭabarzad.* Sugar-candy.

A. طبع *ṭab'.* Nature, stamp, temperament; printing.

A. طبعی *ṭab'iy.* Natural.

A. طبق *ṭabaḳ.* The story of a house; a dish, a lid; anything which fits or matches another.

A. طبقات *ṭabaḳát.* Degrees, steps, stories.

A. P. طبقچه *ṭabaḳcha.* A small dish.

A. طبقه *ṭibḳah.* A degree, category, stage, story; a class of men.

A. P. طبقهٔ بالا *ṭabaḳa ï bálá.* An upper story.

A. P. طبقهٔ پائین *ṭabaḳa ï páïn.* The lower story.

A. طبل *ṭabl.* A drum.

A. طبله *ṭabla.* A wooden tray; a little drum.

A. طبی *ṭibbíy.* Medical.

A. طبیب *ṭabíb.* A physician.

A. طبیخ *ṭabíkh.* A decoction.

P. طپیدن *ṭapídan.* To flutter; to palpitate.

A. طبیعت *ṭabíʿat.* Nature, temperament.

A. طبیعی *ṭabíʿiy.* Natural, innate.

A. طحال *ṭiḥál.* The spleen, the milt.

A. طرار *ṭarrár.* A cut-purse.

P. طراز *ṭaráz.* An ornament; fashion.

P. ترازیدن *ṭarázídan.* To embroider.

A. طراوت *ṭaráwat.* Freshness, moisture.

A. طرب *ṭarab.* Cheerfulness, mirth.

A. طرح *ṭaraḥ.* Foundation; style, mode بطرح دادن *ba ṭarḥ dádan.* To compel to purchase at a fixed price.

A. P. طرح افکندن *ṭarḥ afgandan.* To lay a foundation; to practise.

A. P. ترخون *ṭarkhún.* Tarragon (a herb).

A. طرز *ṭarz.* Form, manner, habit.

A. طرف *ṭarf.* Side, quarter.

A. طرفاء *ṭarfáʾ.* The tamarisk-tree.

A. طرفة العين *ṭarfat ul ʿain.* The twinkling of an eye.

A. P. طرفدار *ṭaraf-dár.* Partial; an officer of the revenue.

A. طرفگی *ṭurfagí.* Rarity.

A. طرفه *ṭurfa.* A wonder, a rare thing.

A. طرفین *ṭarafain.* Both sides. (Arabic dual of طرف *ṭaraf.*)

A. طرق *ṭuruḳ.* Roads, ways. (pl. of طریق *ṭaríḳ.*)

P. طره *ṭurra.* A waving ringlet; a lock of hair.

A. طری *ṭaríy.* Fresh, moist.

A. طریق *ṭaríḳ.* Road, manner.

A. طریقت *ṭaríḳat.* Rite, profession, doctrine, sect. پیر طریقت *pír i ṭaríḳat.* The chief of a religious order.

A. طریقه *ṭaríḳa.* Rule, custom, manner.

A. طشت *ṭasht.* A large basin, a wash-trough.

A. طعام *ṭaʿám.* Food, victuals.

A. طعم *ṭaʿm* or *ṭuʿm.* Tasting, taste.

A. طعمه *ṭuʿmat.* Fodder; a bait.

A. طعن *ṭaʿn.* A reproach, chide.

A. P. طعنه زنان *ṭaʿna-zanán.* Jeering, gibing.

A. طغرا *ṭughrá.* The imperial signature; a sort of writing. This word is used technically in speaking of the number of letters, &c. چهار طغرا مکتوب *chehár ṭughrá maktúb*. Four letters.

A. طغیان *ṭughyán*. Rebellion, disobedience.

A. طفل *ṭifl*. A child, infant.

A. P. طفلانه *ṭiflána*. Childish, infantine.

A. طفوء *ṭufú'*. Quenching, extinguishing.

A. طفولیت *ṭufúlíyet*. Infancy, childhood.

A. طفیل *ṭufeil*. A sponge; a parasite.

A. طل *ṭall*. Dew.

P. طلا *ṭilá*. Gold, gilding.

A. طلاسم *ṭalásim*. Talismans. (pl. of طلسم *ṭilsam*.)

A. طلاق *ṭaláḳ*. Divorce.

A. طلاقت *ṭaláḳat*. Glibness (of tongue).

A. P. طلا کاری *ṭilá-kárí*. Gilding.

A. طلاوت *ṭiláwat*. Beauty, grace.

P. طلاءی *ṭiláí*. Golden.

A. طلایه *ṭaláya*. Piquets, reconnoitring parties.

A. طلب *ṭalab*. Demand, summons; wages.

A. طلباء *ṭulabá*. Students.

A. طلبکار *ṭalab-karí*. Demanding, requiring.

A. طلبنامه *ṭalab-náma*. A summons, citation.

A. طلبی *ṭalabí*. Requisite, demandable.

A. P. طلبیدن *ṭalabídan*. To summon, demand, inquire.

A. طلسم *ṭilsam*. A talisman.

A. طلعت *ṭala't*. Appearance, aspect.

A. طلق *ṭalḳ*. Talc.

A. طلوع *ṭulú'*. The rising of the sun, &c.

A. طلیعه *ṭalí'at*. The vanguard, a scout.

A. طمطراق *ṭamṭuráḳ*. Pomp, magnificence.

A. طمع *ṭama'*. Avidity, covetousness.

T. طمغا } طمغه } *ṭamghá*. A grant of land in perpetuity. A royal edict (see تمغه).

A. طناب pronounced تنف *ṭenef*. A tent rope.

A. P. طناب انداختن *ṭenef andákhtan*. To strangle, to bowstring.

A. طنبور *ṭambúr*. A tambourine.

A. طنز *ṭanz*. Sarcasm, irony.

A. طنطنه *ṭanṭana*. Pomp, clangour.

A. طنین *ṭanín*. A buzzing, a din.

A. طواف *ṭawwáf*. Circumambulating (the Kaabah at Mecca, &c.)

A. طوال *ṭawál*. Length, duration.

A. طوالع *ṭawáli'*. Horoscopes.

A. طوائف *ṭawáif*. Peoples, nations.

A. طوبی *ṭubá*. Well done! Name of a tree in paradise.

A. طور *ṭaur.* *ṭúr.* } Manner, mode, fashion.

A. طور سیناء *ṭúr síná'.* The mount Sinai.

A. طوطی *ṭúṭí.* A parrot.

A. طوع *ṭau'.* Obedience.

A. طوعاً *ṭau'an.* Willingly.

A. طوعاً و کرهاً *ṭau'an u karhan.* *Nolens volens.*

A. طوفان *ṭúfán.* A deluge; a hurricane.

A. طوق *ṭauḳ.* A collar. Power, capacity.

A. طول *ṭúl.* Longitude, length.

A. طومار *ṭúmár.* A roll, volume.

A. طومار جمع *ṭumár i jama'.* A rent-roll.

A. طویت *ṭawíyet.* Intention, design.

A. طویل *ṭawíl.* Long, tall; extensive.

A. طویله *ṭawíla.* A stable.

A. طهارت *ṭahárat.* Ceremonial purification.

A. طی *ṭai.* Rolling, folding; travelling; name of an Arabian tribe.

A. طیار *ṭaiyár.* Flying; fleet.

A. طیاش *ṭaiyásh.* Inconstant.

A. طیب *ṭaiyib.* Good, excellent.

A. طیب *ṭíb.* Fragrance; aromatic odour; goodness.

بطیب نفس *ba ṭíbi nafs.* With a willing mind.

A. طیر *ṭáir.* Flying; a bird.

A. طیران *ṭayarán.* Flight.

A. طیش *ṭaish.* Levity, folly.

A. طیف *ṭaif.* A phantom, a spectre. The form of a loved one seen in a dream.

A. طی کردن *ṭai kerdan.* To fold; to travel.

A. طیلسان *ṭailasán.* A mantle.

A. طین *ṭín.* Earth, clay.

A. طینت *ṭínat.* Nature, constitution.

A. طینی *ṭíní.* Earthy, innate, of clay.

A. طیور *ṭuyúr.* Birds.

A. طیوری *ṭuyúrí.* A dealer in birds.

ظ

ظ *ẓá.* Ẓ. The seventeenth letter of the Arabic and twentieth of the Persian alphabet.

A. ظافر *ẓáfir.* A conqueror.

A. ظالم *ẓálim.* A tyrant; unjust.

A. ظامی *ẓámí.* Thirsty.

A. ظان *ẓánn.* Suspicious.

A. ظاهر *ẓáhir.* Apparent, external.

A. ظاهر پرست *ẓáhir-parast.* A superficial observer.

A. ظاهری *ẓáhirí.* Exterior, apparent.

A. ظبی *żaby.* A gazelle.

A. ظرافت *żaráfat.* Elegance, wit.

A. ظرف *żarf.* (pl. ظروف *żurúf.*) A vessel; an adverb of time or place.

A. ظریف *żaríf.* Ingenious, graceful, witty.

A. ظفر *żafar.* Victory, triumph.

A. ظفرة *żafarat.* A cataract in the eye.

A. ظل *żill.* A shade, shadow; protection.

A. ظل الله *żill u' llah.* The shadow of God; title given to the Shah.

A. ظلم *żulm.* Tyranny, oppression.

A. ظلمانی *żulmániy.* Dark, obscure.

A. ظلمت *żulmat.* Darkness.

A. ظلم پیشه *żulm-písha.* A tyrant, oppressor.

A. ظلمت کده *żulmat-keda.* The mansion of darkness, this world.

A. ظلمیت *żulmíyet.* Tyranny, iniquity.

A. ظلوم *żalúm.* Tyrannical.

A. ظما *żama'.* Thirst.

A. ظن *żann.* Opinion, suspicion.

A. ظنون *żunún.* Thoughts, suspicions.

A. ظنه *żinnah.* Suspicion.

A. ظنی *żanní.* Suspicious.

A. ظواهر *żawáhir.* Appearances externals.

A. ظهر *żuhr.* Midday.

A. ظهر *żahr.* The back.

A. ظهور *żuhúr.* Appearing, arising.

A. ظهیر *żahír.* Supporter, protector.

ع

ع *'ain.* '. The eighteenth letter of the Arabic and twenty-first of the Persian alphabet.

A. عابد *'ábid.* A worshipper.

A. عابدانه *'ábidána.* Devout.

A. عابر *'ábir.* A passenger, traveller.

A. عاج *'áj.* Ivory.

A. عاجب *'ájib.* Exciting astonishment, or admiration.

A. عاجز *'ájiz.* Impotent.

A. عاجل *'ájil.* Quick, hasty.

A. عاجلانه *'ájilána.* Hastily.

A. عادة *'ádat.* (pl. عادات *'ádát.*) Custom, usage, practice.

A. عادل *'ádil.* Just, equitable.

A. عادی *'ádí.* An enemy, transgressing.

A. عار *'ár.* Disgrace.

A. عارج *'árij.* Ascending.

A. عارض *'áriz.* An accident; the cheek.

A. عارضی *'árizíy.* Accidental.

A. عارف *'árif.* Knowing (God). The highest grade to which a mystic or theologian can attain.

A. عارفانه *'árifána.* Like an *'árif.*

A. عاری *'ári.* Naked, deprived of.

A. عاریت *'áriyet,* A loan, anything borrowed.

A. عاریتی *'áriyetíy.* Borrowed.

A. عازم *'ázim.* Intending, determining.

A. عاشر *'áshir.* A tenth; a collector of tithes.

A. عاشق *'áshiḳ.* A lover.

A. عاشقانه *'áshiḳána.* Amorously.

A. عاشورا *'áshúrá.* The first days of the festival of Moharram.

A. عاصم *'áṣim.* Innocent, chaste.

A. عاصی *'áṣi.* A sinner, rebel.

A. عاطر *'áṭir.* Noble, odoriferous.

A. عاطف *'áṭif.* Benevolent; the conjunction.

A. عاطفت *'áṭifat.* Kindness.

A. عافیت *'áfiyet.* Health, welfare.

A. عاقبت *'áḳibat.* Conclusion, issue; the future life.

A. عاقر *'áḳir.* Barren (animal), unfruitful.

A. عاقر قرحا *'áḳir ḳarḥá.* Dracunculus, pellitory.

A. عاقل *'áḳil.* Intelligent, rational.

A. عاقلانه *'áḳilána.* Rationally, prudently.

A. عاکف *'ákif.* A devotee, devotion.

A. عالم *'álam.* (pl. عالمین *'álimin.*) The world, the universe; a state or condition.

A. عالم *'álim.* Learned, knowing.

A. عالمی *'álamíy.* Worldly.

A. عالمیان *'álamiyán.* People, men.

A. عالی *'áliy.* High, sublime.

A. عالی جناب *'álí janáb.* Excellency, highness.

A. عالی حضرت *'álí ḥaẓrat.* Majesty.

A. عالی قدر *'álí ḳadr.* High rank.

A. عالی مقام *'álí muḳám.* High station.

A. عالی مقدار *'álí miḳdár.* High in dignity.

A. عام *'ámm.* Common, universal.

A. عامر *'ámir.* Abundant.

A. خزینه عامره *khazína i 'ámira.* The public treasury.

A. عامل *'ámil.* A doer; a collector of revenue. (In grammar) a governing particle.

A. عامه *'ámmah.* The vulgar; plebeians.

A. عاند *'ánid.* Obstinate, refractory.

A. عائد *'áid.* Returning; relative.

A. عایق *'áiḳ.* Hindering.

A. عباء *'abá'.* A cloak worn by Dervishes and Bedouin Arabs.

A. عباب *'ubáb.* A wave, surge, billow.

A. عباد *'ibád.* Servants, worshippers.

A. عبادت *'ibádat.* Worship, service.

A. عبارت *'ibárat.* Style, phraseology.

A. عبارت سنج *'ibárat-sanj.* Attentive to style.

A. عباس *'abbás.* The name of Mohammed's grandfather.

A. عباسی *'abbású.* A coin current in the reign of Sháh 'Abbás = 4 sháhís of the present coinage.

A. عبث *'abs.* Vain, absurd, idle.

A. عبد *'abd.* A servant (of God), a man; a slave.

A. عبرت *'ibrat.* An example, warning..

A. عبری *'ibriy.* Hebrew.

A. عبودیت *'ubúdíyet.* Servitude, slavery.

A. عبور *'ubúr.* Passing, crossing (a river).

A. عبوس *'abús.* Austere, scowling.

A. عبید *'abíd.* Slaves, servants.

A. عبهر *'abhar.* The narcissus; dark-coloured (hair).

A. عبیر *'abír.* Ambergris, a perfume.

A. عتاب *'itáb.* Reproach.

A. عتائق *'atáïk.* Antiquities.

A. عتبه *'ataba.* A threshold.

A. عتق *'itk.* Liberty, manumission.

A. عتیق *'atík.* Old, ancient.

T. عثمانلو *'osmanlú* or *osmanlí.* Turkish, Ottoman.

A. عجائب *'ajáïb.* Wonders.

A. عجائز *'ajáiz.* Old women. (pl. of عجوز.)

A. عجب *'ajab.* Wonderful; wonder.

A. عجبا *'ajbá.* (fem.) A prodigy (of beauty).

A. عجز *'ajz.* Weakness, wretchedness.

A. عجل *'ijl.* A calf.

A. عجلت *'ajlat.* Haste, hurry.

A. عجم *'ajam.* Persia, any country but Arabia.

A. عجمی *'ajamíy.* A Persian, a barbarian.

A. عجوز *'ajúz.* An old woman.

A. عجیب *'ajíb* Wonderful, surprising.

A. عجیل *'ajíl.* Making haste.

A. عجین *'ajín.* Dough, paste, an electuary.

A. عد *'add.* Numeration, number.

A. عدالت *'adálat.* Justice, equity, law.

A. عداوت *'adáwat.* Enmity, hostility.

A. عداوت گزین *'adáwat guzín.* Hostile, inimical.

A. عدة *'iddat.* The time which must expire before a divorced woman can be remarried.

A. عدد *'adad.* Number.

A. عدس *'adas.* A lentil.

A. عدل *'adl.* Justice, equity.

A. عدم *'adam.* Non-existence, privation.

A. عدمی *'adamíy.* Privative, non-existent.

A. عدو *'adúw.* An enemy.

A. عدول *'adúl.* Swerving, refusing.

A. عدیل *'adíl.* Equal, a load balancing another.

A. عدیم *'adím.* Destitute of, deprived.

A. عذاب *'aẓáb.* Torment, punishment.

A. عذار *'iẓár.* The cheek.

A. عذال *'aẓẓál.* A railer, an accuser.

A. عذب *'aẓb.* Sweet (water).

A. عذر *'uẓr.* An excuse, pretext.

A. P. عذر خواستن *'uẓr khástan.* To beg pardon.

A. P. عذر خواه *'uẓr-kháh.* Seeking an excuse.

A. P. عذر نهادن *'uẓr nihádan.* To excuse.

A. عذوبت *'uẓúbat.* Sweetness.

A. عرابه *'arába.* A cart, wheeled-carriage.

A. عراده *'arráda.* A balista, an engine for hurling missiles.

A. عراق *'irák* Babylonia, Chaldea.

A. عراقی *'irákíy.* Belonging to Irac or Chaldea.

A. عرائس *'aráïs.* Brides. (pl. of عروس.)

A. عرائض *'aráïẓ.* Petitions. (pl. of عریضة.)

A. عرب *'arab.* Arabia, an Arab.

A. عربون *'arbún.* Earnest-money.

A. عربده *'arbada.* Conflict, dispute; a drunken brawl.

A. عربستان *'arabistán.* Arabia.

A. عربی *'arabíy.* Arabia, the Arabic language.

A. عرس *'urs.* A marriage-feast, a spouse.

A. عرش *'arsh.* A throne; the highest heaven.

A. عرصه *'arṣah.* A space (of time); an area, a plain.

A. P. عرصه زمین *'arṣa ï zamín.* The surface of the earth.

A. عرض *'arẓ.* Breadth; a petition.

A. عرضداشت *'arẓ-dásht.* A petition.

A. عرض گاه *'arẓ-gáh.* A rendezvous for troops.

A. عرضه *'urẓah.* Intention, project; credit.

A. عرضی *'arẓí.* A petition, memorial.

A. عرف *'urf.* Known, notorious; common parlance.

A. عرفاء *'urafá.* Intelligent persons. (pl. of عارف.)

A. عرفان *'irfán.* Knowing, intelligent.

A. عرفی *'urfí.* Public, notorious.

A. عرق *'araḳ.* Juice, essence, sweat; distilled spirit.

A. P. عرق کشیدن *'araḳ keshídan.* To distil spirituous liquors.

A. P. عرق سه اتشی *'araḳ i sih átishí.* Extra-strong spirit.

A. عرق *'irḳ.* A root, base.

A. عرق النسا *'irḳ un nisá.* The sciatica.

A. عروج *'uruj.* Ascent, ascension.

A. عروس *'arús.* A bride.

A. عروسی *'arúsí.* Bridal, nuptials.

A. عروض *'arúẓ.* Prosody.

A. عروق *'urúḳ.* Veins. (pl. عرق *'irḳ.*)

A. عریان *uryán.* Naked.

A. عریض *'aríẓ.* Broad, wide.

A. عریضه *'aríẓa.* A petition.

A. عز *'izz.* Glory, grandeur.

A. عزا *'azá.* Condolence.

A. عزازیل *'azázíl.* The devil.

A. عزب *'azab.* An unmarried person.

A. P. عزب دفتر *'azab-dafter.* A clerk, registrar.

A. عزت *'izzat.* Honour, respect.

A. عزرائیل *'azráïl.* The angel of death.

A. عزل *'azl.* Removal from office.

A. عزلت *'uzlat.* Retirement.

A. عزم *'azm.* Design, intention.

A. عز و جل *'azza wa jall.* May He be honoured and glorified! (applied to God.)

A. عزیز *'azíz.* Dear, beloved, darling, precious.

A. عزیز مصر *'azíz i misr.* Joseph, the sovereign of Egypt.

A. عزیمت *'azímat.* Purpose, determination.

A. عساکر *'asákir.* Armies. (pl. of عسکر.)

A. عسر *'usr.* Difficulty.

A. عسرت *'usrat.* Difficulty, distress.

A. عسس *'aṣas.* The patrol night-watch.

A. عسکر *'askar.* An army.

A. عسل *'asal.* Honey.

A. عسیر *'asír.* Difficult.

A. عشا *'ashá.* The first watch of the night; supper.

A. عشاق *'usshák.* Lovers. (pl. of عاشق.)

A. عشائر *'ashaïr.* Kindred, clansmen.

A. عشر *'ushr.* A tithe.

A. عشر *'ashar.* Ten.

A. عشرت *'ishrat.* Pleasure, delight.

A. عشرین *'ishrín.* Twenty.

A. عشق *'ishḳ.* Love, affection.

A. عشق باز *'ishḳ-báz.* A ladies' man.

A. عشق حقیقی *'ishḳ i haḳíḳíy.* Love (for a mistress, &c.).

A. عشق مجازے *'ishḳ i mujázíy.* Paternal, filial, &c. love.

A. عشوه *'ishwat.* Wanton coquetry.

A. عشى *'ashíy.* The evening.

A. عشر *'ashír.* A tenth.

A. عصا *'aṣá.* A staff, wand.

A. عصاة *'uṣát.* Rebels, sinners.

A. عصار *'aṣṣár.* An oil-presser.

A. عصاره *'uṣárah.* Expressed juice.

A. عصافر *'aṣáfír.* Sparrows. (pl. of عصفور.)

A. عصب *'aṣab.* A tendon, sinew.

A. عصر *'aṣr.* Time, an age; the afternoon.

A. عصرانه *'aṣrána.* A five-o'clock meal.

A. عصفور *'aṣfúr.* A sparrow.

A. عصمت *'iṣmat.* Chastity, continence.

A. عصيان *'isyán.* Rebellion, sin.

A. عضد *'azud.* An arm.

A. عضلة *'azalat.* A muscle.

A. عضو *'azúw.* A limb, a member.

A. عطاء *'aṭá'.* A gift, favour, grant.

A. عطار *'aṭṭár.* A druggist, a perfumer.

A. عطارد *'uṭárid.* The planet Mercury.

A. عطاس *'uṭás.* Sneezing; the dawn aurora.

A. عطايا *'aṭáyá.* Gifts, presents. (pl. of عطيه *'aṭíyeh.*)

A. عطب *'aṭab.* Destruction.

A. عطر *'iṭr.* Perfume, essence, odour.

A. عطريات *'iṭríyát.* Perfumes.

A. عطس *'aṭs.* Sneezing.

A. عطسه زدن *'aṭsa zadan.* To sneeze.

A. عطش *'aṭsh.* Thirst.

A. عطشان *'aṭshán.* Thirsty.

A. عطف *'aṭf.* Favour; inclination; (in grammar) a conjunction. عطف بيان *'aṭf i baiyán.* Apposition.

A. عطل *'uṭal.* Privation.

A. عطوف *'aṭúf.* Favourable, kind.

A. عطوفت *'uṭúfat.* Favour, affection.

A. عطيه *'aṭíyeh.* A gift, present.

A. عظم *'aẓm.* A bone. (pl. عظام *'iẓám.*)

A. عظم *'uẓm.* Greatness; large.

A. عظماء *'uẓamá'.* Grandees.

A. عظمت *'aẓamat.* Greatness, magnificence.

A. عظيم *'aẓím.* Great, mighty.

A. عف *'iff.* } Chastity,
A. عفت *'iffat.* } continence.

A. عفاف *'afáf.* Chastity, continence.

A. عفريت *'ifrít.* A demon.

A. عفص *'afiṣ.* A styptic, an astringent.

A. عفو *'afw.* Pardon, forgiveness.

A. عفونت *'ufúnat.* Corruption, infection.

P. عفيدن *'afídan.* To bark.

A. عفيف *'afíf.* Abstinent, chaste.

A. عقاب *'uḳáb.* An eagle.

A. عقاب *'iḳáb.* Chastisement.

A. عقارب *'aḳárib.* Scorpions. (pl. of عقرب.)

A. عقائد *'aḳáid.* Articles of faith. (pl. of عقيدة.)

A. عقب *'aḳab.* Behind, after; the heel.

A. عقبى *'uḳbá.* Futurity, end.

A. عقد *'aḳd.* A knot.

A. P. عقد بستن *'aḳd bastan.* To betroth, to tie a knot.

A. P. عقد نكاح *'aḳd i nikaḥ.* The marriage-tie.

A. عقدة *'uḳdah.* A knot, a node.

A. عقده كشا *'uḳda-kushá.* Resolving difficulties.

A. عقر *'aḳr.* Being barren (an animal).

A. عقرب *'aḳrab.* A scorpion.

A. عقل *'aḳl.* Intellect.

A. عقلاء *'uḳalá.* Intelligent people.

A. عقلى *'aḳlíy.* Judicious, reasonable.

P. عقوبت *'uḳúbat.* Punishment, torment.

A. عقود *'uḳúd.* Knots.

A. عقول *'uḳúl.* Intelligences.

A. عقيدت *'aḳídat.* Faith, belief.

A. P. عقيدت كيش *'aḳídat-kísh.*
A. P. عقيدت منش *'aḳídat-manish.* } Faithful.

A. عقيق *'aḳíḳ.* A cornelian, a ruby.

A. عقيم *'aḳím.* Barren.

A. عكس *'aks.* Reflection, inversion; a shadow.

A. علاء *'alá'.* Height, sublimity.

A. على *'alá.* Above, upon, on.

A. علاج *'iláj.* A remedy.

A. P. علاج پذير *'iláj-pażír.* Curable.

A. على الخصوص *'ala 'lkhuṣúṣ.* Especially; perpetually.

A. على الصباح *'ala ṣṣabáḥ.* Early in the morning.

A. على الاطلاق *'ala 'l iṭláḳ.* Universally, absolutely.

A. علاف *'alláf.* A seller of horse-provender.

A. علاقه *'aláḳah.* Connection.

A. علامة *'alámat.* A sign, symptom. (pl. علامات *'alámát.*)

A. علامه *allámah.* A very learned man.

A. علانية *'aláníyet.* Public life, external deportment.

A. علاوه *'aláwa.* Besides, moreover.

A. علاوه برين *'aláwa barín.* Moreover, besides this.

A. علائق *'aláiḳ.* Connections.

A. علت *'illat.* Cause, reason; disease.

A. علت فاعلی *'illat i fá'ilíy.* Efficient cause.

A. علت مادی *'illat i máddíy.* Material cause.

A. علت صوری *'illat i ṣúríy.* Apparent cause.

A. علت غائی *'illat i ghá'íy.* Final cause.

A. علحده *'alá-ḥidda.* Separate, apart.

A. علف *'alaf.* Forage, fodder.

A. علف زار *'alaf-zár.* A pasture.

A. علم *'alam.* A flag, banner; a proper name.

A. علم *'ilm.* Knowledge, science, theory.

A. علماء *'ulamá.* Learned men.

A. علم دار *'alam dár.* A standard, banner.

A. علمی *'ilmíy.* Scientific, theoretic.

A. علو *'ulúw.* Sublimity, height.

A. علوفه *'ulúfah.* Provender, money, subsistence for an army.

A. علوم *'ulúm.* Sciences. (pl. of علم *'ilm.*)

A. علوی *'alawíy.* A descendant from 'Alí.

A. علیاء *'ulyá* (fem. of علی.) Eminent, most high. ید علیاء *yad i 'ulyá.* The upper or bestowing hand.

A. علیک *'alaika.* Above, on or to thee.

A. علیل *'alíl.* Sick, indisposed.

A. علیم *'alím.* Wise, learned.

A. علیه *'alaih.* Upon him or it.

A. عم *'amm.* Paternal uncle.

A. عماد *'imád.* Pillar, support.

A. عمارت *'imárat.* Building; an edifice.

A. عمال *'ummál.* Agents, tax-gatherers.

A. عمامه *'amáma.* A turban.

A. عمد *'amd.* Intention, purpose. بلا عمد *bilá 'amdin.* Unintentionally.

A. عمداً *amdan.* Deliberately, purposely.

A. عمدة *'umdat.* A pillar, a prop; a noble.

A. عمر *'umr.* Life-time, age.

A. عمرو *'Amr.* A fictitious name used in legal and scholastic works: see Zeid.

A. عمق *'amḳ* or *'umḳ.* Depth, profundity.

A. عمل *'amal.* Action, possession; practice (opposed to علم *'ilm.* Theory).

A. عملی *'amalíy.* Practical, forged.

A. عمو *'ammú.* A paternal uncle.

A. عمود *'amúd.* A pillar, a prop.

A. عموم *'umúm.* Common, universal.

A. عموماً *'umúman.* Generally, universally.

A. عمه *'ammah.* Paternal aunt.

A. عمی *'amíy.* Blind.

A. عمیق *'amík.* Deep, profound.

A. عمیم *'amím.* Universal, general.

A. عن *'an.* Of, from, on, after, &c.

A. عنا *'ana.* Care, trouble.

A. عناب *'unnáb.* The jujube fruit.

A. عناد *'inád.* Contumacy.

A. عنادل *'anádil.* Nightingales. (pl. of عندلیب.)

A. عناصر *'anásir.* The elements. (pl. of عنصر.)

A. عناقید *'anákíd.* Bunches, clusters.

A. عنان *'inán.* Reins.

A. عنایت *'ináyat.* Favour, assistance, present.

A. عنب *'anab.* A grape.

A. عنبر *'amber.* Ambergris; a perfume.

A. عنبر بار *'amber-bár.* Odoriferous, fragrant.

A. عنبرین *'amberín.* Of ambergris.

A. عند *'ind.* (An adverb of time and place), near, with, about, &c. عند الفرصة *'ind al fursat.* At your leisure.

A. عندلیب *'andalíb.* A nightingale.

A. عنصر *'unsur.* An element.

A. عنصری *'unsurí.* Elementary.

A. عنف *'unf.* Severity, rigour, violence.

A. عنفوان *'unfuwán.* The flower of youth.

A. عنق *'ank.* The neck.

A. عنقا *'anká.* A fabulous bird, the phœnix; also called سیمرغ *símurgh,* q. v.

A. عنقریب *'an-karíb.* Nearly, almost.

A. عن قبله *'an kibalih.* On his part.

A. عنکبوت *'ankabút.* A spider.

A. عنوان *'unwán.* A preface; the address of a letter.

A. عنید *'aníd.* Refractory.

A. عنیف *'aníf.* Severe, rigorous.

A. عنین *'anín.* Impotent.

A. عوارض *'awáriz.* Accidents.

A. عواطف *'awátif.* Favours, affections.

A. عواقب *'áwákib.* Ends, consequences.

A. عوام *'awwám.* The common people.

A. عوام الناس *'awwám un nás.* The vulgar, the masses.

A. عوامل *'awámil.* Performers, tax-gatherers.

A. عوائد *'awáïd.* Gains, profits, returns.

A. عوائق *'awáïk.* Impediments.

A. عوج *'awaj.* Crooked, curved.

A. عود *'úd.* Fragrant aloes wood.

A. عود *'aud.* Returning.

A. عورت *'aurat.* A woman; the *pudenda.*

A. عوض *'iwaz.* Recompense, compensation, equivalent, substitute.

A. عون *'aun.* Aid, assistance.

A. عہد *'ahd.* Promise, treaty; season.

A. عہد و پیمان *'ahd u paimán.* Bargain and agreement.

A. عہد نامہ *'ahd-náma.* A treaty.

A. عہدہ *'uhda.* Office, trust.

A. عہدہ بندے *'uhda bandí.* A stated time for payment.

A. عہدہ دار *'uhda-dár.* An officer.

A. عہود *'uhúd.* Promises.

A. عیاذًا باللہ *'iyázan billah.* God forbid!

A. عیار *'iyár.* Mark, proof, standard.

A. عیار *'aiyár.* A cheat, sly.

A. عیار گرفتن *'iyár giriftan.* To try, to assay.

A. عیار گیر *'iyár-gír.* An assayer.

A. عیارے *'aiyárí.* Deceit, imposture.

A. عیاش *'aiyásh.* A jovial fellow; a *bon-vivant.*

A. عیال *'iyál.* Family, children.

A. عیان *'aiyán.* Clear, manifest.

A. عیب *'aib.* A defect, blemish, fault, vice.

A. عیب جوی *'aib júí.* Cavilling.

A. عیب ناک *'aib-nák.* Defective.

A. عید *'íd.* A festival, holiday.

A. عید غدیر *'íd i ghadír.* Feast in commemoration of the day when Mohammed appointed 'Alí his successor.

A. عید فطر *'íd i fatr.* Feast at the end of the fast of Ramazán.

A. عید قربان *'íd i kurbán.* The feast of sacrifices.

A. عید مولود *'íd i maulúd.* Feast of the nativity (of Mohammed).

A. عید نوروز *'íd i nau-rúz.* New year's day.

A. عیدے *'ídíy.* Belonging to a festival.

A. عیسی *'ísá.* Jesus.

A. عیسوے *'ísawíy.* Christian.

A. عیش *'aish.* Pleasure, delight.

A. عین *'ain.* The eye, sight; a fountain; the essence of a thing, the thing itself; as عین کمال *'ain i kemál.* Perfection itself.

A. عینک *'ainak.* Spectacles.

A. عینی *'ainí.* Real.

A. عینین *'ainain.* The two eyes. (An Arabic dual of عین.)

A. عيوب *'uyúb.* Vices, defects. (pl. of عيب.)

A. عيون *'uyún.* Eyes, fountains. (pl. of عين.)

غ

غ *ghain.* Gh. The nineteenth letter of the Arabic, and twenty-second of the Persian alphabet.

A. غابن *ghábin.* An impostor, a cheat.

A. غادر *ghádir.* A traitor.

A. غار *ghár.* A cave, a hollow.

A. غارت *ghárat.* Rapine, plunder.

P. غازه *gháza.* Rouge.

A. غازى *ghází.* A warrior.

A. غاشيه *gháshiyeh.* A saddle-cloth.

A. غاصب *ghásib.* An usurper.

A. غافل *gháfil.* Negligent.

A. غالب *ghálib.* A conqueror, overcoming.

A. غالبًا *gháliban.* Chiefly, principally.

A. P. غالبانه *ghálibána.* Triumphant.

A. غالى *ghálí.* Dear, valuable.

A. غاليه *ghúliyeh.* Civet, perfume.

A. غامر *ghámir.* Flooded, overwhelmed.

A. غامض *ghámiz.* Obscure.

A. غانية *gháníyet.* A lady.

A. غائب *gháíb.* Absent.

A. P. غائبانا *gháíbána.* Invisible.

A. غايت *gháyat.* The end, extremity.

A. غائط *gháít.* Excrement.

A. غب *ghibb.* An intermittent fever.

A. غبًا *ghibban.* Every second day; at intervals.

A. غبار *ghubár.* Dust, a vapour.

A. غبغب *ghabghab.* A dewlap, a double chin.

A. غبن *ghabn.* Cheating, gulling.

A. غبى *ghabíy.* A dolt.

A. غد *ghadd.* To-morrow.

A. غدار *ghaddár.* Perfidious.

A. غدر *ghadr.* Perfidy, treachery.

A. غدير *ghadír.* A pool, a pond.

A. غذاء *ghizá.* Diet.

A. غراء *gharrá.* Bright, splendid.

A. غراب *ghuráb.* A crow; a corvette (ship).

A. غرامت *gharámat.* Mulct, fine.

A. غرائب *gharáib.* Wonders. (pl. of غريبة.)

A. غرب *gharb.* Sunset, the west.

A. غرباء *ghurabá*. The poor, strangers. (pl. of غريب.)

A. غربت *ghurbat*. Foreign travel, exile.

A. غربال *ghirbál*. A sieve.

A. غربی *gharbíy*. Western, westerly.

A. غرشیدن *gharshidán*. To be angry.

A. غرض *gharẓ*. A design, an object; a grudge.

A. P. غرضمند *gharẓ-mand*. Self-interested.

A. غرغره *ghar-ghara*. A gargle.

A. غرفه *ghurfah*. An upper chamber.

A. غرق *gharḳ*. Drowned, immersed.

A. P. غرقاب *gharḳ-áb*. Deep water, a whirlpool.

A. T. غرما *ghuramá*. Composition of a bankrupt with his creditors.

P. غرنده *gharenda*. Roaring, furious.

A. غروب *ghurúb*. Sunset.

A. غرور *ghurúr*. Pride, conceit.

A. غره *ghurra*. The "blaze" or white star on a horse's forehead; the first day of the month.

P. غره *gharra*. Deluded; proud.

A. غريب *gharíb*. Poor, rare, a stranger.

P. غریدن *ghurídan*. To thunder, roar; to yawn.

A. غریزی *gharízíy*. Innate, natural.

A. غريق *gharíḳ*. Immersed, drowned.

P. غريو *ghiríw*. Clamour.

A. غزا *ghazá*. A war, a raid.

A. غزال *ghazál*. A gazelle.

A. غزل *ghazal*. (pl. غزليات *ghazalíyát*.) A sonnet.

P. غزلاغ *ghazlágh*. A lark.

A. غزو *ghazw*. Making war, fighting, a raid.

A. غزير *ghazír*. Copious.

A. غسل *ghusl*. Washing, ablution.

A. غشاوة *ghasháwat*. Dimness of eye-sight.

A. غشی *ghashy*. Fainting.

A. غصب *ghaṣb*. Usurpation.

A. غصب *ghuṣn*. A branch. (pl. غصون *ghuṣún*.)

A. غصه *ghuṣṣa*. Suffocation; anger, anguish.

A. غضب *ghaẓab*. Anger, rage.

A. غضبان *ghaẓbán*. Enraged.

A. P. غضبناك *ghaẓab-nák*. Angry.

A. غضروف *ghuẓrúf*. (pl. غضاريف *ghaẓáríf*.) A gristle.

A. غضنفر *ghaẓanfar*. A lion.

A. غفار *ghaffár*. A pardoner, forgiver.

A. غفران *ghufrán*. Pardon, forgiveness.

A. غفلت *ghaflat.* Negligence.

A. غفور *ghafúr.* Forgiving.

A. غل *ghull.* A fetter, yoke.

A. غل *ghill.* Perfidy, guile.

A. غلات *ghallát.* Grain.

A. غلاف *ghiláf.* A cover, a scabbard.

A. غلام *ghulám.* A slave, boy; a page of the imperial household.

P. غلبة *ghalabat.* Superiority, excelling, conquering.

A. غلط *ghalaṭ.* An error, blunder.

P. غلطان *ghalṭán.* Rolling, wallowing.

P. غلطيدن *ghalṭídan.* To tumble, to roll.

A. غلظت *ghalẓat* or *ghulẓat.* Thickness, grossness.

P. غلغل *ghulghul.* Tumult, clamour.

A. غلف *ghalaf.* The prepuce.

A. غلمان *ghilmán.* Boys, pages. (pl. of غلام.)

A. غلوله *ghalúla.* A ball.

A. غلة *ghallah.* Grain.

A. غليظ *ghalíẓ.* Thick, gross.

P. غليواج *ghalíwáj.* } A kite

P. غليواز *ghalíwáz.* } (bird).

A. غم *ghamm.* Sorrow, grief, care.

A. غماز *ghammáz.* An eavesdropper.

A. غمازی *ghammází.* Slander, eaves-dropping.

A. P. غمخوار *gham-khár.* Commiserating.

A. P. غم خوردن *gham-khurdan.* To grieve; to commiserate.

A. غمز *ghamz.* A signal; conniving.

A. P. غمزدگی *gham-zadagí.* Grief.

A. P. غمزده *gham-zada.* Grieved, afflicted.

A. غمزه *ghamza.* Ogling, connivance.

A. P. غمگسار *gham-gusár.* Condoling, pitying.

A. غمگین *gham-gín.* Sorrowful.

A. غموم *ghumúm.* Sorrows. (pl. of غم.)

P. غمیار *gham-yár.* Yawning, gaping.

A. غناء *ghaná.* Riches, sufficiency.

A. غناء *ghiná.* A song.

A. غنائم *ghanáim.* Spoils, plunder. (pl. of غنيمة.)

P. غنج *ghanj.* An amorous gesture.

P. غنچه *ghuncha.* A bud, blossom.

P. غنجيدن *ghanjídan.* To toy.

A. غنم *ghanam.* Sheep; plunder.

P. غنودن *ghunúdan.* To slumber.

A. غنی *ghaníy.* Rich, contented.

A. غنيم *ghaním.* An enemy, a plunderer.

A. غنيمة *ghanímat.* Gain,

plunder; a godsend. غنیمت شمردن *ghanímat shumurdan.* To esteem as a privilege; to make the most of.

A. غواشی *ghawáshí.* Saddle-cloths. (pl. of غاشه.)

A. غواص *ghawwáṣ.* A diver.

A. غوایت *ghawáyet.* Extremities.

A. غوث *ghauṡ.* A cry for help. i. q. ابدال *abdál,* q. v.

T. غوچ *ghúch.* A ram.

A. غور *ghaur.* Deliberation, depth; lowlands.

A. P. غور رسی *ghaur-rasí.* Deep research.

P. غوره *ghúra.* Unripe grapes or dates.

A. غوطه *ghauṭah.* Plunging, diving.

A. P. غوطه خور *ghauṭa-khur.* A diver.

P. غوغا *ghaughá.* A noise, uproar.

P. غوك *ghúk.* A frog.

A. P. غول *ghúl.* An ogre; a demon of the waste.

A. غیاث *ghiyáṡ.* Succour, redress; a redresser.

A. غیب *ghaib.* The invisible; the inscrutable.

A. غیبت *ghaibat.* Absence; backbiting.

A. P. غیب دان *ghaib-dán.* Omniscient.

A. غیث *ghaiṡ.* Rain; widespread clouds.

A. غیر *ghair.* Another, different, except, (in comp.) not, un-. بغیر *bighair.* Without.

A. غیرت *ghairat.* Emulation, zeal; jealousy.

A. غیر جنس *ghair-jins.* A different species.

A. غیر حاضر *ghair-ḥáẓir.* Absent.

A. غیر منتهای *ghair-muntahái.* Unlimited.

A. غیظ *ghaiẓ.* Anger, rage.

A. غیوب *ghuyúb.* Invisible (things).

A. غیور *ghaiyúr.* Jealous, high-minded.

ف

ف *fá.* F. The twentieth letter of the Arabic, and twenty-third of the Persian alphabet.

A. فاتح *fátiḥ.* One who opens; a conqueror.

A. فاتحه *fátiḥah.* The first chapter of the Ḳorān; prayers for the dead.

A. P. فاتحا خوانی بر چیدن *fátiḥa kh'ání bar chídan.* To break up an assembly convened to offer prayers for the dead.

A. فاتر *fátir.* Weak, languid.

A. فاتك *fátik.* Intrepid, strong.

A. فاتن *fátin.* A tempter; fascinated.

A. فاجر *fájir.* (fem. فاجره *fájirah.*) An adulterer.

A. فاحش *fáḥish.* Obscene, indecent.

A. فاحشه *fáḥishah.* A harlot.

P. فاخته *fákhta.* A ring-dove.

A. فاخر *fákhir.* Sumptuous.

A. فأر *fa'r.* A rat, mouse.

P. فارس *fárs.* Persia.

A. فارس *fáris.* A horseman.

A. فارسی *fársí.* Persian.

A. فارغ *fárigh.* Free, at leisure.

A. فارغ البال *fárigh ul bál.* Contented, independent.

A. T. فارغخطی *fárigh-khaṭṭí.* An acquittance.

A. فارق *fáriḳ.* Distinguishing, dividing.

P. فازہیدن *fázhídan.* To yawn, to gape.

A. فاسد *fásid.* Vicious, corrupt.

A. فاسق *fásiḳ.* A fornicator.

P. فاش *fásh.* Apparent.

A. فاصل *fáṣil.* A separator; deciding.

A. فاصله *fáṣilah.* Distance.

A. فاضل *fáẓil.* An accomplished person.

A. فاطر *fáṭir.* The Creator.

A. فاعل *fá'il.* An agent; making; (in grammar) the active participle; the subject of a verb.

A. فاقه *fákah.* Starvation.

A. فاکهه *fákihah.* Fruit.

A. فال *fa'l* or *fál.* An omen, presage.

A. P. فال گرفتن *fál giriftan.* To take an omen from the poems of Hafiz, after the manner of the *sortes Virgilianæ.*

A. فالج *fálij.* The palsy.

A. فال گو *fál-gú.* Soothsayer.

A. فالق *fáliḳ.* Splitting, cleaving.

P. فام *fám.* An affix implying colour as سیاه‌فام *siyáh-fám.* Blackish.

A. فانوس *fánús.* A lamp shade, a paper lantern.

A. فانه *fána.* A wedge.

A. فانی *fání.* Transitory, perishable.

A. فائده *fáida.* Profit, gain, advantage.

A. فائده مند *fáida-mand.* Profitable, useful.

A. فایز *fáiz.* Overtaking, obtaining.

A. فایض *fá'iẓ.* Abundant, liberal.

A. فایق *fáiḳ.* Superior.

A. فبها *fabihá.* Well.
اگر این کارها صورت میدهید فبها و الا جواب صریح بدهید تا خودم تمام کنم *agar ín kár-há ṣúrat mí-dihíd fabihá; wa illá javáb i ṣaríḥ bidihíd tá khudam tamám kunam.* If you can manage this business, well; if not give me a decisive answer that I may finish it myself.

P. فتادن *futádan.* To fall.

A. فتاده *futáda.* Fallen.

A. فتح *fatḥ.* Victory; opening.

A. فتحه *fatḥah.* The vowel-point َ.

P. فتراك *fitrák.* Saddle-straps.

A. فتر *fatar.* Languor; intermission.

A. فترة *fitrat.* An interregnum.

A. فتق *fatḳ.* Bursting; splitting.

A. فتنه *fitnah.* (pl. فتن *fitan.*) Sedition, trouble.

A. P. فتنه انگيز *fitna-anghíz.* Seditious, an agitator.

A. فتوى *fatwá.* A judicial sentence (especially on a point of religious jurisprudence).

A. فتوت *futúwat.* Generosity, liberality.

A. فتوح *futúḥ.* } Victories.
A. فتوحات *futúḥát.* }

A. فتور *futúr.* Languor, weakness.

A. P. فتيله *fatíla.* The wick of a candle.

A. فتى *fatá.* A youth, a boy.

A. فجر *fajr.* The morning, dawn.

A. فجل *fujuḷ.* A radish.

A. فجور *fujúr.* Adultery.

A. فحش *faḥsh.* Obscenity; bad language.

A. فحوى *faḥwá.* (pl. فحاوى *faḥáwí.*) Signification, purport.

A. فخر *fakhr.* Glory; boasting.

A. فدا *fidá.* Sacrifice, devoting.

A. P. فدايت شوم *fidáyet shavam.* May I be your ransom; (used in addressing princes, or from children to parents. In petitions to the Sháh the Arabic formula روحنا فداه *rúḥuná fidáhu.* "May our souls be his ransom" is used.)

A. فدوى *fidawí.* A devoted servant.

A. فديه *fidya.* A ransom.

P. فر *far.* Pomp, splendour.

P. فرا *fará.* Above, upon; behind.

P. فرا پيش *fará-písh.* Before, anterior.

A. فرات *furát.* The Euphrates.

P. فرا چنك اوردن *fará chang áwardan.* To get in one's grasp.

P. فراخ *farákh.* Wide, ample.

P. فراختن *farákhtan.* To exalt.

P. فراخروى *ferákh-rúí.* Pleasant, countenance.

P. فراخروے *ferákh-raví.* Width of step; extravagance.

P. فراخور *ferákh-khur.* Worthy, fit, conformable to.

P. فراخى *ferakhí.* Abundance, amplitude.

P. فرا خيز *ferá-khíz.* A tottering pace.

A. فراداً *furádan.* Separately.

A. فرار *ferár.* Flight, desertion.

P. فرا رسیدن *fará rasídan.* To arrive.

P. فرا رفتن *fará-raftan.* To go, to proceed.

P. فرا روی *fará raví.* Progress.

A. فراری *farárí.* A runaway, deserter.

P. فراز *faráz.* Exalting, high.

P. فرازے *farází.* Exaltation.

P. فرا زدن *fará-zadan.* To open, to discover.

P. فرازندہ *farázenda.* A raiser.

P. فرازیدن *farázídan.* To erect.

A. فراست *firásat.* Sagacity.

P. فراستوك *farástúk.* A swallow.

A. فراش *farásh.* A butterfly, moth.

A. فراش *farrásh.* A carpet-spreader; a footman, a butler.

A. فراغبال *farágh i bál.* Tranquillity.

A. فراغت *farághat.* Leisure, ease.

A. فراق *firák.* Separation, absence.

P. فرا گرفتن *fará girifian.* To envelop, to assume.

P. فراموش *farámúsh.* Forgetful.

P. فراموشی *farámúshí.* Forgetfulness.

P. فراموشیدن *farámúshidan.* To forget.

A. فرامین *farámín.* Mandates, orders. (pl. of P. فرمان.)

P. فرا نمودن *fará namúdan.* To show, to exhibit.

P. فراوان *faráwán.* Much, abundant.

P. فراهم *faráham.* Collection.

A. فرائد *faráid.* Unique pearls.

A. فرائض *faráiz.* The Mohammedan law of succession. Precepts.

P. فربه *farbih.* Fat, corpulent.

P. فربهی *farbihí.* Fatness.

P. فرتوت *fartút.* A decrepit old man.

A. فرج *farj.* *Pudenda mulieris.*

A. فرج *faraj.* Joy, comfort.

P. فرجام *farjám.* End, conclusion, issue.

A. فرح *farah.* Gladness, joy.

A. P. فرحناك *farah-nák.* Joyful.

P. فرخ *farrukh.* Happy, fortunate.

P. فرخندگی *farkhundagí.* Happiness, prosperity.

P. فرخنده *farkhunda.* Happy, fortunate.

P. A. فرخنده مال *farkhunda-ma'ál.* Of happy issue.

P. فرخی *farrukhí.* Prosperity.

A. فرد *fard.* Single, one. A list or schedule.

A. P. فرد اعلی *fard i a'lá.* Best quality (goods).

P. فردا *fardá.* To-morrow. پس فردا *pas-fardá.* The day after to-morrow. پسین فردا *pasín-fardá.* Three days hence.

A. P. فردوس *firdaus.* A garden, paradise.

P. فرزام *farzám.* Worthy, suiting.

P. فرزان *farzán.* } Wisdom, science.
P. فرزانگی *farzánagí.* }

P. فرزانه *farzána.* Learned, wise.

P. فرزند *farzand.* A child, son or daughter.

P. فرزین *farzín.* The queen at chess (see شطرنج).

A. فرس *faras.* A mare; the knight at chess.

P. فرستادن *faristádan.* To send.

P. فرسنگ *farsang.* A parasang, a league.

P. فرسودن *farsúdan.* To rub, erase, obliterate.

P. فرسوده *farsúda.* Torn, worn.

A. فرش *farsh.* A bed, carpet. يك دست فرش *yek dast farsh.* One carpet.

P. فرشته *firishta.* An angel.

A. فرصت *furṣat.* Opportunity, leisure.

A. فرض *farẓ.* A duty; a necessary (religious) observation.

A. فرط *farṭ.* Plenty, superfluity.

A. فرع *far'.* A branch.

A. فرعون *fir'aun.* Pharaoh.

A. فرعی *far'íy.* Derivative.

P. فرفر *farfar.* Hurry.

A. فرقان *furḳán.* The Koran (lit. a means of discriminating).

A. فرقت *furḳat.* Separation.

A. فرقدان *farḳadán.* Two stars near the pole; the greater and the lesser Bears.

P. فرقه *firḳa.* A sect, a party.

P. فرکندن *far-kandan.* To destroy; to dig.

P. فرما *farmá.* (In comp.) commanding.

P. فرمان *farmán.* A mandate, order.

P. فرمان بردار *farmán-bardár.* Obedient, submissive.

P. فرمان ده *farmán-dih.* }
P. فرمان روا *farmán-ravá.* }
A sovereign ruler.

P. فرمایش *farmáyish.* An order; (pl. فرمایشات *farmáyishát*).

P. فرمودن *farmúdan.* To order.

P. فرنگ *firang.* A European, a Frank.

P. فرنگستان *firangistán.* Europe.

P. فرنگی *firangí.* A European.

P. فرو *farú.* Below, downward.

P. فرو بستن *farú bastan.* To tie down.

P. فرو بردن *farú burdan.* To carry down, to swallow.

P. فروتر *farú-tar.* Lower, inferior.

P. فرو ترین *farú-tarín.* Lowest.

P. فرو تن *farú-tan.* Humble.

P. فروخت *farúkht.* Sale.

P. فروختن *farúkhtan.* To sell.

P. فرو خواندن *farú-kh'ándan.* To hold forth, to utter.

P. فرود *farúd.* Under, down.

P. فرودست *farú-dast.* Inferior, powerless.

P. فرود گاه *farúd gáh.* A halting-place.

P. فروردین *farvardín.* The first Persian month (March).

P. فروز *furúz.* Kindling, inflaming.

P. فروش *farúsh.* Selling; a seller.

P. فروغ *furúgh.* Splendour, brightness.

P. فرو رفتن *farú raftan.* To go down, to sink.

P. فرو گذاشت *farú-guzásht.* Relinquishment; pardon.

P. فرو گذاشتن *farú-guzáshtan.* To quit; to relinquish.

P. فرو کوفتن *farú-kúftan.* To knock down, to bruise.

P. فرو ماندگی *farú-mándagí.* Helplessness; indigence.

P. فرو ماندن *farú-mándan.* To be distressed.

P. فرو مانده *farú-mánda.* Tired, dejected.

P. فرو مایگان *farú-máyagán.* Base people.

P. فرو مایه *farú-máya.* Mean, worthless.

P. فروند *farvend.* Winged, furnished with sails; a word used in numbering ships. دو فروند کشتی *dú farvend kishtí.* Two ships.

P. فرو هشتن *farú hishtan.* To hang down.

P. فرهنگ *farhang.* Science; a lexicon.

A. فره *farih.* Brisk, active; saucy.

P. فرهیخته *farhíkhta.* Polite, well educated.

P. فرهاد *farhád.* Name of a celebrated Persian statuary; a stone-cutter.

P. فرهد *farhad.* A handsome youth.

P. فریاد *faryád.* Lamentation; cry for help.

P. فریاد رس *faryád-ras.* A redresser of grievances.

P. فریاد رسی *faryád-rasí.* Redress of grievances.

P. فریادے *faryádí.* Complainant, plaintiff.

P. فریب *faríb.* Deceit, fraud.

P. فریبنده *faríbanda* A cheat,

A. فرید *faríd.* Single, unique.

A. فریسه *farísa.* A lion's prey.

A. فریضه *faríẓa.* An ordinance of God.

P. فریفتن *faríftan.* To seduce; to deceive.

P. فریفته *farífta.* Deceived; enamoured.

A. فریق *faríḳ.* A troop, a sect. فریقین *faríḳain.* The two parties in a dispute; battle, &c.

P. فزا *fazá.* (In comp.) augmenting.

A. فزع *faza'.* Fear.

P. فزودن *fuzúdan.* To increase, to augment.

P. فزون *fuzún.* Increase, more.

P. فزونی *fuzúní.* Augmentation.

A. فساد *fasád.* Depravity, iniquity.

A. فسادی *fasádí.* Quarrelsome.

P. فسان *fasán.* A whetstone.

P. فسانه *fasána.* A fable, a story.

A. فستق *fustuḳ.* A pistachio; a pine.

A. فسحت *fusḥat.* Space, amplitude.

A. فسر *fasr.* Explanation.

P. فسردگی *fusurdagí.* Congelation.

P. فسردن *fusurdan.* To congeal.

A. فسق *fisḳ.* Iniquity, sin.

P. فسوس *fisús.* See افسوس.

A. فسوق *fusúḳ.* Immorality.

P. فسون *fusún.* Incantation, fascination.

A. فسیح *fasíḥ.* Ample, capacious.

P. فشان *fishán.* (In comp.) scattering, diffusing.

P. فشاندن *fishándan.* To scatter.

P. فشردن *fashurdan.* To squeeze.

A. فص *fuṣṣ.* The stone of a signet-ring.

P. فصاحت *faṣáḥat.* Eloquence.

A. فصاد *faṣṣád.* A phlebotomizer.

A. فصاد *fiṣád.* Bleeding, phlebotomy.

A. فصل *faṣl.* (pl. فصول *fuṣul.*) A section; season; distinction (between right and wrong).

A. فصیح *faṣíḥ.* Eloquent.

A. فصیل *faṣíl.* A rampart, breastwork.

A. فضاء *faẓá'.* A plain, area.

A. فضاحت *faẓáḥat.* Disgrace, ignominy.

A. فضائح *faẓáïḥ.* Disgraceful acts. (pl. of فضیحة.)

A. فضایل *faẓáïl.* Virtues, excellencies. (pl. of فضیلت.)

A. فضل *faẓl.* Excellence, virtue, favour.

A. فضلاء *fuẓulá.* Accomplished persons.

A. فضلات *fazalát.* Redundancies, leavings, orts. (pl. of فضله *fazlah.*)

A. فضول *fuzúl.* Extravagant, profuse; idle talk.

A. P. فضولی *fuzúli.* Excess.

A. فضه *fizzah.* Silver.

A. فضیحت *fazíhat.* Ignominy, disgrace.

A. فضیلت *fazílat.* Excellence, perfection.

A. فطام *fitám.* Weaning.

A. فطر *fitr.* Breaking a fast.

P. فطرت *fitrat.* Nature; complexion; tendency. Alms given on breaking the fast of Ramazán (عید الفطر).

A. فطریت *fitríyet.* Alms given at the عیدالفطر above-mentioned.

A. فطنت *fitnat.* Sagacity, wisdom.

A. فطن *fatn.* Comprehending.

A. فظ *fazz.* Inhuman, harsh.

A. فظاعت *fazá'at.* Being disagreeable.

A. فعال *fa''ál.* A doer, an agent.

A. فعل *fi'l.* Action; a verb.

P. فغان *fighán.* Lamentation.

A. فقاع *fuká'.* Beer.

A. فقدان *fikdán.* Deprivation, loss.

A. فقر *fakr.* Poverty.

A. فقراء *fukará.* The poor.

A. فقره *fikra.* A clause, a sentence; the vertebræ.

A. فقط *fakat.* Only, merely, no more.

A. فقه *fikh.* Religious jurisprudence.

A. فقهاء *fukahá.* Jurisprudists. (pl. of فقیه).

A. فقیر *fakír.* A poor man, a religious mendicant.

A. فقیرانه *fakírána.* Poorly, like a mendicant.

A. فقیری *fakírí.* Poverty, indigence.

A. فقیه *fakíh.* A jurisprudist, theologian, doctor.

A. فك اعلی *fakk i a'lá.* The upper jaw.

A. فك اسفل *fakk i asfal.* The lower jaw.

A. فكاك *fikák.* Redeeming a pledge, prisoner, &c.

A. فكر *fikr.* Thought, reflection.

A. فكرمند *fikr-mand.* Anxious.

A. فكنت *fuknat.* Regret.

P. فكندن *fikandan.* To throw down, to overset.

A. فكيف *fa-keif.* How then? how much more then?

P. فگار *figár.* Galled, crippled.

A. فلاح *faláh.* Prosperity.

A. فلاح *felláh.* A husbandman, a peasant.

A. فلاحت *faláhat.* Agriculture.

P. فلاخن *falákhan.* A sling.

A. فلاسفه *falásifeh.* Philosophers. (pl. of فيلسوف.)

A. فلاكت *falákat.* Adversity, misfortune.

A. فلان *fulán.* Such a one.

A. فلت *falat.* Escape.

P. فلج *falj.* A lock or bolt.

A. فلز *filizz.* Metal.

A. فلزى *filizzíy.* Metallic.

A. فلس *fils.* A small copper coin; a fish's scale.

G. فلسفه *falsafa.* Philosophy.

A. فلفل *filfil.* Pepper.

A. فلك *fulk.* A ship.

A. فلك *falak.* The sky, heaven.

A. فلكى *falakíy.* Astronomical.

A. فلوس *fulús.* Small copper coins. (pl. of فلس.)

A. فلهذا *faliházá.* Therefore.

A. فم *fam.* The mouth.

A. فن *fann.* Science, art.

A. فنا *fand.* Mortality, frailty; transientness.

A. P. فنا پذير *fand-pazír.* Transitory, frail.

A. P. فندق *funduk.* A filbert-nut.

P. فندق سيم *funduk i sím.* The stars.

P. فنودن *funúdan.* To deceive.

A. فنون *funún.* Sciences, arts. (pl. of فن.)

A. فو *fú.* The mouth.

A. فوات *fawát.* Dying, passing away.

A. فواحش *fawáhish.* Shameful things.

A. فوارس *fawáris.* (pl. of فارس.) Cavaliers.

A. فواره *fawwára.* A fountain, a jet of water.

A. فواضل *fawázil.* Learned men.

A. فواق *fuwák.* The hiccough, the last breath.

A. فواكه *fawákih.* Fruits. (pl. of فاكهة.)

A. فوايد *fawáid.* Advantages. (pl. of فائده.)

A. فوت *faut.* Death; elapsing.

A. فوج *fauj.* An army, a regiment. The divisions, gradations of rank, &c. of the Persian army are as follows:

فوج *fauj.* A regiment.

دسته *dasta.* A company. The 1st of the 10 *dasta* of which a *fauj* is composed is called بهادران *bahádurán.* Heroes; the 10th مخبران *mukhbirán.* Scouts.

سر باز *sar-báz.* A private.

ده باشى *dih-báshí.* A commander of 10.

وكيل *wakíl* or بيك زاده *beg-záda.* } 1st non-commissioned officer.

وكيل دوم *wakíl i dúvum.* 2nd non-commissioned officer.

وكيل اول *wakíl i awwel.* Superior non-commissioned officer.

نائب دوم *náib i dúvum.* Ensign.

(فوج continued).

نائب اول *náïb i awwel.* Lieutenant.

سلطان *sulṭán.* Captain.

یاور دوم *yáver i dúvum.* 2nd major.

یاور اول *yáver i awwel.* 1st major or chief of battalion.

سرهنك *sarhang.* Lieutenant-colonel.

سرتیب سیوم *sartíb i síyum.* Colonel.

سرتیب دوم *sartíb i dúvum.* General of brigade.

سرتیب اول *sartíb i awwel.* General of division.

امیر تومان *amír i túmán.* Chief of 10000 men.

امیر نویان *amír i núyán.* General commander-in-chief (chief of 20000 men).

امیر توپخانه *amír i túpkhána.* Chief of artillery.

امیر نظام *amír i niẓám.* Marshal.

A. P. فوجدار *fauj-dár.* (In India) a police-magistrate.

A. فور *faur.* Haste.

A. فوراً *fauran.* Immediately.

A. فوز *fauz.* Victory; escape; obtaining.

A. فوطه *fúṭa.* An apron; a testicle; a purse.

A. فوق *fauḳ.* Above.

A. فوقانی *fauḳání.* Superior, supreme.

P. فولاد *fúlád.* Steel.

A. فهام *fahhám.* Very intelligent.

A. فهد *fahd.* A cheeta or hunting panther.

P. فهرست *fihrist.* }
A. فهرس *fihris.* } An index, list, catalogue.

A. فهم *fehm.* (pl. فهوم.) Understanding.

A. P. فهمانیدن *fehmánídan.* To inform, explain.

A. P. فهمیدن *fehmídan.* To understand.

A. فهیم *fahím.* Intelligent.

A. فی *fí.* In, upon. فی من *fí man.* Per pound. فی صد *fí ṣad.* Per cent.

A. فیاض *faiyáẓ.* Liberal.

A. فی الحال *fi 'l ḥál.* Immediately, at once.

A. فی الجمله *fi 'l jumlah.* In short.

A. فی الحقیقة *fi 'l ḥaḳíḳat.* In truth.

A. فی المثل *fi 'l maṡal.* As for example.

A. فی الواقع *fi 'l wáḳiʿ.* In fact.

A. فیروز *fírúz.* Victorious, fortunate.

P. فیروزه *fírúza.* A turquoise.

A. فیصل *faiṣal.* }
A. فیصله *faiṣala.* } A decision, decree.

A. فیض *faiẓ.* Bounty, plenty.

A. P. فیل *fíl.* An elephant.

P. فیلبان *fíl-bán.* An elephant-driver.

G. فیلسوف *feilasúf.* A philosopher.

P. فِل مرغ *fíl-murgh.* A turkey.

A. فيما بين *fímá-bain.* Between, reciprocal.

A. في نفسه *fí nafsihi.* Personally.

A. فيوض *fuyúẓ.* Bounties, overflowing.

ق

ق *ḳáf.* Ḳ. The twenty-first letter of the Arabic and twenty-fourth of the Persian alphabet.

A. قابض *ḳábiẓ.* A seizer; an astringent.

A. قابض الارواح *ḳábiẓ ul arwáḥ.* The angel of death.

A. قابل *ḳábil.* Skilful, capable.

A. قابلة *ḳábilat.* The next night.

A. قابله *ḳábila.* A midwife.

A. قابليت *ḳábilíyet.* Capacity, skill.

P. قابو *ḳábú.* Opportunity, power.

A. قاتل *ḳátil.* A murderer, deadly.

A. قادر *ḳádir.* Potent, powerful.

T. قارچ *ḳárch.* A mushroom.

T. قارغه *ḳárgha.* A crow.

A. قاروره *ḳárúra.* A urinometer.

A. قارئ *ḳárí.* A reader.

A. قارون *ḳárún.* Korah; Crœsus; the two being confounded in the Koranic legend.

P. قاز *ḳáz.* A goose.

A. قاسم *ḳásim.* A distributor.

T. قاش *ḳásh.* A bit, a slice.

A. قاشر *ḳáshir.* Excoriating the skin.

T. قاشق *ḳáshiḳ.* A spoon.

A. قاصد *ḳáṣid.* A courier, messenger; aiming at.

A. قاصر *ḳáṣir.* Failing in duty.

A. قاضى *ḳáẓí.* A judge.

A. قاطبًا *ḳáṭiban.* Universally.

T. قاطر *ḳáṭir.* A mule.

T. قاطرچى *ḳáṭirchí.* A muleteer.

A. قاطع *ḳáṭiʿ.* Cutting; decisive.

A. قاطع الطريق *ḳáṭiʿ uṭ ṭaríḳ.* A highway-robber.

A. قاطن *ḳáṭin.* An inhabitant.

A. قاع *ḳáʿ.* A plain.

A. قاعد *ḳáʿid.* Sitting.

A. قاعده *ḳáida.* A rule, custom; the capital of a column.

A. قاف *ḳáf.* A fabulous chain of mountains said to surround the whole world.

A. قافله *ḳáfila.* A body of travellers, a caravan.

A. قافيه *ḳáfiyeh.* Rhyme, cadence.

A. P. قافيه تنگ شدن *ḳáfiyeh i tang shudan.* To be at a loss.

A. قاقله *ḳákullah.* Cardamums.

P. قاقم *ḳáḳum.* The ermine.

A. قال *ḳál.* A word, a saying. قيل و قال *ḳíl u ḳál.* Gossip, chattering.

A. قال *ḳál.* He said.

A. قالب *ḳálib.* A mould, form.

P. قالى *ḳálí.* A large carpet.

P. قاليچه *ḳálíche.* A small carpet.

A. قامت *ḳámat.* The stature.

A. قامع *ḳámiʿ.* Smiting down, subduing.

A. قاموس *ḳámús.* The ocean; a lexicon.

A. قانت *ḳánit.* Godly.

A. قانص *ḳániṣ.* A hunter; prey, game.

A. قانط *ḳániṭ.* Despairing.

A. قانع *ḳániʿ.* Contented, satisfied.

G. قانون *ḳánún.* A canon, rule; a dulcimer.

A. قاه *ḳáh.* Obedience; dignity, power.

A. قاهر *ḳáhir.* Subduing; violent, mighty.

A. قايد *ḳáïd.* A leader, a commander.

A. قايل *ḳáïl.* Speaking, speaker; one who assents to or maintains an opinion.

A. قايم *ḳáïm.* Standing, durable, firm.

T. قايمق *ḳáymaḳ.* Clotted cream.

A. قايم مقام *ḳáïm maḳám.* A lieutenant-governor (in Turkey); deputy Prime Minister (in Persia).

P. قبا *ḳabá.* An upper garment, an overcoat.

A. قباب *ḳibáb.* Towers, vaults, cupolas. (pl. of قبة.)

P. قباچه *ḳabáche.* A little tunic.

P. قباحت *ḳabáḥat.* Baseness.

P. قباس *ḳubás.* The sun.

A. P. قباله *ḳabála.* A contract, deed, bill of sale, security.

A. قبايح *ḳabáïḥ.* Crimes.

A. قبايل *ḳabáïl.* Tribes, families. (pl. of قبله.)

A. قبح *ḳubḥ.* Baseness, deformity.

A. قبر *ḳabr.* A tomb, grave.

A. P. قبرستان *ḳabristán.* A burying ground.

A. قبض *ḳabẓ.* Grasping, seizing.

A. قبض الوصول *ḳabẓ ul wuṣúl.* A receipt, a discharge.

A. قبضه *ḳabẓa.* A handful; grasp, clutch; the closed fist.

A. قبل *ḳabl.* Before, prior.

A. قبل *ḳibal.* Presence; part. من قبل *min ḳibal.* In respect of.

A. قبله *ḳibla.* A point of adoration; Mecca.

A. قبله *ḳublah.* A kiss.

A. P. قبله گاه *ḳibla-gáh.* A point of adoration; a parent.

A. P. قبله نما *ḳibla-numá.* The mariner's compass.

A. قبله عالم *ḳibla i 'álam.* Cynosure of the universe (used in addressing H. M. the Sháh).

A. قبور *ḳubúr.* Tombs.

A. قبول *ḳubúl.* Consent, acceptance.

A. قبه *ḳubbah.* A vault; arch; a dome.

A. P. قبه اب *ḳubba i áb.* A bubble of water.

A. P. قبه زرين *ḳubba i zarrín.* The sun.

A. قبيح *ḳabíḥ.* Base, ugly.

A. قبيله *ḳabílah.* A tribe, a family.

A. قتال *ḳitál.* Battle, slaughter.

A. قتل *ḳatl.* Slaughter, killing.

A. قتل گاه *ḳatl gáh.* The seat of carnage. A place of execution.

A. قتيل *ḳatíl.* Killed, slain.

A. قحبه *ḳaḥbah.* A prostitute.

A. قحط *ḳaḥṭ.* Drought, famine.

A. P. قحط سال *ḳaḥṭ-sál.* A famine, a barren year.

A. قحف *ḳiḥf.* The skull.

A. قد *ḳadd.* Stature.

A. قدام *ḳudám.* Ancient, anterior, prior.

A. قدام *ḳaddám.* A leader.

A. قدامت *ḳadámat.* Priority.

A. قدح *ḳadḥ.* A cup, goblet.

A. قدر *ḳadr.* Rank, quality.

A. قدر *ḳadar.* Value, quantity.

A. قدر *ḳidr.* A kettle, a caldron.

A. قدرت *ḳudrat.* Power.

A. P. قدری *ḳadrí.* Somewhat, a little.

A. P. قد زن *ḳad-zan.* A bone for nibbing pens on.

P. قدس *ḳuds.* Sanctity, holiness.

P. قدغن *ḳadaghan.* Order, prohibition.

A. قدم *ḳadam.* A foot, a pace.

A. قدماء *ḳudamá.* The ancients.

A. قدوس *ḳadús.* Holy.

A. قدوی *ḳadwá.* Rectitude.

A. قدوم *ḳudúm.* Arrival.

A. قدوة *ḳadwat.* A leader, chief.

A. قدير *ḳadír.* Powerful.

A. قديم *ḳadím.* Ancient, old, former.

A. قرے *ḳurá.* Villages. (pl. of قريه *ḳaryat.*)

A. قراءت *ḳirá'at.* Reading (especially the Korán).

A. قرابت *ḳarábat.* Relationship, propinquity.

T. قراسوران *ḳurá súrán.* Escort for the mail; a sentinel.

P. قرابه *ḳarába.* A large flagon.

P. قرار *ḳarár.* Stability; confession.

A. P. قرار داد *ḳarár-dád.* Established, ratified.

P. قراشه *ḳurásha.* A fever in which the hair stands on end.

A. قراضه *ḳuráẓa.* Filings.

T. قراغوش *ḳarághúsh.* A sparrow-hawk.

A. قرآن *ḳur'án.* The Koran.

A. قران *ḳirán.* Conjunction.

P. قراول *ḳaráwul.* Picquets, out-guards.

A. قرب *ḳurb.* Propinquity, kindred.

A. قرباء *ḳurabá.* Relations.

A. قربان *ḳurbán.* A sacrifice.

A. قربت *ḳurbat.* Affinity, proximity.

A. قربى *ḳurbá.* Relationship, consanguinity.

A. قربه *ḳirba.* A water-skin.

A. قرة *ḳurrat.* Coolness and lustre in the eyes.

A. قرح *ḳarḥ.* A wound, a scar.

A. قرحة *ḳarḥat.* A sore.

A. قرد *ḳird.* A monkey.

A. قرص *ḳurṣ.* A disc; a round loaf.

A. قرص سمين *ḳurṣ i símín.* The moon.

A. قرض *ḳarẓ.* A debt, a loan.

A. P. قرض خواه *ḳarẓ-kh'áh.* A creditor.

A. P. قرض دار *ḳarẓ-dár.* A debtor.

A. قرطاس *ḳirṭás.* Paper.

A. قرع *ḳar'.* A gourd.

A. قرعة *ḳar'at.* A lot, chance.

A. قرمز *ḳirmiz.* Crimson.

A. قرمز فرنگى *ḳirmiz i firengí.* Cochineal.

A. قرمزى *ḳirmizí.* Crimson.

A. قرن *ḳarn.* A horn; a century, an age.

A. قرنفل *ḳaranful.* Cloves.

A. قروح *ḳuruḥ.* Ulcers.

A. قرون *ḳurún.* Horns, ages. (pl. of قرن.)

A. قريب *ḳaríb.* Near, about, kin.

A. قريش *ḳuraish.* A noble tribe in Arabia, to which Mohammed belonged.

A. قرين *ḳarín.* Connected with, joined.

A. قرينه *ḳarína.* Conjecture; context.

A. قريه *ḳaryah.* A village.

P. قز *ḳaz.* Coarse, raw silk.

A. قزاق *ḳazzák.* A robber, a cossack.

T. قزلباش *ḳazal-básh.* "Red-head"; a moghul soldier.

A. قساوت *ḳasáwat.* Hardness.

A. قسط *ḳasṭ.* A division; instalment.

A. P. قسطبندى *ḳasṭ-bandí.* A settlement by instalment.

A. قسم *ḳism.* A kind; share.

A. قسم *ḳasm.* An oath.

قسم خوردن *ḳasm khurdan.* To swear.

A. قسمت *ḳismat.* Fate, share.

A. قشر *ḳishr.* Bark, peel, husk.

A. قشف *ḳashf.* Squalor, scurf.

A. قص *ḳaṣṣ.* Shaving, shearing.

A. قصاب *ḳaṣṣáb.* A butcher.

A. قصاص *ḳiṣaṣ.* The law of retaliation for homicide.

A. قصائد *ḳaṣáïd.* Odes. (pl. of قصيده.)

A. قصب *ḳaṣab.* A reed, pen; muslin.

A. قصبه *ḳaṣbah.* A town, small city.

A. قصد *ḳaṣd.* Intention, attempt.

A. قصر *ḳaṣr.* A palace; deficiency.

A. قصص *ḳiṣaṣ.* Tales. (pl. of قصة.)

A. قصوى *ḳaṣwá.* The extremity.

A. قصور *ḳuṣúr.* Fault, failure, deficiency.

A. قصة *ḳiṣṣah.* A history, tale.

A. P. قصه خوان *ḳiṣṣa-kh'án.* A story-teller.

A. P. قصه كو *ḳiṣṣa-gú.* A story-teller.

A. قصيده *ḳasída.* An ode.

A. قصير *ḳaṣír.* Short.

A. قضا *ḳaẓá.* Decree, fate.

قضارا *ḳaẓárá.* By chance.

A. قضاة *ḳuẓát.* Judges. (pl. of قاضى.)

A. قضا و قدر *ḳaẓá wa ḳadar.* Fate and destiny.

A. قضايا *ḳaẓáyá.* Affairs, lawsuits. (pl. of قضية.)

A. قضبان *ḳaẓbán.* Branches.

A. قضيب *ḳaẓíb.* A branch.

A. قضيه *ḳaẓíyeh.* A dispute, a proposition.

A. قطا *ḳaṭá.* A sand-grouse (famous for its ingenuity in discovering water in the desert).

A. قطار *ḳiṭár.* A row, rank.

A. قطاع الطريق *ḳuṭṭá' uṭ ṭaríḳ.* Highwaymen.

A. قطاف *ḳaṭáf* or *ḳiṭáf.* The vintage.

A. قطب *ḳuṭb.* The polar star, pole, &c.

A. قطر *ḳaṭr.* A diameter line; a region.

A. قطرات *ḳaṭarát.* Drops.

A. قطران *ḳaṭrán.* Dropping, distilling; pitch.

A. قطره *ḳaṭrah.* One drop.

A. قطع *ḳaṭ'.* Cutting.

A. قطع رحم *ḳaṭ' i raḥim.* Renunciation of one's kindred.

A. قطعا *ḳaṭ'an.* Never, by no means.

A. P. قطع كردن *ḳaṭ' kardan.* To cross, to traverse.

A. قطع نظر *ḳaṭ' i naẓr.* Overlooking (a fault, &c.).

A. قطعه *ḳaṭ'ah.* A piece; a strophe.

A. قطف *ḳaṭaf.* A vestige.

A. قطن *ḳuṭn.* Cotton.

A. قطين *ḳaṭín.* Domestics.

A. قعر *ḳa'r.* The bottom, the depths (of the sea, &c.).

A. قفا *ḳifá.* The nape of the neck.

A. قفص *ḳafaṣ.* Net-work; a cage.

A. قفل *ḳufl.* A lock.

A. قفيز *ḳafíz.* A measure, weight.

A. قلاش *ḳallásh.* Cunning, crafty.

A. قلاع *ḳilá'.* Castles, forts. (pl. of قلعة.)

P. قلاوزى *ḳaláwuzí.* Guidance.

A. قلب *ḳalb.* The heart; centre; inversion. Base coin.

P. قلبه *ḳulba.* A plough.

P. قلبه ران *ḳulba-rán.* A ploughman.

A. قلبى *ḳalbí.* Hearty, cordial.

A. قلة *ḳillat.* Scarcity, want.

A. قلت *ḳalt.* Saxifrage.

P. قلتبان *ḳaltabán.* A pimp.

A. قلع *ḳal'.* Extraction, pulling out.

A. قلعه *ḳal'ah.* A fort, castle.

A. قلعى *ḳal'íy.* Made of or containing tin.

P. قلفت *ḳuluft.* Big, bulky.

A. قلق *ḳalaḳ.* Agitation, perturbation.

A. قلم *ḳalam.* A pen, a reed.

A. P. قلم تراش *ḳalam-tarash.* A penknife.

A. P. قلم دان *ḳalam-dan.* A pen-case.

A. P. قلم در كشيدن *ḳalam dar kashídan.* To obliterate.

A. P. قلمرو *ḳalam-rav.* Jurisdiction; an empire.

A. P. قلمزن *ḳalam-zan.* A scribe.

A. قلم كار *ḳalam-kár.* A painter.

A. P. قلم موى *ḳalam i múí.* A hair-pencil.

A. قلمون *ḳalamún.* A chameleon.

A. قلندر *ḳalandar.* A kind of monk.

A. قلوب *ḳulúb.* Hearts. (pl. of قلب.)

A. قله *ḳullah.* Top, summit.

A. قلى *ḳalí.* Alkali.

A. قليل *ḳalíl.* Few, little.

P. قليان *ḳaliyán.* } A hookah
P. قليون *ḳaliyún.* } or narghileh.

A. قليه *ḳalíyah.* A fricassee; a curry.

A. قمار *ḳumár.* Dice; any game of hazard.

A. P. قمار باختن *ḳamár bákhtan.* To game, to gamble.

P. قماش *ḳumásh.* Piece goods.

T. قمچى *ḳamchí.* A whip.

A. قمر *ḳamar.* The moon.

A. قمرى *ḳamaríy.* Lunar.

A. قمرى *ḳumríy.* A ring-dove.

A. قمع *ḳam'.* Battering, bruising.

A. قمل *ḳamal.* A louse.

A. قميص *ḳamíṣ.* A shirt.

A. قنات *ḳanát.* The walls of a tent.

A. قنادیل *ḳanádíl.* Chandeliers; candles.

A. قناعت *ḳiná'at.* Content, abstinence.

A. قنب *ḳinnab.* Hemp.

P. قند *ḳand.* Sugar-candy.

A. قندیل *ḳindíl.* A candle.

A. قنوط *ḳunúṭ.* Despair.

P. قو *ḳú.* A swan.

T. قو *ḳú.* Tinder.

A. قوی *ḳuwá.* Powers, faculties. (pl. of قوة.)

A. قواعد *ḳawá'id.* Rules, customs.

A. قوال *ḳawwál.* A singer, an orator.

A. قوام *ḳawám.* Pillar, support.

A. قوانین *ḳawánín.* Canons, regulations.

A. قوائم *ḳawáïm.* Pillars.

A. قوت *ḳút.* Aliment, food.

A. قوت *ḳúwat.* Strength, power.

P. قوتی *ḳútí.* A box.

T. قوچ *ḳúch.* A ram.

A. قور *ḳaur.* Riband, tape.

P. قور خانه *ḳúr-khána.* An arsenal.

P. قوری *ḳúrí.* A tea-pot.

A. قوس *ḳaus.* A bow, Sagittarius.

A. قوس قزح *ḳaus i ḳuzaḥ.* The rainbow.

T. قوش *ḳúsh.* A bird of prey, a falcon. یك بهله قوش *yek bahla ḳosh.* One falcon.

A. قول *ḳaul.* Saying, speech.

T. قولتوق *ḳúltúḳ.* A gulf.

A. قول و فعل *ḳaul u fi'l.* Word and deed.

A. P. قولنامه *ḳaul-náma.* A treaty.

A. G. قولنج *ḳulinj.* The cholic.

A. قولی *ḳaulí.* Verbal.

A. قوم *ḳaum.* A tribe, nation.

A. قوی *ḳawíy.* Strong, robust.

A. قویم *ḳawím.* Valiant, steadfast.

A. قهر *ḳahr.* Rage, fury, wrath.

A. قهار *ḳahhár.* Powerful; avenger.

A. قهقهه *ḳahḳahah.* Loud laughter.

A. قهوه *ḳahweh.* Coffee.

A. قی *ḳai.* Vomiting.

A. قیاس *ḳiyás.* Conjecture, guess; analogy.

A. قیاسی *ḳiyásí.* Conjectural.

A. قیافه *ḳayáfá.* Physiognomy.

A. قیام *ḳayám.* Standing, permanence.

A. قیامت *ḳiyámat.* The resurrection.

T. قیچی *ḳaichí.* Scissors.

A. قیح *ḳaiḥ.* Matter, pus.

A. قید *ḳaid.* Restraint, confinement.

A. قیدی *ḳaidí.* A prisoner.

P. قیر *ḳír.* Pitch.

A. قیراط *ḳíráṭ.* A carat.

A. قیس *ḳais.* Comparing.

A. قیصر *ḳaiṣar.* Cæsar; an emperor.

A. قیظ *ḳaiẓ.* Midsummer.

G. قیفال *ḳífál.* The cephalic vein.

A. قیق *ḳíḳ.* Foolish, giddy; clucking like a hen.

A. قیل و قال *ḳil u ḳál.* Conversation.

A. قیلوله *ḳailúla.* Sleeping at midday.

A. قیمت *ḳímat.* Price, value.

A. قیمتی *ḳímatíy.* Valuable.

T. قیمق *ḳaimaḳ.* See قایمق.

P. قیمه *ḳíma.* Minced meat.

A. قیود *ḳuyúd.* Stipulation.

A. قیوم *ḳaiyúm.* Eternal.

ک

ک *káf.* K. The twenty-second letter of the Arabic and twenty-fifth of the Persian alphabet.

P. ک *-ak.* A diminutive termination, as پسرک *pisarak.* A little boy.

A. کابت *kábit.* Melancholy.

P. کابتره *kábtara.* Foolish discourse.

A. کابوس *kábús.* The nightmare.

P. کابین *kábín.* A marriage-settlement.

A. کاتب *kátib.* A writer, secretary.

P. کاچه *kácha.* The side of a mountain.

P. کاخ *kákh.* An upper gallery or balcony; a house built upon an elevation.

A. کاذب *kázib.* A liar, impostor.

P. کار *kár.* Business, work.

P. کار اگاه *kár-ágáh.* Skilful.

P. کار امدنی *kár-ámadní.* Useful.

P. کار پرداز *kár-pardáz.* A manager.

P. کار خانه *kár-khána.* A workshop, a manufactory.

P. کارد *kárd.* A knife.

A. کارز *káriz.* A preacher.

P. کار زار *kár-zár.* Battle, conflict.

P. کار شناس *kár-shinás.* A man of business, skilful.

P. کار فرما *kár-farmá.* A minister, ruler.

P. کار گذار *kár-guzár.* Discharging one's duty.

P. کارگر *kárgar.* Effectual, effective.

P. کار کن *kár-kun.* A director, a record-keeper.

A. کاروان *kárawán.* A caravan.

P. کاروان سرای *kárawán saráí.* An inn.

P. کار و بار *kár u bár.* Negotiation, business.

P. کار و باری *kár u bárí.* A trader, a transactor of business.

P. کاری *kárí.* A champion; an affair.

P. کاریدن *káridan.* To sow seed.

P. کاریز *káríz.* A canal for irrigation.

P. کاریگر *kárigar.* An artificer; a workman.

P. کاز *káz.* Shears, scissors; the branch of a tree.

A. کاسب *kásib.* A receiver, gainer, acquirer.

A. کاس *kás.* A cup.

P. کاست *kást.* Diminution.

P. کاستن *kástan.* To decrease.

A. کاسد *kásid.* Deficient; not current.

A. کاسر *kásir.* A breaker.

P. کاسنی *kásní.* Endive, white succory.

A. P. کاسه *kása.* A cup, goblet; porcelain.

P. کاسهٔ سر *kása i sar.* The skull.

P. کاش *kásh.* Would that!

P. کاشانه *káshána.* A bird's nest; a house.

P. کاشتن *káshtan.* To sow, to cultivate the land.

A. کاشح *káshiḥ.* A secret enemy.

A. کاشف *káshif.* A detector, discoverer.

A. کاظم *káẓim.* One who restrains his anger.

P. کاغذ *kághaẓ.* Paper; a letter.

P. کاغذ باد *kághaz i bád.* A paper-kite.

P. کاغذ زر *kághaẓ i zar.* Gold leaf.

P. کاغذ وصلی *kághaẓ i waṣlí.* Pasteboard.

P. کافتن *káftan.* To dig; to split.

A. کافر *káfir.* An infidel; an unbeliever.

A. کافر نعمت *káfir i ni'mat.* Ungrateful.

A. کافل *káfil.* A sponsor, surety.

A. کافور *káfúr.* Camphor; a white wax-candle; a nickname given to black eunuchs, "snowball."

A. کافوری *káfúrí.* An eunuch; camphorated.

A. کافه *káfa.* All, the whole.

A. کافهٔ انام *káfa i anám.* All mankind.

A. کافی *káfí.* Sufficient.

P. کاک *kák.* Biscuit.

P. کاکل *kákul.* A curl, lock, ringlet.

P. کاکنج *kákenj.* A species of nightshade.

P. کالا *kálá.* Things, necessaries, goods.

P. کالبد *kálbad.* The human body, form, figure; mould.

RUSS. کالسکه *káluska.* A carriage.

P. کالبد گر *kálbad-gar.* A sculptor.

P. کام *kám.* Desire, wish; the palate.

P. کام جو *kám-jú*. Seeking enjoyment.

P. کامران *kám-rán*. Happy, felicitous.

P. کامرانی *kámrání*. Felicity, fruition.

P. کامروا *kám-rawá*. Enjoying, gratified.

P. کامزن *kám-zan*. One who intends doing anything.

A. کامل *kámil*. Perfect, entire.

P. کام نا کام *kám-ná-kám*. Willing or unwilling.

A. کامن *kámin*. Lying in ambush.

P. کامیاب *kám-yáb*. Prosperous, successful.

P. کامیابی *kám-yábí*. Fruition, prosperity.

P. کان *kán*. A mine, quarry.

A. کانون *kánún*. A chafing-dish, a fireplace.

A. کانون الاخر *kánún ul ákhir*, or
A. کانون الثانی *kánún us ṡání*.
A Syrian month (January).

A. کانون الاول *kánún ul awwal*. A Syrian month (December).

P. کانی *kání*. Mineral.

P. کاو *káv*. Digging, hollowing out.

P. کاواك *kávák*. A hollow thing, cavity.

P. کاورك *káwark* A bird's nest.

P. کاوش *kávish*. Digging; meditating.

P. کاویدن *kávídan*. To dig.

P. کاه *káh*. Straw.

P. کاهبان *káh-bán*. Stubble, a stubble-field.

P. کاه ربا *káh-rubá*. Amber.

P. کاه ربای *káh-rubáí*. Electricity.

P. کاهش *káhish*. Diminution.

P. کاهریز *káh-ríz*. Straws, rubbish.

A. کاهل *káhil*. Slothful, lazy.

A. P. کاهلی *káhilí*. Sloth, indolence.

A. کاهن *káhin*. A soothsayer.

P. کاهو *káhú*. Lettuce, salad.

P. کاهیدن *káhídan*. To diminish.

A. کائن *káïn*. Being, existing; a creature.

A. کائنات *káïnát*. Creatures, beings.

A. کب *kabb*. Overthrowing; inverting.

A. P. کباب *kebáb*. Roasted meat.

A. کبابه *kebába*. Cubebs.

A. کباد *kubád*. Disease of the liver.

A. کبار *kibár*. Grandees, nobles.

A. کبد *kibd*. The liver, the heart.

A. کبر *kibr*. Grandeur, pride.

A. کبراء *kubará*. Great men, grandees. (pl. of کبر.)

A. كبرة *kibrat.* Grandeur.

A. كبريا *kibriyá.* Grandeur; power. The Most High.

A. كبريت *kibrít.* Sulphur.

P. كبگ *kabg.* A species of partridge.

A. كبل *kebl.* A large chain, or fetter.

P. كبوتر *kabútar.* A pigeon.

P. كبود *kabúd.* Blue, azure.

P. كبه *kaba, kuba* or *kubba.* A cupping-glass.

P. كبى *kabí.* An ape, monkey.

A. كبير *kabír.* Great, large.

A. كبيسه *kabísa.* Intercalary.

A. كتاب *kitáb.* A book, letter, epistle.

A. كتاب *kuttáb.* A school.

A. كتابت *kitábat.* Writing.

H. كتاره *katára.* A dagger.

A. كتان *kettán.* Linseed; linen.

A. كتب *kutub.* Books. (pl. of كتاب.)

A. P. كتب خانه *kutub-khána.* A library.

P. كتخدا *kat-khudá.* The master of a family, bridegroom. (pronounced in Turkish *k'yáha.*)

P. كتخدائے *kat-khudáí.* Marriage; housebreaking.

A. كتف *katif.* The shoulder; blade-bone.

P. كتكنه *kat-kena.* Portion of a farm re-let.

A. كتم *katm.* Concealment.

A. كثافت *kaśáfat.* Density.

A. كثرت *kaśrat.* Abundance, excess.

A. كثير *kaśír.* Many, much, abundant.

A. كثيف *kaśíf.* Dense, thick.

P. كژ *kaj.* Crooked, curved, bent.

P. كجا *kujá.* Where.

P. كژ اكند *kaj-ágand.* A quilted silk-jacket worn under armour.

P. كجاوه *kajáva.* A camel-litter.

P. A. كژ طبع *kaj-ṭab'.* Perverse, crooked-tempered.

P. كجك *kajak.* A hook for driving elephants.

P. كجى *kají.* Crookedness, curvature.

A. كحال *kuḥḥál.* An oculist.

A. كحل *kuḥl.* Collyrium.

A. كد *kadd.* Trouble, inconvenience.

A. كداس *kudás.* Sneezing (of animals).

P. كدام *kudám.* Which; what; whether.

P. كد بانو *kad-bánú.* A lady, matron.

A. كدر *kadar.* Turbidness.

P. كدو *kaddú.* A gourd.

P. كدوخ *kadúkh.* A bath; a cup.

A. كدورت *kudúrat.* Turbidness.

P. كده *keda.* A locative termination, as اتش كده *átish-keda.* A fire-temple.

A. كذا *każá.* Thus, so.

A. كذاب *każżáb.* A great liar.

A. كذب *kiżb.* A lie, lying.

A. كذوب *każúb.* i. q. كذاب.

P. كر *kar.* Deaf.

P. كرا *kirá.* To whom.

A. كرات *karrát.* Times, many times.

A. كراث *karrás.* A leek.

A. كراز *kuráz.* A small bottle or phial.

A. كرام *kirám.* Beneficent or noble men.

A. كرامت *karámat.* Liberality; a lesser miracle.

P. كران *karán.* } Margin,
P. كرانه *karána.* } border, edge.

A. كراهت *karáhat.* } Aver-
A. كراهيت *karáhiyat.* } sion, disgust.

A. كرايه *kiráyah.* Rent, hire.

P. كرب *karb.* Being afflicted, melancholy.

A. كربال *kirbál.* A bow for carding cotton.

A. كربت *kurbat.* Affliction, distress.

A. كرة *karrat.* Once, one time, an assault.

P. كرجى *karají.* A little boat.

P. كردار *kardár.* Action, deed.

P. كردگار *kardagár.* The Creator.

P. كردن *kerdan.* To do.

P. كردنى *kardaní.* Practicable, fit to do.

A. كرسى *kursíy.* A chair, a throne; the highest heaven.

P. كرشمه *kirishma.* A wink, nod, glance. بيك كرشمه دو كار *biyek kirishma du kár.* To kill two birds with one stone.

A. كرفس *karafs.* Parsley.

T. كرك *kurk.* A pelisse.

A. كركدن *karkaddan.* A rhinoceros.

P. كركس *kargas.* A vulture.

A. كرم *karam.* Liberality, beneficence.

P. كرم *kirm.* (pl. كرمان *kirmán.*) A worm.

P. كرم پيله *kirm i píla.* A silk-worm.

P. كرم شب تاب *kirm i shab-táb.* A glow-worm, firefly.

P. كرموش *kar-músh.* A musk-rat.

P. كرنا *karná.* A trumpet, clarion.

A. كرنب *kurnub.* A cabbage.

A. P. كرنب رومى *kurnub i rúmí.* A cauliflower.

HEB. كروبى *karrúbíy.* A cherub.

P. كروه *kurúh.* A measure of length, two miles.

P. كرويا *karwiyá.* Carraway-seed.

P. كره *kara.* Fresh butter.

A. كره *kurrah.* A globe, sphere.

P. كره *kurra.* A colt, foal.

A. كريم *karím.* Bountiful, liberal, gracious.

A. كريه *karíh.* Detestable.

P. كژ *kazh.* Crooked.

P. كژ اغند *kazh-ághand.* See كژ اكند.

P. كس *kas.* A person, an individual.

P. كس *kus.* Pudendum muliebre.

A. كساد *kasád.* Badness of market, not current.

A. كسافت *kasáfat.* Sediment; an eclipse.

A. كسالت *kasálat.* Sluggishness, slowness.

A. كسب *kasb.* Trade, occupation, industry.

A. كسبر *kusbar.* An ivory bracelet.

A. P. كسبى *kasbí.* A prostitute.

P. كستى *kustí.* A belt worn by Parsis.

A. كسر *kasr.* Fracture.

A. كسره *kasrah.* The vowel ِ.

A. كسرى *kasrá.* Khosroes, name of several kings of Persia.

A. كسل *kasl.* Slowness, sickness.

A. كسلمند *kasl-mand.* Sick, relaxed.

A. كسوت *kiswat.* Dress, habit.

A. كسوف *kusúf.* An eclipse of the sun.

P. كشادگى *kushádagí.* Amplitude, expansion.

P. كشادن *kushádan.* To open, to subdue.

P. كشاده *kushádan.* Open, subdued, cheerful.

A. كشاف *kashsháf.* One who reveals or discloses.

P. كشاكش *kashákash.* Perplexity, attraction.

P. كشان *keshán.* Drawing (in comp.).

P. كشان *kushán.* Killing (in comp.)

P. كشايش *kusháyish.* An opening, subduing.

P. كشت *kisht.* A sown field.

P. كشت زار *kisht-zár.* Cultivated land.

P. كشت كار *kisht-kár.* A husbandman.

P. كشتن *kishtan.* To sow, to till.

P. كشتن *kushtan,* To kill.

P. كشتى *kishtí.* A boat; a ship.

P. كشتى *kushtí.* Wrestling.

P. كشتى بان *kishtí-bán.* A pilot, steersman.

P. كشتى شكسته *kishtí-shikasta.* Shipwrecked.

P. كشتى گذاره *kishtí i guzára.* A ferry-boat.

P. كشتى گير *kishtí-gír.* A wrestler.

P. كش ران *kash i rán.* The groin.

P. كشش *kashish.* Attraction, allurement.

A. كشف *kashf.* Opening, revealing.

A. كشكول *kashkúl.* A beggar's wallet.

P. كشمش *kishmish.* Raisins.

P. كشنز *kishníz.* Coriander seed.

P. كشودن *kashúdan.* To open.

P. كشور *kishvar.* Climate, region.

P. كشور كشا *kishvar-kushá.* A conqueror.

P. كشيدن *kashídan.* To pull, attract, draw out; to suffer.

P. كعب *ka'b.* The ankle, cube.

A. كعبه *ka'bah.* The temple of Mecca.

A. كف *kaff.* The palm, hand.

P. كف *kaf.* Scum, froth.

A. كفار *kuffár.* Infidels.

A. كفارت *kafárat.* Penitence, atonement.

A. كفاف *kafáf.* Daily bread.

A. كفالت *kafálat.* Guarantee, security.

A. كفاية *kifáyat.* Sufficiency; economy.

A. P. كف پا *kaff i pá.* The sole of the feet.

P. كفچه *kafché.* A ladle.

A. P. كف دشت *kaff i dast.* The palm of the hand.

A. كفر *kufr.* Infidelity, blasphemy; ingratitude.

A. كفران *kufrán.* Ingratitude.

P. كف زدن *kaf zadan.* To foam, froth.

P. كفرك زدن *kaff-rag zadan.* To bleed a horse's hoof.

P. كفش *kafsh.* A shoe, slipper.

P. كفش دوز *kafsh-dúz.* A shoe-maker.

P. كفگير *kaf-gír.* A skimmer.

A. كفل *kafl.* The buttocks

A. كفن *kafan.* A winding-sheet.

A. P. كفه *kaffa.* The tray of a pair of scales.

A. كفو *kafw.* Equal.

A. كفور *kafúr.* Impious, ungrateful.

A. كفيل *kafíl.* A security, surety, bail.

A. كل *kull.* The whole, all.

P. كل *kal.* Bald, baldness.

P. كلا *kalá.* A frog.

A. كلاب *kaláb.* Hydrophobia.

P. كلابه *kalába.* Raw thread; yarn.

P. كلاخ *kalákh.* A fillet, a head-band.

P. كلار *kalár.* A frog.

A. كلاسه *kalása.* Wells, where travellers drink.

P. كلاغ *kalágh.* A crow.

A. كلال *kalál.* Weakness, fatigue.

P. كلاله *kulála.* Ringlets; a nosegay.

A. كلام *kalám.* Speech, a word.

P. كلان *kalán.* Large, great.

P. كلانى *kalání.* Greatness.

P. كلاوه *kaláva.* A skein or ball of thread.

P. كلاه *kuláh.* A tall Persian cap.

A. كلب *kalb.* A dog.

A. كلبتان *kalbatán.* Tongs, pincers.

P. كلجه *kulaja.* A frock-coat.

P. كلخان *kalkhán.* } A furnace for heating a bath.
P. كلخن *kalkhan.* }

P. كلبه *kulba.* A closet, cell.

A. كلس *kils.* Quick-lime for making mortar.

A. كلف *kalaf.* A spot in the face; being in love.

A. كلفت *kulfat.* Trouble, vexation, distress.

P. كلك *kilk.* A pen, reed.

P. كلم *kilim.* A carpet.

A. كلمات *kalimát.* Discourses.

A. كلمه *kalima.* A word, speech, saying. The Mohammedan profession of faith.

P. كلند *kaland, kuland.* A mattock, spade.

P. كلنك *kulank.* A crane.

A. كلوب *kallúb.* Forceps, pincers.

P. كلوخ *kulúkh.* A clod of earth.

P. كلوخ كوب *kulúkh-kúb.* A mallet for breaking clods.

P. كلوخ انداز *kulúkh-andáz.* A slinger.

P. كله *kalla.* A flock, herd.

P. كله *kalla.* A head, a sugar-loaf.

P. كله پاچه *kalla-pácha.* Sheep's trotters.

P. كله سر *kalla i sar.* The crown of the head.

A. كلى *kullíy.* Universally, totally.

A. كليات *kullíyát.* The collected works of an author.

P. كليد *kilíd.* A key.

P. G. كليسه *kalísa.* A church.

A. كليم *kalím.* An interlocutor. كليم الله *kalím alláh.* Moses.

A. كليه *kulya.* The kidneys, reins.

P. كم *kam.* Few, less, wanting.

A. كم *kam.* How much?

A. كما *kamá.* As.

A. كم *kumm.* A sleeve.

A. كماد *kimád.* Fomentation.

P. كماش *kumásh.* Fustian.

A. كمال *kamál.* Perfection.

P. كمان *kamán.* A bow.

P. كمانچه *kamánché.* A violin.

P. كماندار *kamán-dár.* An archer.

A. كما ينبغى *kamá yambaghi.* As it ought to be.

P. کم بخت *kam-bakht.* Unfortunate, wretched.

P. کمتر *kamtar.* Less, fewer, inferior.

P. کمخاب *kam-kháb.* Brocade.

A. کمر *kamar.* The loins, waist, middle.

A. P. کمر بسته *kamar-basta.* Ready.

A. P. کمر بند *kamar-band.* A belt, girdle.

P. کم رنگ *kam-rang.* Pale.

A. کمرے *kamaríy.* Weak in the loins (a horse).

P. A. کم عیار *kam aiyár.* Below standard (coin).

P. کمک *kumak.* Auxiliaries.

P. کمند *kamand.* A noose, halter, lasso.

P. کم و کاست *kam u kást.* Defect and diminution.

A. کمون *kammún.* Cummin-seed.

A. کمه *kamah.* Blind from the birth.

P. کمی *kamí.* Paucity, scarcity.

A. کمی *kamíy.* A hero, a mailed warrior.

P. کمیاب *kam-yáb.* Rare, scarce.

A. کمیت *kumaít.* A bay horse.

A. کمیت *kamíyet.* Quantity.

P. کمیز دان *kumíz-dán.* The urine-bladder.

A. کمین *kamín.* An ambush.

P. کمین *kamín.* } Mean,
P. کمینه *kamína.* } base, abject.

A. کن *kun.* Be thou.

P. کن *kun.* Do thou.

P. کن *kan.* Dig thou; (in composition) a digger.

P. کناد *kunád.* May (God) do!

P. کنار *kanár.* Side, brink.

P. کنار *kinár.* A lap; an embrace.

P. کناره *kinára.* Beach, shore, margin.

A. کناس *kannás.* A sweeper.

A. کنایه *kináyah.* Sign, allusion, metaphor.

P. کنایس *kanáis.* Churches. (pl. of کنیسه.)

P. کنج *kunj.* A corner, angle.

P. کنجشک *kunjishk.* A sparrow.

P. کند *kund.* Blunt, stupid.

P. کندن *kandan.* To dig, engrave; to pluck up.

P. کنشت *kunisht.* A church, synagogue; a profession.

P. کنز *kanz.* A treasure.

A. P. کنعان *kan'án.* Canaan.

A. کنف *kanaf.* A wing, side.

P. کنکاش *kunkásh.* Conference, especially of conspirators.

P. کنگره *kungura.* A battlement.

P. کننده *kanenda.* A digger.

A. کنوز *kunúz.* Treasures.

P. کنون *kanún.* Now, at present.

A. کنه *kunh.* Substance, mode.

P. کنیز *kaníz.* A maid-servant.

P. کنیزك *kanízah.* A little girl.

P. کنیسه *kanísah.* A church.

A. کواکب *kawákib.* Stars. (pl. of کوکب.)

P. کوب *kúb.* Bruise thou; bruising.

P. کوبیدن *kúbídan.* To beat, bruise.

P. کوتاه *kútáh.* Short, contracted.

P. کوتاهی *kútáhí.* Shortness.

A. کوثر *kauśar.* Name of a stream in paradise.

P. کوچ *kúch.* Marching, decampment; (colloquially) family, household.

P. کوچك *kúchak.* Little, small.

P. کوچه *kúcha.* A lane, a street.

P. کودك *kúdak.* A boy, youth.

P. کودن *kaudan.* A block-head, stupid.

P. کور *kúr.* Blind.

P. کور دل *kúr-dil.* Lazy, careless.

P. کورنش *kúrnish.* } Obeisance,
P. کورنشات *kurnishát.* } salutation.

P. کوره *kúra.* A fireplace, forge.

P. کوری *kúrí.* Blindness.

P. کوز *kúz.* Crooked.

P. کوز پشت *kúz-pusht.* Hump-backed.

A. P. کوزه *kúza.* A jug.

P. کوس *kús.* A kettle-drum.

P. کوشش *kúshish.* Effort, attempt.

P. کوشك *kúshk.* A palace, kiosk.

P. کوشیدن *kushídan.* To strive, endeavour.

A. کوفه *kúfa.* Kufa, a city on the Euphrates. In Kufa and Bosra were rival schools of learning.

P. کوفتن *kúftan.* To bruise, to smite.

P. کوفته *kúfta.* A rissole.

A. کوکب *kaukab.* A star.

A. کوکبه *kaukebah.* Attendants, satellites.

P. کوك کردن *kúk-kerdan.* To wind up (a watch); to tune (a musical instrument).

P. کوکلتاش *kúkal-tash.* A foster-brother.

P. کوکو *kúkú.* The cuckoo.

T. کومك *kúmak.* Assistance.

P. کون *kún.* The podex; anus.

A. کون *kaun.* Existence.

A. کون مکان *kaun makán.* The world, existence.

A. کونین *kaunain.* Both states of existence.

P. کونی *kúní.* A pæderast.

P. کوه *kúh.* A hill, mountain.

P. کوهان *kúhán.* A camel's or bullock's hump.

P. کوهسار *kúh-sár.* Mountainous.

P. کوهستان *kúhistán.* A hilly country.

P. کوی *kúy.* A street, lane.

P. که *ki.* Who; that.

A. کهان *kuhhán.* Soothsayers.

A. کهانت *kahánat.* Soothsaying.

P. کهتر *kih-tar.* Less, junior.

P. کهربا *kah-rubá.* Attracting straws, (amber).

P. کهربای *kahrubáí.* Electricity.

A. کهف *kahf.* A cave, a large cavern. اصحاب کهف *aṣḥáb i kahf.* The seven sleepers of Ephesus.

P. کهکشان *kah-kashán.* The milky way, the galaxy.

P. کهن *kuhn.* Old, ancient, worn.

P. کهنه *kuhna.* Old, ancient.

P. کهواره *kahwára.* A cradle.

P. کی *kai.* When? ; an emperor.

A. کی *kai.* Cautery.

A. کیاست *kiyásat.* Ingenuity.

P. کیان *kaiyán.* The Kayánian dynasty.

P. کیانی *kaiyání.* Imperial, of the Kyanian race.

P. کی خسرو *kai-khusrav.* Kai-Khosrau, Cyrus.

A. کید *kaid.* Deceit, fraud. stratagem.

P. کیر *kír.* Membrum virile.

A. کیس *kais.* Sagacity, ingenuity.

P. کیست *kíst.* Who is it? = که است.

A. P. کیسه *kísa.* A bag, a purse.

P. کیسه بر *kísa-bur.* A cut-purse.

P. کیش *kísh.* Religion; faith; a quiver; a kind of diaper. Name of an island at the entrance of the Persian Gulf.

P. کیغ *kígh.* The matter adhering to the corners of the eyes.

A. کیف *kaif.* How.

T. کیف *kaif.* Being cosy, comfortable, amused.

A. کیفیت *kaifíyet.* State, condition, circumstances.

P. کیك *kaik.* A flea.

A. کیل *kail.* A measure of grain.

P. کیمخت *kímukht.* Leather of horse's or ass's hide.

G. کیموس *kaimús.* Chyle.

G. کیمیا *kímíyá.* Chemistry, alchymy.

P. کیمیا کر *kímíyá-gar.* A chemist, alchymist.

P. کینه *kína.* Malice, wrath.

P. کینه کش *kína-kesh.* Vindictive.

P. کیوان *kaiván.* The planet Saturn.

P. کیهان *kíhán.* The world.

گ

گاف *gáf.* G. The twenty-sixth letter of the Persian alphabet.

P. گاذر *gáżur* or گازر *gázur.* A fuller, a washerman.

P. گار *gár.* An affix denoting agency.

P. گاز *gáz.* Tongs.

P. گام *gám.* A step, pace.

P. گاو *gáu.* A cow. ریش گاو *rísh i gáu.* A fool.

P. گاو اهن *gáu u áhan.* A ploughshare.

P. گاو دم *gáu-dam.* A trumpet; a tapering tube.

P. گاو زبان *gáu-zabán.* Bugloss.

P. گاو زور *gáu-zúr.* Rude, brutal.

P. گاو شنگ *gáu-shang.* An ox-goad.

P. گاو میش *gáu-mísh.* A buffalo.

P. گاه *gáh.* Time, place.

P. گاه گاه *gáh-gáh.* Sometimes, now and then.

P. گائیدن *gáïdan.* To copulate.

P. گبر *gabr.* A worshipper of fire, follower of Zoroaster; an infidel.

P. گچ *gach.* Mortar, plaster.

P. گدا *gadá.* A beggar.

P. گداختن *gudákhtan.* To melt, to dissolve.

P. گدازش *gudázish.* Liquefaction.

P. گدازنده *gudázenda.* A solvent.

P. گدائی *gadáï.* Beggary.

P. گدو *gaddú.* A pumpkin.

P. گذار *gużár.* A passage; a ferry.

P. گذاردن *gużárdan.* To perform.

P. گذارش *gużárish.* Representation; presenting a memorial, &c.

P. گذاشتن *gużáshtan.* To quit; to leave; to allow; to present.

P. گذاف *gużáf.* Boasting.

P. گذر *gużar.* Pass thou.

P. گذر *gużar.* A passage; a ferry; passing.

P. گذر نامه *gużar-náma.* A passport.

P. گذران *gużrán.* Passing, spending.

P. گذرانیدن *gużránídan.* To cause to pass; to present.

P. گذر بان *gużar-bán.* A road-watch.

P. گذر گاه *gużar-gáh.* A ford, a ferry.

P. گذشتن *gużashtan.* To pass.

P. گذشته *gużashta.* Past.

P. گر *gar.* If.

P. گرامی *garámí.* Dear, respectable, excellent.

P. گران *garán.* Heavy; dear.

P. گرانی *garání.* Scarcity, dearth; weight.

P. گراى *garáï.* Inclination.

P. گرائيدن *garáïdan.* To incline towards; to explore, examine.

P. گربال *girbál.* A sieve.

P. گربه *gurbah.* A cat.

P. گربه مسكين *gurba-i-miskín.* A rogue; poor-puss.

P. گربهٔ ابى *gurba i ábí.* An otter.

P. گربز *gurpuz.* Artful, seductive.

P. گرچه *gar-chí.* Although.

P. گرد *gard.* Dust.

P. گرد *gird.* Round; circuit.

P. گرد *gurd.* A hero.

P. گرداب *girdáb.* A whirlpool.

P. گرداگرد *gird á gird.* Round about.

P. گرد امدن *gird ámadan.* To gather round.

P. گردان *gardán.* Turning, revolving.

P. گردانيدن *gardánídan.* To alter, to turn, to cause, to become.

P. گرد اورى *gird-áwarí.* Watching, guarding.

P. گرد باد *gird-bád.* A whirlwind.

P. گردش *gardish.* Revolution.

P. گرد شهر *gird i shahr.* Suburbs.

P. گردكان *gurdagán.* A walnut.

P. گرد كردن *gird-kardan.* To surround, to invest.

P. گردن *gardan.* The neck.

P. گردن فراز *gardan-faráz.* Proud, haughty.

P. گردن كشيدن *gardan keshídan.* To rebel.

P. گردون *gardún.* The celestial sphere; a wheel.

P. گردو *girdú.* } A nut.
P. گردوى *girdúy.* }

P. گرده *gurda.* A kidney; courage.

P. گرده *girda.* A wafer, cake; a shield; a round pillow.

P. گرديدن *gardídan.* To become; to wander.

P. گرز *gurz.* A mace or club.

P. گرستن *giristan.* To weep, to cry.

P. گرسنگى *gursnagí.* Hunger.

P. گرشمه *girishma.* An amorous glance. See كرشمه.

P. گرسنه *gursna.* Hungry.

P. گرفتار *giriftár.* Seized, a captive.

P. گرفتارى *giriftárí.* Captivity, bondage.

P. گرفتن *giriftan.* To take; seize.

P. گرگ *gurg.* A wolf.

P. گرم *garm.* Hot, warm.

P. گرمابه *garmába.* A warm bath.

P. گرم خيز *garm-khíz.* Active; an early riser.

P. گرم سير *garm-sír.* A warm climate.

P. گرمی *garmí.* Heat, warmth.

P. گرمیدانه *garmídána.* A rush.

P. گرنه *gar-na.* Unless.

P. گرو *girav.* A pledge, pawn.

P. گروه *gurúh.* Band, troop.

P. گرویدن *girawídan.* To follow, to imitate, to be attached.

P. گره *girah.* A knot.

P. گریان *giryán.* Weeping, lamenting.

P. گریانیدن *giryánídan.* To cause to cry.

P. گریبان *garíbán.* The collar or breast of a garment.

P. گریختن *guríkhtan.* To flee, desert.

P. گریز *guríz.* Flight, defeat.

P. گریزان *gurízán.* Taking flight.

P. گریزانیدن *gurízánídan.* To put to flight.

P. گریستن *giristan.* To cry, to weep.

P. گریوه *girívа.* A steep acclivity.

P. گریه *girya.* Weeping.

P. گز *gaz.* An ell; a tamarisk.

P. گزاف *guzáf.* Boasting, foolish talking.

P. گزان *gazán.* Biting, pungent.

P. گزر *gazar.* A carrot.

P. گزند *gazand.* Injury, damage.

P. گزنه *gazna.* A nettle.

P. گزیدن *guzídan.* To choose, to select.

P. گزیدن *gazídan.* To bite

P. گزیده *guzída.* Chosen, selected.

P. گزیر *guzír.* Aid, remedy.

P. گستاخ *gustákh.* Rude.

P. گستاخی *gustákhí.* Rudeness.

P. گستر *gustar.* One who spreads, diffusive.

P. گسترانندن *gustarándan.* }
P. گسترانیدن *gustaránídan.* }
To cause to spread.

P. گستردن *gustardan.* To spread.

P. گسستن *gusistan.* } To
P. گسیختن *gusíkhtan.* } tear, or twist off.

P. گسلیدن *guslídan.* }
P. گسلانیدن *guslánídan.* }
To snap asunder.

P. گشت *gasht.* Walking, going round.

P. گشتن *gashtan.* To become; to turn.

P. گشته *gashta.* Became; changed.

P. گفت *guft.* He spoke.

P. گفتار *guftár.* To speak.

P. گفتگو *guft-gú.* }
P. گفت و شنید *guft u shunid.* }
Conversation.

P. گل *gul.* A flower; a rose; the snuff of a candle.

P. گل *gil.* Clay, mud.

P. گلاب *guláb*. Rose-water.

P. گلاب پاش *guláb-pásh*. A bottle for sprinkling rose-water.

P. گل ارمنی *gil í armaní*. Bole armenic.

P. گلبن *gulbun*. A rose-tree.

P. گلخن *gulkhan*. The stove of a warm-bath.

P. گلدسته *guldasta*. A nosegay.

P. گل رخ *gul-rukh*. Rosy-cheeked.

P. گلستان *gulistán*. A rose-garden.

P. گل سفید *gil i safeid*. Chalk.

P. گل شکر *gul-shakar*. Conserve of roses.

P. گلشن *gulshan*. A rose-garden.

P. گل فام *gul fám*. Like the rose; a mistress.

P. گل قند *gul-ḳand*. Conserve of roses.

P. گلگیر *gul-gír*. A pair of snuffers.

P. گلنار *gulnár*. Pomegranate-blossoms.

P. گلو *gulú*. The throat.

P. گلو بند *gulú-band*. A necklace; neckcloth.

P. گلو گرفتن *gulú giriftan*. To have a sore throat.

P. گلوله *gulúla*. A bullet.

P. گله *gila*. Murmuring, complaint.

P. گله *gala*. A herd.

P. گله بان *gala-bán*. A pastor.

P. گله بانی *gala-báni*. Pastoral care.

P. گلی *gilí*. Earthen.

P. گلیم *gilím*. A blanket.

P. گم *gum*. Lost, missing.

P. گماشتن *gumáshtan*. To commission, depute.

P. گماشته *gumáshta*. An agent, factor.

P. گمان *gumán*. Suspicion, conjecture.

P. گمراه *gum-ráh*. Lost, erring, abandoned.

P. گمراهی *gum-ráhí*. Error; wandering.

P. گمرك *gumruk*. From the Greek κουμερκί the Custom-house. The Excise is called راهداری q.v.

P. گناه *gunáh*. Sin, crime, fault.

P. گناهگار *gunáh-gár*. A sinner, culprit.

P. گنجایش *ganjáyish*. Capacity, holding.

P. گنجیدن *ganjídan*. To hold, contain.

P. گنجفه *ganjífa*. A pack of cards.

P. گنجور *ganjvar*. A treasure.

P. گنجینه *ganjína*. A treasury, magazine.

P. گندم *gundam*. Wheat.

P. گندم بریان *gundam i biriyán*. Parched corn.

P. گندم گون *gundam-gún*. Swarthy.

P. گندانا *gandáná.* A leek.

P. گنده *gunda.* Coarse, thick.

P. گنده *ganda.* Fetid.

P. گندیدن *gandídan.* To putrefy; to stink.

P. گنگ *gung.* Dumb.

P. گنه *gunah.* A crime, fault.

P. گنهگار *gunahgár.* A sinner.

P. گو *gú.* Speak, say (from گفتن *guftan*). A ball.

P. گوار *gawár.* } Digestible,
P. گواره *gawára.* } agreeable.

P. گواه *gawáh.* A witness, evidence.

P. گواهی *gawáhí.* Testimony, evidence.

P. گوپال *gupál.* An iron mace.

P. گور *gúr.* A grave, a tomb.

P. گور *gúr.* The wild ass.

P. گورستان *gúristán.* A burying-place.

P. گوز *gúz.* Crepitatio ventris.

P. گوزن *gauzan.* An elk.

P. گوساله *gausála.* A calf.

P. گوسپند *gúspend.* A goat, a sheep.

P. گوش *gúsh.* An ear. گوش تو دو دادند و زبان تو یکی *gúsh i tú dú dádand u zabán i tú yekí.* Talk less and listen more.

P. گوشت *gúsht.* Flesh, meat.

P. گوش مال *gúsh-mál.* Chastisement; pulling the ears.

P. گوشواره *gúshwára.* An ear-ring; the abstract of an account.

P. گوشه *gúsha.* A corner, angle.

P. گوشه نشین *gúsha-nishín.* Sitting in a corner; retiring.

P. گوگرد *gaugird.* Sulphur.

P. گول *gúl.* An idiot.

P. گوله *gúla.* A cannon-ball.

P. گون *gún.* A particle implying colour.

P. گوناگون *gún á gún.* Various.

P. گونه *gúna.* Colour; sort, form. چه گونه. *che gúna ï.* "How are you?"

P. گوه *gúh.* Excrement.

P. گوهر *gauhar.* Essence; a gem.

P. گوهری *gauharí.* A jeweller.

P. گوی *gúy.* A ball; a globe. (In comp.) speech.

P. گویائی *gúyáï.* Speech.

P. گوینده *gúyanda.* Speaking; a speaker.

P. گه *gah.* Time; place.

P. گهر *guhar.* A jewel, gem; race, family.

P. گهواره *gahwára.* A cradle.

P. گیاه *giyáh.* Grass; herbage.

P. گیتی *gítí.* The world, universe.

P. گیتی ارا *gítí-árá.* Adorning the world.

P. گیتی فروز *gítí farúz.* World-illuminating.

P. گیج *gíj.* Vertigo.

P. گیر *gír.* Seizing; seize thou.

P. گیر و دار *gír u dár.* Dominion.

P. گیرا *gírá.* One who holds.

P. گیسو *gísú.* A knot of hair, ringlet.

P. گیلاس *gílás.* A cherry.

P. گین *gín.* A termination signifying affected with, as اندوه گین *andúh-gín.* Full of grief.

P. گیوه *gíva.* White kid, or cotton shoes.

ل

ل *lám.* L. The twenty-third letter of the Arabic, and twenty-seventh of the Persian alphabet.

A. لا *lá.* No, not.

A. لابث *lábis.* Delaying, dilatory.

A. لا بد *lá budd.* Necessarily, infallibly.

P. لابه *lábah.* Desire; flattery.

A. لا جرم *lá jaram.* Necessarily.

A. لاجورد *lájward.* Lapis lazuli, azure.

A. لاحق *láḥiḳ.* Adjoining, attached to.

A. لا حول *lá ḥaul*, abbreviated for لا حول و لا قوة الا بالله *lá ḥaula wá lá kúwata illá billáh.* There is no strength nor power but in God. Used as an expression of astonishment especially at an unexpected misfortune.

P. لاخ *lákh.* A termination signifying place, as, سنگلاخ *sang-lákh.* A stony place.

A. لا خراج *lá kharáj.* Rent-free.

A. لا دوا *lá dawá.* Incurable.

A. لا زال *lá zál.* May it endure!

A. لازب *lázib.* Firm, solid.

A. لازم *lázim.* Incumbent, necessary.

A. لازمی *lázimí.* Necessary.

P. لاژه *lázha.* Wild saffron

P. لاش *lásh.* A corpse.

P. لاشخور *lásh-kh'ur.* A carrion-bird.

A. لاشك *lá shakk.* Doubtless.

P. لاشه *lásha.* A dead body, corpse, carcass.

A. لاصق *laṣiḳ.* Adhering.

A. لا طائل *lá ṭáil.* Absurd, useless, unprofitable.

A. لاعب *lá'ib.* A player, gamester.

P. لاغ *lágh.* Jest, burlesque.

P. لاغر *lághar.* Lean, thin.

P. لاف *láf.* Boasting, vanity.

P. لاف زدن *láf-zadan.* To brag, to boast.

P. لاك *lák.* Gum-lac.

A. لا كلام *lá kalám.* Without dispute. Ineffable.

P. لال *lál.* Dumb; red.

P. لاله *lála.* A tulip.

A. لآلى *la'álí.* Pearls. (pl. of لؤلؤ.)

A. لامس *lámis.* Touching, feeling.

A. لامسه *lámisah.* The sense of feeling.

A. لامع *lámi'.* Splendid, bright.

A. لا و نعم *lá wa na'm.* Yes and no.

P. لاوه *láwa.* Supplication.

A. لاوى *láwíy.* A Levite; Levitical.

A. لاهوت *láhút.* Divinity.

A. لائح *láïḥ.* Evident.

A. لا يعنى *lá ya'ní.* Absurd, meaningless.

A. لايق *láïḳ.* Worthy, deserving, fit.

A. لايم *láïm.* A reprover, slanderer.

A. لا يموت *lá yamút.* Immortal.

A. لا ينبغى *la yambaghí.* Indecent, impertinent, improper.

P. لاييدن *láyídan.* To complain, talk snappishly; to bark.

P. لب *lab.* The lip, brink, margin.

A. لبّ *lubb.* The pith, marrow; essence.

A. لباب *lubáb.* The best and purest of anything.

A. لبّاده *labbáda.* A felt overcoat.

A. لباس *libás.* Dress, apparel.

A. لباسى *libásí.* Forgery, deception.

P. لبالب *lab álab.* Brimful.

A. لبان *libán.* Benzoin.

P. لبريز *labríz.* Running over.

A. لبس *labs.* Putting on a garment.

A. لبلاب *labláb.* Ivy, bindweed, pellitory.

P. لبلبو *lablabú.* Beetroot.

A. لبن *laban.* Soured milk.

A. لبنان *libnán.* Mount Lebanon.

A. لبيب *labíb.* Prudent, wise.

A. لبيك *labbaik.* Here am I! used in addressing the Deity.

A. لت *lat.* A blow, stroke.

P. لتره *latra.* A part, fragment.

A. لثم *latm.* A slap; striking.

A. لثق *laṡaḳ.* Being moist, or bedewed.

A. لثم *laṡm.* Kissing; veiling the face.

A. لجاج *lajáj.* Contest, litigation.

A. لجام *lijám.* A bridle, reins.

A. لحاظ *laḥáẓ.* Scrutiny.

A. لحاف *liḥáf.* A coverlid.

A. لحام *laḥḥám*. A butcher.

A. لحس *laḥs*. Licking; eating.

A. لحظة *laḥẓat*. A moment; a glance.

A. لحم *laḥm*. Flesh, meat.

A. لحن *laḥn*. Melody, tune.

A. لحية *liḥyat*. A beard.

P. لخت *lakht*. A bit, a piece.

P. لختی *lakhtí*. Somewhat, some; a little while.

A. لدام *ladám*. A patch.

A. لدغ *ladgh*. Biting, stinging.

A. لذت *lażżat*. Pleasure; taste.

A. لذيذ *lażíż*. Delicious, sweet.

P. لرزه *larza*. Tremor.

P. لرزيدن *larzídan*. To tremble.

A. لزوم *luzúm*. Necessity, expediency.

A. لسان *lisán*. (pl. السنه.) The tongue; language.

A. لسان الثور *lisan us ṡaur*. Bugloss.

A. لسع *lasʻ*. The stinging (of a scorpion, &c.).

P. لشكر *lashkar*. An army.

P. لشكر گاه *lashkar-gáh*. A camp.

P. لشكر كش *lashkar-kesh*. A general.

P. لصوق *luṣúḳ*. Adhesion, conjunction.

A. لطافت *laṭáfat*. Elegance, beauty.

A. لطائف *laṭáïf*. (pl. of لطيفه.) Jests, witticisms.

A. لطخ *laṭkh*. Staining; smearing; defaming.

A. لطف *luṭf*. Favour, kindness. لطف شما كم نشود *luṭf i shumá kam nashawad*. Thank you.

A. لطمه *laṭmah*. A blow, a box.

A. لطيف *laṭíf*. Elegant, agreeable.

A. لطيفه *laṭífah*. A jest, a witticism.

A. لظى *lażá*. Hell, or hell-fire.

A. لعاب *luʻáb*. Sliminess, viscosity.

A. لعب *laʻb*. Playing; a play, game.

A. لعبة *laʻbat*. A puppet.

A. P. لعبت بازی *laʻbat bází*. A puppet-show.

A. لعل *laʻl*. A ruby.

A. لعنت *laʻnat*. A curse.

A. لعين *laʻín*. Execrable.

A. لغات *lughát*. Languages.

A. لغت *lughat*. Speech; language; a dictionary.

A. لغز *laghz*. An enigma, riddle.

P. لغزان *laghzán*. Slipping, sliding.

P. لغزيدن *laghzídan*. To slip.

A. لغو *laghw*. An inconsiderate speech.

A. لغوی *laghawí*. Belonging to language.

A. لفاح *luffáḥ*. Mandragora.

A. لفافه *lifáfah.* An envelope.

A. لفظ *lafẓ.* A word, speech.

A. لفق *lafḳ.* Stitching together.

A. لف و نشر *laff u nashr.* A figure in rhetoric, in which several subjects are first mentioned, and the predicates given in a separate clause.

A. لفيف *lafíf.* A crowd.

A. لقاء *liḳá'.* A visit, interview.

A. لقب *laḳab.* A surname, nickname.

A. لقلق *laḳlaḳ.* A stork.

A. لقمان *luḳmán.* The great Eastern fabulist, Æsop.

A. لقمه *luḳmah.* A mouthful, morsel.

P. لك *lak.* Lac.

P. لكام *lagám.* The bit of a bridle.

P. لكد *lakd.* A kick.

P. لكد و كوب *lakd u kúb.* Assault and battery.

A. لكن *lakan.* Stammering.

P. لكن *lakan.* A bason; a tub.

A. لكنت *laknat.* Stammering, stuttering.

P. لكه *lakka.* A spot, a blemish.

P. لله *lala.* A mentor, a tutor.

A. لله الحمد *lilláhi 'l ḥamd.* God be praised.

A. لما *lammá.* When.

A. لما *limá.* Why?

A. لمحه *lamḥah.* A moment; a glance, a wink.

A. لمس *lams.* The touch, handling, feeling.

A. لمع *lam'.* Splendour, brilliancy.

A. لمعان *lama'án.* Shining, glittering.

P. لنك *lang.* Lame.

P. لنكر *langar.* An anchor.

P. لنكيدن *langídan.* To limp.

A. لواء *liwá'.* A standard, banner.

A. لواحق *lawáḥiḳ.* Domestics, dependants.

A. لوازم *lawázim.* Necessaries, requisites.

A. لوامع *lawámi'.* Rays, lights.

A. لوبيا *lubiyá.* A species of bean.

A. لوث *laus.* Defilement, impurity.

A. لوح *lauḥ.* A plank, board, tablet.

P. لوچ *lúch.* Squint-eyed.

A. لوز *lauz.* An almond.

A. P. لوزينه *lauzína.* A confection of almonds.

A. لوطى *luṭíy.* A sodomite.

A. لؤلؤ *lú'lu'.* A pearl.

P. لوله *lúla.* The mouth or barrel of a firearm.

P. لولى *lúlí.* A courtezan; singing girl.

P. لولين *lúlín.* An earthenware vessel.

A. لوم *laum.* Blame, censure.

A. لون *laun.* Colour; species.

P. لوند *lawand.* Free; ignorant, foolish; poor; a soldier.

T. له *lah.* A Pole; Polish.

A. لهاب *laháb.* } Flame.
A. لهب *lahab.* }

A. لهجة *lahjat.* Pronunciation.

A. لهذا *lihází.* Therefore.

A. لهو *lahw.* Playing.

A. لهو و لعب *lahw wa la'b.* Sport.

A. ليالى *layálí.* Nights. (pl. of ليلة.)

A. ليام *liyám.* Sordid men.

A. ليت و لعل *lait u la'all.* Procrastination, prevarication.

A. ليث *lais.* A lion.

P. ليزم *lízam.* A kind of bow.

P. ليزيدن *lízídan.* To slip.

P. ليسيدن *lísídan.* To lick.

P. ليك *laik.* } But,
A. P. ليكن *laikin.* } notwithstanding.

A. ليل *lail.* The night.

A. ليلى *lailá.* A celebrated heroine of Persian poetry, the mistress of Majnún.

A. ليمون *laimún.* A lemon.

A. لينة *línat.* Mildness, softness; a kind of palm.

A. ليم *liyam.* Vile, base.

A. ليمان *límán.* Base men.

م

م *mím.* M. The twenty-fourth letter of the Arabic, and twenty-eight of the Persian alphabet.

P. م *-am.* (Affixed pronoun) me, my.

A. ما *má.* What; why; no, not.

P. ما *má.* We, us, our.

A. ماء *má.* Water, juice.

A. ماء الجبن *má ul jibn.* Whey.

A. ماء الحياة *má ul ḥaiyát.* The water of life.

A. ماب *ma'áb.* A resort.

A. ماباقى *mábáḳí.* } The remainder,
A. ما بقى *má baḳí.* } the rest.

A. مابون *mábún.* Infamous, suspected.

A. ما بين *ma bain.* Between.

A. مات *mát.* He is dead.

T. P. مات *mát.* Astonished, amazed.

A. ما تقدم *má taḳaddam.* The past; antiquity.

P. ماتم *mátum.* Mourning.

P. ماتم پرسى *mátum-pursí.* Condolence.

P. ماتمى *mátumí.* Belonging to mourning.

A. ماتى *ma'tá.* The face, appearance.

A. ماثر *ma'ásir.* Marks, signs, memorials.

A. ماثل *mașil.* Standing.

A. ماثور *ma'șúr.* History, tradition.

A. ماثوم *ma'șúm.* A guilty or suspected person.

A. ماجد *májid.* Noble, praiseworthy.

A. ما جرے *má jará.* An event, incident. (Though used in Persian as a noun, this is a complete clause in Arabic, signifying "what has occurred.")

P. ماجو *máj'ú.* A gall-nut.

A. ماجوج *májúj.* Magog the son of Japhet; Eastern Tartary.

P. ماچ و موچ *mách u múch.* Kissing and licking as a cat her kittens.

A. ماجور *ma'júr.* Recompensed, paid.

P. ماچین *máchín.* The empire of China.

A. ما حصل *má ḥașal.* Anything collected, produce.

A. ما حضر *má ḥazar.* Whatever is at hand.

A. ماحی *máḥí.* Obliterating.

A. ماخذ *ma'khaz.* The original or source of anything.

A. ماخوذ *ma'khúz.* Received, taken.

A. ماحور *mákhur.* A tavern.

A. ما دام *má dám.* Whilst, during, until.

A. مادح *mádiḥ.* A eulogist.

P. مادر *mádar.* A mother.

P. مادر پدر *mádar i padar.* Paternal grandmother.

P. مادر روزکار *mádar i rúzgár.* Dame nature.

P. مادر زاد *mádar-zád.* Innate, from the birth.

P. مادر مادر *mádar i mádar.* Maternal grandmother.

P. مادری *mádarí.* Maternal.

A. ماده *máddah.* The first principle; subject.

P. ماده *máda.* Female.

A. مادی *máddíy.* Material, essential.

P. مادیان *mádiyán.* A mare, a she-ass.

A. مادیت *máddíyat.* Substantialness.

A. ماذون *ma'zún.* Permitted, allowed.

P. مار *már.* A snake.

A. مار *már.* A lord; a saint.

P. مارا *márá.* Us, to us.

P. ماراب *máráb.* Recent good fortune.

A. مارب *ma'árib.* Important affairs.

P. مار چوبه *már-chúba.* Asparagus.

P. مار گیر *már-gír.* A snake-catcher.

P. مار گزیده *már-gazída.* Snake-bitten.

P. مار ماهی *már i máhí.* An eel.

P. مارندر *márandar.* A mother-in-law.

P. ماروت *márút*. One of two angels; *Hárút* and *Márút*, punished for falling in love with mortal women. They are supposed to be suspended head downwards in a well at Bábel, where they teach men sorcery.

A. ماروك *ma'rúk*. An origin, a root.

P. مازو *mázú*. A gall-apple.

A. ما سبق *má sabaḳ*. That which precedes.

P. ماست *mást*. Coagulated or curded milk.

A. ماسك *másik*. Holding, retentive.

A. ما سلف *má salaf*. The past.

A. ما سوا *má siwá*. Besides, except.

P. ماش *másh*. A kind of pea.

P. ماشه *másha*. A small weight; tweezers.

A. ماشی *máshí*. Walking; a pedestrian.

A. ماص *máṣṣ*. Slipping; sucking.

A. ما صدق *má ṣudiḳ*. Anything verified.

A. ماضی *máẓí*. The past; the preterite tense.

A. ماضغه *maẓighah*. That part with which one masticates.

A. ماطر *máṭir*. Rainy.

A. ماعز *má'iz*. A goat-herd; goats' leather.

A. ما فات *má fát*. That which has elapsed.

A. ما فوق *má fauḳ*. Beyond, above, superior.

A. ما قبل *má ḳabal*. Antecedent.

P. ماکو *makú*. A weaver's shuttle.

A. ماکول *ma'kúl*. Eaten; food, victuals.

P. ماکیان *makíyán*. A fowl, a hen.

A. مال *mál*. Wealth, property.

A. مآل *ma'ál*. Consequence, end, issue.

A. مال و اموال *mál u amwál*. Riches, money, wealth.

A. ما لا کلام *má lá kalím*. Ineffable.

A. P. مالامال *mál-á-mál*. Full, heaped up.

A. مآل اندیش *ma'ál-andísh*. Forecast.

A. ما لا یعنی *má lá ya'ní*. Meaningless.

A. P. مالپرست *mál-parast*. A worshipper of wealth.

A. مالح *máliḥ*. Salted, savoury.

G. مالخولیا *málikhúliya*. Melancholy.

A. P. مالدار *máldár*. Wealthy.

A. P. مالداری *máldárí*. Opulence.

A. ما لزم *má lazam*. That which is necessary.

P. مالش *málish*. Rubbing, friction.

A. P. مالضامن *mál-ẕámin.* Surety in sum.

A. مالك *málik.* Proprietor, master, owner.

A. P. مالكانه *málikána.* The proprietor's share of the produce of the soil.

A. P. مالگذاری *málguzárí.* Land-tax, revenue.

A. مالكيت *málikíyet.* Proprietaryship.

A. مال و متاع *mál u mitá'.* Property and effects.

A. مالوف *ma'lúf.* Familiar.

P. ماله *mála.* A trowel.

A. مالی *máliy.* Belonging to riches.

A. ماليت *máliyet.* Wealth, value.

P. ماليدن *málídan.* To rub, to anoint.

P. ماليده *málída.* Bread made with milk, flour, &c.

A. مالی و ملکی *málí wa mulkí.* Finance and government.

P. ماما *mámá.* Mother, (old women in general are so called).

P. مامك *mámak.* (Diminutive of the above) goody.

A. مأمن *ma'man.* Refuge, asylum.

A. مأمور *ma'múr.* Ordered, established.

A. مأمول *ma'múl.* Hoped for, expected.

A. مأمون *ma'mún.* Preserved, secured, guarded.

P. ماند *mánad.* From ماندن *mándan.* It remains. From مانستن *mánistan.* It resembles.

P. ماندگی *mándagí.* Fatigue, lassitude.

P. ماندن *mándan.* To remain.

P. مانده *mánda.* Fatigued, tired; left.

P. مانستن *mánistan.* To resemble.

A. مانع *máni'.* Obstacle, prohibition.

P. مانند *mánand.* Alike, resembling.

A. مانوس *ma'nús.* An intimate friend.

P. مانی *mání.* Manes, a celebrated heresiarch and painter, the founder of the Manichæan sect.

A. ماوا *máwá.* A dwelling, abode, habitation.

A. ما ورا *má wará.* Beyond, over, behind.

A. ما وراء النهر *má wará an nahr.* Transoxania.

A. ما وقع *má waḳa'.* An event.

P. ماه *máh.* The moon; a month.

P. ماهانه *máhána.* Monthly; monthly wages.

P. ماه بماه *máh ba máh.* Monthly.

P. ماهتاب *máh-táb.* Moonlight; the moon.

A. ماهر *máhir.* Skilful, experienced.

P. ماهرو *máh-rú*. Moon-faced, beautiful as the moon.

P. ماه کنعانی *máh i kin'ání*. The moon of Canaan, i.e. Joseph.

P. ماه نو *máh i nau*. The new moon.

P. ماهوار *máhwár*. Monthly.

P. ماهواری *máhwárí*. Monthly wages.

P. ماهوت *máhút*. Cloth.

P. ماهی *máhí*. A fish.

P. ماهیانه *máhiyána*. Monthly.

A. ماهیت *máhíyet*. State, value, substance.

P. ماهی خوار *máhí-khár*. A heron.

P. ماهی گیر *máhí-gír*. A fisherman; an otter.

A. مائی *má'í*. Watery, aquatic.

P. مایٔی و منی *má'í u maní*. Pride and egotism.

A. مائده *máidah*. A table covered with victuals.

A. مایع *máï'*. Liquid.

A. ما یقرا *ma yukrá*. Legible.

A. مایل *máil*. Inclined, towards.

A. مایوس *ma'yús*. Desperate, hopeless.

P. مایه *máya*. Stock; wealth, matter.

A. مایة *mi'at*. A hundred.

P. مایه دار *máya-dár*. A man of property.

P. مایهٔ شیر *máya e shír*. Rennet.

A. مباح *mubáh*. Lawful, allowable; allowed to be shed with impunity (blood).

A. مباحت *mabáhat*. Sincerity.

A. مباحث *mubáhis*. A disputant, disputing.

A. مباحثه *mubáhasah*. Dispute, debate.

P. مبادا *mabádá*. God forbid!

A. مبادر *mubádir*. Preceding, anticipating.

A. مبادرت *mubádarat*. Precedence, anticipating.

A. مبادله *mubádalah*. Exchange, barter.

P. مباش *ma-básh*. May it not be! stay not.

A. مبادے *mabádí*. Beginnings, origins.

A. مبارز *mubáriz*. A warrior, a champion.

A. مبارك *mubárak*. Happy, fortunate. This term is applied to all public and imperial institutions in Persia.

A. مبارك باد *mubárak-bád*. May it be fortunate!

A. P. مبارك بادی *mubárak-bádí*. Congratulation.

A. P. مبارکی *mubárakí*. Auspiciousness, happiness.

P. مباش *mabásh*. Be not.

A. مباشر *mubáshir*. A supervisor, inspector.

A. مباشر چاپار خانه *mubáshir i chápár-khána*. Chief of the Post.

A. مباشرت *mubásharat.* Management; copulation.

A. مباعدت *mubá'adat.* Distance.

A. مبالغ *mabáligh.* Sums of money. (pl. of مبلغ.)

A. مبالغه *mubálaghah.* Hyperbole; exaggeration.

A. مبانی *mabání.* Edifices.

A. مباهات *mubáhát.* Glory, honour.

A. مباهجت *mubáhajat.* Conviviality.

A. مباهلت *mubáhalat.* Behaving foolishly.

A. مباهی *mubáhí.* Glorious; arrogant, proud.

A. مبایعت *mubáya'at.* Commerce, traffic.

A. مباینت *mubáyanat.* Separation.

A. مبتلی *mubtalá.* Tired, afflicted.

A. مبداء *mabdá'.* The beginning.

A. مبتداء *mubtadá'.* Commencement, principle.

A. مبتدے *mubtadí.* A beginner, innovator.

A. مبتدع *mubtadi'.* A beginner, learner.

A. مبتشر *mubtashir.* A receiver of good news.

A. مبتغیات *mubtaghayát.* Requisitions.

A. مبتلاء *mubtalá.* Afflicted, distressed.

A. مبتهج *mubtahij.* Exalting, rejoicing.

A. مبحث *mabhas.* Subject of disputation.

A. مبدء *mabda'.* The beginning, origin.

A. مبدع *mubdi'.* Creator; inventor.

A. مبدل *mubaddal.* Changed, altered.

A. مبده *mibdah.* An improvisatore.

A. مبده *mubdah.* Extempore, irregular.

A. مبذر *mubazzir.* Prodigal, expensive.

A. مبذول *mabzúl.* Bestowed, expended.

P. مبر *mabar.* Do not carry or take.

A. مبرا *mubarrá.* Free, absolved, exempted.

A. مبرات *mabarrat.* Good works, beneficences.

A. مبرح *mubarrih.* Severe, heavy, distressing.

A. مبرد *mubarrid.* Cooling, refreshing.

A. مبرد *mibrad.* A file.

A. مبرز *mibraz.* A field of battle; a privy.

A. مبرور *mabrúr.* Purified, absolved, pious.

A. مبروص *mabrús.* Leprous, a leper.

A. مبرهن *mubarhan.* Demonstrative, evident.

A. مبسوط *mabsút.* Spread, extended; happy.

A. مبشر *mubasshar.* Rejoiced with good news.

A. مبشر *mubasshir.* A bearer of good news; an evangelist.

A. مبصر *mubṣir.* Seeing; a spectator.

A. مبطل *mubṭal.* Abolished, annihilated.

A. مبعوث *mab'ús.* Sent; Raised up.

A. مبلغ *mabligh.* A sum, ready money.

A. مبلل *muballil.* Moistening well.

A. مبنى *mabní.* Founded, constructed.

A. مبهج *mubhij.* Rejoicing, recreating.

A. مبهم *mubham.* Occult; doubtful.

A. مبهوت *mabhút.* Astonished, confounded.

A. مبيت *mabít.* A place in which to pass the night.

A. مبيع *mabí'.* Sold, bought.

A. مبين *mubayyin.* Explaining, dividing.

A. مبين *mabín.* Manifest, evident.

A. متى *matá.* When.

A. متابد *muta'abbid.* Wild, scared.

A. متابع *mutábi'.* A follower; obedient.

A. متابعت *mutába'at.* Imitation; obeying; following.

A. متاثر *muta'assar.* Impressed.

A. متاخر *muta'akkhar.* Behind; modern.

A. متاخرين *muta'akhkharín.* The moderns.

A. متادے *muta'addí.* Prepared, arranged.

A. متاذے *muta'azzí.* Injured, afflicted.

A. متاسد *muta'assad.* Furious, enraged.

A. متاسف *muta'assif.* Regretting, groaning.

A. متاع *mutá'.* Goods, effects.

A. متاعب *matá'ib.* Vexatious, affliction.

A. متالف *muta'allif.* Familiarized, associated.

A. متالم *muta'allim.* Grieved, sad, afflicted.

A. متامل *muta'ammil.* Considering, contemplative.

A. متامن *muta'ammin.* Confiding in, secure.

A. متانت *matánat.* Firmness, solidity.

A. متاهل *muta'ahhal.* Having a family; worthy.

A. متباين *mutabáyin.* Distinct, separate.

A. متبدل *mutabaddal.* Inverting, changing.

A. متبحر *mutabaḥḥir.* Profoundly learned.

A. متبدل *mutabaddal.* Changed, altered.

A. متبرك *mutabarrak.* Blessed, fortunate, happy.

A. متبرى *mutabarrí.* Freed, absolved.

A. متبنى *mutabanna.* An adopted son.

A. متبنى *mutabanní.* Adopting.

A. متبوع *matbú'.* Obeyed.

A. متبين *mutabaiyin.* Rendering clear.

A. متجاسر *mutajásir.* Bold, magnanimous.

A. متجاوز *mutajáwiz.* Exceeding; transgressing.

A. متجاهل *mutajáhil.* Feigning ignorance.

A. متجسس *mutajassis.* Exploring; playing the spy.

A. متجلى *mutajallí.* Illuminating; splendid.

A. مجتمع *mujtama'.* United, collected.

A. متحد *muttahid.* United, made one.

A. متحرك *mutaharrik.* Moveable, moved.

A. متحصن *mutahassin.* In garrison (troops).

A. متحقق *mutahakkik.* Verifying, true.

A. متحقق *mutahakkak.* Verified, true, certain.

A. متحلى *mutahallá.* Adorned.

A. متحمل *mutahammil.* Supporting, forbearing.

A. متحير *mutahaiyir.* Astonished.

A. متخاصم *mutakhásim.* Disputing, litigation.

A. متخاصمين *mutakhasimain.* (Dual of the above.) Plaintiff and defendant.

A. متخلف *mutakhallif.* Backing out of a promise.

A. متخيل *mutakhaiyil.* Imagining.

A. متخيله *mutakhaiyalah.* The imagination, fancy.

A. متداول *mutadáwil.* Customary, usual.

A. متدين *mutadaiyin.* Orthodox, firm in religion.

A. مترادف *mutarádif.* Successive.

A. متراكمه *mutarákamah.* Accumulation.

A. متراتب *mutarátab.* Arranged, sorted.

A. مترجم *mutarjim.* A translator, interpreter.

A. متردد *mutaraddid.* Perplexed, hesitating.

A. مترسل *mutarassil.* A correspondent, a secretary.

A. مترسم *mutarassim.* Contemplative.

A. مترصد *mutarassid.* Watching, expecting.

A. مترقب *mutarakkib.* Expecting, hoping.

A. متركب *mutarakkib.* Composing, compounding.

A. مترنم *mutarannim.* Singing, modulating.

A. متروك *matrúk.* Abandoned, left.

A. متروكات *matrúkát.* Legacies, the estate of a deceased person.

A. متزايد *mutazáyid.* Increasing.

A. متزلزل *mutazalzal.* Agitated, trembling.

A. متساوى *mutasáwí.* Equal, parallel.

A. متسع *muttasiʻ.* Large, expanding.

A. متسلط *mutasalliṭ.* Having absolute dominion.

A. متسلم *mutasallam.* Delivered, consigned.

A. متسلى *mutasallí.* Consoled, satisfied, comforted.

A. متشابه *mutashábih.* Resembling, like.

A. متشرع *mutasharriʻ.* Skilled in the law.

A. متشكك *mutashakkik.* Doubting.

A. متشكل *mutashakkil.* Like, resembling.

A. متشكى *mutashakkí.* Complaining.

A. متشنج *mutashannaj.* Convulsed.

A. متصاعد *mutaṣáʻid.* In ascending scale.

A. متصدع *mutaṣaddiʻ.* Vexing, troubling.

A. متصدى *mutaṣaddí.* A clerk, writer.

A. متصرف *mutaṣarrif.* Possessing, occupying; a local governor.

A. متصف *muttaṣif.* Qualified, endowed with.

A. متصل *muttaṣil.* Contiguous to.

A. متصور *mutaṣawwar.* Imagined.

A. متضعف *mutaẓaʻif.* Enfeebled.

A. متضمن *mutaẓammin.* Including.

A. متعارف *mutaʻárif.* Mutually known.

A. متعاقب *mutaʻáḳib.* Successive, following.

A. متعال *muttaʻál.* High, sublime.

A. متعبد *mutaʻabbid.* Devout.

A. متعجب *mutaʻajjib.* Admiring, astonished.

A. متعدد *mutaʻaddid.* Many, a great number.

A. متعدى *mutaʻaddí.* An active, transitive, or causal verb; an invader, oppressor.

A. متعذر *mutaʻaẓẓir.* Apologizing.

A. متعرض *mutaʻarriẓ.* Opposing.

A. متعرق *mutaʻarriḳ.* Sweating, perspiring.

A. متعسر *mutaʻassir.* Difficult, intricate.

A. متعصب *mutaʻaṣṣib.* Partial, bigoted.

A. متعلق *mutaʻallaḳ.* Belonging to, concerning.

A. متعلم *mutaʻallim.* A student.

A. متعندان *mutaʻannidán.* Enemies.

A. متعوب *matʻúb.* Fatigued, oppressed.

A. متعهد *mutaʻahhid.* Undertaking, engaging.

A. متعين *muta'ayin.* Constituted, appointed, fixed, deputed.

A. متغير *mutaghaiyar.* Disturbed, altered.

A. متفاوت *mutafáwit.* Different, distinct.

A. متفتش *mutafattish.* Inquiring.

A. متفرع *mutafarra'.* Branched out, divided.

A. متفرق *mutafarraḳ.* Separated; distinct; dispersed.

A. متفق *muttafiḳ.* United, concurring.

A. متفكر *mutafakkir.* Thoughtful.

A. متقاضى *mutaḳáẓí.* Importuning.

A. متقاعد *mutaḳá'id.* Desisting, receding.

A. متقدم *mutaḳaddim.* Anterior, preceding.

A. متقدمين *mutaḳaddimín.* The Ancients.

A. متكبر *mutakabbir.* Proud, haughty.

A. متكفل *mutakaffil.* Becoming surety or responsible.

A. متكلف *mutakallif.* A troubler, vexer.

A. متكلل *mutakallal.* Crowned.

A. متكلم *mutakallim.* A speaker; the first person.

A. متكى *muttakí.* Relying upon, leaning; a couch.

A. متلاحق *mutaláḥaḳ.* Added, augmented.

A. متلاطم *mutaláṭim.* Buffeting, dashing.

A. متلاف *mitláf.* Extravagant.

A. متلالى *mutalá'lí.* Shining, glittering.

A. متلذذ *mutalaẓẓiẓ.* Relishing.

A. متلقى *mutalaḳḳí.* Visiting, meeting.

A. متلون *mutalawwin.* Various, fickle.

A. متمادى *mutamádí.* Prolonging.

A. متمايل *mutamáyil.* Inclining.

A. متمتع *mutamatti'.* Enjoying.

A. متمرد *mutamarrid.* Stubborn, disobedient.

A. متمسك و متثبت *mutamassak wa mutaśabbat.* Based and founded on.

A. متمكن *mutamakkin.* Powerful; residing.

A. متمم *mutammim.* A finisher.

A. متمنى *mutamanní.* Wishing, hoping.

A. متن *matn.* The text, the loins.

A. متموج *mutamawwij.* Dashing (waves).

A. متناهى *mutanáhí.* Terminated, finished.

A. متنبه *mutanabbih.* Circumspect, vigilant.

A. متنعم *mutana'am.* Affluent.

A. متنفر *mutanaffir*. Abhorring.

A. متنوع *mutanawwa'*. Different, various.

A. متواتر *mutawátir*. Successively.

A. متوارے *mutawárí*. Absconding, concealing, lurking.

A. متوازے *mutawází*. Parallel.

A. متواضع *mutawáẓi'*. Humble.

A. متوافر *mutawáfir*. Numerous, plenty.

A. متوالی *mutawálí*. Successive, consecutive.

A. متوجه *mutawajjih*. Looking towards, attentive.

A. متوحش *mutawaḥḥish*. Terrified, scared; savage.

A. متورع *mutawarri'*. Abstinent.

A. متوزع *mutawazzi'*. Dividing, dealing.

A. متوسل *mutawassil*. Having recourse to.

A. متوصل *mutawaṣṣil*. Connected, related.

A. متوطن *mutawaṭṭin*. Inhabiting; naturalized.

A. متوفی *mutawaffí*. Deceased.

A. متوقع *mutawaḳḳi'*. Expecting, hoping.

A. متوقف *mutawaḳḳif*. Delaying; stopping for.

A. متوکل *mutawakkil*. Trusting in God.

A. متولد *mutawallad*. Born, generated.

A. متولی *mutawallí*. Superintending religious endowments.

A. متوهم *mutawahhim*. Suspecting, fearing.

A. متهاون *mutaháwin*. Negligent, slothful.

A. متهم *muttaham*. Suspected, accused.

A. متهور *mutahawwir*. Furious.

A. متیقن *mutayaḳḳin*. Knowing for certain.

A. متیقنه *mutayaḳḳana*. Ascertained.

A. متین *matín*. Strong, firm, solid.

A. مثاب *muśáb*. Recompensed.

A. مشابه *muśábih*. Resembling. A step, degree, point.

A. مثال *miśál*. Similitude, parable, proverb.

A. مثانه *maśánah*. The urine-bladder.

A. مثانی *maśání*. The first section of the Koran.

A. مثبت *muśabbit*. Establishing, fixed.

A. مثقال *miśḳál*. A weight of about a dram and a half.

A. مثقب *muśaḳḳib*. An instrument for boring.

A. مثل *maśal*. An example, parable, proverb.

A. P. مثل زدن *maśal zadan*. To give an example, quote a proverb.

A. مثلا *maśalan*. For example.

A. مثلث *muśallaś.* Triple, triangular.

A. مثمر *muśmir.* Fruitful (tree).

A. مثمن *muśamman.* Octagonal.

A. مثمور *maśmúr.* Abounding (in wealth).

A. مثنی *maśníy.* Doubled, bent.

A. مثنوی *maśnaví.* A poem consisting of rhyming couplets.

A. مثوب *muświb.* Recompensing.

A. مثوبات *maśúbát.* Good works.

A. مثوی *maśwá.* A dwelling, habitation.

A. مجادل *majádil.* Contentious.

A. مجادلت *mujádalat.* Contention, dispute.

A. مجاری *majárí.* Channels.

A. P. مجارے اب *majárí ab.* The bed of a river.

A. مجاز *mujáz.* A metaphor.

A. مجازات *mujázát.* Compensation.

A. مجازے *mujází.* Hypothetical, metaphoric.

A. مجال *majál.* Power, strength.

A. مجالبت *majálabat.* Assistance.

A. مجالس *majális.* Assemblies, sessions. (pl. of مجلس.)

A. مجالست *mujálasat.* Sitting together, conference.

A. مجامع *majámi'.* Congregations.

A. مجامعت *mujáma'at.* Copulation.

A. مجانبت *mujánabat.* Avoiding, receding from.

A. مجاوبت *mujáwabat.* Answering one another.

A. مجاور *mujáwir.* A neighbour.

A. مجاورت *mujáwarat.* Neighbourhood; intimacy.

A. مجاوز *mujáwiz.* Transgressing, exceeding bounds.

A. مجاوعت *mujáwa'at.* Hunger.

A. مجاهد *mujáhid.* A warrior (especially in a religious war).

A. مجاهدة *mujáhadat.* Exertion, striving.

A. مجاهرت *mujáharat.* Conquering, prevailing over.

A. مجبور *majbúr.* Constrained, forced.

A. مجتبی *mujtabá.* Elected, chosen.

A. مجتمع *mujtama'.* Assembling, coming together.

A. مجتنب *mujtanib.* Abstaining from.

A. مجتوی *mujtawí.* Abhorring, detesting.

A. مجتهد *mujtahid.* Striving. The title given to the highest ecclesiastical dignitaries in Persia.

A. مجد *majd.* Glory, grandeur, greatness.

A. مجداف *mijdáf.* An oar.

A. مجدد *mujaddid.* Renewing.

A. مجدداً *mujaddadan.* Afresh, newly.

A. مجذوب *majżúb.* Drawn, attracted.

A. مجرب *mujarrab.* Tried; expert.

A. مجرد *mujarrad.* Solitary, alone, only, single. به مجرد *ba mujarrad.* Immediately upon.

A. مجرم *mujrim.* A criminal, sinner.

A. مجروح *majrúḥ.* Wounded.

A. مجری *mujrí.* Causing to flow.

A. مجسم *mujassam.* Corporal.

A. مجعد *muja''id.* Crisped or curling hair.

A. مجلی *mujallá.* Made brilliant; illuminated.

A. مجلد *mujallid.* A bookbinder.

A. مجلس *majlis.* An assembly, meeting, a session.

A. P. مجلس عام *majlis i 'ám.* A levee.

T. مچلکه *muchalka.* An obligation in writing.

A. مجمد *mujammad.* Congealed, frozen.

A. مجمر *mijmar.* A censer for incense.

A. مجمع *majma'.* Confluence.

A. مجمل *majmal.* A summary, abstract.

A. مجملاً *majmalan.* Summarily.

A. مجموع *majmú'.* A collection, all, the whole.

A. مجن *majinn.* A shield.

A. مجناء *mujná'.* A shield without iron in it.

A. مجند *mujannid.* Collecting an army.

A. مجنون *majnún.* Insane; name of a celebrated hero of Arab Romance (see *Lailá*).

A. مجوس *majús.* A Magian.

A. مجوسی *majúsí.* A Magian.

A. مجوسیة *majúsíyet.* The Magian religion.

A. مجوف *mujawwaf.* Hollow, concave.

A. مجهد *mujhid.* Striving, strenuous.

A. مجهور *majhúr.* Purified, cleaned.

A. مجهول *majhúl.* Unknown.

A. مجیب *mujíb.* Accepting, agreeing to.

A. مجید *majíd.* Honourable, noble.

A. مجیء *mají'.* Coming, arrival.

P. مچک *machak.* A lentil.

A. محابا *muḥábá.* Connivance; ceremony.

A. محاذی *muḥáżí.* Opposite, facing.

A. محارب *muḥárib.* A warrior, combatant.

A. محاربة *muḥárabat.* War, battle.

A. محاریب *maḥáríb*. Niches. (pl. of محراب.)

A. محاسب *muḥásib*. One who settles accounts.

A. محاسبت *muḥásabat*. Computation, settlement of accounts.

A. محاسن *maḥásin*. Virtues, merits.

A. محاصر *muḥáṣir*. Besieging, surrounding.

A. محاصره *muḥáṣarah*. A siege, blockade.

A. محاط *muḥáṭ*. Besieged, surrounded.

A. محافر *muḥáfir*. One who digs.

A. محافظ *muḥáfiẓ*. A guard, keeper.

A. محافظت *muḥáfaẓat*. Guardianship, custody.

A. محافل *maḥáfil*. Assemblies.

A. محافه *maḥáfa*. A litter.

A. محاکات *muḥákát*. Relating stories.

A. محاکمت *muḥákamat*. Bringing a suit before a judge.

A. محال *maḥál*. Impossible.

A. محال *maḥáll*. Places, districts. (pl. of محله *maḥallah*.)

A. محالات *maḥálát*. Impossibilities.

A. P. محال اندیش *maḥál-andísh*. A visionary.

A. محامد *maḥámid*. Laudable actions.

A. محاوره *muḥáwarah*. Phraseology; familiar use; the art of conversation.

A. محب *muḥibb*. A lover, a friend.

A. محبت *maḥabbat*. Love, affection, friendship.

A. P. محبت نگار *maḥabbat-nigár*. Impressing with affection.

A. P. محبت ورزیدن *maḥabbat warzídan*. To display affection.

A. محبوب *maḥbúb*. Beloved.

A. محبوبه *maḥbúbah*. (Feminine of the above.)

A. محبوس *maḥbús*. Confined, imprisoned.

A. P. محبوس خانه *maḥbús khána*. A prison.

A. محتاج *muḥtáj*. Needy, indigent.

A. محتاط *muḥtáṭ*. Circumspect.

A. محتبس *muḥtabis*. Restrained, imprisoned.

A. محتجب *muḥtajib*. Retired; sequestered.

A. محترف *muḥtarif*. An artificer.

A. محترم *muḥtaram*. Honoured, revered.

A. محتسب *muḥtasib*. A police officer who examines weights and measures, and takes cognizance of offences against public morality.

A. محتشم *muḥtashim*. Powerful, having many followers.

A. محتکر *muḥtakir*. Monopolizing grain.

A. محتمل *muḥtamil*. Probable.

A. محتوی *muḥtawí*. Comprehending, embracing.

A. محجوب *maḥjúb*. Veiled, modest.

A. محجور *maḥjúr*. Prohibited.

A. محدب *maḥdab*. Convex.

A. محدث *muḥdis*. Inventor, innovator.

A. محدث *muḥaddis*. A relator, narrator.

A. محدود *maḥdúd*. Limited, bounded.

A. محذوف *maḥẓúf*. Apocopated.

A. محراب *miḥráb*. A prayer-niche, an arch.

A. محرب *muḥrib*. Stirring up battles.

A. محرر *muḥarrir*. A writer, clerk.

A. محرض *muḥarriẓ*. Enticing, exciting.

A. محرق *muḥriḳ*. Burning; incentive.

A. محرك *muḥarrik*. A mover.

A. محرم *muḥarram*. The first month of the Mohammedan year.

A. محرمات *muḥramát*. Things prohibited.

A. P. محرمان *maḥramán*. Those who are permitted to enter the haram.

A. P. محرم راز *maḥram i ráz*. A confidant.

A. محرور *maḥrúr*. Hot. Written.

A. محروس *maḥrús*. Protected, preserved.

A. محروق *maḥrúḳ*. Burnt.

A. محروم *maḥrúm*. Excluded; unfortunate.

A. محزون *maḥzún*. Grieved.

A. محسن *muḥsin*. Benefiting, generous.

A. محسوب *maḥsúb*. Computed, reckoned.

A. محسود *maḥsúd*. Envied.

A. محسوس *maḥsús*. Felt, perceived.

A. محشر *maḥshar*. The last judgment; a place of assembly.

A. محشو *maḥshúw*. Solid, stuffed.

A. محصل *muḥaṣṣil*. Collecting, gathering.

A. محصود *maḥṣud*. Reaped.

A. محصور *maḥṣúr*. Besieged, surrounded.

A. محصول *maḥṣúl*. Custom; duties; the produce of anything.

A. محض *maḥẓ*. Pure, merely.

A. محضر *maḥẓar*. A citation, summons. (In comp.) disposition, temper; as نیك محضر *ník-maḥẓar*. Good-natured.

A. محظور *maḥẓúr*. Forbidden, unlawful.

A. محظوظ *maḥẓúẓ*. Delighted.

A. محفل *maḥfil*. An assembly, banquet.

A. محفوظ *maḥfúẓ*. Guarded, preserved.

A. محقر *muḥaḳḳar*. Despised.

A. محقق *muḥaḳḳiḳ*. Verifying, ascertaining.

A. P. محققانه *muhakkikána.* Truly; spiritual.

A. محك *mahakk.* A touchstone.

A. محكم *muhkam.* Firm, strong.

A. محكمه *mahkama.* A tribunal. A court, an office.

A. محكوم *mahkúm.* Subjected; commanded.

A. محل *mahall.* A place, station.

A. محله *mahallah.* (pl. محلات *mahallát.*) A quarter of a town.

A. محمد *muhammad.* Praised; Mohammed.

A. محمدى *muhammadí.* Mohammedan.

A. محمل *mahmil.* A camel-litter.

A. محمول *mahmúl.* Loaded.

A. محموم *mahmúm.* Warmed, feverish.

A. محنت *mihnat.* (pl. محن *mihan.*) Labour, toil.

A. P. محنتى *mihnatí.* Laborious.

A. محو *mahw.* Erasing, cancelling.

A. محور *mihwar.* The axis (of a sphere).

A. محيى *muhyí.* Reviving.

A. محيط *muhít.* Surrounding. The ocean.

A. مخادعات *mukháda'át.* Deceits.

A. مخارج *makhárij.* Egresses, issues.

A. مخازن *makházin.* Magazines.

A. مخاصمت *mukhásamat.* Animosity, enmity.

A. مخاط *mukhát.* The mucus of the nose.

A. مخاطب *mukhátib.* The second person.

A. مخاطبة *mukhátabat.* Speaking, addressing anyone.

A. مخاطر *mukhátir.* Dangerous.

A. مخافات *mukháfát.* Dreads, terrors.

A. مخالطة *mukhálatat.* Mixing together in society.

A. مخالف *mukhálif.* Contrary, opposing.

A. مخالفت *mukhálafat.* Contrariety, opposition.

A. مخاوف *makháwif.* Dreadful places.

A. مخبر *mukhbir.* Announcing; an informer.

A. مخبط *mukhabbat.* Disordered; insane.

A. مختار *mukhtár.* Exercising freewill. Select.

A. P. مختار كار *mukhtár-kár.* A free agent.

A. P. وزير مختار *vazír i mukhtár.* Envoy extraordinary and minister plenipotentiary.

A. مخترع *mukhtari'.* An author, inventor.

A. مختص *mukhtass.* Appropriated.

A. مختصر *mukhtasar.* Abridged; an epitome.

A. مختفى *mukhtafí.* Hidden, concealed.

A. مختل *mukhtall.* Disturbed, confused.

A. مختال *mukhtál.* Arrogant, vain.

A. مختلف *mukhtalif.* Different, various, discordant.

A. مختوم *makhtúm.* Sealed.

A. مختون *makhtún.* Circumcised.

A. مخدر *mukhaddir.* A narcotic.

A. مخدر *mukhaddar.* Senseless, stupefied.

A. مخدره *mukhaddarah.* A matron, a virtuous woman.

A. مخدوم *makhdúm.* Obeyed, waited upon; a master.

A. مخذول *makhżul.* Contemptible.

A. مخرج *makhraj.* The time or place of going forth.

A. مخروب *makhrúb.* Ruined, desolated.

A. مخروط *makhrúṭ.* Turned in a lathe.

A. مخزن *makhzan.* A magazine, storehouse.

A. مخسور *makhsúr.* Suffering loss, damaged.

A. مخصوص *makhṣúṣ.* Particular, especial.

A. مخضر *mukhazzar.* Verdant.

A. مخضرم *mukhazram.* One who lived between the end of the Pagan and the beginning of the Mohammedan times.

A. مخطط *mukhattaṭ.* A garment marked with stripes.

A. مخطور *makhṭúr.* Dreadful. Imagined.

A. مخفف *mukhaffif.* Alleviated; lightened.

A. مخفوض *makhfúẓ.* Submissive, subjected.

A. مخفی *makhfí.* Hidden, clandestine.

A. مخل *mukhill.* Spoiling, disturbing.

A. مخلب *mikhlab.* A claw; a sickle.

A. مخلد *mukhallad.* Eternal.

A. مخلص *mukhliṣ.* Sincere, loyal.

A. P. مخلصانه *mukhliṣána.* Sincerely.

A. مخلوط *makhlúṭ.* Mixed, blended.

A. مخلوق *makhlúḳ.* Created, produced.

A. مخلوقات *makhlúḳát.* Created beings; the creation.

A. مخمر *mukham-mar.* Leavened, kneaded.

A. مخمس *mukhammas.* Pentagonal.

A. مخمل *makhmal.* Velvet.

A. مخمور *makhmúr.* Drunken, leavened.

A. مخنث *mukhannaṡ.* An hermaphrodite; effeminate.

A. مخوق *mukhawwif.* Dreadful, dangerous.

A. مخوف *mukhawwaf.* Terrified, dreadful.

A. مخیل *mukhaiyil.* Imagining.

A. مخیم *mukhaiyam.* A camp.

A. مد *madd.* Extension; the flow of the tide.

A. مداح *maddáḥ.* A eulogizer, encomiast.

A. مداحی *maddáḥí.* Encomium.

A. مداخل *madákhil.* Receipts, income.

A. مداخلت *mudákhalat.* Interference; undertaking.

A. مداد *midád.* Ink.

A. مدار *madár.* A centre, a pivot.

P. A. مدارا *madára.* Courtesy, dissimulation.

A. مدارج *madárij.* Steps, dignities.

A. مدارس *madáris.* Colleges.

A. مدارست *mudárasat.* Giving lessons.

A. P. مدار کار *madár i kár.* The chief or manager of a business.

A. مدار المہام *madár ul mahámm.* Chief Secretary.

A. مدافع *mudáfi'.* Repulsing.

A. مدافعت *mudáfa'at.* Repulsion.

A. مدام *mudám.* Always, perpetual. Old wine.

A. مداومت *mudáwamat.* Perpetuity, continuance.

A. مداوات *mudáwát.* Applying a remedy.

A. مدایح *madáiḥ.* Laudable actions.

A. مداین *madáin.* Cities. (pl. of مدینه.)

A. مدبر *madabbir.* Regulating; a minister.

A. مدبر *mudbir.* Retiring.

A. مدبول *madbúl.* Tanned dressed (leather).

A. مدت *muddat.* A space of time.

A. مدح *madḥ.* Praise, eulogium.

A. مدخل *madkhal.* Entrance; income.

A. مدخول *madkhúl.* Entered.

A. مدخوله *madkhúla.* A concubine.

A. مدد *madad.* Aid, assistance.

A. مد و جزر *madd u jazr.* The flood and ebb tides.

A. مدد گار *madad-gár.* Supporter, aider.

P. مدر *madar.* A clod.

A. مدرس *mudarris.* A professor, schoolmaster.

A. مدرسه *madrasah.* A college, public school.

A. مدرك *mudrik.* Understanding, comprehending.

A. مدركه *madrikah.* The understanding.

A. مدعی *mudda'iy.* The plaintiff.

A. مدعی علیه *mudda'á 'alaih.* The defendant (masc.).

A. مدعی علیها *muda'á alaihá.* The defendant (fem.).

A. مدعی علیهم *mudd'á 'alaihim.* The defendants.

A. مدعو *mad'ú.* Invited, called.

A. مدغم *mudgham.* Coalesced, assimilated.

A. مدفون *madfún.* Buried.

A. مدلل *mudallal.* } Demon-
A. مدلول *madlúl.* } strated, proof.

A. مدله *mudallah.* Insane; distracted with love.

A. مدن *mudun.* Cities. (pl. of مدينه.)

A. مدور *mudawwer.* Round, circular.

A. مدون *mudawwan.* Arranged as a *díván* (poems).

A. مدهوش *madhúsh.* Astonished, amazed.

A. مديد *madíd.* Long, extensive.

A. مدير *mudír.* Causing to turn round. The manager of an institution (see ادارة).

A. مدينه *madínah.* A city.

A. مديون *madyún.* Indebted, a debtor.

A. مذاب *mużáb.* Liquid, melted.

A. مذاق *mużáḳ.* Tasting; the taste; the palate.

A. مذاكرات *mużákarát.* Conversations, conference.

A. مذاهب *mażáhib.* Sects, religions.

A. مذبح *mażbaḥ.* An altar for sacrifice.

A. مذبذب *mużabżab.* Hesitating, irresolute.

A. مذبوح *mażbúḥ.* Slaughtered, sacrificed.

A. مذكر *mużakkar.* Masculine.

A. مذكور *mażkúr.* Mentioned, aforesaid.

A. مذلت *mażallat.* Baseness.

A. مذمت *mażammat.* Blame, reproach.

A. مذموم *mażmúm.* Blameable, contemptible.

A. مذنب *mużnib.* A criminal.

A. مذهب *mażhab.* A sect.

A. مر *murr.* Bitter; myrrh.

P. مر *mar.* A pleonastic particle placed before the oblique case of nouns, as مراورا *mar-ú-rá.* To him.

P. مرا *mará.* Me, to me.

A. مرآت *mar'át.* A mirror.

A. مراتب *marátib.* Ranks, degrees; times.

A. مراجحت *murájaḥat.* Having preference over.

A. مراجعت *murája'at.* Return.

A. مراحل *maráḥil.* Journeys, day's journey.

A. مراحم *maráḥim.* Favours, benefits.

A. مراد *murád.* Desire, will; meaning.

A. P. مراد بخش *murád-bakhsh.* Granting desire.

A. مرادفت *murádafat.* Succession.

A. مرارت *marárat.* Bitterness.

A. مراره *marárah.* The gall-bladder.

A. مراسلت *murásalat.* (pl. مراسلات *murásalát.*) Epistolary correspondence; despatches.

A. مراسم *marásim.* Usages, customs.

A. مراضعت *muráza'at.* Suckling a child.

A. مراعات *murá'át.* Taking care of, favouring.

A. مراغبت *murághabat.* Propensity.

A. مرافعت *muráfa'at.* Reference; appeal.

A. مرافقت *muráfakat.* Companionship.

A. مراقب *murákib.* Contemplating; an observer.

A. مراقبت *murákabat.* Observance; watching.

P. مرال *marál.* A mountain-goat, ibex.

A. مرام *murám.* Desire, wish.

A. مراودت *muráwadat.* Relation.

A. مراهم *maráhim.* Plasters, dressings for wounds.

A. مربی *murabbá.* Educated; preserved.

A. مربع *murabba'.* Square, quadrilateral.

A. مربوط *marbút.* Bound, fastened.

A. مربی *murabbá.* Confectionary, preserved in syrup, jam.

A. مربی *murabbí.* A guardian, patron.

A. مرت *marrat.* One time, turn.

A. مرتب *murattab.* Arranged, adjusted.

A. مرتبط *murtabat.* Bound, fastened.

A. مرتبة *martabah.* Rank, degree; a time or turn.

A. مرتفع *murtafi'* Elevated.

A. مرتقی *murtakí.* Advancing, progressing.

A. مرتکب *murtakib.* Perpetrating.

A. مرتهن *murtahin.* A mortgagee.

A. مرثیه *marsíyah.* An elegy.

A. مرجان *marján.* Coral.

A. مرجح *murajjah.* Superior, preferred.

A. مرجع *marji'.* The place of return; refuge.

A. مرجل *mirjal.* A large caldron.

A. مرجو *marjú.* Hoped, expected.

A. مرجوح *marjúh.* Excelled, surpassed.

A. مرحبا *marhabá.* Hail! welcome!

A. مرحله *marhalah.* A halting-place.

A. مرحمت *marhamat.* Pity, compassion.

A. مرحوم *marhúm.* Deceased.

A. مرخص *murakkhas.* Permitted.

P. مرد *mard.* A man.

P. مرداد *mardád.* The fifth Persian month (July).

P. مردار *murdár.* Carrion.

P. مردان *mardán.* Men.

P. مردانگی *mardánagí.* Bravery, manliness.

P. مردانه *mardána.* Manly, bravery.

P. مردك *mardak.* A contemptible fellow.

P. مردگان *murdagán.* The dead.

P. مردم *mardum.* A man, mankind.

P. مردم ازار *mardum-ázár.* Injuring mankind.

P. مردم خوار *mardum-kh'ár.* A cannibal.

P. مردمان *mardumán.* Mankind, people.

P. مردمك چشم *mardumak i chashm.* The pupil of the eye.

P. مردمی *mardumí.* Humanity.

P. مردن *murdan.* To die.

A. مردود *mardúd.* Repulsed, rejected.

P. مرده *murda.* Dead; a corpse.

P. مردی *mardí.* Manhood.

P. مرز *marz.* A region, country.

P. مرزا *mirzá.* See میرزا.

P. مرزبان *marz-bán.* A governor on the borders of a hostile country.

P. مرز بوم *marz-búm.* A place of residence.

P. مرزغان *marzaghán.* Hell; a chafing-dish.

A. مرسل *mursal.* An ambassador, an apostle.

A. مرسله *mursala.* An epistle, a letter.

A. مرسلین *mursalín.* Apostles.

A. مرسوم *marsúm.* Marked, addressed; pay, stipend; a letter.

A. مرشا *marshá'.* Evil, malignant.

A. مرشد *murshid.* A spiritual guide.

A. مرصع *muraṣṣa'.* Studded with jewels.

A. مرض *maraẓ.* Disease, malady.

A. مرضع *murẓi'.* Suckling; a wet-nurse.

A. مرضی *marẓí.* Concurrence; satisfactory.

A. مرطبان *marṭabán.* A glazed vessel.

A. مرطوب *marṭúb.* Moïstened; full of humours.

A. مرعی *mar'á.* Pasture.

A. مرعوب *mar'úb.* Terrified.

A. مرعی *mar'í.* Governed, guarded.

P. مرغ *murgh.* A bird; a fowl.

P. مرغابی *murgh-ábí.* A water-fowl.

P. مرغزار *murgh-zár.* A verdant meadow, pasture.

P. A. مرغ سحر *murgh i siḥar.* The bird of dawn, i.e. the cock, or nightingale.

A. مرغوب *marghúb.* Desirable.

A. مرفق *mirfaḳ.* The elbow.

A. مرفوع *marfú'.* Exalted.

A. مرفوع القلم *marfú' ul ḳalam.* Absolved, remitted.

A. مرفه *muraffah.* Quiet, contented.

A. مرقد *markad.* A sepulchre.

A. مرقع *murakka'.* Patched, ragged.

A. مرقم *markam.* A pen, a style.

A. مرقوم *markúm.* Written; above-mentioned.

P. مرك *marg.* Death.

A. مركب *markab.* A horse; slip.

A. مركب *murakkab.* Compound. Ink.

A. مركز *markiz.* A centre.

A. مركوز *markúz.* Concentred.

A. مرمت *marammat.* Repairing.

P. مرمر *marmar.* Marble.

A. مرواريد *marwáríd.* A pearl.

A. مروت *murúwat.* Courtesy, politeness.

A. مروج *murawwaj.* Current, in use.

A. مروحه *mirwahah.* A fan.

A. مرور *murúr.* Passing, elapsing.

A. مرهم *marham.* A plaster.

A. مرهوب *marhúb.* Terrible, dreadful.

A. مرهون *marhún.* Pledged.

A. مرئ *marí'.* The windpipe; the gullet.

A. مريخ *mirríkh.* The planet Mars.

A. مريد *muríd.* A disciple.

A. مريد *maríd.* Contumacious.

A. مريض *maríz.* Sick, infirm.

A. مزاج *mizáj.* Temperament, constitution.

A. P. مزاج شريف چه طوراست *mizáj i sharíf ché túrást.* How do you do?

A. مزاح *mazáh.* } Joking,
A. مزاحت *mazáhat.* } pleasantry.

A. مزاحم *muzáhim.* Hindering, molesting.

A. مزاحمت *muzáhamat.* Impediment.

A. مزاد *muzád.* A sale by auction.

A. مزار *mazar.* A shrine.

A. مزارع *muzári'.* A husbandman, sower.

A. مزارع *mázári'.* Sown fields.

A. مزامير *mazámír.* Flutes, psalteries.

A. مزبله *mazbala.* A cesspool.

A. مزبور *mazbúr.* Beforementioned.

A. مزج *mazaj.* Mixing, tempering.

A. مزجات *mazaját.* A trifle.

A. مزخرف *muzkharif.* Glossed over.

P. مزد *mazd.* A recompense, wages, fee.

P. مزدور *mazdúr.* A hired labourer.

P. مزدوری *mazdúrí.* Labour; wages.

P. مژده *muzhda.* Glad tidings.

A. مزرع *mazra'.* A field ready for sowing.

A. مزروع *mazru'.* Sown (a field or seed).

A. مزعفر *muza'far.* Saffron-coloured.

A. مزکی *muzakká.* Purified, sacrificed; capital less 2½ per cent. زکات or alms.

P. مژکان *mazhagán.* The eyelashes.

A. مزلات *mazallát.* Slippery places.

A. مزلقه *mazlakah.* A slippery place.

A. مزمار *mizmár.* A flute.

A. مزور *muzawwir.* A cheat, deceiver.

A. مزور *muzawwar.* Falsified.

P. مزه *maza.* Taste, flavour, relish.

P. مژه *mizha* or *muzha.* (pl. مژکان *muzhagán.*) Eyelash.

P. مزه دار *maza-dár.* Relishing, delicious.

A. مزیت *maziyet.* Excellence.

A. مزید *mazíd.* Augmentation.

A. مزین *muzaiyan.* Adorned; signed and sealed by the Sháh.

A. مس *mass.* Handling, rubbing.

P. مس *miss.* Copper.

A. مساء *masá.* The evening.

A. مسابقت *musábakat.* Racing.

A. مساجد *masájid.* Mosques.

A. مساح *masáh.* A land-measurer.

A. مساحت *masáhat.* Measurement.

A. مسارعت *musára'at.* Haste.

A. مسارقت *musárakat.* Theft.

A. مساس *misás.* Touching, feeling.

A. مساعد *musá'id.* Assisting.

A. مساعدت *musá'adat.* Assistance.

A. مسافت *masáfat.* (pl. مسافات *masáfát.*) Distance.

A. مسافر *musáfir.* A traveller.

A. مسافرت *musáfarat.* Travelling.

A. مساکن *masákin.* Habitations; the poor.

A. مسالك *masálik.* Ways, roads.

A. مسأله *mas-ala.* A question.

A. مسام *masám.* Pores of the body.

A. مسامحت *musámahat.* Complaisance; leniency.

A. مسامع *masámi'.* Ears.

A. مساوات *musáwát.* Equation, evenness.

A. مساودت *musáwadat.* Contention for dominion.

A. مساوی *masáwí.* Parallel; equivalent.

A. مساهلت *musáhalat.* Negligence, indifference.

A. مساهم *musáhim.* A partner, sharer; a shareholder.

A. مساهمت *musáhamat.* Distribution, division, allotment of shares.

A. مسائل *masáil.* Questions.

P. مست *mast.* Intoxicated, libidinous.

A. مستاجر *musta'jar.* A farmer, contractor.

A. مستاصل *musta'ṣil.* Eradicating.

A. مستانه *mastána.* Like one intoxicated.

A. مستبشر *mustabshir.* Announcing good news.

A. مستبصر *mustabṣir.* Considering attentively.

A. مستبعد *mustab'id.* Wishing anything far off.

A. مستتر *mustatar.* Hidden, concealed.

A. مستثنى *mustaṡní.* Exceptional.

A. مستجاب *mustajáb.* Acceptable, answered.

A. مستجاب الدعوات *mustajáb ud da'wát.* One whose prayers are heard.

A. مستجب *mustajib.* Desirable.

A. مستجر *mustajirr.* Drawing, carrying off.

A. مستحسن *mustaḥsin.* Laudable.

A. مستحق *mustaḥikk.* Deserving, worthy.

A. مستحكم *mustaḥkam.* Firm, strong.

A. مستخرج *mustakhraj.* Extracted, drawn out.

A. مستخلص *mustakhlaṣ.* Released, liberated.

A. مستدام *mustadám.* Perpetual.

A. مستدعى *mustad'í.* Imploring, supplicating.

A. مستدل *mustadill.* Adducing proofs.

A. مستدير *mustadír.* Round, spherical.

A. مسترد *mustaradd.* Returned, restored.

A. مسترشد *mustarshid.* Orthodox teaching.

A. مستسعد *mustas'ad.* Gratified, happy.

A. مستسقى *mustaskí.* Dropsical.

A. مستطاب *mustaṭáb.* Good, agreeable.

A. مستظهر *mustaẓhar.* Supported, aided.

A. مستعار *musta'ár.* Borrowed.

A. مستعان *musta'án.* One whose aid is implored (God).

A. مستعجل *musta'jil.* Hasty, hurried.

A. مستعد *musta'idd.* Prepared, ready.

A. مستعرب *musta'rab.* A naturalized Arabian.

A. مستعصى *musta'ṣí.* Rebellious.

A. مستعقب *musta'kib.* Following.

A. مستعمل *musta'mal.* Practised, used.

A. مستغرق *mustaghraḳ*. Immersed, overwhelmed.

A. مستغفر *mustaghfir*. Penitent.

A. مستغنی *mustaghní*. Independent.

A. مستغیث *mustaghís*. A complainant.

A. مستفاد *mustafád*. Benefited, acquired.

A. مستفاض *mustafáẓ*. Divulged; revealed.

A. مستفید *muṣtafíd*. Profiting by.

A. مستفیض *mustafíẓ*. Diffused.

A. مستقبح *mustaḳbiḥ*. Odious, deformed.

A. مستقبل *mustaḳbil*. Future, the future tense.

A. مستقر *mustaḳirr*. Firm, constant.

A. مستقل *mustaḳill*. Absolute; independent sovereignty.

A. مستقیم *mustaḳím*. Straight, strong.

A. مستکبر *mustakbír*. Proud.

A. مستکره *mustakrih*. Abominable, disagreeable.

A. مستکمل *mustakmil*. Seeking perfection.

A. مستلذات *mustalażżát*. Delicacies.

A. مستلزم *mustalzim*. Requiring, exacting.

A. مستمال *mustamál*. Comforted, soothed.

A, مستمر *mustamirr*. Firm, constant.

A. مستمسك *mustamsik*. Bound to perform.

A. مستمع *mustami'*. Hearing, a listener.

P. مستمند *mustmand*. Afflicted, melancholy, poor.

A. مستنبط *mustambiṭ*. Extracting, finding out.

A. مستند *mustanad*. An official document.

A. مستنشی *mustanshí*. Smelling.

A. مستوجب *mustaujib*. Deserving, worthy.

A. مستوحش *mustauḥish*. Afflicted, mournful.

A. مستودعات *mustauda'át*. Deposits.

A. مستور *mastúr*. Concealed, veiled.

A. مستوره *mastúra*. A modest woman.

A. مستوفی *mustaufí*. An official; a controller.

A. مستوقد *mustauḳid*. Kindling fire.

A. مستولی *mustaulí*. Overcoming, dominant.

A. مستوهب *mustauhib*. Asking for a present.

A. مستوی *mustawí*. Equal, straight.

A. مستهام *mustaḥám*. Astonished, distracted.

A. مستهان *mustaḥán*. Despised, abject.

A. مستهزی *mustahzí*. Ridiculing.

A. مستهل *mustahill*. Cheerful, bright.

A. مستهلك *mustahlak.* Destroyed, ruined.

P. مستی *mastí.* Intoxication, drunkenness; lust.

A. مستيقظ *mustaiḳaẓ.* Awaking, vigilant.

A. مسجد *masjid.* A mosque.

A. مسجع *musajja'.* Rhythmical.

A. مسجل *musajjal.* Stamped, registered (a document).

A. مسجون *masjún.* Imprisoned.

A. مسح *masḥ.* Wiping.

A. مسحاة *masḥát.* A shovel.

A. مسحوق *masḥúḳ.* Worn; powdered, brayed.

A. مسخ *maskh.* Metamorphosis.

A. مسخر *musakhkhar.* Compelled to work without wages; subdued.

A. مسخرگی *maskharagí.* Drollery, buffoonery.

A. مسخره *maskhara.* A buffoon.

A. مسدود *masdúd.* Shut, obstructed.

A. مسرة *masarrat.* (pl. مسرات *masarrát.*) Joy.

A. مسرج *musarraj.* Saddled (horse).

A. مسرع *musri'.* Quick, making haste.

A. مسرف *musrif.* Prodigal, extravagant.

A. مسرور *masrúr.* Glad, gay.

A. مسروق *masrúḳ.* Stolen, robbed.

A. مسطح *misṭaḥ.* A level.

A. مسطر *masṭar.* A rule.

A. مسطور *masṭúr.* Described, delineated.

A. مسعود *mas'úd.* Happy, fortunate.

A. مسكر *muskir.* Intoxicating.

P. مسگر *miss-gar.* A brasier.

A. مسكن *maskan.* Habitation.

A. مسكنة *maskinah.* Poverty.

P. مسكه *maska.* Butter.

A. مسكين *miskín.* Poor, weak.

A. مسكينی *miskíní.* Poverty.

A. مسئلت *mas'alat.* A question, proposition.

A. مسلح *musallaḥ.* Armed.

A. مسلسل *musalsal.* Consecutive.

A. مسلط *musallaṭ.* Superior, dominant, ruling over.

A. مسلك *maslik.* A road, way, conduct.

A. مسلم *muslim.* A Moslem.

A. مسلم *musallam.* Intrusted to, resigned.

A. مسلمان *mussalmán.* A Moslem.

A. مسلمانی *mussalmání.* The Mohammedan religion.

A. مسلمين *muslimín.* The Faithful.

A. مسلوك *maslúk.* Practised.

A. مسلول *maslúl.* Unsheathed, drawn (a sword).

A. مسمی *musammá.* Named, called.

A. مسمار *mismár.* A nail, peg.

A. مسمع *misma'.* The organ or sense of hearing.

A. مسموع *masmú'.* Heard, audible.

A. مسموم *masmúm.* Poisoned.

A. مسند *masnad.* A throne.

A. P. مسند ارا *masnad-ára.* Adorning the throne, reigning.

A. مسواك *miswák.* A stick of bitter wood used as a tooth-brush.

A. مسوده *musawwadah.* A sketch, rough draft.

A. مسئول *mas'úl.* Asked.

A. مسهل *mus-hil.* A purgative.

A. مسهل *mus-hal.* Purged.

A. مسيح *masíh.* The Messiah.

A. مسير *masír.* Travelling; a journey.

A. مشابه *mushábih.* Like, resembling.

A. مشابهت *mushábahat.* Similitude.

A. مشاتمت *mushátamat.* Abuse, vituperation.

A. مشار *mushár.* Signified, indicative.

A. مشار اليه *mushár ilaih.* Indicated, aforesaid.

A. مشارب *mashárib.* Drinking places.

A. مشاربت *mushárabat.* Drinking with or to another.

A. مشارع *mashári'.* Highways.

A. مشارفت *musharafat.* Eminence.

A. مشارق *masháriḳ.* Eastern places.

A. مشارك *masháriк.* Associates, comrades.

A. مشاركت *mushárakat.* Partnership.

A. مشاطه *mashsháṭa.* A tire-woman.

A. مشاع *mushá'.* Divulged, undistributed.

A. مشاعر *masha'ir.* The external senses.

A. مشاعره *mushá'arah.* A poetical contest.

A. مشاعل *mashá'il.* Torches.

A. مشاغل *mashághil.* Employments, occupations.

A. مشافهت *musháfahat.* Speaking to one's face.

A. مشاكل *mushákil.* Resembling.

A. مشاكلت *mushákalat.* Resemblance.

A. مشام *mashámm.* The sense of smell.

A. مشاورت *musháwarat.* Debate, consultation.

A. مشاهد *musháhid.* Seeing, contemplating.

A. مشاهده *musháhadah.* Contemplation, view.

A. مشاهره *musháharah.* Monthly allowance.

A. مشاهير *masháhír.* Renowned persons.

A. مشايخ *masháikh.* Sheikhs, elders. (pl. of شيخ.)

A. مشايعت *musháya'at.* Accompanying; escorting home.

A. مشبك *mushabbak.* Latticed.

P. مشت *musht.* The fist; a handful.

A. مشتاق *mushták.* Desirous, longing.

A. مشتبه *mushtabih.* Ambiguous, obscure.

A. مشترك *mushtarik.* A partner.

A. مشترى *mushtarí.* A purchaser; the planet Jupiter.

P. مشت زدن *musht zadan.* To box.

A. مشتغل *mushtaghal.* Employed.

A. مشتق *mushtakk.* Derived, derivative.

A. مشتكى *mushtakí.* Complaining.

A. مشتمل *mushtamil.* Comprehending, containing. (Construed with the preposition بر.)

A. مشتهر *mushtahar.* Proclaimed.

A. مشتهى *mushtahí.* Desiring.

A. مشجر *mushajjar.* Wooded (country); damasked silk.

A. مشحون *mashhún.* Filled, laden.

A. مشخص *mushakkas.* Estimated, defined.

A. مشدد *mushaddad.* Corroborated.

A. مشرب *mashrab.* A drinking place; behaviour.

A. مشرط *mishrat.* A surgeon's scalpel.

A. مشرع *mashra'.* A street.

A. مشرف *musharraf.* Ennobled, honoured.

A. مشرق *mashrik.* The east.

A. P. مشرقى *mashrikí.* Eastern.

A. مشرك *mushrik.* A polytheist, an idolater.

A. مشروب *mashrúb.* Drinkable.

A. مشروح *mashrúh.* Explained, illustrated.

A. مشروط *mashrút.* Stipulated.

A. مشروع *mashrú'.* Legal; ordained by law.

A. مشط *masht.* A comb.

A. مشعبد *musha'bid.* A juggler.

A. مشعر *mush'ir.* Signifying.

A. مشعل *mash'al.* A torch.

A. T. مشعلچى *mash'alchí.* A torch-bearer.

A. مشعله *mash'alah.* A small torch.

A. مشعوف *mash'úf.* Pleased, satisfied.

A. مشغوف *mashghúf.* Inflamed with love.

A. مشغله *mashghalah.* Business, occupation.

A. مشغول *mashghúl.* Busied, employed.

A. مشفق *mushfik.* Courteous, a friend.

A. P. مشفقانه *mushfikána.* Kindly, courteously.

A. مشق *mashḳ.* Exercise, practice.

A. مشقت *mashaḳḳat.* Distress.

P. مشك *mashk.* A skin for water or milk.

A. مشك *mushk.* Musk.

A. مشك بو *mushk-bú.* Musk-scented.

A. مشكل *mushkil.* Difficult.

A. مشكلات *mushkilát.* Difficulties.

A. مشكوت *mishkút.* The lanthorn (of a building).

A. مشكور *mashkúr.* Thanked; (*colloquially* grateful).

A. مشكوك *mashkúk.* Doubtful.

A. مشكين *mishkín.* Musky, black.

A. مشلول *mashlúl.* Paralytic.

A. مشمش *mishmish.* An apricot.

A. مشمول *mashmúl.* Comprehended, contained.

A. مشموم *mashmúm.* Odoriferous.

A. مشورت *mashwarat.* Council, deliberation.

A. مشوش *mushawwash.* Disturbed.

A. مشهد *mashhad.* A place of martydom.

A. مشهود *mashhúd.* Beheld.

A. مشهور *mashhúr.* Celebrated, notorious.

A. مشى *mashy.* Walking.

A. مشيت *mashíyet.* Will, desire.

A. مشيد *mushaiyad.* Strengthened.

A. مشير *mushír.* A counsellor.

A. مشيمه *mashímah.* The placenta.

A. مصابح *maṣábíḥ.* Lamps. (pl. of مصباح.)

A. مصابرت *muṣábarat.* Forbearance.

A. مصاحب *muṣáḥib.* An *aide de camp*; a favourite; an attaché.

A. مصاحبت *muṣáḥabat.* Society, conversation.

A. مصاحف *maṣáḥif.* Volumes. Copies of the Ḳorán.

A. مصادر *maṣádir.* Infinitives of verbs.

A. مصادره *muṣádarah.* Fining, amercing.

A. مصادقت *muṣádaḳat.* Sincere friendship.

A. مصارعة *muṣára'at.* Wrestling, throwing down.

A. مصارف *maṣárif.* Expenses, disbursements.

A. مصارفت *muṣárafat.* Acting slily (with one).

A. مصاعب *maṣá'ib.* Difficulties.

A. مصاف *maṣáff.* Ranks (of soldiers); a field of battle.

A. مصافات *muṣáfát.* Good understanding, harmony.

A. مصافحه *muṣáfaḥah.* Shaking hands.

A. مصالح *maṣáliḥ.* Affairs.

A. مصالحت *maṣálaḥat.* Pacification.

A. مصائب *maṣáïb.* Misfortunes. (pl. of مصيبت.)

A. مصباح *miṣbáḥ.* Lamps.

A. مصبغ *muṣabbagh.* Tinged, dyed.

A. مصحح *muṣaḥḥiḥ.* An emendator.

A. مصحف *masḥaf.* A book (especially a copy of the Korán).

A. مصدر *maṣdar.* Source, origin; the infinitive of a verb.

A. مصدع *muṣaddiʿ.* A troubler.

A. مصدق *muṣaddiḳ.* Verifying.

A. مصداق *miṣdáḳ.* Rectifying, verifying.

A. مصدور *maṣdúr.* Derived, issuing.

A. مصر *miṣr.* Egypt, Cairo.

A. مصر *muṣirr.* Persevering, insisting.

A. مصراع *miṣráʿ.* A hemistich.

A. مصرح *muṣarriḥ.* Manifesting; serene (sky).

A. مصرف *muṣrif.* Prodigal, extravagant.

A. مصروع *maṣrúʿ.* Afflicted with the epilepsy.

A. مصروف *maṣrúf.* Expended, employed.

A. مصطفى *muṣṭafá.* Selected, chosen. A name of Mohammed.

A. مصطلح *muṣṭaliḥ.* Technical.

A. مصفى *muṣaffá.* Clarified.

A. مصقول *maṣḳúl.* Polished, furbished.

A. مصلح *muṣliḥ.* Rectifier, restorer.

A. مصلحت *maṣliḥat.* An affair; the proper course to pursue; one's interest.

A. مصلحت اميز *maṣliḥat-ámíz.* Conciliatory.

A. مصلحت جو *maṣliḥat-jú.* A reformer.

A. مصلوب *maṣlúb.* Crucified.

A. مصلى *muṣallá.* A place of prayer; name of a place near Shíráz.

A. مصمم *muṣammim.* Firm, determined.

A. مصنف *muṣannif.* An author.

A. مصنفات *muṣannafát.* Literary composition.

A. مصنوع *maṣnúʿ.* Made, artificial.

A. مصور *muṣawwir.* A painter.

A. مصون *maṣún.* } Guarded,
A. مصيون *maṣyún.* } preserved.

A. مصيبت *maṣíbat.* Misfortune.

A. مصيبت زده *maṣíbat zada.* Unfortunate.

A. مصير *maṣír.* Residence, receptacle.

A. مضاجع *maẓájiʿ.* Bedchambers.

A. مضاد *muẓádd.* An opponent.

A. مضادت *muẓáddat.* Opposition.

A. مضارع *muzári'*. The aorist.

A. مضاعف *muzá'af*. Doubled, increased.

A. مضاف *muzáf*. Annexed; a governing noun.

A. مضافات *muzáfát*. Annexations.

A. مضاف اليه *muzáf ilaih*. The noun governed.

A. مضامين *mazámín*. Significations, contents. (pl. of مضمون.)

A. مضايق *muzáik*. Narrow places, straits.

A. مضايقه *mazáikah*. Distress, trouble. هيچ مضايقه ندارد *hích mazáikah na dárad*. It does not matter.

A. مضبوط *mazbút*. Strong, robust; that which may be relied upon.

A. مضجع *muzja'*. A bed; a tomb.

A. مضحك *muzhik*. Ridiculous, laughable.

A. مضحكات *muzhikát*. Jests, jokes.

A. مضر *muzirr*. Hurtful, injurer.

A. مضرت *mazarrat*. (pl. مضرات.) Detriment, injury.

A. مضرور *mazrúr*. Damaged, injured.

A. مضطر *muztarr*. Distressed.

A. مضطرب *muztarib*. Agitated, afflicted.

A. مضغ *mazgh*. Chewing, mastication.

A. مضل *muzill*. One who leads astray.

A. مضمحل *muzmahill*. Digested; fading.

A. مضمر *muzmar*. Implied, suppressed.

A. مضموم *mazmúm*. Joined; having the vowel *zammah* ُ.

A. مضمون *mazmún*. The contents of a letter or document.

A. مضيق *muzík*. A narrow place, strait.

A. مطا *matá*. The back.

A. مطابق *mutábik*. According to, conformable.

A. مطابقت *mutábakat*. Conformity.

A. مطارح *matárih*. Places of conference.

A. مطارحه *mutárahah*. Conference, conversation.

A. مطاع *mutá'*. Obeyed.

A. مطاعم *matá'im*. Meats.

A. مطاف *mutáf*. A place, such as the Ka'bah at Mecca, round which the ceremony of circumambulation is performed.

A. مطالب *matálib*. Demands; objects. (pl. of مطلب.)

A. مطالبه *matálabah*. Asking, requisition.

A. مطالعه *matála'ah*. Consideration, perusal.

A. مطاوعة *mutáwa'ah*. Obedience, submission.

A. مطاهر *mutáhir*. Purifying.

A. مطايبات *mutáyibát*. Jokes, pleasantries.

A. مطايا *maṭáya.* Riding-horses or camels. (pl. of مطيه.)

A. مطبخ *maṭbakh.* A kitchen.

A. مطبوخ *maṭbúkh.* Cooked.

A. مطبوع *maṭbúʿ.* Impressed, stamped, printed; agreeable.

A. مطر *maṭar.* Rain.

A. مطرب *muṭrib.* A musician, singer.

A. مطرح *maṭrah.* A place where anything is thrown.

A. مطرد *maṭrad.* Flowing; current.

A. مطرود *maṭrúd.* Expelled.

A. مطعون *maṭʿún.* Taunted.

A. مطفی *muṭfí.* An extinguisher.

A. مطلی *muṭallá.* Gilded.

A. مطلب *maṭlab.* Desire, object.

A. مطلع *maṭlaʿ.* The East; exordium.

A. مطلع *muṭṭaliʿ.* Informed.

A. مطلق *maṭlak.* Absolute.

A. مطلوب *maṭlúb.* Required, necessary.

A. مطموع *maṭmúʿ.* Desired.

A. مطمئن *muṭmaïn.* Enjoying repose.

A. مطوے *maṭwí.* Folded, complicated.

A. مطهر *muṭahhir.* A purifier.

A. مطیب *muṭaiyeb.* Aromatic.

A. مطیر *muṭír.* Rainy, showery.

A. مطیع *muṭíʿ.* Obedient.

A. مظالم *mażálim.* Tyrannies, oppressions.

A. مظاهر *mażáhir.* Objects, spectacles.

A. مظافر *mużáfir.* Victorious, a conqueror.

A. مظفر *mużfir.* Victorious, triumphant.

A. مظلم *mużlim.* Dark.

A. مظلمت *mażlamat.* Oppression, tyranny.

A. مظلوم *mażlúm.* Oppressed.

A. مظنون *mażnún.* Thought; suspected.

A. مظنه *mażannah.* Opinion, thought.

A. مظهر *mużhar.* Object, view.

A. مع *maʿ.* With, together.

A. معا *miʿá.* A gut.

A. معاً *maʿan.* Together, along with.

A. معابد *maʿábid.* Sacred sites.

A. معابر *maʿábir.* Passes; fords, ferries.

A. معاتب *muʿáteb.* Reprehended.

A. معاتبت *muʿátabat.* Chiding, reprehension, expostulation.

A. معاد *miʿád.* The place to which one returns; the resurrection.

A. معادل *muʿádil.* Equal, equivalent.

A. معادلت *muʿádalat.* Equity.

A. معادن *maʿádin.* Mines, minerals.

A. معاذ *maʿáż.* Refuge.

A. معاذ الله *ma'áz alláh.* "God is my refuge." An exclamation of horror.

A. معاذیر *ma'ázír.* Excuses.

A. معارج *ma'árij.* Ascents. (pl. of معراج.)

A. معارض *mu'áriz.* Opposing.

A. معارضت *mu'árazat.* Opposition.

A. معارف *ma'árif.* Sciences, virtues.

A. معارك *ma'árik.* Fields of battle.

A. معارکة *mu'árakat.* Fighting, a conflict.

A. معاش *ma'ásh.* Means of living.

A. معاشر *ma'áshir.* A companion.

A. معاشرت *mu'ásharat.* Intercourse.

A. معاصات *mu'áṣát.* Rebellion, defection.

A. معاصر *mu'áṣir.* Contemporary.

A. معاضدت *mu'áẓadat.* Mutual aid.

A. معاطفت *mu'áṭafat.* Favour, courtesy.

A. معاف *mu'áf.* Pardoned, exempted.

A. P. معاف بفرمائید *mu'áf bifarmáyíd.* I beg your pardon.

A. معافی *mu'áfá.* Exempted, privileged.

A. معاقب *mu'áḳib.* A punisher.

A. معاقبت *mu'áḳabat.* Punishment.

A. معاقد *mu'áḳid.* Confederated, bound.

A. معاقد *ma'áḳid.* Knots.

A. معاقدت *mu'áḳadat.* League, confederacy.

A. معالج *mu'álij.* Applying a remedy.

A. معالجه *mu'álajah.* A cure, remedy.

A. معامله *mu'ámalah.* Business, negotiation.

A. P. معامله کردن *mu'ámalah kardan.* To trade, to negotiate.

A. معالی *ma'álí.* Eminences, elevations.

A. معاند *mu'árid.* Inimical, refractory.

A. معاندت *mu'ánadat.* Obstinacy, opposition.

A. معانق *mu'ániḳ.* Embracing.

A. P. معانقه کردن *mu'ánaḳah kerdan.* To embrace.

A. معانی *ma'ání.* Meanings. (pl. of معنی.)

A. معاودت *mu'áwadat.* Returning.

A. معاوضت *mu'áwaẓat.* Barter, exchange.

A. معاون *mu'áwin.* An assistant.

A. معاونت *mu'áwanat.* Mutual aid.

A. معاویة *mu'áwiyah.* A whelp; a lynx.

A. معاهد *mu'áhid.* Confederated.

A. معاهده *mu'áhadah.* Confederacy, alliance.

A. معايب *ma'áïb.* Vices.

A. معايش *ma'áyish.* Necessaries, victuals.

A. معاينة *mu'áyanah.* Inspection.

A. معبد *ma'bad.* A place for worship.

A. معبد *mu'abbid.* Worshipper.

A. معبر *mi'bar.* A pass, ferry, ford.

A. معبود *ma'búd.* Adored; a deity.

A. معتاد *mu'tád.* Accustomed, habituated, used to.

A. معتبر *mu'tabar.* Respectable, reputable, legal.

A. معتد *mu'tadd.* Numbered, computed.

A. معتدل *mu'tadil.* Temperate, equal.

A. معتذر *mu'tazir.* Excusing one's self.

A. معترض *mu'tariz.* Opposing, objecting.

A. معترف *mu'tarif.* Acknowledging, confessing.

A. معتزل *mu'tazil.* A seceder.

A. معتقد *mu'takid.* A believer.

A. معتكف *mu'takif.* A devotee.

A. معتمد *mu'tamad.* Confidential, trustworthy.

A. معجب *mu'jib.* Admiring one's self; agreeable.

A. معجزه *mu'jizah.* (pl. معجزات *mu'jizat.*) A miracle.

A. معجل *mu'ajjil.* Causing to make haste.

A. معجمه *mu'jamah.* Having a diacritical point, (a letter).

A. معجون *ma'jún.* Kneaded; an electuary.

A. معدلت *ma'dalat.* Equity, justice.

A. معدم *mu'dim.* Depriving, annihilating. Destitute.

A. معدن *ma'dan.* A mine, a mineral.

A. معدنى *ma'daní.* Mineral, fossil.

A. معدود *ma'dúd.* Numbered.

A. معدول *ma'dúl.* Swerved.

A. معدوم *ma'dúm.* Non-existent.

A. معده *mi'dah.* The stomach.

A. P. معده سنگی *mi'da-sangí.* Dyspepsia.

A. معذر *mu'zir.* An apologist.

A. معذره *ma'zarah.* An excuse, apology.

A. معذور *ma'zúr.* Excused, excusable.

A. معراج *mi'ráj.* An ascent, especially the supposed ascent of Mohammed into heaven.

A. معربد *mu'arbid.* A drunkard.

A. معرض *mu'riz.* Averse; turning away from.

A. معرف *mu'arrif.* Making known.

A. معرفت *ma'rifat.* Knowledge, acquaintance; by means of.

A. معرکه *ma'rikah.* A field of battle.

A. معروض *ma'rúẓ.* Represented, requested.

A. معروف *ma'rúf.* Known,

A. معزز *mu'azzaz.* Honoured, revered.

A. معزول *ma'zul.* Dismissed from office.

A. معسکر *ma'askar.* A camp.

A. معشر *ma'shar.* A company, a troop.

A. معشوق *ma'shúḳ.* (fem. معشوقه *ma'shúḳah.*) Beloved.

A. معصر *ma'ṣar.* A press.

A. معصم *mi'ṣam.* The wrist.

A. معصور *ma'ṣúr.* Expressed (juice, &c.), squeezed.

A. معصوم *ma'ṣúm.* Innocent.

A. معصیت *ma'ṣíyet.* Defection, rebellion.

A. معضلات *mu'ẓilát.* Intricacies, knotty points.

A. معطر *mu'aṭṭar.* Perfumed, fragrant.

A. معطش *mu'ṭish.* Exciting thirst.

A. معطل *mu'aṭṭal.* Abandoned; obsolete.

A. معطوف *ma'ṭúf.* Turned towards; favoured.

A. معطی *mu'ṭí.* A giver; bestowing.

A. معظم *mu'aẓẓam.* (fem. معظمه *mu'aẓẓamah.*) Honoured.

A. معقد *mu'aḳḳad.* Intricate, knotty.

A. معقود *ma'ḳúd.* Knotted, fastened.

A. معقول *ma'ḳúl.* Reasonable, pertinent.

A. معکوس *ma'kús.* Inverted, reverted.

A. معلی *mu'allá.* High, sublime.

A. معلف *ma'laf.* A manger.

A. معلف *mi'laf.* A nosebag.

A. معلق *mu'allaḳ.* Suspended, hung up.

A. معلق زن *mu'allaḳ-zan.* A tumbler, rope-dancer.

A. معلم *mu'allim.* A preceptor.

A. معلم *mu'lam.* Marked.

A. معلن *mu'lin.* A revealer, divulger.

A. معلوم *ma'lúm.* Known, notorious.

A. معمی *mu'ammá.* An enigma.

A. معمار *mi'már.* An architect, bricklayer.

A. معماری *mi'márí.* Architecture, building.

A. معمور *ma'múr.* Cultivated, inhabited.

A. معموری *ma'múrí.* Population, cultivation.

A. معمول *ma'múl.* Accustomary, usual.

A. معنبر *ma'amber.* Perfumed with ambergris.

A. معنوے *ma'nawí.* Intrinsic; significant, logical.

A. معنی *ma'ná.* Sense, meaning.

A. معوضت *ma'úzat.* A thing given for another.

A. معول *mu'awwal.* Relied upon.

A. معونة *ma'únat.* Help, aid.

A. معهود *ma'húd.* Customary, wonted, usual.

A. معيت *ma'iyet.* Conjunction, society.

A. معير *mu'aiyir.* An assayer of metals.

A. معيشت *ma'íshat.* Livelihood.

A. معيل *mu'íl.* Wanting, indigent, helpless.

A. معين *mu'ín.* An assistant.

A. معين *mu'aiyan.* Fixed, determined.

A. معيوب *ma'yúb.* Vicious, defective.

P. مغ *mugh,* A fire-worshipper; a tavern-keeper.

A. مغاره *magháralı.* A cave.

P. مغاك *maghák.* A pit.

A. مغالطت *mughálaṭat.* Leading into error.

A. مغاير *mugháyir.* Contrary, adverse.

A. مغايره *mugháyarah.* Disagreement.

A. مغايرة *mugháyarat.* Exchanging.

A. مغبون *maghbún.* Deceived, cheated.

A. مغرب *maghrib.* The west.

A. مغربی *maghribí.* Western; African.

A. مغرق *mugharrak.* Gilded; silvered.

A. مغرور *maghrúr.* Proud, arrogant.

A. مغروری *maghrúrí.* Pride.

A. مغروق *maghrúḳ.* Immersed, sunk.

P. مغز *maghz.* The brain; marrow, pulp, pith.

A. مغسل *maghsal.* A place for washing (especially of dead bodies).

A. مغسول *maghsúl.* Washed.

A. مغشی *maghshí.* Covered, feigning.

A. مغص *maghaṣ.* Colic.

A. مغضوب *maghẓúb.* Angered.

A. مغفر *mighfar.* A helmet.

A. مغفرت *maghfirat.* Pardon, remission.

A. مغفور *maghfúr.* Pardoned, deceased.

P. مغل *mughal.* A Mogul, Mongolian.

A. مغلطه *maghliṭa.* Confusion.

A. P. مغلطه کردن *maghliṭa kerdan.* To jabber.

A. مغلق *mughlaḳ.* Abstruse, difficult.

A. مغلوب *maghlúb.* Conquered, subjected.

A. مغلوق *maghlúḳ.* Locked, barred.

A. مغموم *maghmúm.* Grieved.

A. مغنی *mughanní.* (fem. مغنیه *mughanniyah.*) A singer.

A. مغير *mughaiyir.* One who alters.

A. مغيلان *mughailán*. The acacia mimosa.

A. مفاتح *mafátih*. Keys. (pl. of مفتاح *miftáh*.)

A. مفاجات *mufáját*. Suddenness.

P. A. مرگ مفاجات *marg i mufáját*. Sudden death.

A. مفاخر *mufákhir*. Glorying, boasting.

A. مفاخرت *mufákharat*. Glorying, boasting one against another.

A. مفارق *mufárik*. Separating.

A. مفارقت *mufárakat*. Separation, absence.

A. مفازه *mafázah*. A desert. (pl. مفاوز *mafáwiz*.)

A. مفاسد *mafásid*. Evils.

A. مفاصل *mafásil*. Joints.

A. مفاصلة *mufásalat*. Distance between two places.

A. مفاضت *mafázat*. Consignment; a despatch.

A. مفاوضت *mufáwazat*. Commerce, intercourse.

P. مفت *muft*. Gratuitously, gratis.

A. مفتاح *miftáh*. A key.

A. مفتتن *muftatin*. Bewitched, infatuated.

A. مفتخر *muftakhir*. Glorious.

A. مفترع *muftari'*. Violating, ravishing.

A. مفترق *muftarik*. Dispersed.

A. مفتری *muftarí*. A slanderer, a deviser of false tales.

A. مفتش *mufattish*. An inquisitor.

A. مفتقر *muftakar*. Reduced to poverty.

A. مفتل *muftall*. Twisted.

A. مفتن *mufattan*. Bewitched, infatuated.

A. مفتوح *maftúh*. Open, conquered.

A. مفتول *maftúl*. Twisted.

A. مفتون *maftún*. Fascinated.

A. مفتی *muftí*. A magistrate; one who gives a فتوے *fatwá*, q. v.

A. مفخر *mufakhkhar*. Glorified, glorious.

A. مفخم *mufakkham*. Magnified, glorious.

A. مفر *mafarr*. A place of refuge.

A. مفرح *mufarrih*. Exhilirating.

A. مفرد *mufrad*. Singular, alone, unique.

A. مفرط *mufrit*. Causing to exceed, excessive.

A. مفروش *mafrúsh*. Spread, expanded.

A. مفروض *mafrúz*. Enjoined (by law).

A. مفروق *mafrúk*. Separated, scattered.

A. مفسد *mufsid*. Spoiling, making bad.

A. مفسدت *mafsadat*. Anything pernicious.

A. مفسر *mufassir*. Interpreting.

A. مفصد *mifsad*. A lancet.

A. مفصل *mufaṣṣil.* Discriminating, detailing.

A. مفصل *mufaṣṣal.* Detailed.

A. مفضول *mafẓúl.* Overcome, conquered.

A. مفطر *mufṭir.* One who breaks a long fast.

A. مفعول *maf'úl.* Done, made.

A. مفقر *mufḳar.* Impoverished.

A. مفقود *mafḳúd.* Lost, non-existent.

A. مفكوك *mafkúk.* Freed, loosed.

A. مفلج *mufallaj.* Paralysed.

A. مفلح *mufliḥ.* Prosperous.

A. مفلس *muflis.* Poor, bankrupt.

A. مفلسی *muflisí.* Poverty.

A. مفلوج *maflúj.* Paralysed.

A. مفلی *muflí.* Having a yearling colt (a mare).

A. مفوض *mufawwaẓ.* Entrusted to.

A. مفهوم *mafhúm.* Understood.

A. مفید *mufíd.* Profitable.

A. مفیض *mufíẓ.* Pouring, streaming on; hastening.

A. مفیق *mufíḳ.* Convalescent.

A. مقابر *maḳábir.* Tombs, sepulchres.

A. مقابل *muḳábil.* Opposite, comparing.

A. مقابله *muḳábalah.* Comparison.

A. مقاتل *muḳatil.* Fighting.

A. مقاتله *muḳátalah.* Combat.

A. مقارب *muḳárib.* Middling, mediocre.

A. مقارن *muḳárin.* Simultaneous.

A. مقارنت *muḳáranat.* Simultaneity.

A. مقاسات *muḳását.* Endurance.

A. مقاسمه *muḳásamah.* Division, partition.

A. مقاصد *maḳáṣid.* (pl. of مقصد.) Objects.

A. مقاطر *maḳaṭir.* Drops.

A. مقاطع *maḳáṭí'.* Cut off, stragglers.

A. مقال *maḳál.* Talk, conversation.

A. مقام *muḳám.* A place, a station.

A. مقامات *muḳámát.* Sessions.

A. مقامر *muḳámir.* An antagonist at play, a gambler.

A. مقامرت *muḳámarat.* Gambling.

A. مقاوم *muḳawim.* Persevering.

A. مقاومت *muḳáwamat.* Perseverance.

A. مقبره *maḳbarah.* A sepulchre, a graveyard.

A. مقبل *muḳbil.* Approaching.

A. مقبوض *maḳbúẓ.* Grasped.

A. مقبول *maḳbúl.* Accepted, agreeable.

A. مقتبس *muḳtabas.* Quoted (especially from the Ḳorán).

A. مقتدی *muḳtadí.* An imitator, a follower.

A. مقتدر *muḳtadir.* Powerful.

A. مقتر *muḳtir.* Parsimonious.

A. مقتصر *muḳtaṣar.* Abridged.

A. مقتضی *muḳtaẓá.* Required, demanded.

A. مقتضی *muḳtaẓí.* Requiring, demanding.

A. مقتفی *muḳtafá.* Preferred, set over.

A. مقتل *maḳtal.* A place of slaughter.

A. مقتول *maḳtúl.* Slain.

A. مقدار *miḳdár.* Size, measure.

A. مقدر *muḳaddar.* Decreed.

A. مقدس *muḳaddas.* Holy. Jerusalem.

A. مقدم *muḳaddam.* Prior, precedent.

A. مقدم *muḳaddam.* Previous, preceding.

A. مقدمه *muḳaddamah.* A preface; a case (lawsuit.)

A. مقدور *maḳdúr.* Fate, power, ability.

A. مقر *muḳirr.* Confessing.

A. مقراض *miḳráẓ.* Scissors, shears.

A. مقرب *muḳarrab.* Brought near; a courtier, one near the throne.

A. مقربت *muḳrabat.* Relationship, propinquity.

A. مقرر *muḳarrar.* Appointed, established.

A. مقروض *maḳrúẓ.* Indebted, lent.

A. مقرون *maḳrún.* Joined to, connected with.

A. مقرونیت *maḳrúníyet.* Conjunction.

A. مقسوم *maḳsúm.* Allotted, partitioned.

A. مقشر *muḳashshar.* Barked, peeled.

A. مقشور *maḳshúr.* Peeled.

A. مقصد *maḳṣad.* An object.

A. مقصود *maḳṣúd.* Kept in view, an object.

A. مقصور *maḳṣúr.* Shortened, curtailed.

A. مقصر *muḳaṣṣar.* Defective.

A. مقصی *muḳṣá.* Remote.

A. مقضی *maḳẓí.* Completed, decreed.

A. مقطر *muḳaṭṭar.* Distilled, falling drop by drop.

A. مقطع *maḳṭaʿ.* A cut, a place of cutting, a separation, a ford.

A. مقطوع *maḳṭúʿ.* Cut.

A. مقعد *maḳʿad.* A seat.

A. مقفار *miḳfár.* A desert.

A. مقفی *muḳaffá.* Pursued; rhymed.

A. مقل *muḳill.* Poor, indigent.

A. مقلب *muḳallab.* Inverted.

A. مقلت *muḳlat.* The eyeball.

A. مقلد *muḳallad.* Imitated.

A. مقلو *maḳlúw.* Fried.

A. مقلوب *maḳlúb.* Inverted.

G. A. مقناطيس *maḳnáṭís.* A magnet.

A. مقنع *maḳnaʿ.* Sufficient, satisfactory.

A. مقنن *muḳannin.* One who institutes.

A. مقود *miḳwad.* A halter, a leading string.

A. مقوس *miḳwas.* A quiver, a bow.

A. مقوم *muḳawwam.* Straightened.

A. مقوم *muḳawwim.* One who rectifies.

A. مقوى *muḳawwá.* Strengthened.

A. مقهور *maḳhúr.* Subdued.

A. مقيى *muḳaiyí.* An emetic.

A. مقياس *miḳyás.* A meter, a measure. The Nilometer.

A. مقيت *muḳít.* Powerful, a guardian.

A. مقيد *muḳaiyad.* Diligent, registered, engaged.

A. مقيم *muḳím.* Dwelling, an inhabitant.

P. مقيمى *maḳímí.* Brokerage.

A. مقى *muḳíy.* An emetic.

A. مكاتب *makátib.* Schools. (pl. of مكتب.)

A. مكاتبة *mukátabat.* Correspondence by letter. (pl. مكاتبات *mukátabát.*)

A. مكاتيب *makátíb.* Letters, writings. (pl. of مكتوب.)

A. مكار *makkár.* A cheat, an impostor.

A. مكارم *makárim.* Generous actions.

A. مكاره *makárih.* Abominations.

A. مكاسب *makásib.* Acquisitions.

A. مكاشفة *mukáshafah.* Displaying, disclosure.

A. مكافات *mukáfát.* Recompense, retribution.

A. مكالمة *mukálamah.* Conversation.

A. مكامن *makámin.* Hiding-places, ambuscades.

A. مكان *makán.* A house, a dwelling.

A. مكايد *makáïd.* Frauds, snares.

A. مكايل *mukáïl.* Measuring.

A. مكب *mukibb.* Depressing, humiliating.

A. مكتب *maktab.* A school.

A. مكترى *muktarí.* Hiring.

A. مكتسب *muktasab.* Acquired.

A. مكتفى *muktafí.* Content, having a sufficiency.

A. مكتوب *maktúb.* Written; a writing, a letter.

A. مكتوم *maktúm.* Hidden, concealed.

A. مكث *makṡ.* Delaying, delay.

A. مكدر *mukaddar.* Turbid, vexed, uneasy.

A. مكر *makar.* Fraud, deceit.

P. مگر *magar*. Except, unless, yet.

A. مکرر *mukarrar*. Repeated; a postscript.

A. مکرم *mukarram*. Noble, respected.

A. مکرمت *makrumat*. Honour, respectability.

A. مکروه *makrúh*. Odious, hated, detestable.

P. مگس *magas*. A fly.

A. مکسب *maksab*. Gain, acquisition.

A. مگس ران *magás-rán*. A fly-flap.

A. مگس عسل *magas i 'asal*. A honey-bee.

A. مکسور *maksúr*. Broken; marked with the vowel *kasrah* ـِ.

A. مکشوف *makshúf*. Revealed, disclosed.

A. مکلف *mukallif*. Putting to inconvenience.

A. مکلل *mukallal*. Ornamented with a wreath or garland.

A. مکمل *mukammal*. Perfect, complete.

A. مکمن *makman*. A hiding-place.

A. مکمون *makmún*. In ambush, concealed.

A. مکنت *maknat*. Power, strength.

A. مکنون *maknún*. Hidden, concealed.

A. مکیال *mikyál*. A vessel to measure with.

A. مکیده *makídah*. A ruse, a stratagem.

P. مکیدن *makídan*. To suck.

A. مکین *makín*. Firmly fixed.

A. مکیول *makyúl*. Measured.

P. مل *mul*. Spirituous liquor.

A. ملاء *malá'*. The public.

A. P. بر ملاء افتادن *bar malá' uftádan*. To be made public.

A. ملا *mullá*. A learned man, a schoolmaster.

A. ملاء *malá'*. Full.

A. ملابس *malábis*. Garments.

A. ملابست *mulábasat*. Commerce, intercourse.

A. ملاح *malláḥ*. A sailor, boatman.

A. ملاحت *maláḥat*. Beauty, elegance.

A. ملاحدة *maláḥidah*. Atheists, infidels.

A. ملاحظه *muláḥaẓah*. Contemplation, inspection, perusal.

A. ملاذ *maláẕ*. An asylum, protection.

A. ملازمت *mulázamat*. Service, interview.

A. ملازم *mulázim*. A servant, attendant.

A. ملاصق *muláṣiḳ*. Contiguous, adjoining.

A. ملاطف *muláṭif*. Courteous, civil.

A. ملاطفه *muláṭafah*. Courtesy; an epistle.

A. ملاعب *malá'ib*. Jests, pleasantries.

A. ملاعبت *muláʿabat.* Playing, toying together.

A. ملاعنة *muláʿanat.* Mutual execration.

A. ملاعين *maláʿín.* Accursed persons. (pl. of ملعون.)

A. ملاقات *mulákát.* A meeting; an interview.

A. ملاقی *muláḳí.* Meeting, conversing with.

A. ملاکت *malákat.* Possession.

A. ملال *malál.* } Sadness,
A. ملالت *malálat.* } ennui.

A. ملام *malám.* } Re-
A. ملامت *malámat.* } proach, censure.

A. ملامست *malámasat.* Handling, feeling.

A. ملاهی *maláhí.* Pastimes; musical instruments.

A. ملائک *maláik.* } Angels.
A. ملائکه *maláikah.* } (pl. of ملك *malak.*)

A. ملایم *muláyim.* Mild, soft, tender.

A. ملایمة *muláyamat.* Softness, gentleness.

A. ملبس *mulabbas.* Clothed, dressed; confused.

A. ملبوس *malbús.* Put on (garments).

A. ملبوسات *malbúsát.* Garments, clothes.

A. ملت *millat.* Religion, faith.

A. ملتجم *multajam.* Bridled.

A. ملتجی *multají.* Taking refuge.

A. ملتحم *multaḥim.* Healed (a wound).

A. ملتحی *multaḥí.* Getting a beard.

A. ملتزم *multazim.* Constrained, compelled.

A. ملتصق *multaṣiḳ.* Conjoined, adhering.

A. ملتفت *multafit.* Shewing respect, paying attention.

ملتفت شدید *multafit shudíd.* Are you attending?

A. ملتقط *multaḳiṭ.* Gathering, collecting.

A. ملتقی *multaḳí.* Meeting.

A. ملتمس *multamis.* Supplicating, petitioning.

A. ملتوی *multawí.* Crooked, delayed.

A. ملتهب *multahib.* Inflamed, burning.

A. ملجأ *maljáʾ.* An asylum.

P. ملچخ *malchakh.* A stone for a sling.

A. ملح *milḥ.* Salt.

A. ملحد *mulḥid.* An atheist.

A. ملحق *mulḥaḳ.* Added, annexed, adhering.

A. ملحوظ *malḥuẓ.* Contemplated, considered.

A. ملخ *milkh.* A locust.

A. ملخ خورد *milkh i khurd.* A grasshopper.

A. ملزم *mulzam.* Confuted, convicted.

A. ملزوم *malzúm.* Obliged; attached.

A. ملسق *mulassaḳ.* Adoptive, adscititious.

A. ملصق *mulaṣṣaḳ*. Conjoined, united.

A. ملعون *mal'ún*. Damned, cursed.

A. ملفوف *malfúf*. Enveloped, enclosed.

A. ملق *maliḳ*. Bland, flattering.

A. ملقب *mulaḳḳab*. Surnamed.

A. ملك *mulk*. A kingdom, country.

A. ملك *málik*. A king.

A. ملك *malak*. An angel.

A. ملك *milk*. Property, estate.

A. ملك الموت *malak ul maut*. The angel of death.

A. ملك رانی *mulk-rání*. Sovereign sway.

A. ملك گیری *mulk-gírí*. Conquest.

A. ملکوت *malkút*. The kingdom of heaven.

A. ملك و مال *mulk u mál*. Land and money.

A. ملکه *malikah*. A queen.

A. ملکی *malikí*. Royal, kingly.

A. ملکی *mulkí*. Belonging to a country.

A. ملل *milal*. Religious. (pl. of ملة.)

A. ملمع *mulamma'*. Plated.

A. ملوث *mulauwas̤*. Polluted, defiled.

A. ملوك *mulúk*. Kings.

A. ملوکانه *mulúkána*. Royal, princely.

A. ملول *malúl*. Tired, afflicted with tedium.

A. ملول شدن *malúl shudan*. To be tired of anything; to feel *ennui*.

A. ملوم *malúm*. Reprehended.

A. ملون *mulawwán*. Coloured, variegated.

A. ملوی *malwíy*. Distorted, crooked.

P. ملهتی *malhatí*. Liquorice.

A. ملهم *mulham*. Inspired.

A. ملهوب *malhúb*. Kindled, inflamed.

A. ملی *malíy*. Lasting long.

A. مليح *malíḥ*. Beautiful, agreeable.

A. ملين *mulaiyin*. Softening, emollient.

A. ممات *mumát*. Death.

A. مماثل *mumás̤il*. Alike, resembling.

A. ممارست *mumárisat*. Practice, management.

A. ممالك *mamálik*. Kingdoms, provinces.

A. ممالیك *mamálík*. Slaves.

A. ممانعت *mumána'at*. Prohibition, hindrance.

A. ممتاز *mumtáz*. Distinguished, eminent.

A. ممتثل *mumtas̤il*. Obedient, obsequious.

A. ممتد *mumtadd*. Extended, prolonged.

A. ممتزج *mumtazaj*. Mixed, tempered.

A. ممتلی *mumtalí*. Full, replete.

A. ممتنع *mumtana'.* Prohibited, impassable.

A. ممد *mumidd.* Extending, prolonging.

A. ممدود *mamdúd.* Extended.

A. ممر *mamarr.* A pass, passage, transit.

A. ممزوج *mamzúj.* Mixed, tempered.

A. ممسك *mumsik.* Seizing; stingy.

A. ممسوح *mamsúḥ.* Wiped, cleaned; anointed.

A. ممشوط *mamshúṭ.* Combed.

A. ممطول *mamṭúl.* Hammered, extended. Put off (a creditor).

A. ممقوت *mamḳút.* Hated.

A. ممكن *mumkin.* Possible.

A. مملكة *mamlikat.* An empire, realm.

A. مملو *mamlúw.* Full, replete.

A. مملوك *mamlúk.* A purchased slave.

A. مملوكة *mamlúkat.* Property, estate.

A. ممنوع *mamnú'.* Prohibited.

A. ممنون *mamnún.* Obliged, under obligation.

A. ممهد *mumahhid.* Confirming, founding.

A. ممهور *mamhúr.* Sealed.

A. مميز *mumaiyiz.* Discriminating.

P. من *man.* I.

P. من *man.* A weight equal to 80 lbs.

A. من *min.* From.

A. من *mann.* Imposing a feeling of obligation.

A. من الان *min al'án.* Henceforth, after this.

A. من اجل *min ájl.* For the sake of.

A. مناب *munáb.* Acting as a *locum tenens.*

A. منابر *manábir.* Pulpits, rostrums, &c.

A. مناة *manát.* An idol of the Pagan Arabians.

A. مناجات *munáját.* Addresses to the Deity.

A. مناخر *manákhir.* The nostrils.

A. منادي *munádí.* A crier, proclaimer.

A. منادم *munádim.* A boon-companion.

A. منادمت *munádamat.* Joining in a drinking bout.

A. مناديل *manádíl.* Napkins, pocket-handkerchiefs.

A. منار *minár.* A large lanthorn, a light-house.

A. منارة *minárah.* A turret, a minaret.

A. منازع *munázi'.* Contending, litigating.

A. منازعت *munáza'at.* Contest, litigation.

A. منازل *manázil.* Mansions, stages.

A. مناسب *munásib.* Proper, fit, suitable.

A. مناسبت *munásabat.* Suitability.

A. مناشیر *manáshír.* Royal mandates.

A. مناصب *manáṣib.* Offices, dignities. (pl. of منصب.)

A. مناصحت *munáṣaḥat.* Admonition.

A. مناصفه *múnáṣafah.* Halving.

A. مناظره *munáẓarah.* Controversy.

A. مناع *manná'.* Strongly prohibiting.

A. مناعت *maná'at.* Inaccessibility.

A. مناعم *muná'im.* Tender, soft, gentle.

A. مناف *manáf.* Name of a pagan Arabian idol.

A. منافذ *manáfiẑ.* Holes, fissures.

A. منافر *munáfir.* Abhorring.

A. منافع *manáfi'.* Profits, gains.

A. منافق *munáfiḳ.* A hypocrite.

A. مناقشه *munáḳashah.* Contention.

A. مناقض *munáḳiẓ.* Contradictory, opposite.

A. مناقضت *munáḳaẓat.* Contradiction, opposition.

A. مناكحة *munákaḥat.* Marriage.

A. مناكير *manákír.* Iniquitous things.

A. منال *munál.* Profit, means of gain.

A. منام *munám.* Sleep.

A. منان *mannán.* Beneficent.

A. مناهج *manáhij.* Roads, ways.

A. مناهل *manáhil.* Watering-places.

A. مناهى *manáhí.* Prohibited things.

A. منايا *manáyá.* Deaths.

A. منبر *mimbar.* A pulpit.

A. منبسط *mumbasiṭ.* Rejoicing.

A. منبع *mimba'.* Fountain, spring, source.

A. من بعد *min ba'd.* Afterwards.

A. منبعث *mumbá'is.* Excited; sent.

A. منبه *munabbih.* An admonisher, an awakener.

A. منت *minnat.* An obligation, favour.

A. منتهج *múntahij.* Deducing.

A. منتخب *muntakhib.* Chosen, selected.

A. منتزع *muntazi'.* Seizing, taking.

A. منتسب *muntasib.* Compared, referred to.

A. منتشر *muntashir.* Diffused, dispersed.

A. منتصب *muntaṣab.* Erect, set up.

A. منتصر *muntaṣir.* Conquering, overcoming.

A. منتظر *muntaẓir.* Expecting, waiting.

A. منتظم *muntaẓam.* Ordered, arranged.

A. منتفع *muntafiʿ.* Gaming, enjoying.

A. منتفی *muntafí.* Dissipated, destroyed.

A. منتقض *muntaḳiz.* Demolishing.

A. منتقل *muntaḳil.* Emigrating.

A. منتقم *muntaḳim.* Avenging.

A. منتقی *muntaḳí.* Selecting.

A. منتن *muntin.* Fetid.

A. P. منت نهادن *minnat nihádan.* To confer a favour.

A. منتهی *muntahá.* Finished, terminated, ending.

A. منجر *munjarr.* Drawn, dragged.

A. منجر شدن *munjarr shudan.* To be finished.

A. منجس *munajjas.* Polluted.

A. منجل *minjal.* A sickle, scythe.

P. منجلاب *manjaláb.* Polluted water.

A. منجلی *munjalí.* Conspicuous, apparent.

A. منجم *munajjim.* An astronomer, astrologer.

A. منجمد *munjamid.* Congealed.

P. منجو *manjú.* A lentil.

A. منجور *manjúr.* Planed, cut.

A. منحوس *manḥús.* Unfortunate.

A. منخر *minkhar.* A nostril.

A. منخرط *munkhariṭ.* Turned (on a lathe).

A. منخرق *munkhariḳ.* Split, lacerated.

A. منخرم *munkharim.* Chopping, splitting.

A. منخل *minkhal.* A sieve.

P. مند *-mand.* A termination signifying "possessed of".

A. مندرج *mundarij.* Including, containing.

A. مندرس *mundaris.* Obliterated, cancelled.

A. مندس *mundass.* Hid, buried.

A. مندفع *mundafiʿ.* Repulsed, removed.

A. مندوب *mandúb.* Lamented, mourned.

A. مندیل *mandíl.* A napkin.

A. منزل *manzil.* A day's journey; a halting-place.

A. منزلت *manzilat.* Dignity, rank.

A. منزوع *manzúʿ.* Polluted.

A. منزوی *munzawí.* A solitary man, hermit.

A. منزه *munazzah.* Pure, holy.

A. منسج *minsaj.* A loom.

A. منسلب *munsalib.* Plundered.

A. منسلك *munsalik.* Joined, connected.

A. منسوب *mansúb.* Related, ascribed.

A. منسوج *mansúj.* Woven.

A. منسوخ *mansúkh.* Obsolete, cancelled, abrogated.

A. منسى *mansíy.* Forgotten.

P. منش *manish.* Mature, temperament.

A. منشاء *manshá'.* Principle, origin, beginning.

A. منشات *munshát.* Letters, compositions.

A. منشار *minshár.* A saw.

A. منشر *munshir.* (God) reviving, bringing to life.

A. منشعب *munsha'ab.* Branching off, divided.

A. منشق *munshaḳḳ.* Spilt.

A. منشور *manshúr.* Diffused, promulgated.

A. منشى *munshí.* A secretary.

A. منصب *manṣab.* Dignity, office, station.

A. P. منصب دار *manṣab-dár.* An office-holder.

A. منصبغ *munṣabagh.* Dyed, tinged.

A. منصرف *munṣarif.* Turned back.

A, منصف *munṣif.* Just, equitable; a judge.

A. منصوب *manṣúb.* Erected, constituted.

A. منصور *manṣúr.* Victorious, aided.

A. منصوص *manṣúṣ.* Manifested, declared.

A. منصه *manaṣṣah.* Front, forehead.

A. منضم *munẓamm.* Joined.

A. منطبق *munṭabiḳ.* Congruous, consonant.

A. منطفى *munṭafí.* Distinguished.

A. منطق *manṭiḳ.* Logic.

A. منطقه *manṭiḳah.* A girdle, zone.

A. منطقة البروج *manṭiḳat ul burúj.* The zodiac.

A. منطوق *manṭúḳ.* Said, spoken, enunciated.

A. منطوى *munṭawí.* Folded, involved.

A. منظر *manẓar.* The countenance, aspect; a view.

A. منظور *manẓúr.* Agreeable.

A. منظوم *manẓúm.* Arranged, metrical.

A. منظومه *manẓúmah.* Versified.

A. منع *man'.* Hinderance, prohibition.

A. منعدم *mun'adim.* Annihilated.

A. منعدى *mun'adí.* Contagious.

A. منعطف *mun'aṭif.* Turned, inclined to.

A. منعقد *mun'aḳid.* Tied, bound.

A. منعكس *mun'akis.* Inverted, contrary.

A. منعم *mun'im.* A benefactor.

A. منعم *muna'am.* Affluent.

A منفتح *munfatiḥ.* Subdued, conquered.

A. منفتق *munfatiḳ.* Split, cleft.

A. منفجر *munfajir.* Flowing; dawning.

A. منفخ *minfakh.* A pair of bellows.

A. منفذ *manfaẕ*. A hole, vent, passage.

A. منفر *munfir*. Terrifying, putting to flight.

A. منفرج *munfarij*. Open, separated.

A. منفرح *munfariḥ*. Exhilarated.

A. منفرد *munfarid*. Alone; simple.

A. منفصل *munfaṣil*. Separated, detached.

A. منفطر *munfaṭir*. Split, splitting.

A. منفعت *manfiʻat*. Profit, advantage.

A. منفعل *munfaʻil*. Bashful, ashamed.

A. منفق *munfiḳ*. Expending.

A. منفك *munfakk*. Dislocated, disjointed.

A. منفوض *manfúẓ*. Shaken, concussed.

A. منفى *manfí*. Repulsed; negative.

A. منقاد *minḳád*. Submissive.

A. منقار *minḳár*. The beak of a bird.

A. منقاش *minḳásh*. Pincers, tweezers.

A. منقبت *manḳabat*. (pl. مناقب.) Virtue, a noble mind.

A. منقبض *munḳabiẓ*. Constipated, contracted.

A. منقح *munaḳḳaḥ*. Cleansed.

A. منقذ *munḳiẕ*. Liberating.

A. منقرض *munḳariẓ*. Extinct, elapsed.

A. منقسم *munḳasim*. Divided into parts.

A. منقش *munaḳḳash*. Painted, embroidered.

A. منقشر *munḳashir*. Peeled, skinned, barked.

A. منقصت *manḳaṣat*. Detriment, loss.

A. منقضى *munḳaẓí*. Past, elapsed.

A. منقطع *munḳaṭaʻ*. Broken off, terminated.

A. منقلا *manḳalá*. The advanced guard, an ambassador.

A. منقلب *munḳalib*. Changed, inverted.

A. منقلع *munḳalaʻ*. Torn out, extracted.

A. منقوب *manḳúb*. Undermined.

A. منقوش *manḳúsh*. Engraved.

A. منقوص *manḳúṣ*. Damaged.

A. منقول *manḳúl*. Copied, recounted, removed.

A. منقى *munaḳḳí*. Detergent.

A. منكار *munkár*. Wicked.

A. منكر *munkir*. Denying, refusing.

A. منكرم *munkarim*. Honoured.

A. منكشف *munkashif*. Displayed, revealed.

A. منكوب *mankúb*. Miserable.

A. منكوحه *mankúḥah*. A lawful wife.

A. منكوس *mankús*. Inverted; perverted.

P. منکه *man ki.* I who am.

P. منگ *mang.* A die, dice; custom, habit; a thief, robber.

P. منم *manam.* I am.

A. منوال *minwál.* Mode, rule.

A. منور *munawwar.* Illuminated.

A. منوط *manúṭ.* Fastened; dependent on.

A. منوی *manwíy.* Intended, proposed.

A. منهج *minhaj.* A highway, a road.

A. منهدم *munhadim.* Destroyed.

A. منهزم *munhazim.* Defeated, put to flight.

A. منهضم *munhaẓim.* Well digested.

A. منهل *minhall.* A watering place.

A. منهی *munhí.* Announcing.

A. منهی *manhí.* Forbidden, prohibited.

A. منی *miná.* Semen virile.

A. منیت *munyat.* Wish, desire.

A. منیت *maníyat.* Death.

A. منیر *munír.* Shining.

A. منیع *muníʿ.* Inaccessible, impregnable.

A. منیف *muníf.* Eminent, sublime.

P. مو *mú.* Hair.

A. موات *mawát.* Death.

A. مواثیق *mawásík.* Confederacies, compacts.

A. مواجب *mawájib.* Causes, reasons; salary, wages.

A. مواجهة *muwájahat.* Facing, beholding.

A. مواخات *muwákhát.* Fraternity.

A. مواخذ *muwákhiż.* Seizing, chastising.

A. مواخذة *muwákhażat.* Remonstrance; calling to account.

A. مواد *mawádd.* Matters, points. (pl. of مادة.)

A. موارد *mawárid.* Watering-places; focuses.

A. موازنة *muwázanat.* Equilibrium, being equal.

A. موازے *muwází.* Quantity; nearly; sets, pairs, &c.

A. موازین *mawázín.* Balances. (pl. of میزان.)

A. مواسا *muwásá.* Society fellowship.

A. مواسات *muwását.* Brotherly affection.

A. مواشی *mawáshí.* Cattle, quadrupeds.

A. مواصلت *muwáṣalat.* Interview; conjunction.

A. مواضع *mawáẓiʿ.* Places, villages. (pl. of موضع.)

A. مواطات *muwáṭát.* Emulating, levelling.

A. مواطن *mawáṭin.* Native countries.

A. مواظبت *muwáẓabat.* Perseverance.

A. مواعدت *muwáʿidat.* Promise, agreement.

A. مواعظ *mawáʿiẓ.* Exhortation, advice.

A. موافق *muwáfiḳ.* Conformable, suiting, favourable.

A. موافقت *muwáfaḳat.* Conformity, analogy.

A. مواقع *mawáḳi'.* Occurrences.

A. مواقف *mawáḳif.* Stations, posts. (pl. of موقف.)

A. مواکب *mawákib.* Cavalcades. (pl. of موکب.)

A. موالات *muwálát.* Friendship.

A. موالی *mawálí.* Lords, friends, slaves. (pl. of مولی.)

A. موالیا *muwáliyá.* Seriatim.

A. موالد *mawálid.* Offspring.

A. موانست *muwánasat.* Intimacy, familiarity.

A. موانع *mawáni'.* Impediments.

A. مواهب *mawáhib.* Gifts.

A. مواهبت *muwáhabat.* Contending in liberality.

A. مواهنت *muwáhanat.* Remissness.

A. موبد *mobed.* A Zoroastrian priest.

A. موءبد *mu'abbid.* Eternal, perpetual.

P. مو بمو *mú-ba-mú.* Hair by hair.

A. موت *maut.* Death.

A. موتی *mautá.* The dead. (pl. of میت *maiyit.*)

A. موءتجر *mu'tajar.* Mercenary, hired.

P. موتراش *mú-tarásh.* A hair-cutter.

A. موءتمر *mu'tamar.* Obsequious, submissive.

A. موءتمن *mu'taman.* Trusty.

A. موثر *muśir.* Making an impression on, efficacious.

A. موثق *múśiḳ.* Strengthening.

A. موثقه *mauśiḳah.* Confidence.

A. موثوق *mauśúḳ.* Firm, constant.

A. موج *mauj.* A wave.

A. موجب *mújib.* A cause, motive.

A. موجد *mújid.* An author, cause.

A. موجز *mújiz.* A compendium, epitome.

A. موجع *muja'.* In pain.

A. موج زدن *mauj-zadan.* To surge, to billow.

A. موءجل *mu'ajjal.* Appointed time.

A. موجود *maujúd.* Existing, present.

A. موجه *muwajjah.* Approved.

P. موچینه *mú-chína.* Tweezers.

A. موحد *muwaḥḥid.* One who believes in the unity of God.

A. موحش *múḥish.* Terrifying, dismal.

A. موءخر *mu'akkhar.* Posterior, consequent.

A. موءدے *mu'addá.* Paid, performed.

A. موءدب *mu'addib.* A preceptor.

A. مودت *muwaddat.* Friendship, love.

A. مودی *mu'addi.* Paying, performing.

A. موذن *mu'azzin.* The crier of a mosque.

A. موذے *mu'zí.* Noxious, hurtful.

P. مور *múr.* An ant.

P. مورچانه *múrchána.* Rust on iron.

A. مورخ *mu'arrikh.* A historian.

A. مورخ *mu'arrakh.* Dated.

A. مورد *maurid.* A focus.

P. مورد *múrd.* Myrtle.

A. موروث *maurús.* Inherited.

A. موروثی *maurúsí.* Hereditary, hereditaments.

A. موریانه *muriyána.* Rust.

A. موز *mauz.* A plantain.

A. موزون *mauzún.* Weighed, measured.

P. موزه *múza.* A stocking, a boot.

P. موژ *múzh.* Grief, sorrow.

A. موسس *mu'assis.* A founder.

A. موسم *mausam.* Season, time.

A. موسوم *mausúm.* Marked, signed, named.

G. موسیقی *musíkí.* Music.

P. موش *músh.* A mouse, rat.

A. موشح *muwasshah.* Wearing a scarf, ornamented. Odes with varied rhymes.

P. موش پران *músh i parrán,* or,
P. موش پرنده *músh i paranda.* } A squirrel.

P. موش خور *músh-khúr.* A kite.

P. موش دشتی *músh i dashtí.* A field-mouse.

P. موش کور *músh i kúr.* A mole.

A. موصی اليه *muwaṣṣá ilaíh.* A legatee.

A. موصل *múṣil.* A carrier, bearer. Leading to.

A. موصوف *mauṣúf.* Described, before-mentioned.

A. موصول *mauṣúl.* Collected, delivered.

A. موصی *muwaṣṣí.* A testator, bequeathing.

A. موضح *múẓiḥ.* Clearing up, manifesting.

A. موضع *mauẓi'.* A place.

A. موضوع *mauẓú'.* Placed; an object.

A. موطاء *muwaṭṭá'.* Levelled, trampled.

A. موطن *mauṭin.* A dwelling.

A. موطی *mauṭí.* A footprint.

A. موظف *muwaẓẓaf.* Fixed pay or tribute.

A. موعد *mau'id.* A promise.

A. موعذت *mauïzat.* Exhortation.

A. موعظت *mauïẓat.* Preaching, admonition.

A. موعود *mau'úd.* Promised, predicted.

A. موفر *muwaffar.* Profuse.

A. موفق *muwaffiḳ.* Prospering, aiding.

A. موفور *maufúr.* Copious, plenty, full.

A. موفى *muwaffá.* Satisfied, paid, performed.

A. موقت *muwaḳḳat.* Restricted to a certain time.

A. موقر *muwaḳḳar.* Honoured, respected.

A. موقع *mauḳi'.* A place; a contingency.

A. موقف *mauḳif.* A station.

A. موقوف *mauḳúf.* Deferred, delayed, stopped.

A. موقى *muwaḳḳá.* One who is feared.

P. موك *múk.* The sting of an insect.

A. موكب *maukab.* A cavalcade.

A. موءكد *mu'akkad.* Confirmed.

A. موكل *muwakkal.* Appointed guardian.

A. مولى *maulá.* A master, lord; a slave.

A. مولانا *mauláná.* Our lord.

A. مولد *maulid.* Nativity, native place.

A. مولع *múla'.* Excited, desirous.

A. موءلف *mu'allif.* A compiler (of a book, &c.)

A. مولفات *mu'allafát.* Compilations.

A. موءلم *mu'allam.* Afflicted, distressed.

A. مولود *maulúd.* Generated, born.

A. مولوى *maulawí.* A learned man, my Lord.

A. P. موم *múm.* Wax.

P. موم جامه *múm-jáma.* Cerecloth, wax-cloth.

A. موءمر *mu'ammar.* In command (a general).

A. موءمل *mu'ammil.* Hoping.

A. موءمن *mú'min.* A true believer.

P. مومى *múmí.* Waxen.

A. موءمى *mú'mí.* Pointing out, beckoning.

A. موءمى اليه *mú'má ilaih.* Above-mentioned.

A. موميا *múmiyá.* Petroleum.

A. مومیائے *múmiyáï.* A mummy.

A. مئونت *ma'únat.* Provisions.

A. موءنث *mu'annaṡ.* Feminine.

A. موءنس *mu'nis.* A familiar, an intimate.

A. موهب *mauhib.* A present, gift.

A. موهوب *mauhúb.* Given, presented.

A. موهوم *mauhúm.* Imagined, suspected.

A. موهون *mauhún.* Enervated, weak.

P. موى *múy.* Hair.

P. مويار *múyár.* Wearing long hair.

A. موءيد *mu'aiyad.* Strengthened, aided.

P. مويز *maviz.* Raisins.

P. موبه *múyah.* Weeping, lamenting.

P. مه *mah.* The moon, a month.

P. مه *ma.* No, not, (with the imperative).

P. مه *mih.* Great.

P. مها *mahá.* Great.

A. مهاب *muháb.* Awful, revered (man).

A. مهابت *mahábat.* Majesty, reverence, awe.

A. مهاجر *muhájir.* A fugitive; a companion of Mohammed's flight.

A. مهاجرت *muhájarat.* Separation.

A. مهاد *mahád.* Cradles; a throne, bed.

A. مهار *mihár.* A camel's bridle.

A. مهارت *mahárat.* Expertness.

A. مهالك *mahálik.* Dangerous places.

A. مهام *muhám.* An important business.

A. مهان *muhán.* Despised, slighted.

P. مهان *mihán.* Great people.

A. مهب *mahabb.* A place whence the wind blows.

A. مهبط *mahbiṭ.* A place of descent.

P. مه پاره *mah-pára.* A mistress.

P. مهتاب *mah-táb.* Moonlight.

A. مهتدی *muhtadí.* Directed, guided.

P. مهتر *mihtar.* Greater; a chief.

P. مهترے *mihtarí.* Greatness, superiority.

A. مهجور *mahjúr.* Separated, forsaken.

P. مهچه *mahché.* A little moon.

A. مهد *mahd.* A cradle; a couch.

A. مهذب *muhażżab.* Refined.

P. مهر *muhr.* A seal; a gold coin.

A. مهر *muhr.* A marriage-portion.

P. مهر *mihr.* Love; the sun.

P. مهربان *mihrbán.* Kind, friendly, a friend.

P. مهربانی *mihrbání.* Kindness, favour.

P. مهرجان *mihrján.* The festival of the autumnal equinox.

P. مهر دار *muhr-dár.* The keeper of the seal.

A. مهر کن *muhr-kan.* A seal-engraver.

P. مهرماه *mihrmáh.* The seventh Persian month (September).

P. مهرو *mahrú.* Beautiful, face like the moon.

P. مهره *muhra.* A shell or coral-bead.

A. مهزول *mahzúl.* Emaciated.

A. مهزوم *mahzúm.* Put to flight.

A. مهضوم *mahẕúm.* Digested.

P. مهل *ma-hil.* Quit not.

A. مهلت *muhlat.* Delay, respite.

A. مهلك *muhlik.* Deadly, fatal.

A. مهلكه *mahlikah.* A dangerous place.

A. مهم *muhimm.* Important. (pl. مهمات *muhimmat.*)

P. مهمان *mihmán.* A guest, stranger.

P. مهمان سرا *mihmán sará.* An inn, a guest-house.

P. مهمانى *mihmání.* Hospitality.

A. مهمل *muhmil.* Negligent.

A. مهميز *mihmíz.* A spur, a goad.

A. مهندس *muhandis.* A geometrician.

P. مهوش *mah-vash.* Beautiful as the moon.

P. مهى *mihí.* Greatness.

A. مهيا *muhaiyá.* Prepared, ready.

A. مهيب *muhíb.* Awful, dreadful.

A. مهيمن *muhaiman.* God.

A. مهين *mihín.* Greater, elder.

A. مهيى *muhyí.* One who prepares.

P. مى *mai.* Wine.

A. ميادين *mayádín.* Fields; camps.

A. ميامن *mayámin.* Benediction, prosperities.

P. ميان *miyán.* The waist, loins, the middle; between.

P. ميان تهى *miyán-tahí.* Empty, hollow.

P. ميانچى *miyánchí.* A mediator.

P. ميانه *miyána.* The middle, between; middling, moderate.

P. ميانه روى *miyána-raví.* Moderation.

A. ميت *maiyit.* A corpse.

A. ميثاق *mísák.* A compact, promise.

P. ميخ *míkh.* A peg, nail.

P. ميخ شكاف *míkh i shikáf.* A wedge.

P. ميخك *míkhak.* Cloves.

P. ميخ كوب *míkh-kób.* A mallet.

P. ميخوش *mai-khush.* Agreeably acid.

A. ميدان *maidán.* A plain.

P. ميده *maida.* Fine flour.

A. P. مير *mír.* A lord, chief.

P. مير *mir* (from مردن *murdan*). Die thou.

A. ميراث *mírás.* Heritage.

P. مير بخشى *mír-bakhshí.* The paymaster-general.

P. مير حج *mír i ḥajj.* The leader of the Hajj caravan.

P. مير ده *mír i dah.* A commander of ten; a superintendent.

P. ميرزا *mírzá.* A Persian title; if it precedes the name it merely signifies "Mr" as ميرزا ابراهيم Mr Ibrahim; but if it follows, it is equivalent to "Prince" as ابراهیم میرزا Prince Ibrahim.

P. میر شکار *mír shikár.* A huntsman.

P. میز *míz.* A table.

P. میزاب *mízáb.* A spout.

A. میزان *mízán.* A balance; the sign Libra.

A. میزان دادن *mízán dádan.* To balance an account.

A. میزبان *míz-bán.* A host, landlord.

P. میزك *mízak.* A mixture.

P. میزه *mízah.* The middle of a saddle.

A. میسر *muyassar.* Facilitated, attainable.

A. میسره *maisarah.* The left side.

P. میش *mísh.* A ram.

A. میشوم *maishúm.* Unfortunate.

A. میعاد *mí'ád.* A rendezvous, the time or place assigned.

P. میغ *mígh.* A cloud.

A. میفاء *mífá'.* Projecting.

P. می فروش *mai-farúsh.* A vintner.

A. میقات *miḳát.* A stated time.

A. میکائیل *míká'íl.* The archangel Michael.

P. میکده *mai-keda.* A tavern.

P. میکسار *mai-gusár.* A connoisseur of wine.

P. میکو *maigú.* A shrimp.

P. میکون *mai-gún.* Wine-coloured.

A. میل *mail.* Propensity, inclination.

A. چه چیز میل می دارید *chi chíz mail mí daríd.* What will you take?

P. میل *míl.* A bodkin, a needle for putting collyrium on the eyes; an instrument for putting out the eyes; a mile.

A. میلاد *míládd.* Nativity, birth.

A. میلان *mílán.* Inclined, desiring.

A. میمنت *maimanat.* Prosperity.

A. میمنه *maimana.* The right side.

A. میمون *maimún.* Happy, fortunate. A monkey, an ape.

P. مینا *míná.* Enamel; the azure sky.

P. مینا کار *míná-kár.* An enameller.

P. مینو *mínú.* Paradise; an emerald.

P. میوه *míva.* Fruits.

P. میوه دار *míva-dár.* Fruitful, bearing fruit.

ن

ن *nún.* N. The twenty-fifth letter of the Arabic, and twenty-ninth of the Persian alphabet.

P. نا *ná*. A negative particle prefixed to nouns.

A. نا *ná*. An affix, signifying our, ours.

P. نا آزموده *ná-ázmúda*. Untried, inexperienced.

P. نا آشنا *ná-áshná*. Unacquainted, stranger.

P. نا استوار *ná ustuwár*. Inconstant.

P. نا امید *ná-ummeid*. Hopeless, desperate.

P. نا امیدی *ná-ummeidí*. Despair.

P. نا انبان *ná-ambán*. A musical instrument.

P. نا اندیش *ná-andísh*. Clear, evident, requiring no thought.

P. A. نا اهل *ná-ahl*. Unfit.

P. ناب *náb*. Clear, pure.

P. نا پاک *ná-pák*. Impure, unclean.

P. A. نا بالغ *ná-báligh*. Under age, immature.

P. نا پایدار *ná-páidár*. Not durable, inconstant.

P. نا بایسته *ná-báyista*. Improper.

P. نا بخرد *ná-bakhirad*. Unwise.

P. نا پدید *ná-padíd*. Invisible, disappearing.

P. نا پروا *ná-parwá*. Fearless, careless.

P. نا پسند *ná-pasand*. Displeasing, disagreeable.

P. نا بسی *ná-basí*. Not existing.

P. نا بکار *ná-bakár*. Useless, vagabond.

P. نا بلد *ná-balad*. One unacquainted with the ways and manners of a country.

P. نا بنوا *ná-binawá*. Useless, spoiled.

P. نا بود *ná-búd*. Annihilated, non-existent.

P. نا بهره *ná-bahra*. Great, choice, excellent; mean, base.

P. نا پیدا *ná-paidá*. Not to be found.

P. نا بینا *ná-bíná*. Blind.

P. نا تراشیده *ná-taráshída*. Rough, uncut.

P. A. نا تمام *ná-tamám*. In complete, imperfect.

P. نا توان *ná-tawán*. Infirm, incapable.

P. نا توان بین *ná-tawán-bín*. Envious, malevolent.

P. نا توانی *ná-tawání*. Infirmity.

P. نا چار *ná-chár*. Helpless, forlorn, destitute.

P. نا چاق *ná-chák*. Unsound; indisposed.

P. A. نا جنس *ná-jins*. Ignoble.

P. ناجود *najúd*. A large cup, a goblet.

A. ناجی *nají*. One who escapes.

P. نا چیده *ná-chída*. Ungathered.

P. نا چیز *ná chíz*. Insignificant, nothing.

P. A. نا حق *ná-hakk*. Unjust.

A. ناحی *nahí.* Side, quarter.

A. ناحیت *náhiyet.* Country, territory.

P. ناخ *nákh.* The navel.

P. ناخدا *nákhudá.* A pilot, helmsman.

A. ناخر *nákhir.* Worn, hollow (as a carious bone).

P. A. نا خلف *ná-khalaf.* Degenerate, ignoble.

P. ناخن *nákhun.* A nail, claw.

P. ناخن بدندان *nákhun ba-dandán.* Sorrowful; astonished.

P. ناخن پال *nákhun-pál.* A whitlow.

P. ناخن پرای *nákhun pairáï.* A barber.

P. ناخنه *nákhuna.* A film on the eye.

P. نا خواست *ná-kh'ást.* Not required.

P. ناخن خامه *nákhun i kháma.* The tip of a pen.

P. نا خواه *ná-kh'áh.* Unwilling, against will.

P. نا خوش *ná-khush.* Displeased, unpleasant.

P. نا دار *ná-dár.* Insolvent, indigent.

P. نا دارے *ná-dárí.* Impudent, indecent.

P. نا داشت *ná-dásht.* Shame, poverty.

P. نا داشتی *ná-dáshtí.* Poverty.

P. نا دان *ná-dán.* Ignorantly, unwillingly.

P. نا دانی *ná-dání.* Ignorance.

A. نادر *nádir.* Rare, precious.

P. نادرست *ná-durust.* Wrong; not true.

P. نادره *nádirah.* A rarity; a witticism.

A. نادم *nádim.* Penitent.

A. نادی *nádí.* Calling, convoking; a crier.

P. نا دیدنی *ná-dídaní.* Invisible, imperceptible.

P. نا دیده *ná-dída.* Unseen.

A. نار *nár.* Fire.

P. نا راست *ná-rást.* Crooked, wrong.

A. P. نار افشاندن *nár-afshándan.* To weep, cry, bewail.

P. A. نا رائے *ná-ráï.* Lazy, careless, indiscreet.

P. ناربن *nárbun.* A pomegranate-tree.

P. نارجیل *nárjíl.* A cocoanut.

P. نارخوك *nárkhúk.* Opium.

P. نا رس *ná-ras.* Unripe.

P. نا رساءی *ná-rasáï.* Incapacity.

P. نا رسیده *ná-rasída.* Unripe, immature.

A. نارنج *náranj.* } An orange.
P. نارنگ *nárang.* }

P. نارنگی *nárangí.* Orange-coloured.

P. نا روا *ná-ravá.* Inadmissible, prohibited.

P. نا روان *ná-raván.* Not current, stagnant.

A. ناری *nárí.* Fiery.

P. ناز *náz.* Blandishment, coquetry.

P. ناز بالش *náz-bálish.* A soft pillow.

P. ناز بوی *náz-búy.* A species of sweet basil.

A. نازح *náziḥ.* Far distant (town).

P. نازك *názuk.* Delicate; elegant.

P. نازك بدن *názuk-badan.* Delicate; a sweetheart. A red flower.

A. نازل *názil.* Descending.

A. نازله *názila.* A calamity (from heaven).

P. نازنده *názanda.* Dissembling, coquetting.

P. نازيدن *názídan.* To dissemble, to coquette.

P. نازو *názú.* A kind of bird; the moon.

P. ناژو *názhu.* A pine, a juniper.

A. ناس *nás.* Mankind.

P. نا ساز *ná-sáz.* Discordant; indisposed.

P. نا سازے *ná-sází.* Disagreement.

P. نا سپاس *ná-sipás.* Unthankful, ungrateful.

P. نا ستوده *ná-sitúda.* Mean, low, worthless.

A. ناسج *násij.* A weaver.

A. ناسخ *násikh.* Abolishing, cancelling.

P. نا سره *ná-sara.* Base coin.

P. نا سزا *ná-sazá.* Unworthy, indecent.

P. نا سفته *ná-sufta.* Unpierced.

P. ناسك *nasik.* Devout.

P. نا سكاليده *ná-sakálída.* Inconsiderate, heedless.

A. ناسوت *násút.* Human kind.

A. ناسور *násúr.* A gangrene.

A. ناسى *násí.* Forgetful.

P. نا شاد *ná-shád.* Cheerless.

P. نا شايسته *ná-sháyista.* Unfit, indecent.

P. ناشته *náshta.* Breakfast.

P. نا شدنى *ná-shudaní.* Impossible, impracticable.

A. ناشر *náshir.* Dispersing.

A. ناشره *náshira.* A blustering wind.

P. نا شسته *ná-shusta.* Unwashed; inelegant.

A. ناشط *náshiṭ.* Active, sprightly.

A. ناشطات *náshiṭát.* Moving stars.

P. نا شكيبائے *ná-shakíbáí.* Impatience.

P. نا شناس *ná-shinás.* Ignorant, unacquainted.

P. نا شنيدنى *ná-shunídaní.* Unfit to be heard.

P. نا شنيده *ná-shunída.* Unheard.

A. ناشى *náshí.* Growing.

A. ناصب *náṣib.* } Erecting,
A. ناصبه *náṣibah.* } planting.

A. ناصح *náṣiḥ.* A monitor.

A. ناصر *náṣir.* An assistant.

A. ناصع *naṣi'.* Pure (colour).

A. نا صواب *ná-ṣawáb.* Not right, sinful.

A. ناصيه *náṣiyeh.* The forehead.

A. ناضب *náẓib.* Far, distant.

A. ناضر *náẓir.* Florid, vivid, splendid.

A. ناطح *náṭiḥ.* Butting with the horns, as a ram.

A. ناطر *náṭur.* See ناطور.

A. ناطق *naṭiḳ.* Speaking; rational.

A. ناطقه *náṭiḳah.* The faculty of speech.

A. نا طلب *ná-ṭalab.* Uncalled.

A. ناطور *náṭúr.* The watchman in a vineyard or garden.

A. ناظر *náẓir.* Seeing; an overseer.

A. ناظم *náẓim.* An adjuster, a ruler.

A. ناظور *náẓúr.* Seeing, observing, inspecting.

A. ناعس *ná'is.* Sleepy, drowsy.

A. ناعم *ná'im.* Soft, tender.

A. ناعمه *ná'imah.* A garden, a meadow.

P. ناغول *nághúl.* A stair; ladder.

P. ناف *náf.* The navel; middle.

P. A. ناف ارض *náf i arẓ.* The navel of the earth (Mecca).

P. نافخ *náfikh.* Blowing; a blower.

A. نافذ *náfiẓ.* Penetrating, effectual.

A. نافر *náfir.* Timid; conquering, a victor.

P. نا فرجام *ná-farjám.* Incomplete, coming to a bad end.

P. نا فرمان *ná-firmán.* Disobedient, rebel.

P. نا فرمانی *ná-firmání.* Disobedience, refractoriness.

P. نا فرهخته *ná-farhikhta.* An ugly, impudent fellow.

A. نافع *náfi'.* Advantageous.

A. نافله *náfilah.* Supererogatory (prayers).

P. نافه *náfa.* A pod of musk.

P. A. نا فهم *ná-fahm.* Stupid, unintelligent.

A. نافی *náfí.* Repelling, negative.

P. A. نا قابل *ná-ḳábil.* Unfit.

A. ناقد *náḳid.* A coiner.

A. ناقز *náḳiz.* Worthless (a gift).

A. ناقص *náḳiṣ.* Imperfect, defective.

A. ناقع *náḳi'.* Penetrating, lodging (venom).

A. ناقل *náḳil.* A reporter, narrator.

A. ناقور *náḳúr.* A trumpet.

A. ناقوس *náḳús.* A bell.

A. ناقه *náḳah.* A she-camel.

P. ناك *nák.* An affix denoting being affected with, as, غمناك affected with grief.

P. نا كاره *ná-kára.* Useless, worthless.

P. نا كاسته *ná-kásta.* Undiminished.

P. نا كام *ná-kám.* Disappointed, discontented.

P. نا كاه *ná-gáh.* Suddenly

A. ناكحة *nákiḥ.* A married woman, a wife.

P. ناكتخدا *ná-katkhudá.* A bachelor.

P. ناكردنى *ná-kerdaní.* Not fit to be done.

P. ناگرفت *ná-girift.* Suddenly, accidentally.

P. ناگريز *ná-guríz.* Inevitable.

P. ناگزران *ná-guzrán.* Helpless, without remedy.

P. ناكس *ná-kas.* Worthless, mean.

P. ناكسى *ná-kasí.* Meanness, abjectness.

P. ناگوار *ná-gawár.* Unwholesome, disgusting.

P. ناگهان *ná-gahán.* Suddenly.

A. نال *nál.* Giving, bestowing, liberal.

P. نالان *nálán.* Lamenting.

P. A. نا لايق *ná-láiḳ.* Improper, unworthy.

P. نالش *nálish.* A complaint.

P. ناله *nála.* Lamentation, complaint.

P. ناليدن *nálidan.* To lament, grieve.

P. نام *nám.* Name; fame.

P. نام اور *nám-ávar.* Illustrious, famous.

P. نام اوردن *nám-ávardam.* To become famous.

P. نام بنام *nám-ba-nám.* Name by name, expressly.

P. نام برده *nám-burda.* Abovenamed.

P. A. نا مبارك *ná-mubárak.* Unfortunate, inauspicious.

P. A. نا متصور *ná-mutaṣawwar.* Inconceivable.

P. A. نا متناهى *ná-mutanáhí.* Infinite.

P. A. نا متوقع *ná-mutawaḳḳí'.* Hopeless, unexpected.

P. نام جو *nám-jú.* Seeking fame.

P. نام جوئے *nám-júí.* The act of seeking fame.

P. A. نا محدود *ná-maḥdúd.* Boundless.

P. A. نا محرم *ná-maḥram.* A stranger; not confidential.

P. A. نا محرمیت *ná-maḥramíyet.* Strangeness.

P. A. نا محصور *ná-maḥṣúr.* Innumerable.

P. A. نا مخصوص *ná-makhṣúṣ.* Unappropriate.

P. نامدار *nám-dár.* Famous, illustrious.

P. A. نا مراد *ná-murád.* Disappointed, frustrated.

A. نا مربوط *ná-marbúṭ.* Unconnected.

P. نا مرد *ná-mard.* A coward; impotent.

P. نا مردمى *ná-mardumí.* Rudeness.

P. نا مردى *ná-mardí.* Cowardice.

P. A. نا مرضى *ná-marẓí.* Disagreeable.

P. A. نا مرغوب *ná-marghúb.* Undesirable; contemptible.

P. نامزد *nám-zad.* Appointed, nominated.

P. A. مساعد نا *ná-musá'id.* Unaided.

P. مستحسن نا *ná-mustaḥsin.* Worthless, censurable.

P. A. مستحق نا *ná-mustaḥıkk.* Undeserving.

P. A. مسعود نا *ná-mas'úd.* Inauspicious.

P. A. معتدل نا *ná-mu'tadil.* Intemperate, immoderate.

P. A. معتمد نا *ná-mu'tamad.* Not trustworthy.

P. A. معدود نا *ná-ma'dúd.* Innumerable.

P. A. معروف نا *ná-ma'rúf.* Not famous, unknown.

P. A. معقول نا *ná-ma'kúl.* Absurd, impertinent.

P. A. معلوم نا *ná-ma'lúm.* Unknown.

P. A. مقبول نا *ná-makbúl.* Unacceptable.

P. A. ملايم نا *ná-muláyim.* Rude, harsh, rough.

P. A. ممیزی نا *ná-mumaiyizí.* Want of discrimination.

P. A. مناسب نا *ná-munásib.* Improper, unsuitable.

P. نامنامی *nám-námí.* Increasing fame.

P. نام نیك *nám i ník.* Good fame.

P. A. موافقت نا *ná-muwákafat.* Contrary, adverse.

P. A. موجه نا *ná-muwajjah.* Disagreeable.

P. نامور *námvar.* Celebrated, famous.

P. ناموری *námvarí.* Fame, renown.

P. A. موزون نا *ná-mauzún.* Discordant, ill-formed.

A. ناموس *námús.* Reputation, fame; low.

P. نامه *náma.* An epistle, book, letter.

A. نامی *námí.* Growing famous.

P. نامیدن *námídan.* To name.

P. A. میسر نا *ná-muyassar.* Unattainable.

A. نامیه *námiyeh.* Growth, vegetation.

P. نان *nán.* Bread.

P. نانا *náná.* A maternal grandfather.

P. نان با *nán-bá.* A baker.

P. نان تنك *nán i tang.* Thin bread, biscuit.

P. نان تهی *nán i tahí.* Bread alone.

P. نان تلخ *nán i talkh.* Stale bread.

P. نان جوی *nán-júí.* A beggar.

P. A. نان حلال *nán i ḥalál.* Bread earned by labour.

P. A. نان خمیری *nán i khamírí.* Leavened bread.

P. A. نان رباط *nán i rubáṭ.* Bread given in monasteries.

P. نان زرین *nán i zarín.* The sun.

P. نان سیمین *nán i símín.* The moon.

P. نان فطیرے *nán i faṭírí.* Unleavened bread.

P. نان كور *nán-kúr.* Ungrateful, mean.

P. نانوا *nánvá.* A baker.

P. A. نان وقف *nán-i wakf.* Bread, left by a charitable bequest.

P. ناو *náv.* A hollow tube; a boat.

P. ناو دان *náv-dán.* A spout.

P. نا وسند *ná-vasand.* Not approved.

P. ناورد *návard.* Battle, combat.

P. ناوك *návak.* A tube for discharging arrows; an arrow.

P. ناهار *náhár.* Unknown, strange.

A. ناهب *náhib.* Plundering.

P. نا همتا *ná-hamtá.* Incomparable.

P. نا هموار *ná-hamvár.* Unlevel, rough, rugged.

P. ها منجار *ná-hanjár.* Improper, unworthy.

A. ناهق *náhiḳ.* Braying (as an ass).

A. ناهى *náhí.* Prohibiting, forbidding.

P. ناهيد *náhíd.* The planet Venus.

P. ناى *náy.* A reed-pipe.

P. نا ياب *ná-yáb.* Undiscoverable, unattainable.

A. نائب *náïb.* A deputy.

A. نائب مناب *náïb munáb.* Performing the functions of, a vicegerent.

P. نائچه *náïchah.* The stem of a hookah or narghilé.

A. نائره *náïrah.* A blaze, arson.

A. نائل *náïl.* Arriving at, obtaining.

A. نائم *náïm.* Sleeping, slumbering.

P. نائيدن *náïdan.* To boast, to flatter.

A. نبات *nabát.* An herb.

A. نبات سكر *nabát i sukkar.* Sugar-cane.

A. نباتات *nabátát.* Herbs, vegetables.

A. نباتى *nabátí.* Vegetable.

A. نباح *nabbáḥ.* Barking (a dog).

A. نباش *nabbásh.* A despoiler of graves, a resurrectionist.

A. نباهت *nabáhat.* Nobleness, celebrity.

P. نبايد *na-báyad.* Not proper.

A. نباه *nabáh.* Celebrated, noble.

A. نبت *nabt.* Growing, germinating.

A. نبث *nabaṡ.* Anger.

A. نبج *nabj.* Oakum.

A. نبخ *nabkh.* The small pox; pustules on the hand from hard labour; barking.

A. نبذة *nubżat.* } A small
A. نبذى *nubżí.* } portion.

P. نبر *nabr.* Lifting, raising.

P. نبراس *nebrás.* A lantern, lamp, light.

P. نبرد *naburd.* A battle, war.

P. نبرد *na-barad.* He bears not.

P. نبرد *na-burad.* He cleaves not.

P. نبرد گاه *naburd-gáh.* A field of battle.

P. نبرده *naburda.* Warlike; chosen, selected.

P. نبریده *na-burída.* A castrated ram with its wool unshorn.

P. نبس *nabas.* A daughter's daughter.

P. نبسه *nabasa.* A daughter's son or daughter.

P. نبشتن *nabishtan.* To write.

A. نبض *nabẓ.* The pulse.

A. نبضان *nabazán.* Beating as an artery.

A. نبضت *nabẓat.* One pulsation.

P. نبناد *nabnád.* Circumspection, innocence.

A. نبوت *nubúwat.* Prophecy.

A. نبور *nabúr.* The buttocks, podex.

A. نبی *nabíy.* A prophet.

P. نپی *nupé* or *nipé.* The words of God, the Koran.

A. نبیذ *nabíẓ.* Wine or beer made of dates, &c.

P. نبیر *nabír.* A son's son, a grandchild.

P. نبیره *nabíra.* A grandson, son's son.

A. نبیل *nabíl.* Excellent, ingenious, generous.

P. نبق *napak.* Dexterous.

A. نتاج *nitáj.* A birth; result.

P. نتاس *nitás.* Good; healthy; cheerful.

A. نتائج *natáij.* Results. (pl. of نتیجة.)

A. نتر *natr.* Corruption, perdition; violence.

A. نتش *natsh.* Pulling off (flesh, hair, &c.) with pincers, &c.

A. نتف *natf.* Pulling out hairs.

A. نتن *natn.* A stink, becoming fetid.

A. نتیجه *natíjah.* A result, an offspring; the conclusion of a syllogism.

P. نتیل *natíl.* Fraud, imposture.

A. نثار *nisár.* Scattering, dispersion.

A. نثاره *nusárah.* Crumbs of bread or meat.

A. نثر *nasr.* Prose; scattering.

P. نج *naj* or *nuj.* The inside of the mouth.

A. نجاء *najá.* Escaping, set free.

A. نجابت *najábat.* Nobility.

A. نجات *naját.* Liberation, freedom.

A. نجاح *najáḥ.* Success.

A. نجاد *nijád.* A sword belt; carpets.

A. نجار *najjár.* A carpenter.

A. نجار *nujár.* Nature; colour; root, origin.

A. نجارت *nijárat.* The trade of a carpenter.

A. نجباء *nujubá'.* Nobles, heroes.

A. نجح *nujḥ.* Success.

A. نجدت *najdat.* Fortitude, boldness.

A. نجز *najz.* Performing (a promise).

A. نجس *najis.* Unclean, dirty.

A. نجش *najsh.* Routing, exciting.

A. نجل *najal.* Having a large eye.

A. نجم *najm.* A star.

P. نجوان *najwán.* Saffron.

A. نجوت *najwat.* High ground.

A. نجوم *nujúm.* Stars. (pl. of نجم.) علم النجوم *'ilm un nujúm.* Astronomy.

A. نجومی *nujúmí.* Astronomical.

A. P. نجوی گفتن *najwá guftan.* To whisper.

A. نجیب *najíb.* Noble, generous.

A. نجیح *najíḥ.* Successful.

A. نجید *najíd.* Bold, brave, strong.

A. نجیع *nají'.* Wholesome, agreeable.

A. نحاة *nuḥát.* Grammarian.

A. نحاس *naḥás.* Copper.

A. نحافت *naḥáfat.* The being emaciated.

A. نحت *naḥt.* Smoothing, planing.

A. نحر *naḥr.* Sacrificing a camel.

A. نحریر *niḥrír.* Learned, wise.

A. نحس *naḥs.* Inauspicious, unlucky.

A. نحل *naḥl.* A bee.

A. نحلت *naḥlat.* Bees.

A. نحو *naḥw.* Grammar, syntax. (*Adverb*). About, nearly.

A. نحوست *nuḥúsat.* Being unlucky.

A. نحوس *naḥús.* Bad, ill, unfortunate.

A. نحوی *naḥawí.* A grammarian.

A. نحیب *naḥíb.* Weeping excessively.

A. نحیف *naḥíf.* Lean, weak.

P. نخ *nakh.* A thread.

A. نخاس *nakhkhás.* A dealer in slaves and cattle.

A. نخاع *nukhá'.* The spinal marrow.

A. نخاعت *nukhá'at.* Phlegm, spittle, mucus.

A. نخبة *nukhbat.* Choice, select.

P. نخجد *nakhjad.* Dross of iron, scales.

P. نخچیر *nakhchír.* Prey, game.

A. نخر *nakhar.* Worn, rubbed to pieces.

P. نخراز *nukhráz.* A ram, a bellwether.

P. نخست *nukhust.*
P. نخستن *nukhustin.*
P. نخستین *nukhustín.*
} The beginning, the first.

P. نخشه *nakhsha.* Proof, demonstration.

A. نخل *nakhl.* The palm tree, a festoon.

A. نخلبند *nakhlband.* Artificial trees or fruits made of wax; a maker of artificial flowers.

A. نخوت *nakhwat.* Pride, haughtiness.

P. نخود *nukhúd.* A pea, vetch, pulse.

A. نخير *nakhír.* Snoring.

P. نخيز *nakhíz.* Coarse, common, low.

P. ند *nad.* Increase, abundance.

A. نداء *nidá.* Proclamation; a clamour.

A. نداف *naddáf.* A cotton-carder.

A. ندامت *nadámat.* Repentance.

A. نداوت *nadáwat.* Moisture (ground).

A. ندبت *nudbat.* Lamentation.

A. ندرت *nudrat.* Rarity.

A. ندس *nadas.* Understanding, cunning, skill.

A. ندش *nadsh.* Dividing, separating, (carding cotton).

A. ندف *nadf.* Carding cotton.

A. ندم *nadam.* Repentance.

A. ندماء *nudamá.* Boon companions.

A. ندو *nadw.* Calling (a council, &c.), assembling.

A. ندوت *nadwat.* An assembly, congress.

A. ندى *nadá.* Liberality; dew.

A. نديف *nadíf.* Carded cotton.

A. نديم *nadím.* A boon companion.

A. نذارت *nażárat.* Warning.

A. نذر *nażr.* A vow, an offering.

A. نذل *nażl.* A low, mean person.

A. نذير *nażír.* One who warns or threatens.

P. نر *nar.* Male, masculine. شير نر *shír i nar.*

P. نرا *nará.* A small wall raised as a screen.

P. نراك *narák.* Always, for ever.

P. نرخ *nirkh.* Price current, tax.

P. نرخ بازار *nirkh i bázár.* The market rate.

P. نرد *nard.* A piece in backgammon, &c.; the game also is so called.

P. نردبان *nardubán.* Ladder, stairs.

P. نرسك *narask.* A lentil.

P. نرگاو *nar-gáu.* A bull.

P. نرگس *nargis.* A narcissus.

P. نرگس و گل *nargis u gul.* (In poetry) the eye and ear.

P. نرگسى *nargisí.* A species of cloth, also of food.

P. نرم *narm.* Soft, tender, gentle.

P. نرماده *nar-máda.* Male and female; a screw or bolt.

P. نرم نرم *narm narm.* Softly, gently.

P. نرمهٔ گوش *narma i gúsh.* The tip of the ear.

P. نرمی *narmí.* Softness, tenderness.

P. نر میش *nar-mísh.* A ram.

P. نره *nara.* Membrum virile, male.

P. نرے *narí.* A dressed sheepskin; a penis. Virility.

P. نریم *narím* or نریمان *narímán.* An old Persian hero, the great grandfather of Rustum.

P. نریمان. See the preceding word.

P. نزار *nizár.* Lean, thin; distressed.

A. نزاع *nizá'* or نزاعت *nazá'at.* Controversy, dispute.

A. نزاکت *nazákat.* Elegance, delicacy.

A. نزالت *nuzálat.* Sperma genitale.

A. نزاهت *nazáhat.* Purity.

P. نزد *nizd.* Near about, with. نزد من *nizd i man.* In my opinion.

P. نزدیک *nazdík.* Near, almost close to.

P. نزدیکی *nazdíkí:* Proximity.

A. نزع *naz'.* Agony.

A. نزغ *nazgh.* Taunting, reproaching.

A. نزك *nizk.* The male lizard.

A. نزك *nazk.* Defaming.

A. نزل *nuzl.* Hospitality; alighting.

A. نزلت *nazlat.* One descent; a catarrh.

A. نزم *nazm.* A severe bite.

A. نزوان *nazawán.* Making an assault.

A. نزول *nuzúl.* A descent, alighting.

A. نزهت *nuzhat.* Delight.

P. نزیدن *nazídan.* To draw out, extract.

A. نزیر *nazír.* Small, moderate.

A. نزیل *nazíl.* A stranger, a foreigner.

P. نژ *nazh.* The wards of a key.

P. نژاد *nizhád.* } Origin,
P. نژاده *nizháda.* } descent.

P. نژغار *nazhghár.* Noise, shout, exclamation.

P. نژم *nizhm* or *nuzhm.* A cloud, fog, mist.

P. نژند *nizhand.* Formidable; tremendous.

P. نژه *nazha.* A thin metal plate; name of a fixed star.

P. نژیدن *nazhídan.* To draw forth, pull out.

P. نس *nus.* A shade; house; the beard; the vulva.

A. نساء *nisá'.* A woman, a lady; the female sex.

A. نسابت *nassábat.* Skilled in genealogy.

A. نساج *nassáj* A weaver.

A. نسائم *nasáïm.* Zephyrs.

A. نسب *nasab.* Lineage, race.

A. نسبة *nisbat.* Relation, reference.

A. نسبت کردن *nisbat kerdan.* To ascribe, refer.

A. نسبتی *nisbatí.* Related.

P. نسترن *nastaran.* A narcissus.

P. نستوه *nastúh.* Disobedient, contentious.

A. نسبی *nasabí.* Of the same race.

A. نسج *nasj.* Weaving.

A. نسخ *naskh.* Obliterating, copying.

A. نسخه *nuskha.* A copy-book; a medical prescription. Rare. A copy.

A. نسخی *naskhí.* The Arabic style of handwriting.

P. نسر *nasar.* Shade, a shady place.

A. نسر *nasr.* A vulture.

A. نسر طائر *nasr i ṭáir.* The sign Aquila.

A. نسرین *nisrín.* The wild white rose.

A. نسق *nasaḳ.* Order, arrangement.

A. P. نسقچی *nasaḳchí.* The imperial body-guard; they are armed with the hatchets called تبرزین q. v.

A. P. نسق کردن *nasaḳ kerdan.* To punish by cutting off the nose or ears, or otherwise mutilating the criminal.

A. نسك *nusk.* Piety, devotion.

P. نسکا *naská.* The earth, ground.

A. نسل *nasl.* Progeny, race.

A. نسمت *nasamat.* A man, the spirit, soul.

A. نسناس *nisnás.* A fabulous being having the form of a man split in halves. A wild man of the woods.

A. نسوان *niswán.* Women.

A. نسوت *niswat.* Women.

P. نسود *nasúd.* Soft, smooth, delicate.

A. نسول *nusúl.* Moulting.

A. نسیان *nisyán.* Oblivion, forgetfulness.

A. نسیب *nasíb.* Celebrating (a mistress) in verse.

A. نسئت *nasi'at.* Buying or selling on credit.

A. نسیج *nasíj.* Texture, anything woven.

A. نسیق *nasíḳ.* Arranged in order.

A. نسیك *nasík.* Gold and silver.

A. نسیم *nasím.* A gentle gale, the zephyr.

A. نسیه *nasiyah.* Credit.

P. نش *nush.* Alike, resembling, equal.

A. نش *nashsh.* A weight of twenty *dirhems.*

A. نشاء *nashá'.* Growing, increasing.

A. نشاب *nushsháb.* Arrows.

A. نشأت *nash'at.* Appearing, being produced. نشأتین *nash'atain.* This world and the next.

P. نشاختن *nisháḳhtan.* To fix in the ground, to establish.

A. نشاد *nishád.* Praying, conjuring.

A. نشادر *nushádir.* Sal-ammoniac.

A. نشارت *nushárat.* Shavings, saw-dust.

P. نشاسته *nasháshta.* Starch.

A. نشاط *nasháṭ.* Joy, alacrity.

P. نشان *nishán.* A sign, a mark; a standard, coat of arms, order of merit, &c.

P. نشاندن *nishándan.* To fix, plant.

P. نشانه *nishána.* A mark, a butt.

P. نشانیدن *nishánídan.* To cause to seat.

P. نشاید *nasháyad.* It is not becoming.

A. نشب *nashab.* Fixed firmly.

P. نشتر *nishtar.* A lancet.

A. نشج *nashaj.* An aqueduct, a canal.

P. نشخوار *nish-khár.* Rumination. The cud.

A. نشد *nashd.* Seeking.

A. نشدان *nishdán.* Seeking, searching.

A. نشدت *nishdat.* A sound, a voice.

A. نشر *nashr.* Diffusion.

A. نشرت *nushrat.* A charm to cure madness or disease.

A. نشری *nashrí.* Dispersive, diffusive.

P. نشستن *nishastan.* To sit down, to recline; to extinguish.

A. نشط *nashṭ.* Going out, exit.

A. نشف *nashaf.* Imbibing water; soaking up.

A. نشق *nashḳ.* Odour, smelling.

P. نشکرده *nishgirda.* A shoemaker's knife.

P. نشکنج *nishkunj.* Tickling; twitching, pinching.

P. نشمن *nashman.* Fortune.

P. نشوان *nashwán.* Intoxicated.

A. نشوب *nushúb.* Becoming fixed.

A. نشوت *nashwat.* Odours, perfume; intoxication.

A. نشور *nushúr.* The resurrection.

A. نشو نما *nashw-namá.* Growing up.

A. نشوع *nushú'.* A medicine either swallowed or snuffed up.

A. نشه *nash.* Intoxication.

A. نشیب *nashíb.* A descent, declivity.

A. نشیط *nashíṭ.* Brisk, cheerful.

P. نشیل *nashíl.* Hanged, suspended.

P. نشیمن *nashíman.* A seat, mansion.

P. نشین *nishín.* (In composition) sitting.

A. نص *naṣṣ.* Elevating, raising, manifesting; the text of a book.

A. نصاب *niṣáb.* A certain estate for which a tax is paid; boundary; root, origin.

A. نصارے *naṣárá.* Christians.

A. نصاف *niṣáf.* Serving.

A. نصافی *naṣáfí.* A kind of Egyptian fabric, half silk and half cotton.

A. نصائح *naṣáïḥ.* Counsels, admonitions. (pl. of نصیحة.)

A. نصب *naṣb.* Erecting, establishing.

A. نصح *nuṣḥ.* Advising, giving counsel.

A. نصر *naṣr.* Assistance.

A. نصرانی *naṣrání.* A Christian.

A. نصرت *nuṣrat.* Assistance, victory.

A. نصف *niṣf.* Half; the middle.

A. نصفت *niṣfat.* Justice, equity.

A. نصل *naṣl.* The point of a spear, a sword.

A. نصوح *naṣúḥ.* Constant, sincere.

A. نصوص *nuṣúṣ.* Demonstrations.

A. نصیب *naṣíb.* Fortune, lot.

A. نصیبه *naṣíbah.* Share, lot.

A. نصیح *naṣíḥ.* Sincere; a monitor.

A. نصیحت *naṣíḥat.* Advice, admonition.

A. نصیر *naṣír.* An assistant, defender.

A. نصیف *naṣíf.* The half of anything.

A. نصیل *naṣíl.* The joint under the jaw between the head and neck.

A. نضار *naẓár.* Gold or silver.

A. نضارت *naẓárat.* Freshness.

A. نضر *naẓr.* Brightness, freshness.

A. نضرت *naẓrat.* Brightness, splendour.

A. نضید *naẓíd.* A cushion, a pillow.

A. نضیر *naẓír.* Gold or silver.

A. نطار *nuṭṭár.* A scarecrow.

A. نطاق *niṭáḳ.* The waist; a girdle.

A. نطح *naṭḥ.* Butting with the horns.

A. نطرون *naṭrún.* Nitre; natron.

A. نطف *naṭf.* Flowing slowly, emission.

A. نطفه *nuṭfah.* Sperma genitale.

A. نطق *nuṭḳ* or نطوق *nuṭúḳ.* Speech, articulation.

A. نطیح *naṭíḥ.* Hateful, detestable.

A. نطیش *naṭísh.* Motion.

A. نظارت *naẓárat.* Inspection, superintendency, viewing.

A. P. نظارگی *naẓẓáragí.* Looking at a spectacle.

A. P. نظارگان *naẓẓáragán.* Spectators.

A. P. نظاره *naẓára.* A spectacle.

A. نظافت *naẓáfat.* Cleanness, neatness.

A. نظام *niẓám*. Arrangement; a ruler.

A. نظائر *naẓáïr*. Resemblances.

A. نظر *naẓar*. A look, sight, glance, observation.

A. نظر بند *naẓar-band*. Under surveillance.

A. نظر باز *naẓar-báz*. A juggler, a spy.

A. نظر ثانی *naẓar i sání*. Revision.

A. نظم *naẓm*. Arrangement, verse.

A. نظم و نسق *naẓm u nasaḳ*. Order and arrangement.

A. نظیر *naẓír*. Alike, resembling.

A. نظیف *naẓíf*. Pure, clean.

A. نعاب *nu'áb*. The croaking of a crow.

A. نعاس *na'ás*. Somnolent, lethargic.

A. نعال *ni'ál*. Horse-shoes.

A. نعام *na'ám*. An ostrich; a desert.

A. نعامت *na'ámat*. A crossbeam, a sandy desert. (pl. نعایم *na'áïm*.)

A. نعامی *nu'áma*. The south wind.

A. نعایم *na'áïm*. The twentieth mansion of the moon. Deserts.

A. نعت *na't*. Praise, especially of Mohammed.

A. نعجه *na'jah*. A white sheep, cow.

A. نعره *ná'rah*. A shout.

A. P. نعره زدن *na'ra zadan*. To shout.

A. نعش *na'sh*. A bier, a coffin.

A. نعل *na'l*. A horse-shoe; shoes, slippers.

A. P. نعل بستن *na'l bastan*. To shoe (a horse).

A. P. نعل بند *na'l band*. A farrier.

A. نعلین *na'lain*. Shoes; sandals.

A. نعلتراش *na'l-tarásh*. A maker of sandals, shoes, &c.

A. نعم *na'am*. Yes. Cattle.

A. نعما *ni'má*. Benefits, comforts.

A. نعما *ni'ammá*. How excellent!

A. نعمان *nu'mán*. Blood. Title of the ancient kings of Ḥírah.

A. نعمت *ni'mat*. Affluence, the comforts of life.

A. نعنع *na'na'*. Mint.

A. نعوت *nu'út*. Encomiums.

A. نعوذ بالله *na'úzu billáhi*. We seek refuge in God!

A. نعوظ *na'úz*. *Erectio penis.*

A. نعومت *nu'úmat*. Being soft, tender.

A. نعی *na'iy*. The messenger of death.

A. نعیب *na'íb*. } Croaking.
A. نعیق *na'íḳ*. }

A. نعیر *na'ír*. Clamour.

A. نعیم *na'ím*. Affluence.

P. نغام *naghám.* Ugly, ill-favoured.

A. نغز *naghz.* Elegant, good, excellent.

A. نغص *naghaṣ.* Disappointment.

A. نغمة *naghmat.* (pl. نغم *nagham* or *naghm.*) Melody, song.

A. نغيق *naghíḳ.* Croaking as a raven.

A. نفاثت *nafáṡat.* Magic, incantation.

A. نفاخ *naffákh.* Flatulent.

A. نفار *naffár.* Scared, frightened.

A. نفاس *nifás.* Rare, valuable.

A. نفاس *nifás.* Childbirth, labour.

A. نفاست *nafásat.* Being exquisite.

A. نفاق *nifáḳ.* Hypocrisy.

A. نفايس *nafáïs.* Delicacies. (pl. of نفيسه *nafísa.*)

A. نفت *nift.* Any combustible matter. i. q. نفط.

A. نفث *nafaṡ.* Blowing (the breath).

A. نفح *nafḥ.* Exhaling odours.

A. نفحت *nafḥat.* A fragrant gale.

A. نفخ *nafkh.* Blowing, inflammation.

A. نفذ *nafẓ.* Penetrating.

A. نفر *nafar.* An individual, a servant, a private soldier.

A. نفرت *nafrat.* Aversion, hate.

A. نفرے *nafarí.* Service, trade.

A. نفس *nafas.* The breath; respiration.

A. نفس *nafs.* A person.

A. نفس الامر *nafs ul amr.* In fact, the thing itself.

A. نفس الاماره *nafs ul imárah.* Sensual appetite, lust.

A. نفسانى *nafsání.* Sensual, carnal.

A. نفسانيت *nafsáníyat.* Sensuality.

A. نفس پرور *nafs-parvar.* Sensual.

A. نفس زدن *nafas-zadan.* To breathe.

A. نفس نفيس *nafas i nafís.* The precious breath, or soul.

A. نفس واپسين *nafas i wapasín.* The last breath.

A. نفسی *nafasí.* An instant.

A. نفسی *nafasí.* Spiritual, vital.

A. نفط *nifṭ.* Naptha.

A. P. نفط اندازى *nifṭ andází.* Fireworks.

A. نفطت *nafṭat* or *nifṭat.* Blisters, pustules.

A. نفع *naf'.* Gain, emolument.

A. نفق *nafaḳ.* Perishing, failing, dying.

A. نفقه *nafaḳat.* Necessary expense.

A. نفل *nafl.* Clear gain; supererogatory devotion.

A. نفوخ *nufúkh.* A medicine snuffed up.

A. نفوذ *nufúż.* Penetrating, impression.

A. نفور *nafúr.* Abhorring, shunning.

A. نفوس *nufús.* Souls, spirits.

A. نفه *nafih.* Lazy, slow.

A. نفی *nafíy.* Negative, forbidding, non-existence.

A. نفیر *nafír.* A wind instrument.

A. نفیس *nafís.* Precious, delicate.

A. نقاب *niḳáb.* A veil.

A. نقابت *naḳábat.* The dignity of a chief.

A. نقاد *naḳḳád.* An assayed coin.

A. نقاره *naḳḳára.* A kettle-drum.

A. نقارچی *naḳḳárachí.* A kettle-drum player.

A. نقاش *naḳḳásh.* An engraver.

A. نقاشی *naḳḳáshí.* The art of engraving.

A. نقاط *nuḳáṭ.* Points, dots, spots.

A. نقاوت *naḳáwat.* Purity.

A. نقاهت *naḳáhat.* Convalescence, feebleness.

A. نقایض *naḳáïẓ.* Damages, injuries; wresting or distorting the meaning of a verse. (pl. of نقیضة.)

A. نقب *naḳb.* A mine dug under walls.

A. نقباء *nuḳabá.* Chiefs. (pl. of نقیب.)

A. نقد *naḳd.* Cash, ready money.

A. نقد و جنس *naḳd u jins.* Money and goods.

A. نقدی *naḳdí.* Belonging to ready money.

A. نقرس *niḳris.* The gout.

A. نقره *nuḳra.* Silver (especially coin).

A. نقرئی *nuḳrat.* Made of silver.

A. نقش *naḳsh.* A picture, an engraving.

A. نقش بند *naḳsh-band.* An engraver.

A. نقش و نگار *naḳsh u nigár.* Painting and ornaments.

A. نقشه *naḳshah.* A map, plan, model.

A. نقص *naḳṣ.* Deficiency, detriments.

A. نقصان *nuḳṣán.* Damage, diminution.

A. نقض *naḳẓ.* Violation, rupture.

A. نقط *naḳṭ.* Dotting, pointing.

A. نقطه *nuḳṭah.* A point, a dot, a spot.

A. نقل *naḳl.* A tale, narrative, change of place; a copy.

A. نقل *nuḳl.* Dessert, dried fruits.

P. نقل مکان *naḳl i makán.* Emigration.

A. نقلی *naḳlí.* Fictitious, copied.

A. نقمت *naḳmat.* Punishment, revenge.

A. نقوت *naḳwat.* The choicest of anything.

A. نقود *nuḳúd.* Sums of ready money.

A. نقوش *nuḳúsh.* Engravings.

A. نقول *nuḳúl.* Copies.

A. نقی *naḳíy.* Pure, clean, excellent.

A. نقیب *naḳíb.* A chief, leader; a warden.

A. نقیصت *naḳiṣat.* A vice, blemish.

A. نقیض *naḳíẓ.* Contrary, opposite.

A. نقیضت *naḳíẓat.* Wresting the meaning of a verse by adding another word or line.

A. نقیع *naḳí'.* Wholesome; steeped, soaked.

A. نقیه *naḳíh.* Feeble, weak.

A. نکات *nukát.* Witticisms, nice points.

A. نکاح *nikáḥ.* Matrimony, marriage.

A. نکاحی *nikáḥí.* Married woman.

P. نکاره *nakára.* Worthless, useless; invalid.

P. نگار *nigár.* A picture.

P. نگار خانه *nigár-khána.* A picture-gallery.

P. نگار عالم *nigár i 'álam.* A miracle of beauty.

P. نگارش *nigárish.* Writing.

P. نگارنده *nigárenda.* A painter; writer.

P. نگاشتن *nigáshtan.* To paint, to write.

A. نکال *nakál.* Punishment, making an example of.

P. نگاه *nigáh.* A look, observation; custody, care.

P. نگاهبان *nigáh-bán.* A guard or keeper.

P. نگاهبانی *nigáh-báni.* Custody, care.

P. نگاهداشت *nigáh-dásht.* Custody, care.

P. نگاهداشتن *nigáh-dáshtan.* To keep, to guard.

P. نگاه کردن *nigáh-kerdan.* To gaze at.

A. نکب *nakb.* Misfortune.

A. نکبت *nakbat.* Adversity, calamity, misfortune.

A. نکته *nuktah.* A quaint conceit, a subtlety.

A. P. نکتا دان *nukta-dán.* Sagacious; a critic.

A. نکته چین *nukta-chín.* A caviller.

A. نکد *nakid.* Miserable.

A. نکر *nakir.* Ignorant; crafty. Not knowing.

A. نکره *nukrah.* Undetermined, indefinite.

P. نگر *nigar.* Look, sight. Behold.

P. نگران *nigrán.* Looking,

P. نگریدن *nigrídan.* }
P. نگرستن *nigristan.* } To look, see, view.
P. نگریستن *nigrístan.* }

A. نکس *niks.* Poor, wretched; topsy-turvy.

P. نکو *nikú.* Good, excellent.

P. نکو خواه *nikú-kháh.* A well-wisher.

P. نکو سیر *nikú-siyar.* Of good disposition.

P. نگون *nigún.* Inverted, bent, hanging down.

P. نکو نام *nikú-nám.* Of good repute.

P. نکوهش *nikúhish.* Reproaching, rejecting.

P. نکوهیدن *nikúhídan.* To despise, to reproach.

P. نکوهیده *nikúhída.* Despicable.

P. نکوی *nikúí.* Goodness.

P. نگه *nigah.* A look.

P. نگهبان *nigah-bán.* A guard, watch.

P. نگهبانی *nigah-báni.* Guard, custody.

A. نکہت *nakhat.* Perfume.

A. نکیر *nakír.* Hateful, detestable; name of one of the angels (Munkir and Nakír) who examine the dead in the tomb.

P. نگین *nigín.* The stone or bezel of a ring.

P. نم *nam.* Moist, wet.

P. نما *namá.* Showing, pointing; an index.

P. نماز *namáz.* Prayer.

P. نمازی *namází.* A person who prays.

A. نمام *nammám.* An informer, accuser.

P. نمایان *namáyán.* Appearing, apparent.

P. نمایش *namáyish.* Appearance, form, face.

P. نماینده *namáyenda.* Showing; a shower.

P. نمچه *namcha.* Germany, Austria.

P. نمد *namad.* Felt, coarse cloth.

P. نمد پوش *namad-púsh.* Clothed in felt.

A. نمر *nimr.* A leopard.

A. نمرود *nimrúd.* Nimrod.

P. نمسه *namsa.* Germany, Austria.

A. نمط *namaṭ.* Mode, manner, way.

P. نمك *namak.* Salt.

P. A. نمك حرام *namak-hárám.* Ungrateful, disloyal.

P. A. نمك حلال *namak-ḥalál.* Grateful, loyal.

P. نمكدان *namak-dán.* A salt-cellar.

P. نمكزار *namak-zár.* A salt-pan.

P. نمكین *namakín.* Salted, savoury; beautiful.

P. نمگین *nam-gín.* Moist, wet, humid.

P. نمگیره *nam-gíra.* A canopy.

A. نمل *naml.* An ant.

P. T. نملو *namlú.* Moist.

A. نمله *namlah.* The ant; a crack in the hoof of a horse.

P. نمناك *nam-nák.* Moist, wet.

A. نمو *namw.* Growing, increasing.

A. نمود *namúd.* Showed; appearance, show.

P. نمودار *namúdár.* Visible.

P. نمودن *namúdan.* To show, to appear, seem.

P. نمونه *namúna.* A model, specimen.

P. نمی *namí.* Humidity, coolness.

A. نمیر *namír.* Wholesome, pure water; many, much.

A. نمیقه *namíkah.* A letter.

P. ننگ *nang.* Reputation; shame.

P. ننگ و ناموس *nang u námús.* Honour, good name.

P. ننگ نامه *nang-náma.* A history of wars.

A. نمیم *namím.* A slanderer.

A. نمیمه *namímah.* Detraction, slander.

P. نو *nau.* New, fresh.

P. نوا *navá.* Song, melody; subsistence.

A. نواب *navváb.* A viceroy, governor. In Persia this title is given to princes of the blood.

P. نوات *nawát.* A date-stone.

A. نواح *nuwáh.* Complaining, a complaint; side.

A. نواحی *nawáhí.* Environs, districts. (pl. of ناحیة.)

P. نواختن *nawákhtan.* To caress, soothe, to play on an instrument.

A. نوادر *nawádir.* Rare things. (pl. of نادره.)

P. نواده *nawáda.* A grandson.

A. نوار *nawár.* Fearful.

A. نوار *niwár.* A broad border round a tent.

P. نواز *nawáz.* Cherishing; a player on an instrument.

A. نواس *nawwás.* Waving, pendulous.

P. نواستن *nawástan.* To contend.

P. نوازش *nawázish.* Kindness. (pl. نوازشات *nawázishát.*)

A. نوازل *nawázil.* Calamities. (pl. of نازله.)

P. نوازندگی *nawázandagí.* Playing on an instrument.

P. نوازنده *nawázenda.* Player; cherisher.

P. نواسا *nawása.* Grandson.

P. نواسی *nawásí.* Granddaughter.

A. نوافل *nawáfil.* Spontaneous acts of devotion.

A. نوال *nawál.* A gift; benefit.

P. نواله *niwála.* A morsel.

P. نو اموز *nau-ámúz.* A learner, noviciate.

A. نو اورد *nau-ávard.* An invention, innovation.

A. نواهی *nawáhí.* Forbidden things.

P. نو ائین *nau-áín.* New regulation, novelty.

A. نوایب *nawáib.* Adversities.

P. نو اینده *nau-áyenda.* A new-comer.

A. نوب *naub.* Being near; returning.

P. نو باوه *nau-báva.* Early fruits.

A. نوبت *naubat.* Time, turn, guard, watch; military music.

A. P. نوبت خانه *naubat-khána.* A music gallery.

P. نو بهار *nau-bahár.* The commencement of spring.

P. نو پدا *nau-paidá.* New, recent.

P. نو جوان *nau-jawán.* Quite young.

A. نوح *nauḥ.* Noah.

A. نوحه *nauḥah.* Lamentation.

A. P. نوحه كر *nauḥah-gar.* A hired mourner.

P. نو خاسته *nau-khásta.* New risen, youthful.

P. نود *navad.* Ninety.

P. نودد *naudad.* A fold.

P. نودره *naudara.* A beloved offspring.

P. نو دميده *nau-damídah.* A new shoot.

A. نور *núr.* Light, splendour.

A. نور *naur.* A blossom.

A. P. نور افشان *núr afshán.* Diffusing light.

A. نورانى *núrání.* Brightness; bright.

A. P. نور بخش *núr-bakhsh.* Bestowing light.

A. P. نور چشم *núr i chashm.* Light of the eye; a beloved child.

P. نورد *navard.* A fold, a ply; war.

A. نوردن *navardan.* To fold, twist; to travel.

P. نو رس *nau-ras.* Fresh, recent.

P. نو روز *nau-rúz.* New year's day.

P. نوزده *núzdah.* Nineteen.

P. نوزدهم *núzdahum.* Nineteenth.

P. نوش *núsh.* Drink thou; a draught; honey; antidote.

A. P. نوشادر *núshádir.* Sal ammoniac.

P. نوشانوش *núshánúsh.* Draught after draught.

P. نوشت *navisht.* He wrote; a writing.

P. نوشتن *navishtan.* To write.

P. نوشته *navishta.* Written, a writing.

P. نوشدارو *núshdárú.* Treacle; any antidote to poison.

P. نوشنده *núshanda.* Drinking, a drinker.

P. نوشيجان *núshíján.* "May it agree with you" said to a person who is eating or drinking.

P. نوشيدن *núshídan.* To drink.

P. نوشين *núshín.* Sweet, wholesome.

A. نوع *nau'.* Species.

A. نوع البشر *nau 'ul bashar.* The human race.

A. P. نوع ديگر *nau' i dígar.* Another kind.

A. P. نو عروس *nau-'arús.* A new bride.

A. نوعی *nau'í.* Specific.

A. نوفل *naufal.* The sea; a munificent man; a present; a handsome youth.

P. نوك *nauk.* Folly; the tip or point of anything, the nib of a pen.

P. نوكر *naukar.* A servant.

P. نوكری *naukarí.* Service.

P. A. نوك قلم *nauk i ḳalam.* The nib of a pen.

P. نول *núl.* The beak of a bird, a spout.

A. نوم *naum.* Sleep, slumber.

P. نومید *naumeid.* Hopeless.

P. نومیدے *naumeidí.* Despair.

A. نون *nún.* A fish.

P. نو نهال *nau-nihál.* A young tree.

P. نو و كهن *nau u kuhn.* New and old.

P. نوئین *núín.* A prince.

P. نوید *naweid.* Good news.

P. نویدن *nawídan.* To lament.

P. نویسنده *nawísanda.* A writer.

P. نوه *nava.* A grandson.

P. نویان *núyán.* A prince of a Turkoman tribe.

P. نه *na.* Not, no, neither.

P. نه *nuh.* Nine.

P. نهاد *nihád.* Nature, constitution.

P. نهادن *nihádan.* To place, apply.

A. نهار *nihár.* The day.

P. نهال *nihál.* A young plant, a shoot.

A. نهام *nahám, nuhám, nihám.* A blacksmith, a carpenter.

P. نهان *nihán.* Hid, concealed.

P. نهانخانه *nihán-khána.* A cabinet, a private apartment.

P. نهان شدن *nihán shudan.* To be concealed.

P. نهانی *nihání.* Privately, secretly.

A. نهایت *niháyet.* The extremity, utmost.

A. نهب *nahb.* Rapine, plunder, spoil.

A. نهج *nahj.* Road; manner.

A. نهد *nahd.* A generous man.

A. نهر *nahr.* A river, stream.

A. نهری *nahrí.* Belonging to a river.

P. نهستن *nihistan.* To put, to place.

A. نهضت *nahẓat.* Departure.

A. P. نهضت فرمودن *nahẓat farmúdan.* To set off on the march.

P. نهفت *nihuft.* He hid.

P. نهفتن *nihuftan.* To hide, conceal.

P. نهم *nuhum.* The ninth.

P. نهمار *nahmár.* Immeasurable, innumerable.

P. نهنك *nihang.* An alligator.

P. نهور *nuhúr.* The eye, sight; an angry look.

A. نهی *nahy.* Prohibition, interdict.

A. نهیب *nahíb.* Plundering, a spoiler.

A. نهیبی *nahíbí.* Plunder, spoil, booty.

P. نهیدن *nahídan.* To place, put, lay.

A. نهیق *nahíḳ.* The braying of an ass.

P. نی *nai.* A reed, tube, flute.

P. نیا *naiyá.* A grandfather; a sheath.

P. نیاب *niyáb.* A sheath; a vessel.

A. نیابت *niyábat.* Vice-royalty, deputyship.

A. نیاح *niyáḥ.* Weeping, lamenting.

P. نیاز *niyáz.* Supplication, petition, indigence.

P. نیاز مند *niyáz-mand.* Indigent, suppliant.

A. نیاق *niyáḳ.* She-camels. (pl. of ناقه.)

A. نیاك *naiyák.* Libidinous.

P. نیام *niyám.* A sheath, scabbard.

P. نیایش *niyáyish.* Praise, blessing.

A. نیت *niyat.* Intention, purpose.

P. نیچه *naicha.* A tube, small pipe.

A. نیدل *nídul.* The nightmare.

A. نیر *naiyar.* The sun; the moon; shining.

A. نیران *nírán.* Fires.

P. نیرنگ *nairang.* Deception, trick, magic.

P. نیرو *nírú.* Strength, power.

P. نیز *níz.* Also, again.

P. نیزه *níza.* A spear, lance, dart.

P. نیزك *nízak.* A javelin.

A. نیسان *naisán.* A Syro-Macedonian month (April).

P. نیست *níst.* It is not.

P. نیستان *naiyistán.* A place where reeds grow.

P. نیست شدن *níst-shudan.* To perish.

P. نیستی *nístí.* Nullity, annihilation.

P. نیش *nísh.* A sting.

P. نیشتر *níshtar.* A lancet.

P. نیش زدن *nísh zadan.* To sting.

P. نیشکر } *nai shakkar.*
P. نی شکر } Sugar-cane.

A. نیفه *nífa.* White cloth, fine linen.

P. نیك *ník.* Good, excellent, beautiful.

P. نیك بخت *ník-bakht.* Fortunate.

P. نیك خو *ník-khú.* Good-nature.

P. A. نیك ذات *ník ẕát.* Of good origin.

P. A. نیك فال *ník-fál.* Of happy omen.

P. نیك فرجام *ník-farjám.* Of issue.

P. نیك خواه *ník-kh'áh.* A well-wisher.

P. نیك مرد *ník-mard.* A good man.

P. نیك نام *ník-nám.* Famous, renowned, of good report.

P. نیك نامی *ník-namí.* Reputation.

P. نیکو *níkú.* Good, beautiful.

P. نیکوی *níkúí.* Goodness.

P. نیکو سیر *níkú siyar.* Well disposed.

P. نیکو کار *níkú-kár.* Benefactor, beneficent.

P. نیکی *níkí.* Goodness, excellence.

P. نیل *níl.* Blue, indigo; the river Nile.

A. نیل *nail.* Acquiring, obtaining.

P. نیلپر *nilupar.* i. q. نیلوفر.

P. نیل کاو *níl-gáu.* The Neelgaw.

P. نیل کون *níl-gún.* Azure, bluish.

P. نیلوفر *nílúfar.* The water lily.

P. نیله *níla.* Blue.

P. نیم *ním.* Half.

P. نیم پخته *ním-pukhta.* Parboiled; half ripe.

P. نیم بسمل *ním-bismal.* Half slaughtered.

P. نیم جوان *ním-jawán.* A middle aged man.

P. نیمچه *ním-cha.* A half or small sword.

P. نیم خورد *ním-khurd.* The remains (of victuals).

P. نیمرنك *ním-rang.* Pale.

P. نیمرو *nímrú.* An omelet.

P. نیمروز *ním-rúz.* Midday; the city of Seistan.

P. نیم روزه *ním-rúza.* Of half a day.

P. نیم شب *ním-shab.* Midnight.

P. نیم کار *ním-kár.* Half used, worn.

P. نیم کرم *ním-garm.* Lukewarm.

P. نیم مرده *ním-murda.* Half dead.

P. نیم مست *ním-mast.* Half drunk.

P. نیمه *níma.* The half of anything.

P. نیمه راه *níma-ráh.* Midway.

P. نی نی *nai-nai.* No no, not at all.

P. نئین *na'ín.* Reedy.

P. نیو *nív.* Strong, powerful.

P. نیوشیدن *naiyúshídan.* To listen, to hear.

P. نی هندی *nai i hindí.* The bamboo cane.

و

و *wáw.* W. The twenty-sixth letter of the Arabic, and thirtieth of the Persian alphabet.

P. وا *wá.* Open. In composition it gives a similar sense to the English prefix *re-* in *return,* &c.

P. وا بستگان *wá-bastagán.* Domestics, dependents.

P. وا بستن *wá-bastan.* To bind, to tie.

P. وا بسته *wá-basta.* Bound; depending on.

P. وا پس *wá-pas.* Restitution.

P. وا پس فرستادن *wá-pas faristádan.* To send back.

ITAL. واپور *vápúr.* A steamship.

P. وا پسین *wá-pasín.* Latter, hindmost.

A. واتن *wátin.* Perpetual, fixed.

A. واثق *wásik.* Firm; confiding.

P. واج *wáj.* Extreme hunger.

A. واجب *wájib.* Necessary, expedient.

A. واجبات *wájibát.* Expediencies.

A. واجب العرض *wájib ul 'arz.* Necessary to be represented.

A. واجب الوجود *wájib ul wajúd.* Necessarily existent (God) as opposed to other beings whose existence is considered only as hypothetical.

A. واجبی *wájibí.* Anything necessary.

A. واجد *wájid.* An inventor.

P. وا جستن *wá-justan.* To inquire, to search.

A. وا چیدن *wá-chídan.* To pick out, to collect.

A. واحد *wáhid.* One, sole, single.

A. واحداً *wáhidan.* Separately.

P. وا خریدن *wá-kharídan.* To redeem.

A. واد *wa'd.* Digging a grave. Burying a daughter alive.

P. وا دادن *wá dádan.* To restore.

P. وا داشتن *wá dáshtan.* To prohibit.

A. وادع *wádi'.* Leaving, depositing.

A. وادی *wádí.* A river-bed, (dry in summer), a valley, a ravine.

P. وا دیدن *wá-dídan.* To gaze at, to regard.

P. وار *wár.* } A termina-
P. ور *war.* } tion implying possession.

A. وارث *wáris.* An heir.

A. وارد *wárid.* Happening, arriving, occurring.

A. واردات *wáridát.* Events, incidents.

P. وا رسیدن *wá-rasídan.* To obtain information.

A. وارغ *wárigh.* Belching.

P. وا رفتن *wá-raftan.* To wander, to walk.

P. واز *wáz.* Open.

P. وازیج *wázíj.* A vine.

P. واژ *wázh.* Inverted.

P. واژ گون *wázh-gún.* Inverted.

P. واس *wás.* An ear of wheat.

A. واسطه *wásiṭa*. Means, intervention.

A. واسع *wási'*. Ample, comprising.

A. والسلام *wa'ssalám*. And peace be on you! = "and that is all, I can say nothing more about it."

P. وا شدن *wá-shudan*. To be open.

A. واشمه *wáshimah*. A female who tattoos herself.

P. واشنگ *wáshing*. A peace-officer.

A. واشی *wáshí*. A whisperer, an eavesdropper.

A. واصف *wáṣif*. One who praises or describes.

A. واصل *wáṣil*. Joined, connected, met.

A. واضح *waẓiḥ*. Clear, manifest.

A. واضع *wáẓi'*. One who establishes.

A. واعد *wá'id*. Promising.

A. واعظ *wa'iẓ*. A monitor, preacher.

A. وافد *wáfid*. An ambassador.

A. وافر *wáfir*. Plenty, many.

A. وافی *wáfí*. Ample, full.

A. واقع *wáḳi'*. Occurring, situate.

A. واقعه *waḳi'ah*. An event; an accident.

A. واقعه دیده *wáḳi'ah dída*. A man of experience.

A. واقعه شدن *wáḳi'ah shudan*. To die.

A. واقعی *wáḳi'í*. Actual.

A. واقف *wáḳif*. Informed, knowing, expert.

A. واقف شدن *wáḳif-shudan*. To be apprized.

P. وا کردن *wá-kerdan*. To open.

P. وا گر نه *wa agar na*. Otherwise, if not.

P. وال *wál*. A whale.

A. وال *wa'l*. Flying to, taking refuge.

P. والا *wálá*. Eminent, exalted.

A. والا *wa illá*. Otherwise, if not.

A. P. والا جاه *wálá-jáh*. Of elevated rank.

A. P. والا شان *wálá-shán*. Of sublime dignity.

A. والد *walid*. A father.

A. والدعا *wa'ddu'á*. Adieu! farewell!

A. والده *wálida*. A mother.

A. والدین *wálidain*. Both parents.

A. والله *walláhi*. By God.

A. والله اعلم *walláhu a'alam*. God knows best.

P. واله *wála*. Distracted, astonished.

A. والی *wálí*. A governor.

P. وام *wám*. A debt.

P. وام خواه *wám kh'áh*. A creditor.

P. وام دادن *wám dádan*. To lend money.

P. وام دار *wám dár*. A debtor.

P. وا ماندن *wá-mándan.* To stay behind.

A. وامق *wámiḳ.* Enamoured.

P. وا نگرستن *wá-nigristan.* To stare.

P. وا نمودن *wá-namúdan.* To show; to open.

A. وا ويلاه *wá-wailáh.* Alas!

P. واه *wáh.* Bravo!

A. واهب *wáhib.* A giver; liberal.

A. واهمه *wáhima.* The imagination.

A. واهى *wáhí.* Weak, feeble.

A. واهيات *wahiyát.* Trifles, nonsense.

A. وبا *wabá.* The plague, pestilence.

A. وبال *wabál.* Misfortune.

A. وبر *wabar.* The hair of camels, goats, &c.

A. وبل *wabl.* Raining heavily.

A. وبه *wabah.* Understanding.

A. وبيض *wabíẓ.* Flashing.

P. وت *wat.* Fur, a fur garment.

A. وتد *watad.* A stake, a tent peg.

A. وتر *watar.* The string of a bow.

A. وترت *watarat.* The bridge of the nose, a cartilage.

A. وتيره *watírah.* A way, path, mode, manner.

A. وثاق *wisáḳ.* A ligature.

A. وثبات *waśabát.* Assaults; irruptions.

A. وثن *waśan.* An idol.

A. وثوب *waśúb.* Jumping, springing.

A. وثوق *waśúḳ.* Reliance, confidence.

A. وثيق *waśíḳ.* Firm, steady, strong.

A. وثيقه *waśíḳa.* A letter, a bond, an obligation.

A. وج *waj.* The sweet cane, galangale.

A. وجاهت *wajáhat.* Presence, aspect.

A. وجد *wajd.* Ecstacy.

A. وجدان *wijdán.* Finding, discovering.

A. وجيز *wajíz.* Abridged.

A. وجع *waj'.* Pain.

A. وجنة *wajnat.* A cheek.

A. وجوب *wujúb.* Obligation, duty.

A. وجود *wujúd.* Existence; invention.

A. وجوه *wujúh.* Faces, phases. (pl. of *wajh.*)

A. وجه *wajh.* A face, mode, manner, phase.

A. وجيه *wajíh.* Specious; a chief; comely.

A. وجيهة *wajíhat.* Beads, &c. worn as a charm against the evil eye.

P. وچر *wachar.* The decree of a judge.

P. وچر گر *wachar-gar.* A judge; a prophet.

A. وحدان *wuhdán.* Units.

A. وحدانيت *waḥdáníyet.* Unity, singularity.

A. وحدت *waḥdat.* Solitude.

A. وحده *waḥdahu.* Single, alone, unity.

A. وحش *waḥsh.* A wild beast.

A. وحشة *waḥshat.* Timidity, a retiring disposition, solitude.

A. وحشی *waḥshí.* Mild, timid.

A. وحل *waḥl.* Clay, mud.

A. وحم *waḥm.* The longing of a pregnant woman.

A. وحوش *wuḥúsh.* Wild beasts.

A. وحی *waḥy.* Revelation; a sound.

A. وحید *waḥíd.* Alone, unique.

A. وخامت *wakhámat.* Indigestion.

P. وخچی *wakhchí.* A date stone.

P. وخشینه *wakhshína.* Anything white.

A. وخفة *wakhfat.* A leathern bag.

A. وخیم *wakhím.* Unwholesome.

A. وداد *widád.* Friendship, love.

A. وداع *widá'.* } Farewell.
A. الوداع *alwidá'.* }

A. ودایع *wadái'.* Deposits, trusts.

A. ودع *wad'.* Parting, leaving.

A. ودیعت *wadí'at.* A deposit, a trust.

A. وذایم *wazáim.* Offerings, especially of cattle at Mecca. (sing. وذیمة.)

P. ور *war.* An affix implying possession, as جانور *jánwar.* Living.

P. و *wa.* And.

A. وراثت *waráśat.* Inheriting.

A. وراع *warrá'.* Moderate; pious.

A. وراق *warráḳ.* Full of leaves.

A. P. ورای *warái.* Behind, besides.

A. ورثة *waraśa.* Heirs.

A. ورد *wird.* Anything constantly repeated; a watering-place.

A. ورد *ward.* A rose.

P. ورد *wird.* A disciple, a pupil.

P. وردانه *wardána.* A rolling-pin.

A. وردی *wardí.* Rosy.

P. ورز *warz.* Gaining, acquiring.

P. ورزش *warzish.* Custom, habit, exercise.

P. ورزیدن *warzídan.* To practise, to exercise.

A. ورطه *warṭa.* A whirlpool, a gulf.

A. ورع *wari'.* Abstinent, scrupulous.

A. ورق *waraḳ.* A leaf.

P. ور کوش *war-gúsh.* An ear-ring.

A. ورم *waram.* A tumour, swelling.

P. ورنان *warnán.* Useful.

P. ورنه *warna.* And if not, otherwise. (for وا گرنه.)

P. وروار *warwár.* A royal seat or throne. A balcony, &c. on a housetop.

A. ورود *wurúd.* Arrival, alighting.

A. وروغ *wurúgh.* Belching, eructing; darkness, obscurity.

P. ورهم *warham.* Harsh words.

A. ورے *wará.* Men, mortals.

P. وريب *waríb.* Crooked, kerned.

A. وريت *waríyat.* Touchwood, tinder.

A. وريد *waríd.* The jugular vein and carotid artery. (See حبل الوريد.)

A. ورع *wari'.* Abstinent, continent.

A. وز *wazz.* A goose, a duck.

A. وزارت *wazárat.* The office of a Vizier.

P. وزان *wazán.* Blowing (a wind).

A. وزر *wizr.* A crime; load.

A. وزراء *wuzurá'.* Viziers, ministers. (pl. of وزير.)

A. وزع *waz'.* Prohibiting, checking.

P. وزق *wazaḳ.* Galangale or sweet cane; a frog.

A. وزن *wazn.* Weight, measure; metre.

P. وزيدن *wazídan.* To blow the wind.

A. وزير *wazír.* A vizier, a prime minister. In Persia the Prime Minister is called صدر اعظم *ṣadr i a'ẓam.*

A. وزين *wazín.* Weighty.

A. وساده *wasádah, wisádah, wusádah,* or

A. وساد *wasád, wisád, wusád.* A pillow, cushion.

A. وساطت *wasáṭat.* Mediation, intervention.

A. وساوس *wasáwis.* Evil suggestions.

A. وسايط *wasáïṭ.* Means.

A. وسايل *wasáïl.* Causes.

A. وسخ *wasakh.* Filth.

P. وسد *wassad.* Coral.

A. وسط *wasṭ.* The middle.

A. وسطى *wasṭí.* The middle finger.

A. وسع *was'.* Possibility; amplitude.

A. حتى الوسع *ḥattá 'l was'.* To the utmost.

A. وسعت *was'at.* Amplitude.

A. وسم *wasm.* A mark, brand.

A. وسمة *wasmah.* } Indigo,
A. وسمت *wasmat.* } a black tincture.

A. وسمى *wasmíy.* Early spring rain; spring herbage.

A. وسن *wasin.* (fem. وسنى *wasná.*) Drowsy, sleepy.

A. وسنان *wasnán.* Sleepy, slumbering.

A. وسواس *waswás.* Doubt, suspense.

A. وسوسه *waswasah.* An evil suggestion.

A. وسيط *wasíṭ.* A mediator, umpire.

A. وسيع *wasí'*, Spacious, extensive.

A. وسيله *wasílah.* A medium, means.

A. وسيم *wasím.* Marked, handsome.

P. وش *-wash.* An affix implying similitude, as ماهوش *máhwash.* Moonlike.

A. وشاة *wushát.* Spies, whisperers.

P. وشت *washt.* Goodness; good, beautiful.

P. وشتا *washtá.* Alive; life.

P. وشتی *washtí.* Beauty, goodness.

A. وشق *wushshaḳ.* Gum ammoniac.

A. وشم *washm.* Tattooing.

P. وشمك *washmak.* A leather shoe or slipper.

P. وشنی *washní.* Rouge.

P. وشه *washa.* Gum ammoniac.

A. وشی *washy.* Painting, dyeing.

A. وشيج *washíj.* Connected by relationship.

P. وشينه *washína.* A cuirass.

P. وشيه *washya.* A jest, a joke.

A. وصاف *waṣṣáf.* One who praises or describes.

A. وصال *wiṣál.* Meeting, interview.

A. وصايا *waṣáyá.* Precepts, testaments. (pl. of وصيه.)

A. وصف *waṣf.* Description, attribute.

A. وصل *waṣl.* Conjunction, meeting.

A. وصلی *waṣlíy.* Copulative, conjunctive.

A. وصول *wuṣúl.* Arrival, conjunction.

A. وصی *waṣíy.* The executor or administrator of a will.

A. وصيت *waṣíyet.* A precept; a will or testament.

A. وضاءت *waẓá'at.* Clean; cleanness.

A. وضاعت *waẓá'at.* Humility, humiliation.

A. وضع *waẓ'.* Mode; gesture.

A. وضعت *waẓ'at.* Childbirth, delivery.

A. وضع كردن *waẓ' kerdan.* To found, institute.

A. وضوء *wuẓú'.* Ablution.

A. وضوح *wuẓúḥ.* Evidence, proof.

A. وضيع *waẓí'.* Base, ignoble.

A. وضيعت *waẓí'at.* Tax, tribute.

A. وطاءت *waṭá'at.* Being flat, level.

A. وطائد *waṭáïd.* Foundation of a house.

A. وطر *waṭar.* A necessary, a thing desired.

A. وطن *waṭan.* A country, native soil. وطن مألوفه *waṭan i ma'lúfa.* One's dear native land.

A. P. وطن كردن *waṭan kerdan.* To make a home.

A. وطواط *waṭwáṭ.* A mountain swallow, a bat.

A. وطيد *waṭíd.* Firm, fixed.

A. وظائف *waẓáïf.* Pensions. stipends. (pl. of وظيفه.)

A. وظيف *waẓíf.* The pastern of a horse.

A. وظيفه *waẓífah.* A stipend, salary.

A. وعاء *wi'á.* A sheath, repository.

A. وعد *wa'd.* Promising.

A. وعده *wa'dah.* A promise, engagement.

A. وعر *wa'r.* Rough, difficult to ascend.

A. وعظ *wa'ẓ.* Exhortation, admonition.

A. وعل *wa'l.* The ibex or mountain goat.

A. وعور *wa'úr.* Difficult to ascend.

A. وعى *wa'y.* Preserving, retaining in the memory.

A. وعيد *wa'íd.* A threat.

A. وغا *wighá.* War.

A. وغيره *waghairah.* Et cetera.

A. وفا *wafá.* Good faith, fidelity.

A. وفات *wafát.* Death, decease.

A. P. وفادار *wafá-dár.* Faithful.

A. P. وفادارى *wafá-dárí.* Fidelity.

A. وفادت *wifádat.* Arrival.

A. وفاق *wifáḳ.* Harmony, unanimity.

A. وفد *wafd.* Arriving, coming.

A. وفر *wafr.* Becoming full, complete; plenty, abundance.

A. وفق *wafḳ.* Conformity.

A. وفود *wufúd.* Arrivals.

A. وفور *wufúr.* Abundance, plenty.

A. وفى *wafíy.* Entire; faithful to an engagement.

A. وقاء *waḳá'.* Preserving, guarding.

A. وقاحت *waḳáḥat.* Impudence.

A. وقاد *waḳád.* Burning, kindling.

A. وقار *wiḳár.* Dignity, grandeur.

A. وقاف *waḳḳáf.* Tardy, dilatory.

A. وقاية *wiḳáyat.* Custody, guardianship.

A. وقايع *waḳá'i.* Events. (pl. of وقعة.)

A. P. وقايع نويس *waḳá'i nawís.* or,
A. P. وقايع نگار *waḳá'i nigár.*
A government reporter.

A. وقت *waḳt.* Time, season.

A. وقح *waḳiḥ.* Impudent, immodest.

A. وقد *waḳd.* Lighting a fire.

A. وقر *waḳr.* Heaviness; a load.

A. وقر *wakr.* Deafness, making deaf.

A. وقعت *wak'at.* A battle, engagement.

A. وقف *wakf.* A bracelet; a pious endowment.

A. وقفت *wakfat.* Restraining, constituting.

A. وقود *wukúd.* Fuel for fire.

A. وقور *wukúr.* Grave, majestic.

A. وقوع *wukú'.* An accident, contingency.

A. وقوف *wukúf.* Experience, knowledge, information.

A. وقية *wukíyat.* An ounce; a weight of $2\frac{1}{4}$ lbs.

A. وقيعت *wakí'at.* Battle; calumny, slander.

A. وكالت *wikálat.* Viceroyalty; agency.

A. P. وكالت نامه *wikálat náma.* A power of attorney; an ambassador's credentials.

P. وگر *wagar.* If, although.

P. وگرنه *wagarna.* If not, otherwise.

A. وكلاء *wukalá'.* Attornies, delegates, deputies. (pl. of وكيل.)

A. وكيل *wakíl.* An agent, attorney.

A. ولاء *wilá'.* Friendship.

A. ولا *wilá.* Time. درينولا *darín wilá.* During all this time.

A. ولاد *wilád,* or } Nativity,
A. ولادت *wiládat.* } birth.

P. ولانه *walána.* A wound.

A. ولايت *wiláyet.* A kingdom, province, region.

A. ولد *walad.* A son, offspring.

A. ولد الزنا *walad uz ziná.* A bastard; a moth.

A. ولدان *wuldán.* Children.

A. ولع *wala'.* Desiring eagerly.

A. ولعت *wula'at.* Desirous of what does not concern him.

A. ولكن *wa lákin.* But, nevertheless.

A. ولوج *wulúj.* Creeping into a hole. Entering.

A. ولوج و خروج *wulúj u khurúj.* Entry and exit.

A. ولوع *wulú'.* Desire, avidity.

A. ولوله *walwalah.* Noise, clamour.

A. وله *walah,* or, } Being
A. ولهان *walhán.* } afflicted, terror, grief, &c.

A. P. ولى *walé.* But, yet, however.

A. ولى *walí.* A friend; a slave; a saint.

A. وليد *walíd.* A child, a son.

A. وليدات *walídát.* Cotemporary.

A. ولى عهد *walí 'ahd.* The heir apparent.

A. وليمه *walíma.* A marriage feast.

A. ولى نعمة *walí ni'mat.* A benefactor, patron.

P. ومر *wamar.* Besides, moreover.

A. ومض *wamẓ.* Glancing, flashing slightly.

A. ومق *wamḳ.* Loving; love.

P. ون *wan.* Sincere.

P. ونا *wana.* A wood pigeon.

P. ونده *wanda.* Cresses.

P. ونكول *wankúl.* Wanting, necessary.

P. ونك *wang* or *wing.* Poor, destitute.

A. وه *wah.* Ah! alas!

A. وهاب *wahháb.* The bestower of benefits (God).

A. وهابى *wahhábí.* A follower of the sect founded by 'Abd ul Wahháb; a very puritanical body of Muslims.

A. وهاج *wahháj.* Burning, flaming, raging.

A. وهام *wahhám.* Suspicious, doubtful.

A. وهب *wahb.* Giving, presenting.

A. وهبى *wahbí.* Bestowed by God.

A. وهجة *wahaj.* The heat of fire, or of the sun.

A. وهل *wahil.* Weak, timid, terrific.

A. وهم *wahm.* Conjecture, imagination.

A. وهمى *wahmí.* Conjectural, imaginary.

A. وهن *wahn.* Weakness; baseness.

A. وهى *wahy.* Being worthless.

A. وهى *wahy.* A rent, fissure, crack.

A. وهيجة *wahíj.* Heat, sultriness.

P. وى *wai.* He, him, to him.

A. ويحة *waiḥ.* Fye! oh!

P. ويرا *wairá.* Him, to him.

P. ويران *wairán.* Desolate, depopulated.

P. ويرانه *wairána.* A desolate spot.

P. ويرانى *wairání.* Desolation, destruction.

T. ويردى *vairdí.* Given, bestowed. Used in forming proper names, as الله ويردى *Alláh vairdé.* Theodore.

P. ويسه *wísa.* Good. Abomination.

P. ويشه *wísha.* Ivy, woodbine; a forest.

A. ويل *wail.* Woe, fye, alas!

P. ويل *wail* or *wíl.* Victory; fortitude.

A. ويه *waih.* Come along; away then!

ه

ه *há.* H. The twenty-seventh letter of the Arabic, and thirty-first of the Persian alphabet.

P. ها *há.* The plural affix for inanimate objects; as كتابها *kitábhá.* Books. خانه ها *khána há.* Houses.

A. هابط *hábiṭ.* Falling, descending.

A. هابيل *hábíl.* Abel, the son of Adam.

A. هات *hát.* Give, grant.

A. هاتف *hátif.* A mysterious voice from heaven, &c.

A. هاجر *hájir.* Abandoning, exiling.

A. هاجى *hájí.* A satirist.

A. هادر *hádir.* Permitting the effusion of blood with impunity.

A. هادم *hádim.* Demolishing.

A. هادى *hádí.* A guide.

A. هذا *háżá.* This.

A. هار *hár.* Weak with age or infirmity.

P. هار *hár.* A string of pearls; row, rank.

A. هارب *hárib.* Flying.

P. هارد *hárad.* The 25th day of the month.

A. هاروت *harút.* The name of an angel (see ماروت).

A. هارون *hárún.* Aaron.

A. هارون الرشيد *Harún ur Rashíd.* The fifth Abbaside khalifeh Haroun el Raschid.

P. هاز *ház.* A curling lock.

A. هازم *házim.* Depressing, oppressing.

P. هاژ *házh.* Clamour, a loud exclamation.

P. هاس *hás.* Also, likewise.

P. هاكره *hákra,* or, } One
P. هاكله *hakla.* } who stutters.

A. هال *hál.* Posterity.

A. هالك *hálik.* (fem. هالكه *hálikah.*) Destructive.

A. هالكى *hálikí.* Blacksmith; a polisher.

A. هاله *hálah.* A halo, or circle round the moon.

P. هامال *hámál.* Concord, harmony.

P. هامون *hamún.* A desert plain.

P. هان *hán.* Have a care; yes.

P. هاون *háwan.* A mortar.

P. هاون دسته *háwan dasta.* A pestle and mortar.

A. هاويه *háwiyeh.* Hell.

P. هاى *hái.* Alas! ah!

A. هايل *háïl.* Terrible, horrible.

A. هايم *háïm.* Astonished, confused.

A. هب *hab.* Grant it, allow it to be so.

P. هباك *habák.* The crown of the head.

A. هبط *habṭ.* Throwing down.

A. هبوب *hubúb.* Blasts or gales of wind.

A. هبوط *hubúṭ.* Descent, declivity.

A. هبه *hibah.* A gift.

A. P. هبه كردن *hiba kerdan.* To give, bestow, present.

A. P. هبه نامه *hiba náma.* A deed of gift.

P. هپاك *hapák.* The crown of the head.

P. هپر *hapar.* The pus, or matter of a sore.

A. هتك *hatk.* Dissipation.

P. هج *haj.* Rectitude.

P. هجاور *hajáwar.* An assembly.

A. هجر *hajr.* Separation, absence.

A. هجرة *hijrah.* Separation; the Mohammedan era.

A. هجو *hajw.* A satire, a pasquinade.

A. هجوع *hujú'.* Sleep, slumber.

A. هجوم *hujúm.* A crowd, an assault.

A. هجير *hajír.* The meridian, mid-day.

A. هدے *hudá.* The right road.

A. هدايا *hadáyá.* Gifts, presents.

A. هدايت *hidáyat.* Guidance, direction.

A. هدر *hadr.* Shedding blood.

A. هدف *hadaf.* A butt, a target.

A. هدم *hadm.* Destruction, demolition.

A. هدنت *hudnat.* Peace, a truce.

P. هدنك *hadang.* A white horse.

A. هدوء *hudú'.* Quiet, calm.

A. هدهد *hudhud.* A lapwing.

A. هديت *hadyat.* Conduct, method.

A. هدية *hadíyat.* A gift, a present.

A. هذا *házá.* This.

A. هذام *huzám.* Sharp (sword).

A. هذب *hazb.* Cutting, cleaning, purifying, flowing.

P. هر *har.* Every, all, everyone.

A. هراء *hurá'.* Speaking indecently.

A. هرات *hirát.* Herát, the capital of Khorasan.

P. هراس *hirás.* Terror, fear, dread.

P. هراسان *hirásán.* Fearing, dreading.

P. هراسه *hirása.* Terror.

P. هراسيدن *hirásídan.* To fear, dread.

P. هراش *harásh.* A vomit; vomiting.

P. هراشيدن *haráshídan.* To vomit.

A. هرانچه *haránchi.* Whatsoever.

A. هرانكه *haránki.* Whosoever.

P. هراول *haráwal.* The vanguard of an army.

P. هرآئنه *haráïna.* Certainly.

A. هرب *harab.* Flight, defeat.

A. P. هرباب *har-báb.* Every chapter, every subject.

A. P. هر بار *har bár.* Every time.

A. هربان *harbán.* Flying, flight.

A. هرت *hirrat.* A she-cat.

P. هرتوز *hartúz.* Truth, speaking the truth.

A. هرج *harj.* Tumult, bother.

P. هر جا *har-já.* Everywhere.

P. هرچند *har-chand.* However much.

P. A. هرجنس *har-jins.* Every kind.

A. هرج مرج *harj-marj.* Anarchy, confusion.

P. هر چه *har-chi.* Whatever.

A. هرد *hurd.* Turmeric.

P. هردو *har dú.* Both.

A. هردے *hurdíy.* Dyed with turmeric root.

P. هر روز *har-rúz.* Daily, every day.

P. هر روزه *har-rúza.* Daily.

P. هرزه *harza.* Absurd.

P. هرزه گردے *harza-gardí.* Vagrancy.

P. هرزه گوے *harza gúí.* Prating, a chatterer.

P. هرسو *har-sú.* Every side.

P. A. هر صورت *har-ṣúrat.* Every manner, anyhow.

در هر صورت *dar har ṣúrat.* In any case.

P. هر کاره *har-kára.* A kettle; a courier.

P. هرگاه *har gáh.* Whenever.

P. هرکش *harkush.* A watch, a sentinel.

P. هرگز *hargiz.* Never.

A. هرم *harim.* A decrepit old man; the mind, understanding. *harm.* Purslain.

P. هرمزد *hurmuzd.* Hormuzd, a king of Persia.

A. هرمی *harmá.* Decrepit; dry wood.

P. هرنوت *harnút.* Fraud, deceit.

P. هرو *harv.* Brave, warlike.

P. هر هفت *har-haft.* The seven kinds of cosmetic used by women.

P. هرین *hurín.* An awful sound, a roar.

P. هز *haz.* Loose, flaccid.

P. هز *haz.* Tribute.

P. هزار *hazár.* A thousand.

A. هزار *hazár.* A nightingale.

P. هزار پا *hazár-pá.* A centipede.

P. هزار چشمه *hazár-chashma.* A cancer.

P. هزاری *hazárí.* What relates to a thousand.

A. هزبر *hizabr.* A lion.

A. هزل *hazl.* Jesting, sportive language.

A. هزليات *hazaliyát.* Jokes, jests.

A. هزم *hazm.* Putting to flight, flight.

P. هزوان *hazwán.* Tongue, speech.

A. هزيمت *hazímat.* Rout, defeat, flight.

P. هزده *hizhdah.* Eighteen.

P. هژیدن *hazhídan.* To dry, to wither.

P. هزینه *hazína*, or, } House-
P. هژینه *hazhína*. } hold expenses.

P. هست *hast*. It is, exists. Existence.

P. هست و بود *hast u búd*. A rent-roll.

P. هستن *hastan*. To be, exist, subsist.

P. هستو *hastú*. Truth, justice, rectitude.

P. هستی *hastí*. Existent. Existence.

P. هسر *hasar*. Ice.

A. هسرت *husrat*. Affinity, kindred, uncles.

P. هش *hush*. See هوش.

P. هش *hish*. The plough-tail.

P. هشت *hasht*. Eight.

P. هشتاد *hashtád*. Eighty.

P. هشتادم *hashtádum*. The eightieth.

P. هشتصد *hasht-ṣad*. Eight hundred.

P. هشتگان *hashtagán*. Eight each.

P. هشتم *hashtum*. The eighth.

P. هشته *hashta*. Hanging loose.

P. هشتیدن *hashtídan*. To whistle; kiss.

P. هشده *hashda*. Eighteen.

P. هشیار *hushyár*. Intelligent, prudent.

P. هشیاری *hushyárí*. Prudence.

A. هضم *hazm*. Digestion.

A. هضمی *hazmí*. Digestible, digestive.

A. هطل *hatl*. Pouring (rain).

P. هف *haf*. A weaver's shop.

P. هفت *haft*. Seven.

P. A. هفت اقلیم *haft iklím*, or }
P. هفت کشور *haft kishwar*. } The seven zones, i.e. the whole world.

P. هفتاد *haftád*. Seventy.

P. هفتادم *haftádum*. The seventieth.

P. هفده *hafda*. Seventeen.

P. هفدهم *hafdahum*. The seventeenth.

P. هفتصد *haftṣad*. Seven hundred.

P. هفتم *haftum*. The seventh.

P. هفته *hafta*. A week.

P. هك *hak*. Full. Hail.

A. هكذا *hákazá*. In this manner.

P. هکك *hikak* or *hukkuk*. Hiccup.

P. هل *hil*. Leave, desist, let go.

P. هلاجن *halájin*. A swing or see-saw.

A. هلاس *hulás*. Consumption, phthisis.

A. هلاك *halák*. } Per-
A. هلاكت *halákat*. } dition, destruction, death.

A. هلال *hilál*. The new moon.

A. هلالی *hiláli*. Resembling the new moon; crescent-shaped.

P. هلانیدن *hilánídan*. To abandon, to dismiss.

A. هلاهل *haláhil*. Deadly (poison).

P. هلدن *hildan.* To dismiss, abandon.

P. هلده *halda.* A kind of orn.

هلكه *hilkah.* Destruction.

A. هلم *halumma.* Come on!

A. هلم جرا *hallumma jarran.* And so on, and so forth.

P. هلندور *halandúr.* Trefoil.

P. هلوجين *halújín.* A swing, or see-saw.

P. هله *hala.* Let alone! desist!

P. هله كردن *hala kerdan.* To advance, to storm.

P. هليدن *hilídan.* To dismiss, to abandon.

P. هليله زرد *halíla i zard.* Yellow myrobalan.

P. هليله سياه *halíla i siyáh.* Black myrobalan.

P. هليوم *halyúm.* Asparagus.

P. هم *ham.* Also, likewise.

A. هم *hamm.* Grief, care.

A. P. هما *humá.* A phœnix; (a fabulous bird, the shadow of which falling on a person's head denotes that he will become a king.)

P. همال *hamád.* All, whole.

P. هماس *humás.* A friend, companion.

P. هماش *hamásh.* Astonished, confounded; mean.

P. همال *hamál.* Equal; coequal, alike.

P. همان *hamán.* Only, solely. That same.

P. همانا *hamáná.* Again; like.

P. هماندم *hamán-dam.* At that moment, suddenly.

P. همانگاه *hamán-gáh,* or
P. همانگه *hamángah.*
As soon as, that very moment.

P همانند *ham-mánand.* Resembling; all as one.

P. هم آواز *ham-áwáz.* Singing in time with another.

P. همايون *humáyún.* Blessed. fortunate. Imperial (from هما q. v.)

P. همباز *ham-báz.* An associate.

A. هم پايه *ham-páya.* A colleague; of equal dignity.

P. هم پشت *ham-pusht.* A companion, an assistant.

P. هم پهلو *ham-pahlú.* An equal, peer; partner, spouse.

P. همتا *ham-tá.* Equal, resembling.

P. همتگ *ham-tag.* A fellow-traveller.

P. همجنگ *ham-jang.* A fellow-soldier.

P. A. همجوار *ham-jawár.* Neighbouring, a neighbour.

P. همچنان *ham-chunán.* In that manner, so.

P. همچنين *ham-chunín,* or
P. همچين *ham-chín.*
In this manner, thus.

P. همچو *hamchú.* Like, thus. such.

P. A. همحال *ham-ḥál.* A companion.

P. A. همخدمت *ham-khidmat.* A fellow-servant.

P. A. همخواب *ham-khawáb.* A bedfellow.

P. همخوے *ham-khúy.* Of the same disposition or habit.

P. همداستان *ham-dástán.* A confidant.

P. همدان *hamażan.* Name of a city and territory in Persia.

A. همدت *hamdat.* Apoplexy.

P. همدرد *ham-dard.* Sympathizing.

P. همدل *ham-dil.* Unanimous.

P. همدم *ham-dam.* An intimate friend.

P. همدیگر *ham-digar.* Both; each other.

P. همدیوار *ham-diwár.* A next door neighbour.

P. همدیهی *ham-dihí.* A fellow-villager.

P. همذات *ham-żát.* Co-existent, consubstantial.

P. همراز *ham-ráz.* A confidant, an intimate friend.

P. همراه *ham-ráh.* A fellow traveller; with, along with.

P. همراهی *ham-ráhí.* Society; companionship in travel.

P. همرقاص *ham-rakkás.* Dancing together.

P. همرنگ *ham-rang.* Of the same colour.

P. همرو *ham-rav.* } A fellow-traveller.
P. همره *ham-rah.* }

A. همز *hamz.* Piercing, pricking.

P. همزاد *ham-zád.* Born together, twins.

P. همزانو *ham-zánú.* Knee to knee, a companion.

P. همزبان *ham-zabán.* One of the same language.

P. همساز *ham-sáz.* Unanimous; a friend.

P. همسایگی *ham-sáyagí* Neighbourhood.

P. همسایه *ham-sáya.* A neighbour.

P. همسبق *ham-sabak.* A school-fellow.

P. همسر *ham-sar.* An associate, a consort.

P. A. همسفره *ham-sufra.* Sitting at the same table.

P. همسنگ *ham-sang.* Of the same weight.

P. همسود *hamsúd.* A rose-bud.

P. A. همشراب *ham-sharáb.* A boon-companion.

P. همشکم *ham-shikam.* Uterine brothers (of the same mother).

P. همشوی *ham-shúy.* A co-wife.

P. همشیر *ham-shír.* A foster brother; a brother.

P. همشیره *ham-shíra.* A sister.

P. همصحبت *ham-suhbat.* An associate.

P. A. همعنان *ham-'inán.* Riding side by side.

P. A. همعهد *ham-'ahd.* Coeval, contemporary.

P. A. همقدح *ham-ḳadḥ.* A pot-companion.

P. A. همقدر *ham-ḳadr.* Equivalent; of equal price.

P. A. همقدم *ham-ḳadam.* A companion, an attendant.

P. A. همقریه *ham-ḳirya.* Of the same village.

P. A. همکاسه *ham-kása.* A pot-companion.

P. همگان *hamagán.* All.

P. همکن *ham-kun.* A companion in travelling or labour.

P. همکیش *ham-kísh.* Of the same religion.

P. همکنان *ham-kunán.* Every person.

P. همگی *hamagí.* All, the whole.

A. همم *himam.* Intentions, aspirations. (pl. of همة.)

P. A. هم معنی *ham-ma'ní.* Synonymous.

P. همنشین *ham-nishín.* An intimate companion.

P. هموار *hamwár.* Plain, even, level.

P. همواره *ham-wára.* Always, constant.

P. A. هموثاق *ham-wiṡáḳ.* Confederated.

P. همون *hamún.* The joists of the roof.

P. A. همونت *ham-waḳt.* At the same time.

P. همون *hamún.* That very.

P. همه *hama.* All, every one.

P. همه جی *hama-jí.* A beetle.

P. همی *hamí.* The poetical and ancient form of the particle می prefixed to the present and preterite imperfect tenses of a verb.

A. همیان *himyán.* A purse or scrip.

P. همیجان *hamíján.* In the same manner.

P. همید *hamíd.* Thus, in this way.

A. همید *hamíd.* Assessed taxes.

P. همیدون *hamídún.* Always: such.

P. همیشگی *hamíshagí.* Eternity, perpetuity.

P. همیشه *hamísha.* Always, ever.

P. همین *hamín.* Only; even this.

P. همینك *hamínak.* Behold now!

P. هن *han.* Gratitude; obligation.

A. هنا *huná.* Here.

A. هنات *hanát.* Small things.

A. هنالك *hunálik.* There, in that place.

P. هنجار *hanjár.* Vexation; grief; conduct. A mason's rule; rectitude.

P. هنجاریدن *hinjárídan.* To travel on.

P. هنجام *hanjám.* A vagrant, wretch.

P. هنجدن *hanjidan.* To vex, grieve, injure.

A. هند *Hind.* India.

A. هندسه *handasah.* Geometry; the Arabic figures or digits.

A. هندسی *handasí.* Geometrical.

P. هندو *hindú.* An Indian.

P. هندوانه *hinduwána.* A water-melon.

P. هندوستان *hindústán.* } India,
P. هندوباز *hindúbáz.* } Hindustan.

P. A. هندی *hindí.* Indian.

P. هنر پرور *hunar-parvar.* An encourager of science.

P. هنر *hunar.* Virtue; science, art.

P. هنر پیشه *hunar-písha.* Virtuous; accomplished.

P. هنر مند *hunar-mand.* An artist.

P. هنگ *hang.* The understanding, wisdom.

P. هنگار *hangár.* Haste, speed.

P. هنگام *hangám.* Time, hour, period.

P. هنگامه *hangáma.* An assembly; disturbance, riot.

P. هنگامه کردن *hangáma kerdan.* To make a noise.

P. هنگامه گیر *hangáma-gír.* Tumultuous.

P. هنگامی *hangámí.* Temporal.

P. هنگفت *hunguft.* Thick, coarse.

A. هنود *hunúd.* Hindoos.

P. هنوز *hanúz.* Yet, still, hitherto.

P. هنومند *hanú-mand.* Shame, modesty.

P. هنه *hana.* Is it not? whether.

A. هنی *haní.* Light, digestible, wholesome.

A. هنیا *haní-an.* May it do you good! a good digestion to you! (said when anyone eats or drinks anything.)

P. هنیار *hanyár,* or } Consort.
P. هنیان *hanyán.* } spouse, partner.

P. هنیز *ha-níz.* Is it not yet?

P. هو *hau.* The moon; a cloud; a fog.

A. هو *hú.* The name of God, Jehovah.

A. هوا *hawá.* Air, atmosphere, ether, the wind. Love, desire.

A. هوا و هوس *hawá u hawwas.* }
A. هوای نفسانی *hawá i nafsání.* }
Lust, concupiscence.

A. P. هوا پختن *hawá pukhtan.* To concoct a fancy.

A. P. هوا پرست *hawá-parast.* Vain; a sensualist.

A. هواجس *hawájis.* Thought; carnal desire.

A. P. هوا خواه *hawá-kháh.* A well-wisher, a friend.

A. P. هوادار *hawá-dár.* Airy; a lover.

A. هوادج *hawádij.* Litters. (pl. of هودج.)

A. P. هوازد *hawá-zad.* Chilled, cold.

A. هواس *hawwás.* Libidinous.

A. هواسیدن *hawásídan.* To convene, to assemble.

A. هوام *hawámm.* Reptiles, serpents, insects.

A. هوام الارض *hawámm ul arz.* The reptiles of the earth.

A. P. هوام ضرر رسان *hawámm i zarar-rasán.* Noxious reptiles.

A. هوان *hawán.* A mortar; contemptible.

A. هواهی *hawáhí.* Follies, trifles.

A. هوائے *hawáiy.* Airy, idle, vain.

P. هوخ *húkh.* The temple of Jerusalem.

P. هوختن *húkhtan.* To draw out, unsheathe.

A. هودج *haudaj.* A litter carried by camels.

P. هور *húr.* The sun, moon.

P. هورخش *húraksh.* The sun.

A. هوز *húz.* Creatures, men.

P. هوزان *húzán.* A narcissus in bloom.

A. هوس *hawwas.* Desire, lust, ambition.

A. هوس باز *hawwas-báz.* Indulging one's passions.

A. P. هوسناک *hawwas-nák.* Ambitious, wishful.

P. هوش *húsh.* Understanding, intellect, the mind, the soul.

P. هوشا *húshá.* Idle, lazy, slow.

P. هوشمند *húsh-mand.* Prudent, wise.

P. هوشمندے *húsh-mandí.* Prudence, intelligence, wisdom.

P. هوشیار *húshyár.* Wise, cautious, prudent.

P. هوشیاری *húshyárí.* Prudence.

P. هوشنگ *Húshang.* Name of the second king of Persia.

P. هوشیدن *húshídan.* To die.

A. هول *haul.* Fright, terror, dread.

P. هول *húl.* High, lofty, eminent.

A. هاولاء *há'ulá'.* These.

A. P. هولناک *haul-nák.* Terrible, dreadful.

A. هون *haun.* Smooth, easy.

P. هوهو *hú-hú.* An owl; a dove.

P. هویدا *huweidá.* Clear, evident, open.

P. هویر *huwír.* One who hopes.

P. هویه *húya.* Shoulder; help, aid.

A. هی *híya.* She.

A. هیات *hai-at.* Aspect.

A. هیاکل *hayákil.* Temples; forms. (pl. of هیکل *haikal.*)

P. هیالیدن *hiyálídan.* To let fall; to dismiss.

A. هیام *huyám.* Distracted with love.

A. هيبت *haibat.* Awe.

A. هيج *haij.* A battle, combat.

P. هيچ *hích.* Nothing. This generally requires another negative, as هيچ نمی دارم *hích na mí dáram.* I have nothing.

A. هيجا *haijá.* War, a battle.

A. هيجان *haiyaján.* Vehemence.

P. هيچكاره *hích-kára.* Unfit for business.

P. هيچكس *hích-kas.* Somebody; nobody.

P. هيچگونه *hích-gúna.* In no form or manner.

P. هيچمدان *hích-madán.* Perfectly; ignorant.

P. هيد *haid.* A winnow.

P. هيدان *haidán.* Timid; covetous.

A. هير *hair.* The north wind.

P. هيرك *hírak.* A kid; a young camel.

P. هيرمند *hirmand.* Humble; obedient.

P. هيزم *heizam.* Timber, firewood.

P. هيزم كش *heizam-kesh.* A woodman.

P. هيزان *hízán.* A beam, a joist.

A. هيضه *haizah.* The cholera morbus.

A. هيف *haif.* Excessive thirst.

A. هيكل *haikal.* A temple; form, aspect.

A. G. هيولا *haiyúlá.* (ἡ ὕλη.) Matter; the first principle of everything.

A. G. هيولانی *haiyulání.* Material.

A. هيهات *haihát.* Alas! a negative exclamation.

A. هيئة *haiát.* Aspect, countenance.

ی

ی *yá.* Y. The twenty-eighth and last letter of the Arabic alphabet, and thirty-second and last of the Persian.

A. يا *yá.* Oh, ah! or, either; a vocative particle.

A. يا الله *yá 'lláh.* O God!

P. ياب *yáb.* Find thou (from يافتن *yáftan,* to find). Used as an affix it implies possession.

P. يابا *yábá.* Finding.

A. يابس *ya'bis.* Dry.

P. يابنده *yabenda.* A finder, gainer.

P. يابو *yábú.* A pony.

A. ياجوج و ماجوج *yájúj u májúj.* Gog and Magog.

P. ياختن *yákhtan.* To draw a sword; to strike; to throw.

P. ياخته *yákhta.* Drawn.

P. ياد *yád.* Memory, recollection.

P. یاد آمدن *yád-ámadan.* To come to mind, to conceive.

P. یاد آوردن *yád áwardan.* To call to mind, to recollect.

P. یاد آوری *yád áwárí.* Remembrance.

P. یاد بودن *yád búdan.* To remain fixed in the memory.

P. یاد دادن *yád-dádan.* To remind.

P. یاد داشت *yád-dásht.* A memorandum.

P. یاد داشتن *yád-dáshtan.* To remember.

P. یاد کردن *yád-kerdan.* To get by heart.

P. یاد گرفتن *yád-giriftan.* To learn.

P. یاد گار *yád-gár.* A monument, keepsake.

P. یاد گاری *yád-gárí.* Remembrance.

P. یار *yár.* A friend, lover, assistant.

P. یارا *yárá.* A friend; boldness; power.

P. یارانه *yárána.* Friendly.

P. یارای *yáráí.* Help, remedy.

A. یا رب *yá rabb.* O Lord! O God!

P. یار باز *yár-báz.* A wanton woman.

A. یار رس *yár-ras.* Aid, help.

P. یارستن *yárastan.* To be able; to inculcate good manners.

P. یارش *yárish.* Friendship, love.

P. یارغو *yárghú.* Strife, contention; litigation.

A. یارق *yáraḳ.* A bracelet.

P. یارکی *yáraki.* Power, strength, ability.

P. یارمند *yár-mand.* Friendly.

P. یاروی *yárúy.* A wound.

P. یار نامه *yár-náma.* Good actions; good name.

P. یاره *yára.* Power; a glove; gauntlet.

P. یاری *yárí.* Friendship; assistance.

P. یاز *yáz.* A countryman, a peasant; yawning; growing.

P. یازابه *yázába.* A pickle.

P. یازده *yázdah.* Eleven.

P. یازدهم *yázdahum.* The eleventh.

P. یازش *yázish.* Gaping, yawning; desire.

P. یازنده *yázenda.* One who resolves and purposes.

P. یازه *yáza.* Yawning, stretching; trembling.

P. یازیدن *yázídan.* To yawn, to stretch out the arms; to wish, desire; to grow.

P. یاژه *yázha.* Foolish words, vain.

A. یاس *yás.* Despair, hopelessness; fear.

P. یاسا *yásá.* A royal mandate.

P. یاساق *yásák*. Explanation, rectification.

P. یاسان *yásán*. Fit, proper, worthy.

P. یاسج *yásij*. A pointed arrow.

A. یاسر *yásir*. Soft, easy, smooth, humane, kind.

P. یاسمین *yásmín*. Jasmine.

P. یاسه *yása*. Law, regulation; desire.

P. یاش *yásh*. A kind of jasper.

P. یاشه *yásha*. A foolish, useless fellow.

T. یاغمه *yághma*. Prey, plunder.

A. یافث *yáfet*. Japhet, son of Noah.

P. یافت *yáft*. He found; income, earnings.

P. یافتن *yáftan*. To find; to obtain, to acquire.

P. یافته *yáfta*. Found, discovered.

P. یافر *yáfer*. A dancer.

A. یافوخ *yáfúkh*. The crown of the head.

A. یافوف *yáfúf*. Timid, fearful; old corn; active, quick.

P. یافه *yáfa*. A foolish speech; missing.

P. یافه داری *yáfa-dárí*. An idle talker.

A. یاقوت *yáḳút*. A ruby.

A. یاقوت خام *yáḳút i khám*. The lip of a sweetheart.

P. یاقوت روان *yáḳút i raván*. Red wine.

A. P. یاقوت احمر *yáḳút aḥmar*. A red gem, a ruby.

A. P. یاقوت کبود *yáḳút kabúd*. A blue gem.

T. یاقین *yáḳín*. Near, nigh to.

P. یال *yál*. A horse's mane · the neck.

P. یالغ *yálagh*. A cup made of horn.

P. یالمند *yál-mand*. A father of many children.

P. یالود *yálúd*. The seashore.

P. یاله *yála*. A cow's horn.

A. یا لیت *yá lait*. Would that!

P. یام *yám*. } A post-horse.
P. یامه *yáma*. }

A. یامن *yámin*. Happy, fortunate.

A. یانع *yániʻ*. Ripe.

P. یاور *yáwar*. An assistant, coadjutor.

P. یاوری *yáwarí*. Assistance; victory.

P. یاوه *yáva*. Vain, foolish, absurd; losing.

A. یا هو *yá hú*. O God!

A. P. یبابگر *yabáb-gar*. A destroyer, a spoiler.

P. یبان *yabán*. A desert; a forest.

A. یبروج *yabrúj*, or } Mandragora.
A. یبروح *yabrúḥ*. }

A. یبس *yabis*. Withered, dry, producing nothing.

A. یبوست *yubúsat*. Dryness, aridity.

A. یتامی *yatámá.* Orphans. (pl. of یتیم and یتیمة.)

A. یتم *yatim.* Lazy, indolent.

A. یتمان *yatmán.* Under age, a pupil, a ward.

A. یتیم *yatím.* An orphan, a pupil, ward.

A. P. یتیم خانه *yatím khána.* A robbers' den.

A. P. یتیم دریا *yatím i daryá.*
A. P. یتیمة *yatíma.*
Unique; a large pearl.

A. یثرب *yathrub.* The ancient name of the city of Medina (مدینه).

A. یحیی *yahya.* The Moslim's name for St John the Baptist; the Oriental Christians call him یحنا *yuhanna.*

A. ابو یحیی *Abu yahyá.* The angel of death (a punning title, یحیی meaning both "he lives" and "John").

P. یخ *yakh.* Ice.

P. یخ بستن *yakh-bastan.* To freeze.

P. یخچه *yakhché.* Hail; a hailstone.

P. یخنی *yakhní.* Cooked, dressed; stored.

P. یخور *yakhwar.* Frozen.

A. ید *yad.* The hand; power.

P. یدک *yadak.* A led horse.

P. یرا *yará.* Because.

A. یراع *yará.* A firefly; a rod.

P. یراغ *yarágh.* A meeting, assembly.

P. یراغه *yarágha.* A reed made for writing.

T. یراق *yarák.* Arms; accoutrements.

A. یربوع *yarbú'.* A jerboa.

P. یرغمال *yarghamál.* A hostage.

P. یرغو *yarghú.* Forbidden; quarrel, dispute; a bailiff.

A. یرقان *yarakán.* The king's evil.

A. یرلیغ *yarlígh.* A royal mandate.

P. یرمر *yarmar.* Expectation.

P. یرمغان *yarmaghán.* Curiosity, rarity.

P. یرمق *yarmak.* Money.

P. یزدان *yazdán.* God.

P. یزدانی *yazdání.* Divine.

P. یزغند *yazghand.* Name of a tree; a hunting-dog.

A. یزک *yazak.* The chief of the night-watch.

P. یزله *yazla.* Hurt, detriment.

A. یسار *yasár.* Left, the left side; plenty.

A. یسارت *yasárat.* Prosperity, happiness.

P. یسال *yasál.* A garland of flowers.

P. یساول *yasáwal.* Horseman; attendants on a man of rank.

A. یستوی *yastawí.* Equality. (Though used in Persian as a noun, it is properly the aorist of the Arabic verb سوی.)

A. يسر *yusr.* Facility, lenity, softness.

A. يسرى *yusrá.* Prosperous; the left hand.

A. يسف *yasuf.* A fly, a gnat.

A. يسور *yasúr.* A gamester.

A. يسير *yasír.* Small, little, easy.

A. يش *yashsh.* Glad, rejoicing.

A. يشب *yashb.* Jasper.

P. يشتن *yashtan.* To supplicate, to intercede; to mutter prayers.

P. يشك *yashk.* A lancet or similar instrument.

P. يشكرده *yashkarda.* A species of lute.

A. يشم *yashm.* A gate.

P. يشمه *yashma.* Raw white leather.

A. يعسوب *ya'shúb.* The king of the bees; a queen bee.

A. يعقوب *ya'kúb.* Jacob, James.

A. يعنى *ya'ní.* That is to say, videlicet.

P. يغلا *yaghlá.* A frying-pan.

P. يغما *yaghmá.* Plunder, spoil.

P. يغماى *yaghmáí.* A plunderer, ravisher.

P. يغناغ *yaghnágh.* An embroidered cap.

A. يقطين *yaktín.* A gourd or any creeping plant.

A. يقظ *yakiz.* Circumspect, wakeful.

A. يقظت *yakzat.* Night-watch, sentry.

A. يقق *yakik.* Cotton; anything very white.

A. يقين *yakín.* Certainly.

A. & P. يقين داشتن *yakín dáshtan.* To be assured.

A. P. يقينى *yakíní.* Certain, unquestionable.

P. يك *yek.* One, once.

P. يكان *yagán.* One, single.

P. يك انداز *yak-andáz.* Of one standard, equal.

P. يكانكى *yagánagí.* Singularity, unity.

P. يكانه *yagána.* One, sole, unique; a friend.

P. يكانيت *yagáníyet.* Solitariness; unity; kindred.

P. يكايك *yekáyek.* One by one; suddenly.

P. يكبار *yak-bár.* Once, one time.

P. يكباركى *yakbáragí.* At once; wholly, universally.

P. يكبرك *yak-barg.* Better, best.

P. يكبن *yak-bun.* Sweet basil.

P. يكپاره *yak-pára.* Solid; one piece.

P. يكتا *yaktá.* Single, simple.

P. يكتاش *Yak-tásh.* Name of a celebrated athlete.

P. يكتاى *yaktáï.* Unique.

P. يكچشم *yak-chashm.* One-eyed.

P. يك چند *yak-chand*. Somewhat.

P. A. يك جهت *yak-jihat*. Of one accord.

P. A. يك جهتی *yak* Unanimity, concord.

P. يك دانه *yak-dána*. a string of pearls.

P. يك دست *yak-dast*. Entire.

P. يكدست جامه *yak-dast i jáma*. A complete dress.

P. يكدگر *yak-digar*. One another.

P. يكدل *yak-dil*. Unanimous, uniform, with one accord.

P. يكدم *yak-dam*. One moment, one breath.

P. يكديگر *yak-dígar*. One another.

P. يكرنك *yak-rang*. Of one colour; sincere.

P. يكروے *yak-rúí*. Unanimous; of one face.

P. يكره *yak-rah*. By one way, at once.

P. يكزبان *yak-zabán*. With one voice, unanimously.

P. يكزده *yak-zada*. By one rule, in one rule.

P. يكزمان *yak-zamán*. Contemporary.

P. A. يكساعت *yak-sá'at*. Momentary.

P. يكساله *yak-sála*. Of one year, one year old.

P. يكسان *yaksán*. Alike, equal, the same.

P. يكسر *yak-sar*. All, generally.

P. يكسو *yaksú*. One side.

P. يكشنبه *yak-shamba*. Sunday.

P. A. يكقلم *yak-kalam*. Together, at one stroke, all at once.

P. يكگونه *yak-gúna*. Of one colour, kind.

P. يكلخت *yak-lakht*. Of one key; most powerful.

P. T. يكلو *yaklú*. Single, simple (thread).

P. يكم *yakum*. The first.

P. يكنفر *yak-nafar*. One man, a certain person.

P. يكونه *yagúna*. Of one; third.

P. يكه *yakka*. One, singular, unique.

P. يكی *yakí*. One, somebody.

P. يكيدن *yakídan*. To become one.

P. يل *yal*. A hero.

P. يلاغ *yalágh*. Anything white.

A. يلب *yalab*. A shield; a coat of mail.

P. يلدا *yaldá*. The longest night of winter.

P. يلدك *yaldak*. Milk and water.

P. يلغز *yalghaz*. The rind of a poppy.

A. يلق *yalak*. White, clear.

P. يلم *yalam*. Glue.

P. يلما *yalmá*. A thing of great bulk, but light.